Coping with Terrorism

SUNY series in the Trajectory of Terror

Louise Richardson and Leonard Weinberg, editors

Coping with Terrorism

Origins, Escalation,
Counterstrategies, and Responses

Edited by
Rafael Reuveny
and
William R. Thompson

Chapter 12 was first published as "Who Supports Terrorism? Insight from Fourteen Muslim Countries." *Studies in Conflict and Terrorism* 29 (1), 51–74 and is reprinted by permission of the publisher (Taylor & Francis).

Published by State University of New York Press, Albany

© 2010 State University of New York

All rights reserved

Printed in the United States of America

No part of this book may be used or reproduced in any manner whatsoever without written permission. No part of this book may be stored in a retrieval system or transmitted in any form or by any means including electronic, electrostatic, magnetic tape, mechanical, photocopying, recording, or otherwise without the prior permission in writing of the publisher.

For information, contact State University of New York Press, Albany, NY
www.sunypress.edu

Production by Cathleen Collins
Marketing by Anne M. Valentine

Library of Congress Cataloging-in-Publication Data

Coping with terrorism : origins, escalation, counterstrategies, and responses / Edited by Rafael Reuveny and William R. Thompson.
    p. cm. — (SUNY series in the trajectory of terror)
  Includes bibliographical references and index.
  ISBN 978-1-4384-3311-0 (hardcover : alk. paper)
  ISBN 978-1-4384-3312-7 (pbk. : alk. paper)
  1. Terrorism—Government policy. 2. Terrorism—Prevention. 3. Liberty—Political aspects. I. Reuveny, Rafael. II. Thompson, William R.

HV6431.C659 2010
363.325—dc22
                                                     2010007183

10 9 8 7 6 5 4 3 2 1

Contents

List of Tables and Figures vii

1. Contemporary Terrorism: Origins, Escalation, Counter Strategies, and Responses 1
   Rafael Reuveny and William R. Thompson

Part One: Origins

2. Precursors of Terror: Origins of European Extremism 25
   Manus I. Midlarsky

3. The Technology of Terror: Accounting for the Strategic Use of Terrorism 53
   Christopher K. Butler and Scott Gates

4. How to Win Enemies and Influence Terrorism: State Repression in Chechnya 75
   Rhonda L. Callaway and Julie Harrelson-Stephens

5. Democratic Pieces: Democratization and the Origins of Terrorism 97
   Erica Chenoweth

Part Two: Escalation and Expansion

6. Internationalizing Domestic Conflict: From Local and Political Insurgency Toward Global Terrorism. The Colombian Case 127
   Sandra Borda

7. Unspoken Reciprocity: The Effect of Major Shifts in Israeli Policy on International Terrorism 149
   David Sobek and Alex Braithwaite

8. Unholy Alliances: How Trans-State Terrorism and
International Crime Make Common Cause 169
Lyubov G. Mincheva and Ted Robert Gurr

Part Three: Counter Strategies

9. Rational Counterterrorism Strategy in Asymmetric Protracted
Conflicts and Its Discontents: The Israeli-Palestinian Case 193
Gil Friedman

10. Getting It Right: Understanding Effective Counterterrorism
Strategies 219
William Josiger

11. Negotiating with Terrorists and the Tactical Question 247
I. William Zartman and Tanya Alfredson

Part Four: Responses

12. Who Supports Terrorism? Evidence from Fourteen
Muslim Countries 287
C. Christine Fair and Bryan C. Shepherd

13. How Northern Norms Affect the South: Adopting,
Adapting, and Resisting the Global War on Terror
in South and Southeast Asia 315
Peter Romaniuk

14. Winners and Losers in the War on Terror: The Problem
of Metrics 349
Michael Stohl

15. Reacting to Terrorism: Probabilities, Consequences, and
the Persistence of Fear 369
John Mueller

About the Contributors 385

Index 393

Tables and Figures

Tables

Table 1.1.	One Hundred Books on Terrorism	3
Table 1.2.	Coding Categories and Operationalizations	8
Table 1.3.	Coding an Amazon Sample of the Current Terrorism Literature	9
Table 1.4.	United Nations' Terrorism Prevention Branch Research Desidrata	11
Table 5.1.	The Relationship Between Competition and Terrorist Group Emergence	111
Table 5.2.	Effects on Executive Constraints on Terrorist Group Emergence	115
Table 5.3.	Nonlinear Effect of Competitive Terrorist Group Emergence	117
Table 6.1.	Internationalization	132
Table 7.1.	Negative Binomial Regressions of Yearly Attacks on Israel	161
Table 7.2.	Negative Binomial Regressions of Quarterly Attacks on Israel	162
Table 9.1.	A Counterterrorism Policy Evaluation Matrix	208
Table 11.1.	A Negotiation Matrix	248
Table 12.1.	Table of Empirical Hypotheses	294
Table 12.2.	Descriptive Statistics for Support for Terrorism (Higher Mean Indicates Greater Support for Terrorism)	296
Table 12.3.	Support for Terrorism Among Those 40 Years and Above and Those Below the Age of 40	297

Table 12.4.	Support for Terrorism Among Married and Unmarried Respondents	297
Table 12.5.	Support for Terrorism Among Males and Females	298
Table 12.6.	Marginal Effects of Various Variables on Support for Suicide Terrorism	299
Table 12.7.	Marginal Effects of Being Female on Support for Terrorism	302
Table 12.8.	Marginal Effects of Threat Perception on Support for Terrorism	303
Table 12.9.	Marginal Effects of Computer Ownership on Support for Terrorism	303
Table 12.10.	Logistic Regression Results for Support for Terrorism (Models 1–5) and Weighted Sample Means	304
Table 13.1.	Interaction of Factors Affecting the Spread of Norms	327
Table 14.1.	Terror and Counterterror Data	355
Table 14.2.	Support for Terrorism and Counterterrorism	359
Table 14.3.	Confidence in the U.S. Government	361
Table 14.4.	Terrorism as an Issue in Exit Polls	362
Table 14.5.	Support for the U.S. President	362
Table 14.6.	Opinions of the U.S.	363

Figures

Figure 6.1.	U.S. Aid to Colombia Since 1997	134
Figure 7.1.	Number of International Terrorist Attacks Against Israel (1968–1998)	160
Figure 7.2.	The Effect of Israeli Dominance and Policy on Quarterly Terrorist Attacks	163
Figure 8.1.	Under What Conditions Do Terrorists Cooperate with Criminals?	177
Figure 8.2.	Under What Conditions Does International Crime Cooperate with Trans-State Terrorism?	182
Figure 9.1.	General Model of the Effects of Counterterrorism/ Insurgency Repression	197

Figure 9.2.	Counterterrorism Repression, Anger, and Hatred, and Willingness to Attack	199
Figure 9.3.	An Elaborated Model of the Effects of Counterterrorism/Insurgency Repression	204
Figure 12.1.	Predicted Probability of Supporting Terrorism by Age, All Else Constant	300
Figure 13.1.	Adoption of Counterterrorist Financing Norms in India and Indonesia, 2001–2006	323
Figure 14.1.	Worldwide Attacks Attributed to al Qaeda	356
Figure 15.1.	International Terrorism and Lightning, 1975–2003	370
Figure 15.2.	Concern About Becoming a Victim of Terrorism, 2001–2006	373
Figure 15.3.	Domestic Communism: The Press and the Public, 1940–1985	379

Chapter 1

Contemporary Terrorism

Origins, Escalation, Counter Strategies, and Responses

Rafael Reuveny and William R. Thompson

Introduction

Terrorism is a tactic of political violence employed by state actors and nonstate actors alike. Generally targeting civilians, terrorists rely on the fear they induce via bombings, assassinations, or kidnappings to meet their goals. Specific motivations vary, but the aim is consistent: encourage the targets and/or their supporters to engage in behaviors desired by the terrorists, such as abandoning resistance to, or support for, an incumbent regime or withdrawing troops from a contested area.

Although terrorism has been employed throughout much of history (for example, first-century Siccari Zealots, thirteenth-century Shi'ite Assassins, and Mongol raiders compensating for their small numbers by destroying towns to demonstrate their determination and ruthlessness), the literature has not fully conceptualized these activities. One indicator of this elusiveness is the tendency of observers to place terrorism somewhere on the continuum spanning between genocide and gang violence.[1] The exact nature of this continuum has yet to be specified, but the underlying message is that terrorism is a criminal justice topic; acts of terrorism, particularly those engaged in by nonstate actors, are often viewed as criminal behavior. Yet this assumption largely stems from rather recently established, Clausewitzian notions that states and their uniformed soldiers should monopolize legitimate warfare and weapons. Nonstate actors attacking state actors are thus illegitimate or criminal.

Contrary to this notion of criminality, many acts of terrorism that capture contemporary imaginations are clearly politically motivated. For example, terrorist tactics were adopted by nineteenth-century socialists and anarchists and twentieth-century colonial nationalists. Marxist revolutionaries employed terrorist tactics in the 1960s and 1970s. More recently, jihadists have relied on terrorism in their efforts to overthrow secular regimes in the Muslim world and to drive Western troops from their homelands.

Conventional academic analysts have been slow to focus on terrorism behavior, as opposed to specialists in criminal behavior and counterinsurgency tactics who have worked extensively on addressing terrorism. This is a tendency that is only gradually being reversed in view of the increasing difficulty of avoiding the subject and the growing realization that terrorist acts involve elements beyond criminal behavior.

One consequence is that a substantial proportion of books written on terrorism either describe groups that employ terrorist tactics (e.g., who they are, what they want, who supports them) or instruct how best to combat their tactics. This statement can be supported empirically, which may help to clarify how this book differs from the terrorism norm.

This Book and the Terrorism Norm

We conducted a search on Amazon.com using the phrase "terrorism." Categorizing the nature of the first 100 titles listed in Table 1.1,[2] we created a set of coding categories based on what seemed to best capture the types of books in the list. Obviously, some entries might qualify for more than one category but our interest was in matching the books to the coding categories that predominately described the approach of each book. We ended up with the 10 categories that are described in Table 1.2 (page 8). The left-hand column in Table 1.1 reports the outcome of our coding.

Table 1.3 (page 9) summarizes the coding outcome. A fifth of the works on the list were general surveys of terrorism that are hard to categorize because they often survey samples of all of the categories in Table 1.2. That is, they look at such topics as the history of contemporary terrorism, trends in activity, representative and well-known groups, and approaches to counterterrorism. Another third of the books were volumes that discussed strategies and tactics for dealing with terrorists. Nine percent were devoted to legal and human rights issues raised by terrorism and counterterrorism practices. Another fifth focused on specific types of terrorism (religious terrorism or weapons of mass destruction—13

Table 1.1. One Hundred Books on Terrorism

Type Code	Authors and Title
O	Hoffman, Bruce. (2006). *Inside terrorism*.
H	Chaliand, Gerand, and Arnaud Blin. (2007). *The history of terrorism: From antiquity to al Qaeda*.
O	White, Jonathan R. (2008). *Terrorism and homeland security: An introduction*.
R	Gabriel, Mark A. (2002). *Islam and terrorism: What the Quran really teaches about Christianity and violence and the goals of the Islamic jihad*.
P	Reich, Walter, and Walter Laqueur. (1998). *Origins of terrorism: Psychologies, ideologies, theologies, states of mind*.
A	Bjorgo, Tore. (2005). *Root causes of terrorism: Myths, reality and ways forward*.
O	Simonsen, Clifford E., and Jeremy R. Spindlove. (2006). *Terrorism today: The past, the players, the future* (3rd ed).
O	Kegley, Charles W. (2002). *The new global terrorism: Characteristics, causes, controls*.
O	O'Neill, Bard E. (2005). *Insurgency and Terror: From Revolution to Apocalypse* (2nd ed., rev.).
W	Clunan, Anne, Peter Lavoy, and Susan Martin. (2008). *Terrorism, War or Disease?: Unraveling the Use of Biological Weapons*.
O	Martin, Clarence A. (2006). *Understanding Terrorism: Challenge, Perspectives, and Issues*.
R	Spencer, Robert. (2007). *Religion of Peace?: Why Christianity is and Islam Isn't*.
P	Bongor, Bruce, Lisa M. Brown, Larry E. Beutler, and James N. Breckenridge. (2006). *Psychology of Terrorism*.
CT	Allison, Graham. (2005). *Nuclear Terrorism: The Ultimate Preventable Catastrophe*.
LHR	Zinn, Howard. (2002). *Terrorism and War*.
P	Post, Jerrold M. (2007). *The Mind of the Terrorist: The Psychology of Terrorism from the IRA to al-Qaeda*.
CT	Davis, Anthony M. (2008). *Terrorism and the Maritime Transportation System*.
CT	Borard, James. (2004). *Terrorism and Tyranny: Triangulating Freedom, Justice and Peace to Rid the World of Evil*.

continued on next page

Table 1.1. (*Continued*)

Type Code	Authors and Title
CT	Pillar, Paul R. (2004). *Terrorism and US Foreign Policy.*
CT	Feith, Doublas J. (2008). *War and Decision: Inside the Pentagon at the Dawn of the War on Terrorism.*
H	Hartwright, Christian. (2002). *The Red Roots of Terrorism.*
W	Levi, Michael. (2007). *On Nuclear Terrorism.*
O	Ross, Jeffry I. (2006). *Political Terrorism: An Interdisciplinary Approach.*
CT	Bevelacqua, Armando S. (2003). *Terrorism Handbook for Operational Responders,* 2nd ed.
LHR	Cole, David, and James K. Dempsey. (2006). *Terrorism and the Constitution: Safeguarding Civil Liberties in the Name of National Security,* revised and updated.
O	Martin, Clarence A. (2007). *Essentials of Terrorism: Concepts and Controversies.*
O	Badey, Thomas J. (2006). *Annual Editions: Violence and Terrorism 07/08.*
CT	Howard, Russell D. James J.F. Forest, and Joanne Moore (2005). *Homeland Security and Terrorism.*
CT	Robb, John, and James Fallows (2008). *Brave New War: The Next Stage of Terrorism and the End of Globalization.*
CT	Webber, Jane, Debra D. Bass, and Richard Yep. (2005). *Terrorism, Trauma, and Tragedies: A Counselor's Guide to Preparing and Responding.*
CT	Walker, Alice, Jodie Evans, Medea Benjamin, and Arundhat Roy. (2005). *How to Stop the Next War Now: Effective Response to Violence and Terrorism.*
LHR	Maggs, Gregory E. (2005). *Terrorism and the Law: Cases and Materials.*
P	Horgan, Jon. (2005). *The Psychology of Terrorism.*
CT	Sheehan, Michael A. (2008). *Crush the Cell: How To Defeat Terrorism Without Terrorizing Ourselves.*
CT	Dershowitz, Alan M. (2003). *Why Terrorism Works, Understanding the Threat, Responding to the Challenge.*
O	Badey, Thomas J. (2008). *Annual Editions: Violence and Terrorism 08/09.*

OTH	Lilley, Peter. (2006). *Dirty Dealing: The Untold Truth About Global Money Laundering, International Crime and Terrorism.*
CT	Rotberg, Robert I. (2005). *Battling Terrorism in the Horn of Africa.*
CT	Hunsicker, A. (2006). *Understanding International Counter Terrorism: A Professional's Guide to the Operational Art.*
LHR	Tsang, Steve. (2008). *Intelligence and Human Rights in the Era of Global Terrorism.*
A	Richardson, Louise. (2006). *The Roots of Terrorism.*
A	Pape, Robert. (2006). *Dying to Win: The Strategic Logic of Suicide Terrorism.*
O	Combs, Cynthia L. (2008). *Terrorism in the 21st Century*, 5th ed.
CT	Howard, Russell D., and Reid L. Sawyer. (2003). *Defeating Terrorism: Shaping the New Security Environment.*
O	White, Jonathan. (2002). *Terrorism: An Introduction*, 2002 update.
CT	Khalsa, Sundri K. (2004). *Forecasting Terrorism: Indicators and Proven Analytical Techniques.*
A	Enders, Walter, and Todd Sandler. (2005). *The Political Economy of Terrorism.*
CT	Burke, Robert. (2006). *Counter-Terrorism for Emergency Responders,* 2nd ed.
W	Howard, Russell D., and James J.F. Forest. (2007). *Weapons of Mass Destruction and Terrorism.*
R	Morse, Chuck. (2003). *The Nazi Connection to Islamic Terrorism: Adolf Hitler and Haj Amin al-Husseini.*
A	Rosen, David M. (2005) *Armies of the Young: Child Soldiers in War and Terrorism.*
CT	Purpura, Philip. (2006). *Terrorism and Homeland Security: An Introduction with Applications.*
CT	Netanuahu, Benjamin. (1997). *Fighting Terrorism: How Democracies Can Defeat Domestic and International Terrorists.*
LHR	Stone, Geoffrey R. (2005). *Perilous Times: Free Speech in Wartime: From the Sedition Act of 1798 to the War on Terrorism.*
SP	Hewitt, Christop. (2002). *Understanding Terrorism in America.*
CT	Cronin, Audrey Kurth, and James M. Ludes. (2004). *Attacking Terrorism: Elements of a Grand Strategy.*
P	Volkan, Vamik. (1998). *Bloodlines: From Ethnic Pride to Ethnic Terrorism.*
O	Whittaker, D. (2002). *The Terrorism Reader.*

continued on next page

Table 1.1. (*Continued*)

Type Code	Authors and Title
SP	William, Philip P. (2002). *Puppetmasters: The Political Use of Terrorism in Italy.*
CT	Bennett, William J. (2003). *Why We Fight: Moral Clarity and the War on Terrorism.*
CT	Lessor, Ian O. (1999). *Countering the New Terrorism.*
CT	Poland, James M. (2004). *Understanding Terrorism: Groups, Strategies, and Responses*, 2nd ed.
LHR	Beckman, James. (2007). *Comparative Legal Approaches to Handle Security and Anti-terrorism.*
O	Martin, Clarence A. (2004). *The New Era of Terrorism: Selected Readings.*
OTH	Kasimenis, George. (2007). *Playing Politics with Terror: A User's Guide.*
LHR	Farer, Tom. (2008). *Countering Global Terrorism and American Neo-Conservatism: The Framework of a Liberal Grand Strategy.*
P	Jones, James. (2008). *Blood That Cries Out From the Earth: The Psychology of Religious Terrorism.*
O	Combs, Cindy C., and Martin W. Slann. (2007). *Encyclopedia of Terrorism.*
CT	Ray, Ellen, and William H. Schaap. (2003). *Covert Action: The Roots of Terrorism.*
LHR	Pious, Richard M. (2006). *The War and Terrorism and the Rule of Law.*
OTH	Van De Ven, Susan Kerr. (2008). *One Family's Response to Terrorism: A Daughter's Memoir.*
SP	Parenti, Michael. (2002). *The Terrorism Trap: September 11 and Beyond.*
W	Falkenrath, Richard A., Robert D. Newman, and Bradly A. Thayer. (1998). *America's Achilles Heel: Nuclear, Biological and Chemical Terrorism and Covert Attack.*
CT	Micheletti, Eric. (2003). *Special Forces: War Against Terrorism in Afghanistan.*
O	Townshend, Charles. (2003). *Terrorism: A Very Short Introduction.*
O	Gupta, Dipak K. (2005). *Current Perspectives: Terrorism and Homeland Security.*

A	Crenshaw, Martha. (1994). *Terrorism in Context.*	
CT	Biersteker, Thomas J., and Sue E. Eckert. (2007). *Countering the Financing of Terrorism.*	
R	Sageman, Marc. (2007). *Leaderless Jihad: Terror Networks in the Twenty-First Century.*	
R	Adams, Neal. (2002). *Terrorism and Oil.*	
CT	Burton, Fred. (2008). *Ghost: Confessions of a Counterterrorism Agent.*	
O	Smith, Paul J. (2002). *The Terrorism Ahead: Confronting Transnational Violence in the Twenty-first Century.*	
SP	Tellis, Ashley J., and Michael Wills. (2004). *Strategic Asia 2004–05: Confronting Terrorism in the Pursuit of Power.*	
W	Boyle, Francis A. (2005). *Biowarfare and Terrorism.*	
R	Emerson, Steven. (2006). *Jihad Incorporated: A Guide to Militant Islam in the US.*	
CT	Posner, Richard A. (2008). *Countering Terrorism: Blurred Focus, Halting Steps.*	
CT	Chandler, Michael, and Rohan Gunaratna. (2007). *Countering Terrorism: Can We Meet the Threat of Global Violence?*	
CT	Heymann, Philip B. (2000). *Terrorism and America: A Commonsense Strategy for a Democratic Society.*	
A	Krueger, Alan B. (2007). *What Makes a Terrorist: Economics and the Roots of Terrorism.*	
CT	Banks, William C., Mitchel B. Wallerstein, and Renee de Nevers. (2007). *Combating Terrorism, Strategies and Approaches.*	
R	Stern, Jessica. (2004). *Terror in the Name of God: Why Religious Militants Kill.*	
O	Thackrah, John R. (2003). *Dictionary of Terrorism.*	
CT	Danieli, Yael, and Danny Brom. (2005). *The Trauma of Terrorism: Sharing Knowledge and Shared Care, An International Handbook.*	
A	Norris, Pippa, Marian R. Just, and Montague Kern. (2003). *Framing Terrorism: The News Media, the Government and the Public.*	
O	Nyatepe-Cao, Akorlie A., and Dorothy Zeisler-Vralsted. (2003). *Understanding Terrorism: Threats in an Uncertain World.*	
LHR	Pohlma, H. (2002). *Terrorism and the Constitution: The Post 9/11 Cases.*	
W	Weinstein, Raymond S., and Ken Albek. (2003). *Biological and Chemical Terrorism: A Guide for Healthcare and First Responders.*	
O	Harmon, Christop. (2007). *Terrorism Today.*	

continued on next page

Table 1.1. (*Continued*)

Type Code	Authors and Title
CT	Kessler, Ronald. (2007). *The Terrorist Watch: Inside the Desperate Race to Stop the Next Attack.*
OTH	Livingstone, David. (2007). *Terrorism and the Illuminati: A Three Thousand Year History.*

Source: Based on a search using the word "terrorism" on Amazon.com in June, 2008.

Table 1.2. Coding Categories and Operationalizations

Category	Definition
CT — Counter terrorism	Focuses primarily on how to defeat terrorists—strongly policy oriented
O — Overviews of the phenomenon	Focuses on providing a survey or overview of the terrorism phenomena, often in textbook format or anthology of collected readings
LHR — Legal/human rights considerations	Focuses primarily on either legal implications or impact on human rights
A — Social science analysis	Focuses primarily on terrorism as a form of political violence utilized to oppose governments within a sociopolitical context
R — Religious/jihadi specific	Focuses primarily on current role of religious fundamentalism/Islam in terrorist activity
W — Weapons of mass destruction	Focuses primarily on chemical, biological, or nuclear weapons and connections to terrorism
P — Psychology of terrorists	Focuses primarily on explaining how terrorists think
SP — Terrorism in specific places	Focuses in various ways on describing terrorism in various locales
H — History of terrorism	Focuses on analyzing terrorism in the past to the current manifestations
OTH — Other	None of the above

Table 1.3. Coding an Amazon Sample of the Current Terrorism Literature

Category	Distribution
Counterterrorism	33
Overviews of the phenomenon	21
Legal/human rights considerations	9
Social science analysis	8
Religious/jihadi specific	7
Weapons of mass destruction	6
Psychology of terrorists	6
Terrorism in specific places	4
Other	4
History of terrorism	2

Note: The numbers represent both absolute and proportional outcomes because the number of books examined totaled 100.

percent in all), terrorism in specific places (4 percent), and the psychology of terrorists (6 percent).

Only 8 percent encompassed what we have labeled as "social science analysis." The label is admittedly awkward, but the entries in this category examine terrorism as merely one type of political violence in the arsenal of dissidents, subject to variations based on the characteristics of the states, societies, and time-periods in which they take place.[3] The emphasis is not to condemn terrorist activity as criminal or evil, nor to propose ways to defeat terrorist activity. Instead, the emphasis is placed on how to explain the causes and impacts of this distinctive type of political behavior, relying on social science theory and methods.[4] The list displayed in Table 1.1 encompasses books written in the last 15 years for the most part, so it is clear that movement toward this type of analysis is slow—on average, one book every two years.

Authors often write books to sell them to the reading public. Therefore, one could look at the list in Table 1.1, shrug, and say that it simply reflects what sells. We have no disagreement with this observation. Our minimal point is merely that neutral analysis of terrorism as a political behavior, whether it sells or not, remains fairly scarce. But something more can be gleaned, we think, from the list in Table 1.1. Standard operating procedure for writing about terrorism tends not to focus on conventional political science or sociology. Journalistic description and policy advocacy is far more common.

We do not say this to denigrate description or policy advocacy. These types of approaches can be valuable. Descriptive information is certainly useful for targets of terrorism in contemplating ways to defend themselves. Analysis of any kind can hardly proceed without empirical data. Given public outrage and insecurities about terrorism, the impulse to discuss preventive policies is certainly understandable. Even so, we suggest there is also a need for more dispassionate study of terrorism as a form of political behavior.

Another way of making our case involves looking at a list of 490 desired research topics recently published. This list was developed initially by the United Nations' Terrorism Prevention Branch and updated by social scientists. It is not surprising that a terrorism prevention branch would place a great deal of emphasis on counterterrorism research topics. That is their mission after all. What is disheartening is that there are so few topics that address interpreting what terrorism is, under what circumstances it is likely to occur and succeed/fail, and what impact terrorism is likely to have on other structures and processes.

There are, to be sure, topics within categories 1 (types), 2 (linkages), 5 (state responses), 11 (evolution), 12 (war), 15 (public), 17 (trends), 18 (consequences), 19 (organization), and 25 (background factors) that are pertinent to the type of analysis of which we would like to see more done. Not coincidentally, the chapters in this book address many of these topics. Yet there is something about terrorism that keeps conventional academic treatments in the minority. Most of the 490 desired research topics summarized in Table 1.4 concern counterterrorism in one way or another. Our rejoinder is that better counterterrorism techniques might be forthcoming if we first had a stronger contextual understanding of what the varieties of terrorist political behavior represent.

We are not so naive to think that counterterrorist policies will wait while our social science understanding catches up to the need for responding to terrorist attacks. Our point is only that we have much to learn about what terrorism is, as well as when, where, why it might occur. Fortunately, research has been done on these topics and more is underway.

Both types of books on terrorism, which either describe groups that employ terrorist tactics or instruct how best to combat their tactics, are valuable; descriptive information is certainly useful for targets of terrorism in contemplating ways to defend themselves. What remain relatively scarce are attempts to bring terrorism within the boundaries of social science explanation, as opposed to a topic awkwardly stuck between genocide and gang violence.

The key to mainstreaming terrorism analyses into regular social science discourse involves two steps. First, avoid treating the terrorism topic as if the word "terrorism" began with a capital T. Terrorism is a violence tactic in the arsenal of groups (and states). Whether we regard it as evil,

Table 1.4. United Nations' Terrorism Prevention Branch Research Desiderata

Research Categories	Number of Topics and Comments
1. Types of terrorism	23 topics on whether different types of terrorists behave differently
2. Linkages	14 topics on whether terrorist organizations have links to other types of networks (criminal, drugs, and political parties)
3. Kidnapping/hostage-taking	6 topics on how kidnapping behavior works
4. International cooperation	22 topics on counterterrorism cooperation among various organizations
5. State responses	19 topics on how different types of states engage in counterterrorism
6. "Best Practices" and "lessons learned": UN member states experiences	14 topics on what works best in counterterrorism
7. Psychological and sociological factors	25 topics on the mindset of terrorists and using psychology for counterterrorism
8. Security	27 topics on preventive counterterrorism
9. Legal efforts	14 topics on legal regulation of terrorist behavior
10. Training	6 topics on training for counterterrorism
11. The evolution of terrorism	11 topics on how terrorist organization and tactics change over time
12. War and terrorism	29 topics on the interactions between war and terrorism and how to use military forces to suppress terrorism
13. Terrorism and the criminal justice system	11 topics on terrorists on trial and in prison
14. Media	12 topics on how terrorism is portrayed in the press and in the cinema
15. Terrorism and the public	6 topics on terrorism's impact on the public and public opinion about terrorism
16. Counterterrorist measures and responses	86 topics on various approaches to counterterrorism
17. Trends and statistics	8 topics on counting different types of terrorism

continued on next page

Table 1.4. (*Continued*)

Research Categories	Number of Topics and Comments
18. Consequences of terrorism	5 topics on assessing the effects of terrorism
19. Terrorist groups: organizations and characteristics	23 topics on how terrorist groups are organized
20. Victims	16 topics on the problems terrorist victims experience
21. Terrorist demands and tactics	54 topics on terrorist tactics and how to deal with them
22. Theoretical/conceptual/definitional considerations	7 topics on how analysts write about terrorism
23. Risk analysis	8 topics on assessing risk and threat
24. Dynamics of terrorism	15 topics on terrorist motives and repertoires and what might be done about them
25. General background factors facilitating international terrorism	21 topics on the domestic and international contexts in which terrorism take place

Source: Based in part on Schmid and Jongman (2007, 268–291).

legitimate or illegitimate, criminal or noncriminal, or a threat to civilization is beside the point. Social scientists study a number of phenomena that they do not necessarily like. But if analysts begin with the assumption that a particular type of behavior should be eliminated altogether from the possible behavioral repertoire of political actors, any subsequent analysis is likely to be strongly influenced by the author's repugnance.

Second, and much more difficult to accomplish, is to analyze terrorism in order to test theories about political violence. Authors on terrorism often choose their topics according to which groups have been most prominent in the media or, alternatively, which groups have been labeled terrorists by antagonistic governments. Area specialists, of course, are most likely to focus on terrorist groups in their selected corner of the world. We propose instead that analysts begin first with a theoretical question and then select appropriate phenomena or groups that allow one to assess the validity of more abstract propositions. In many cases, this type of analysis will not contribute to governmental interests in suppressing terrorism. Nor will it necessarily highlight the clearest threats to political stability. But, it may help us to interpret just where terrorism fits in within the political landscape, and how it relates to political structures and processes.

Accordingly, there are no specific methodological techniques that necessarily deserve priority over others. Case studies, large-N statistical analyses, game theory, polling, interviews, archival investigation, and content analysis are all germane. It is not so much a matter of how one pursues hypotheses about terrorism but rather why. The ideal situation entails pursuing hypotheses about terrorism as a way of assessing theories about political violence—as opposed to only describing, condemning, or praising terrorism, or, alternatively, developing strategies to defeat terrorism. We realize the ideal is not often achieved. Nor is it necessarily a goal in which all analysts of terrorism will be interested. Nonetheless, it remains a goal for social scientists to work toward as much as is feasible.

General Layout of the Book

One complicating factor in bringing terrorism into the social science realm is the tendency of the phenomena to change its shape over time. For instance, it was once conventional wisdom to believe that nonstate terrorists were inclined to minimize casualties so as not to completely alienate their intended audience. Yet the latest form of terrorist behavior by jihadists sometimes seeks to maximize casualties to better gain attention for its cause and weaken the will of its opponents. Terrorist behavior is complex and subject to change. We need to explore the origins of multiple varieties of terrorism, each within its appropriate historical context, examining how and when terrorism tactics escalate. We also need to consider the responses engendered by terrorism tactics, not only in terms of what works or does not work, but as appropriately contextualized, reciprocal behavior between attackers employing terrorist tactics and defenders generating responses.

In short, we must "mainstream" terrorism just as we are coming to terms with asymmetrical warfare in general (e.g., insurgencies and civil wars) as inescapable dimensions of contemporary reality. Terrorism is much more likely to evolve than disappear any time soon. We need to accept this reality and learn how to conceptualize terrorism, theorize about it, and model it, just as we do other phenomena in the social sciences.

Modeling terrorism is what distinguishes this volume from journalistic description and copping strategy advocacy. We organize this work in four parts, each including three or four chapters that share an analytical focus. The first part of the volume includes contributions by Manus Midlarsky, Christopher Butler, and Scott Gates, Rhonda Callaway and Julie Harrelson Stephens, and Erica Chenoweth, focusing on the origins of contemporary terrorism. The second part of the volume includes three articles, written by Sandra Borda, David Sobek and Alex Braithwaite, and Lyubov G. Mincheva and Ted Gurr, which study processes related to the escalation and expansion of contemporary terrorism. A third part includes three chapters focusing on counter strategies in fighting terrorism, written by Gil Friedman, William Josiger, and William Zartman and Tanya Alfredson. Finally, the fourth part of the volume, focusing on broader responses to contemporary terrorism, includes four articles, written by Christine Fair and Bryan C. Shepherd, Peter Romaniuk, Michael Stohl, and John Mueller. Taken together, the 14 chapters paint a holistic picture of origins, escalation, and expansion of terrorism, and counter strategies and responses to cope with it. An overview of the chapters in each section follows.

Part One: Origins

The first part of the volume examines the origins of terrorism and the forces contributing to rise in terrorist acts. The four chapters analyze the roots of twentieth-century political extremism, evaluate the effect of organization patterns, study the effect of state repression in Chechnya, and the role of democracy and democratization in the rise of terrorist activities.

Opening the origins section, Midlarsky focuses on the contexts, etiology, and behavioral traits of the early-twentieth-century European fascism as modal cases of political extremism. He defines them as social movements that pursue goals or programs that existing states view as unacceptable. Another common denominator is that these movements suppress concerns for individual rights in their pursuit of collective goals and are quite prepared to engage in mass killing of any opponents to their programs. Why might this be the case? Midlarsky's explanation focuses on a sequence of initial subservience to external forces, followed by a period of societal gain that is abruptly disrupted by catastrophic losses in population or territory. War losers are especially susceptible to this type of situation. The emotional response is apt to be one of anger over the injustices brought about by some unpopular group that is blamed for the outcome. The intensity of emotion and anger leads to a commitment to doing something radically in order to improve the situation. Midlarsky closes his chapter with the suggestion that this model can be used as a template to understand contemporary terrorist groups, particularly ones engaged in fundamentalist religious programs. In the case of intensely angry jihadis, a long period of subordination to the West was seemingly ended by successes in Afghanistan only to be reversed by the presence of U.S. troops in Saudi Arabia and elsewhere. The commitment to the restoration of a Caliphate is similar to fascist plans to rebuild their states along collectivist lines. Thus, from Midlarsky's perspective, modern terrorism should be viewed as one type of political extremism.

In the second piece, Butler and Gates seek to disentangle the technology of terror. They argue that actors facing a state of unfavorable peace have three primary choices: absorb the losses imposed by this state of affairs, engage in conventional warfare to change the status quo, or engage in unconventional warfare to do so. The choice of unconventional warfare is further disaggregated into activities involving terrorism and guerrilla warfare. Disentangling the technology of terror requires, Butler and Gates argue, a focus on the asymmetrical aspects of the problem, the interactions between superior state forces on one side and the insurgents and their complicit public on the other. Fighting superior state forces is viable as long as the cost of war for the insurgents is not too high. When discontented actors are much weaker than the state forces they face, the costs of conventional and guerilla warfare may be prohibitive. The use of terrorism, in contrast, may entail low enough cost to make it a viable alternative course of action. The focus on asymmetry suggests the state may more successfully quell dissent by "being just" than by increasing its power and investing in defense.

Callaway and Harrelson-Stephens have different curves in mind to explain terrorism. They argue that terrorism is a function of political participation, quality of life, and security but that each variable has a different relationship with the probability of the emergence of terrorist tactics. The relationship between political rights and terrorism is linear and positive. The more open the political system is, the less likely are members of the population to employ terrorist tactics. The quality of life–terrorism relationship resembles an inverted U, with terrorism most likely to be exhibited in the middle of the inverted U. The security-terrorism relationship is more complicated. Regimes capable of total suppression of dissent have less to fear from terrorism than do regimes that fall short of that control extreme. Moreover, the more blatant is the regime's attacks on its population, the greater is the popular support for terrorist activity. Thus, repressive regimes that fall short of complete control are the ones most likely to encourage terrorist attacks.

The authors apply this theory to the growth of terrorism in Chechnya with mixed results. Political rights were and remain limited. The old Soviet regime had approximated the extreme end of the continuum prior to the advent of Gorbachev. The subsequent relaxation of regime control encouraged the emergence of an independence movement. Thus, the political participation and regime security control variables seem to fit. The one variable that does not conform is the quality of life factor, which remained consistently low, thereby neither satisfying a J-curve or an inverted U expectation. Callaway and Harrelson-Stephens conclude with some speculations about intervening variables. One possibility is that political systems with a colonial history of subordination interacting with metropoles of fluctuating strength may exacerbate the probability of violence. Another is that the introduction of foreign fighters into the conflict zone can lead to situations in which the local, extreme dissident movement is basically hijacked by external actors. One or both of these factors may help explain why Chechnya only partially conforms to their analytical expectations. Ultimately, more cases will be needed to sort out the explanatory power of the theory and to establish what are or may be deviant cases.

Concluding the origins section, Chenoweth examines why terrorist groups seem more prevalent in democracies than in autocracies. She argues the answer has to do with intergroup competition among terrorist groups of various ideologies. Motivated by the competitiveness of the political regime in a democracy, the competition between terrorist groups explains, she hypothesizes, an increase in the number of new terrorist groups. She tests this hypothesis by conducting a statistical analysis of 119 countries from 1975 to 1997, employing the number of new terrorist groups as the dependent variable. The key independent variables are agenda competitiveness and intergroup competition. The findings support her hypothesis, but also suggest the relationship is curvilinear: both the most competitive and the least competitive regimes exhibit the largest number of new terrorist groups. Chenoweth concludes that effective counterterrorism policies must consider intergroup dynamics. Officials espousing democratization as a cure for terrorism may have it wrong; intense democratization may actually encourage terrorism.

Part Two: Escalation and Expansion

Moving to the second part of our volume, the escalation and expansion of terrorism processes do not occur randomly. Conditions need to be conducive for terrorism to increase its level of violence or to expand its geographical scope. The three chapters included in this part of the volume shed light on these escalatory and expansionary processes, demonstrating them in three particular cases, Colombia, Israel, and Kosovo.

Escalation processes can seem inadvertent. Two sides engage in tit-for-tat exchanges until one side is seen as responding more violently than the other side's attacks. Suddenly, the exchanges have moved to new heights of lethality without either side fully anticipating the escalation.

Alternatively, escalation can occur when domestic fighting in one country spills over the border into adjacent states. Borda, however, writes about a different type of escalation—one that is explicitly intentional. Prior to September 11, 2001, the U.S. government was aiding the Colombian government in attempting to suppress the flow of drugs from Colombia to North America. At the same time, the U.S. government was reluctant to provide resources that the Colombian government could employ with domestic insurgents. Borda argues that Colombian decision makers began portraying its domestic opponents as terrorists after 9/11 so that they could manipulate the newfound U.S. interest in terrorism suppression to obtain more external military resources. In this the Colombian government was successful, but not without potential costs. Internationalization of a domestic conflict can gain the government more resources but it can also tie its hands should there be an opportunity to negotiate with the opposition. In other words, the trade-off can be resources for decision-making autonomy and possibly more protracted conflict.

In chapter 7, Sobek and Braithwaite address two additional aspects of our problem: the effect of a country's international dominance and its choices of conciliatory or retaliatory responses to attacks by its weaker political foes on the number of terrorist attacks against it in a time period. In previous work, Sobek and Braithwaite have investigated these questions in the context of the U.S. diplomatic and international military dominance and terrorist attacks against U.S. citizens and properties around the world. In this chapter, they shift focus to Israel, ascertaining the effect of Israel's military and economic dominance in the Middle East and concessionary or retaliatory policy choices on the number of attacks occurring within Israel or leading to Israeli casualties abroad in a given year or quarter. The findings suggest that when Israel enjoys high levels of capabilities relative to its neighbors it faces more attacks. Israeli concessions reduce the number of attacks, argue the authors, while retaliatory actions increase attacks.

Concluding the second part of this volume, Mincheva and Gurr study synergies between international terrorism and organized crime. The authors argue that, though the goals of terrorists and criminals differ, the politically motivated terrorist groups and greed-motivated criminal syndicates sometimes work together. Seeking to explain this fact, Mincheva and Gurr's theoretical framework is based on ideas drawn from social movement theory, conflict analysis, and criminology. They propose that one condition for terrorist-criminal collaboration is the existence of trans-state nationalist, ethnic and religious movements, which promotes collaboration based on shared values and mutual trust. Other conditions include the occurrence of an armed conflict, providing incentives and possibilities for cooperation, and forces facilitating transnational illegal exchanges, which often involve intermediaries and corrupt state security forces. Mincheva and Gurr illustrate the operation of their model in the case of the Kosovar Albanian separatist movement, which has evolved into a political-criminal syndicate. Other cases are mentioned in passing, involving Colombia, Afghanistan, and Turkey.

Part Three: Counter Strategies

Moving to the third part of our volume, which focuses on counter strategies employed in the war on terror, we discover the patterns of terrorism and the contexts within which it operates are not uniform across time and space. As a consequence, the counter strategies employed in fighting terrorism and the broader responses of populations to terrorism are apt to be more complex than a simple terrorist action-governmental suppression reaction model might suggest.

Friedman concurs that modeling counterterrorism strategies is a complex undertaking. Focusing on what he calls asymmetric protracted conflicts, he believes it is possible to model the costs and benefits associated with a dominant rival's counterterrorist strategy, but not without bumping into some serious problems. Once violence begins, the dominant rival needs to address the subordinate rival's ability and willingness to engage in violent attacks. Yet once violence is underway, the subordinate rival is all the less likely to be prepared to make concessions and the dominant rival will also avoid concessions for fear of being perceived as lacking in resolve. Should a subordinate rival make concessions, with or without ongoing violence, the dominant rival may lose its motivation to respond appropriately, thereby encouraging the subordinate rival to return to, or to escalate, its level of violence. If the dominant rival responds to subordinate violence with repression, its dilemma is that it must be sufficiently coercive to deter subordinate attacks but must avoid too great of an expansion of anger/hatred within the subordinate population. Throw in such additional ingredients as subordinate organizational disintegration, perceptions of possible settlements, and high religiosity, and the complexity of the asymmetrical protracted conflict situation begins to defy both modeling and operationalization.

Josiger, however, is more sanguine about making generalizations about what works and what does not work in counterterrorism for the older, more affluent states of Europe (in particular, the United Kingdom,

Spain, and France). After several decades of experience, he thinks the following generalizations have support. One, if terrorism lacks domestic support, governments can employ firm responses. But if terrorism enjoys some domestic support, more complex approaches drawing upon political-economic and social changes are necessary if the government hopes to do more than merely contain the violence. Two, contrastingly, under-reaction and/or oscillations in the firmness of the response will work against governmental success. Three, decentralized efforts among different layers of domestic governance tend not to work. Four, terrorists should always be treated as ordinary criminals. Five, international cooperation is absolutely essential.

Friedman and Josiger focus on much different types of political milieu. Zartman and Alfredson further complicate the counter-terrorism guidelines by noting that governments with internal rebels that employ terrorism often end up (80 percent of the time) negotiating with them. Why and when governments and rebel terrorists choose to negotiate is not a straightforward proposition. The rebels may be willing to surrender some goals if they think they can achieve others. Governments may think they can encourage splits within the rebel ranks, isolate the most radical elements, and work out arrangements with the less radical rebels.

Attempting to pin down these circumstances further, Zartman and Alfredson turn to a consideration of five case studies (Rwanda, Sierra Leone, Macedonia, Kosovo, and Palestine). An analysis of the case studies suggest that governments will avoid negotiation unless they feel they have little choice but to make some type of agreement. In this respect, a mutually hurting stalemate can enhance the motivation for both sides to consider coming to terms. So are situations in which third-party mediators lead the way or rebels choose to revise their own goals independently. The irony here is that rebel groups need to stay unified if they hope to moderate their own demands successfully. Otherwise, radical elements will break away and continue the fight. If governments seek to split their opposition, an often-tempting proposition, they may actually make successful negotiations less likely.

Part Four: Responses

Finally, the last part of our volume enlarges the picture to consider the responses to terrorism in a broader sense. Two chapters in this part seek, respectively, to uncover the attributes of people supporting terrorism in Muslim countries, and the effect of Northern norms on the responses of people in South and South East Asia to the global war on terror. The third chapter considers how to measure whether responses, strategies, and actions in the war on terror are successful and efficient. The fourth chapter evaluates the consequences of fear as a persistent factor in the reaction to terrorism.

Beginning this part of our volume, Fair and Shepherd examine determinants of public support for terrorism in Muslim countries. They investigate this subject using data recently made available. The data, which so far have not been used extensively for this purpose, consist of survey responses of 7,849 adults from 14 Asian and African countries with Muslim majorities or large Muslim minorities. The findings suggest that females are often more likely to support terrorism than males, younger persons are more likely to do so than older people, relatively richer people are more likely to do so than the extremely poor, and people believing that religious leaders should play a larger role in politics or that Islam is under threat are more likely to do so than others. Despite these generalizations, Fair and Shepherd stress that the particular effects vary across countries, suggesting that counterterrorism policy interventions must be tailored to the target population in question.

In chapter 14, Stohl observes that officials and scholars who lack appropriate metrics to evaluate whether the global war on terror is being won are politicizing the discussion. The root of this observation is the failure of analysts to ground the existing metrics in a theoretically based understanding of terrorism and counterterrorism. The development of appropriate metrics requires consideration of both the terrorist act and the audience reaction. The governmental counterterrorism tasks involve foiling attacks, arresting terrorists, reducing the risk of attacks, and making the public feel secure and confident in the authorities' actions. Since terrorism crosses borders, foreign perceptions and actions are also important. It follows, argues Stohl, that the metrics need to be multidimensional, including measures such as the number of terrorist attacks across time and space, the extent of networks supporting the terrorists, number of arrests and other disruptions of terrorism, the extent of the counterterrorism global alliance, domestic and foreign publics perceptions of their security and the success of the war on terror, and the condition of human rights in the countries of the anti-terror global alliance.

The last chapter of this volume contributes a sobering note. Mueller argues that terrorism receives a great deal of attention but actually does relatively little damage and claims fewer victims than lightning strikes, bathtub drownings, or allergic reactions to insects (at least in the United States). If the global likelihood of being a victim of a terrorist attack is

1/75,000 to 1/120,000, why are people so fearful of terrorism? The answer is a combination of psychology and structure. Terrorism is an emotional obsession that encourages people to exaggerate its risks without really doing anything concrete about them. At the same time, a number of institutions and politicians are involved in stoking the fear of terrorism. The outcome is a political climate in which politicians seek to outbid one another on who is tougher on terrorism, thereby encouraging more coercive strategies and wars against terrorists in places such as Afghanistan and Iraq. Mueller is not optimistic about weaning ourselves away from such a political climate once it has been established.

Concluding Remarks

This edited volume is not the first collection of social science analyses on terrorism. Nor will it be the last word on the subject. We present it as part of a new wave of scholarly inquiry into a topic once relegated exclusively to specialists in counterinsurgency tactics and criminal behavior. The substantive mix of chapters included in this volume is balanced, we think, with several chapters on each of four subtopics, origins of terrorism, escalation and expansion of terrorism, counter strategies employed in fighting terrorism, and the broader responses to global terrorism. Geographically, the coverage of the chapters is broad, including both global and regional analyses. Academically, we bring together established political scientists (Gates, Midlarsky, Gurr, Zartman, Stohl, and Mueller) with relatively newer political scientists (Alfredson, Butler, Sobek, Braithwaite, Chenoweth, Mincheva, Borda, Fair, Friedman, Josiger, and Romaniuk). The works of these authors combine to create a fresh and exciting look at the complex processes of terrorism, suggesting intriguing and important insights that so far have not received sufficient emphasis in the academic, practitioner, or policy-making communities.

Nor will such insights make much headway in improving our understanding as long as we insist on treating terrorism with a capital "T" or reducing it to a manifestation of political evil. Rather, terrorism is merely a tactic sometimes employed in political combat and violence. We need to develop a better theoretical understanding of who is likely to employ the tactic, in what circumstances and with what effect are they likely to use (and to abandon using) such tactics, and how are their opponents likely to respond, and also to what effect. In brief, we need to make the study of "terrorism" less exceptional and more routine in the same way we study elections, wars, or social movements.

Notes

1. Terrorism studies are found in university library stacks situated between books on genocide and gang warfare.
2. Repeated searches on Amazon.com will not generate the exact same list each time. Our search was conducted in June, 2008.
3. We do not mean to imply that one cannot do counterterrorism or examine human rights issues from a social science perspective. Contrary examples are found in this volume. But most counterterrorism work is oriented toward policy formulation and promotion. Much of the human rights writing is more normative than empirical.
4. One might wish to argue that analyses of the political psychology of terrorists should fall within this category. Some certainly do. We single it out as a special category only because the initial assumption seems to be that terrorists must think differently than nonterrorists—otherwise they would not behave as they do. Analyses in our "social science" category, in contrast, tend to assume that terrorism is a violent tactic that is most likely to be employed by groups that lack the capability to take on their governmental opponents on the battlefield or, alternatively, use terror tactics as a supplement to more conventional internal warfare gambits.

References

Jongman, B. (2007). Research desiderata in the field of terrorism (pp. 255–291) in M. Ranstorp (Ed.), *Mapping terrorism research: State of the art, gaps, and future direction*. London: Routledge.

Part One

Origins

Chapter 2

Precursors of Terror
Origins of European Extremism

Manus I. Midlarsky

Introduction

The purpose of this chapter is to investigate the origins of European fascism as a seminal form of political extremism. Establishing a "baseline" of behavior and etiology is important, for it can then be used to compare fascism with other forms of political extremism such as communism, radical Islamism, rampant militarism, and extreme nationalism.

In addition to fascism, these forms of political extremism are explored in Midlarsky (forthcoming, 2011). How the typical moral restraints that prevent extremist behavior are compromised or indeed obviated also are addressed in that work, as is the extraordinary importance of mortality salience to the extremist enterprise. Applications of this framework lead the personal histories of extremists such as Stalin, Nazi concentration camp guards, leading Ottoman genocidaires in 1915, or radical Islamists in the Madrid bombings of 2004 to assume an importance not previously understood. In the concluding portion of the present chapter, generalizing this etiology to extremist groups such as al Qaeda and the Sri Lankan Liberation Tigers of Tamil Elam (LTTE) is discussed briefly.

To effectively accomplish these tasks, a definition of political extremism is required. Accordingly, political extremism is understood as the will to power by a social movement in the service of a political program typically at variance with that supported by existing state authorities, and for which individual liberties are to be curtailed in the name of collective goals, including the mass killing of those who would actually or potentially disagree with that program. Restrictions on individual freedom in the interests of the collectivity and the willingness to kill massively are central to this definition; note also the importance of the state.

Understanding the origins of fascism, especially its pronounced tendency toward the violation of human rights, even the initiation of mass murder, is the overarching explanatory purpose driving the analysis here. I do not claim that the policy platforms of fascist governments included here are identical, or even have substantial commonalities. Only certain behavioral descriptors and, most important, etiology, are held in common. Etiology is a significant indicator of the ultimate political purposes of extremist movements.

Recent systematic efforts have centered on domestic and rational choice sources of fascism. Spencer Wellhofer (2003), for example, finds that rational choice theory best explains voting for fascism in the 1921 election for the Italian national legislature as did William Brustein (1991). William Brustein (1996) also argues for the "rational fascist" with special attention to Nazism. Thus, "supporters were no different from average citizens, who usually select a political party or candidate they believe will promote their interests" (Brustein, 1996, xii).

Here I propose to examine political extremism from the perspective of the impact of international events on societies that became fascist, and the role of emotional states of being. I then propose to analyze the impact of these explanatory elements on the leaders and early followers of these movements. My emphasis on the origins of fascism in this chapter demands attention to the antecedent international context and emotional variables. Note that the emphasis here on emotions does not preclude rationality. Indeed, analyses of emotions and rational cognition can be supportive at times (Marcus et al., 2000; McDermott, 2004). Election and party membership studies that have supported rational choice are valuable in understanding the pathways to fascist power. However, explanation of the immediate *origins* of the Russian yellow shirts, Italian *fasci di combattimento*, or Nazi brown-shirted *SA,* of course without prior election, requires the approach adopted here.

Initially four instances of European governmental fascism—Italy, Germany, Hungary, and Romania—are compared in their shared propensity toward mass political violence, and similar etiologies. After presenting the common etiology arising from shared origins in war, the centrality of territorial loss within an ephemeral gain based on recent findings on the consequences of emotional states of being, Russian and French proto-fascism also are found to conform. This etiology also reveals an overarching common purpose among the cases of fascism and proto-fascism—the restoration of lost worlds. Apparent exceptions to this uniformity—Austria, Greece, and Bulgaria—countries that experienced loss, but not homegrown governmental fascism (or proto-fascism), are then explained within the confines of the theoretical framework offered here. In addition to contributions to theory, an important policy outcome of this analysis is the capacity to recognize the etiology of embryonic extremist groups *before* the mass killing begins.

An ephemeral gain occurs when a severe loss (e.g., territory, population), typically perceived as a catastrophe, is preceded by a period of societal gain, which in turn is preceded by a period of subordination.

Interpretations of Fascism

Among the many definitions and interpretations of fascism[1], the Columbia historian, Robert Paxton, recently established a point of analytic departure. He defines fascism as

> a form of political behavior marked by obsessive preoccupation with community decline, humiliation, or victimhood and by compensatory cults of unity, energy, and purity, in which a mass-based party of committed nationalist militants, working in uneasy but effective collaboration with traditional elites, abandons democratic liberties and pursues with redemptive violence and without ethical or legal restraints goals of internal cleansing and external expansion. (Paxton, 2004, 235)

Michael Mann defines fascism as "the pursuit of a transcendent and cleansing nation-statism through paramilitarism." (Mann, 2004, 13) establishes paramilitarism as a key similarity among the cases examined here.

Political behavior, not a general program of political change (that may or may not be effected after having been promised [Paxton, 2004]), is the defining feature of fascism. And when one examines the political behavior of these governments directly influenced by fascist movements, a common feature is the willingness to murder large numbers of people for the sake of a political program, however well- or ill-defined. Whatever the differences in practice among the various European fascist governments, they held this behavior in common.

The Willingness to Initiate Mass Murder

Examining only fascist movements that actually captured governmental control in Europe allows us to witness the consequences of fascism in power. Countries that had this experience are: Italy, Germany, Hungary, and Romania. Governments that appeared to be fascist in practice, or had a fascist component, but were in fact military dictatorships are excluded (e.g., Spain; Paxton, 2004, 149–150).

Despite a well-deserved reputation for restraint during the Holocaust that had Italian troops in occupied France and Yugoslavia protecting Jews (and Serbs) from annihilation (Steinberg, 1993), at least until the invasion of Sicily in July 1943[2] (Zuccotti, 2000), this is not the whole story. Fascist governance of Libya (an Italian colony since 1912), in the 1920s resulted in the suppression of resistance in the inland Cyrenaica region that entailed gassing of civilians and confinement of 80,000 Libyans in concentration camps where many perished. It is estimated that approximately one-tenth of the Libyan population died during the period of fascist rule. The Italian invasion of Ethiopia in 1935 also led to the large-scale murder of civilian populations, which, as in Libya, employed chemical weapons of mass destruction. Between 1935 and 1939, 617 tons of gas were shipped to Ethiopia. Altogether, by 1938, 250,000 Ethiopians were dead as a result of gassings and the use of conventional weaponry by the Italians (Ben-Ghiat, 2001, 125–126). Murder on such a grand scale clearly places fascist Italy in the same category as Hungary and Romania, although not at the same level of annihilation as Nazi Germany.

The mass murder of 6,000,000 European Jews by the Nazis during Word War II has few, if any, historical parallels (Hilberg, 2003). Yet the Nazis *in extremis* shared with remaining European fascist governments the willingness to engage in large-scale killing. As in the Italian case, political momentum was accelerated by invasion and war. And despite the virulence of Nazi ideology, it was only after the German invasion of the Soviet Union in June 1941 that Nazi policy was radicalized sufficiently to initiate the genocide of Europe's Jews (Browning, 2004; Midlarsky, 2005b).

Hungary and Romania were much smaller states that in themselves could not initiate major warfare and invasions leading to large-scale killing, yet did participate in the mass murder of perceived internal enemies, especially the Jews. The Hungarian government actually had two fascist incarnations. The first occurred immediately after World War I with the rise of the "Szeged Idea," a form of native Hungarian fascism that included a reversal of massive territorial losses by Hungary in the Trianon treaty of 1920 and virulent anti-Semitism.

Indeed, as early as 1919, Gyula Gömbös, a former captain on the Austro-Hungarian general staff (Deák, 1965, 377) and a leader of the Szeged group, spoke of himself as a Hungarian National Socialist (Weber, 1964, 90). After assuming the post of prime minister in 1932 (but not as a representative of the Szeged group), Gömbös did not initiate any anti-Semitic activity, but did lay the political foundations for later collaboration with the Germans in deporting several hundred thousand Jews after March 1944 (Braham, 2000, 23). According to Mann (2004, 243), "He [Gömbös] moved steadily toward fascism. He declared violence to be 'an acceptable means of statecraft . . . to shape the course of history, not in the interest of a narrow clique, but of an entire nation.' He now embraced corporatist solutions to national unity and moved closer to Mussolini. After Hitler's coup (sic), he promised Göring he would introduce totalitarianism and he wrote to Hitler describing himself as a 'fellow racist.' " Or as Nicholas Nagy-Talavera (2001, 341) avers: "The full responsibility for the year 1944 lies with the Szeged Idea—the line that can be traced from Gömbös straight to Imrédy [Hungarian prime minister at the time of the deportations]. Most of the protagonists of 1944 also came from Szeged."

But the Arrow Cross became the Hungarian fascist political party with the largest electoral mass base, proportionately larger than that of the Nazis in Germany at the height of their electoral success. The Arrow Cross was directly responsible for the deaths of at least 50,000–60,000 Hungarian Jews during its brief tenure in office (Braham, 2000, 253). It was founded in 1935 by Ferenc Szálasi (Payne, 1995, 273), a veteran of World War I and later a member of the general staff, as the Party of the National Will that later in 1938 was transformed into the Arrow Cross party. Shortly after the collaborating government of Admiral Horthy (the Hungarian Regent) declared an armistice, effectively withdrawing from the Axis coalition in October 1944, the Arrow Cross staged a successful coup. It was this government that would be directly responsible for handing over 50,000 Jews to the Germans who did not have the manpower to themselves carry out the deportations. Additional thousands of Jews in Budapest and elsewhere were murdered by Arrow Cross thugs. Only the completed conquest of Hungary by Soviet forces ended this reign of terror (Nagy-Talavera, 2001).

Romanian fascism was represented by the Legion of the Archangel Michael—more commonly known as the Iron Guard—formed in 1927 as an offshoot of the League of National Christian Defense founded by Corneliu Codreanu in 1923 (Weber, 1965b, 517–527). Of all the major European fascist organizations that attained political power,[3] it was the only one with a strong religious base, Eastern Orthodoxy.[4] During the one period in which it directly participated in the Romanian government (September 1940–March 1941), 630 Jews were killed and 400 declared missing (Hilberg, 1985, 764). But the influence of the Iron Guard would extend later to the Iaşi pogrom of June 1941, shortly after the German invasion of the Soviet Union. The number of Jewish dead was forthrightly estimated at 3,000–4,000 (Ioanid, 2000, 77). When the war got well underway, Romanian collaboration with Nazi Germany, again with strong individual Iron Guard participation, would lead to the deaths of 250,000 Jews in Romania and neighboring conquered Soviet territories. According to Raul Hilberg (2003, 809), "no country, besides Germany, was involved in massacres of Jews on such a scale."

The sanctification of violence by means of either a secular or sacred ideation is important. In order to loosen the typical moral restraints on violence, let alone mass murder, the secular or sacred basis of existence must be transformed. Thus, according to Yehuda Bauer, within the framework of the Nazi SS ethos, Heinrich Himmler "changed the biblical 'thou shalt not murder' into a Nazi 'thou shalt murder' . . . a positive commandment. In other words, he did not deviate from accepted moral precepts but stood them on their head" (Bauer, 1994, 116).

Etiology

Having established an important descriptive commonality among our cases of governmental fascism, we now turn to the two basic elements comprising the etiology of political extremism: origins in war and the salience of loss in contrast to gain, after earlier subservience—the ephemeral gain. Emotional states of being are important in understanding the emergence of political extremism.

The Importance of War Experience

On the whole, the immediate origins of European fascism are not in dispute. Virtually all major analysts of the etiology of this phenomenon agree that World War I was crucial (e.g., Weber, 1964; Payne, 1995; Lyttelton, 1996; Mann, 2004; Paxton, 2004). Fundamental causes, or more precisely long term processes as well as ideational content tend to be disputed (e.g., Gregor, 1979, 1999, 2005; Sternhell 1994; Laqueur 1996), but the immediate importance of World War I is seldom contested. Reasons for this emerging consensus are not hard to find. Virtually all of the important fascist leaders of the interwar period experienced battle at the front, or were close to those who did. Simply the return of large numbers of battle-hardened veterans could destabilize societies already exposed to significant economic, social, and especially political strains associated with maintaining the home front intact. For countries that lost the war, these strains would be magnified enormously.

But there is more than simply a general destabilizing impact. For countries that lost the war, or were part of a victorious coalition but were deprived of promised territory at the war's end (Italy), the consequences were severe. Men at the front, who saw their friends die violent deaths, or themselves had debilitating wounds inflicted on them, would be infuriated at the sacrifice in vain. That fury could be mobilized by leaders with political agendas that appeared to address the major concerns of the angry war veterans. The first political organization headed by Mussolini after the war and a direct precursor of the Italian fascist party, was called *fasci di combattimento*, or fraternities of combat, made up of war veterans and other nationalists (Bosworth, 2002, 122; Paxton, 2004, 5). Fascists elsewhere in Europe also were disproportionately involved in the war.

The Salience of Loss

Anger has been found to be associated with loss (Stein et al., 1993). Equally important, anger has been shown to be a significant emotional response to injustice (Haidt, 2003). Aristotle in his Rhetoric (Bk2, Ch2) defined anger as, "an impulse, accompanied by pain, to a conspicuous revenge for a conspicuous slight directed without justification towards what concerns oneself or toward what concerns one's friends." Commenting on Aristotle's definition, Jonathan Haidt (emphasis in original; 2003, 856) notes that "anger is not just a response to insults, in which case it would be just a guardian of self-esteem. Anger is a response to *unjustified* insults, and anger can be triggered on behalf of one's friends, as well as oneself." Thus, anger is categorized by Haidt (2003, 853) as one of the "moral emotions," those "that are linked to the interests or welfare either of society as a whole or at least of persons other than the judge or agent."

People in a state of anger are "more apt to blame others for mishaps that occurred" (Berkowitz, 2003, 816). Further, persons of an ethnicity different from one's own are more likely to be targeted (Bodenhausen et al., 1994, DeSteno et al., 2004). Anger in response to loss also has been associated with the desire to obtain restitution or compensation (Stein et al., 1993), or revenge (Frijda, 1994; Nisbett & Cohen, 1996).

Following this normative theme, Nico Frijda (1986) amplifies: Anger is provoked by a violation of what "ought to be" in the agent's view. Thus, a normative order has been violated, which justifies a challenge to this changing of the rules by the offending party. "Anger implies nonacceptance of the present event as necessary or inevitable; and it implies that the event is amenable to being changed" (Frijda, 1986, 199). Or as a consequence of loss, "anger often carries with it a desire not only to reinstate the goal, but also to remove or change the conditions that lead to goal blockage in the first place" (Stein et al., 1993, 291–294).

Thus, loss generates anger at the injustice of the loss, which in turn can be mobilized by fascist or radical Islamist groups that seek not only to retrieve or redress the loss (as in territory), but also can direct their anger at helpless civilian targets who are somehow implicated, often in the most indirect fashion, in the origins of the loss (Midlarsky, 2005a, b). Recent findings indicate that even routine partisan activity as in an American presidential election can generate emotional responses. When subjects were confronted with information that was inconsistent with their partisan leanings, MRI scanners indicated that the "cold reason" regions of the cortex were relatively quiet. Instead, emotions guided their reactions (Westen et al., 2006).

Why is territorial loss so important? In addition to refugees who flee into the truncated remainder of the country generating feelings of anger toward those who presumably ejected the refugees from the lost territory (Midlarsky, 2005a), territorial loss has additional significance. Territory represents security for the state and its loss inspires feelings of state insecurity. If the nation is an imagined community (Anderson, 1991), then its borders constitute an imagined fortress, a contemporary analog of the medieval castle (Herz, 1957). All that occurs in the form of community development, legal arrangements, and armed defense takes place within the national territorial "walls."

Lost territory represents a breach of those walls, and if for the first time in modern memory after a period of gains, territorial loss is incurred, then that breach becomes more salient. Lost territory now could set the precedent for later additional losses. An even moderately paranoid leader might reach the conclusion that there are enemies both within the state and without who need to be fought mercilessly. Fascism (and proto-fascism) is one manifestation of this tendency: a call to action in the name of restoration. The intractability of territorial conflict has been emphasized in studies such as those of Goertz and Diehl, 1992; Diehl, 1999; Vasquez, 2000; Toft, 2003; and Walter, 2003.

Surprise, Vividness, and a Diachronic Model

An increase followed by a sudden decline constitutes a vivid contrast and surprise at the sudden change in fortune. Surprise has an important consequence in the form of vividness. Both emotional pain and satisfaction can be multiplied substantially by the experience of surprise (Elster, 2004, 160). Or, as Loewenstein and Lerner (2003, 624) suggest, "people respond with greater emotional intensity to outcomes that are surprising—that is, unexpected."

The emotional intensity associated with surprise therefore can lead to vivid information—that which is most likely to be acted upon rapidly (Mele, 2003, 165). Because of the emotional intensity and consequent vividness, a sense of urgency is imparted, or as Frijda (1986, 206) puts it, "Urgency is the irreflexive counterpart of felt emotional intensity." Urgency is demanded without the contemplation and introspection associated with reflexivity (Frijda, 1986, 186–187). Anger can also independently lead to a sense of urgency (Elster, 2004, 154).

In the case of a previous loss prior to the existing one, an individual can explain the current defeat by referring to the earlier one: perhaps a syndrome of defeat stemming from battle against overwhelming odds. Effectively, nothing different had really happened in the second instance that requires explanation. But in the case of an earlier gain prior to the current loss, especially if substantial, then the present loss becomes puzzling, even frightening and then angering, for there must be a special reason for the current defeat. Often the simplest and most readily available explanation, even if erroneous, is seized upon, as in the increased presence of liberals, Jews, or Americans, depending on the particular case in question. Urgent action is then required against the putative offender to redress the loss, or at least to act quickly to prevent further loss.[5]

Equally telling in its ultimate impact is the period *prior* to the increase in authority space. This period is not frequently considered, but is nevertheless important. If the period before the increase consists of a long decline or remains at a consistently small or nonexistent national authority space, then reversion to that condition may be a major fear. The subsequent ascendant portion of the trajectory can then be seen as an exceptional blip in national history—an ephemeral gain—if in turn, followed by the downturn. Authority space is understood as the proportion of society over which governmental influence legitimately extends.

Finally, an important buttressing of the diachronic model emerges from prospect theory. This theory tells us that losses are more highly valued than gains, or put another way, that the lost entity is psychologically more valued than an entirely identical entity that is gained (Kahneman & Tversky, 1979, 2000; Levy, 2000). Experimental evidence has consistently demonstrated the asymmetry between losses and gains, even to the extent that, in contrast to gains, losses can generate extreme responses. Losses as the result of a shrinking spatial environment, therefore, may have a magnified role in the public consciousness, out of all proportion to their real-world consequences. When we add this asymmetry between gains and losses originating in prospect theory alone to the surprise, vividness, and emotional intensity stemming from the contrast between earlier gains and later losses, then these losses can be deeply consequential. Losses also are associated with risky behavior, often associated with extremist movements.

The Cases

Because of the critical importance of territorial loss[6] as an explanatory variable, all European countries that suffered such losses during interstate war,[7] and had the opportunity to embrace fascism thereafter are examined during the period 1900 to 1945.[8] Nine countries emerge from the application of these criteria: Italy, Germany, Hungary, Romania, Russia, France, Austria, Greece, and Bulgaria.

Loss

All of the cases of governmental fascism considered here experienced territorial losses prior to their first entry of fascist government. The German experience was dramatic. If, as did many Germans, one measures the territorial losses from June 1918 when much of Eastern Europe and Ukraine, and portions of France and Belgium were under German and Austro-Hungarian authority, then the contraction would appear to be immense (Evans, 2004, 52–53). Eastern territory that had been German governed for nearly a century and a half now was to be handed over to newly independent Poland. The eastern border with Poland was to be one of the driving forces of German foreign policy until the invasion of Poland in September 1939. And the reversal of these losses in tandem with abrogation of the Treaty of Versailles that mandated them would constitute the major Nazi political demand of the interwar period (Evans, 2004).

Dismemberment of the Austro-Hungarian Empire at the end of World War I led to large swaths of territory ceded to Romania, Czechoslovakia, and the Kingdom of Serbs, Croats, and Slovenes (soon to be called Yugoslavia) as stipulated by the Trianon Treaty of June 4, 1920. Accordingly, Hungary lost "71.4 per cent of her prewar territory, and 63.5 percent of her population. (Of the 325,411 square kilometers that had comprised the lands of the Holy Crown, Hungary was left with only 92,963. Of the population of 20,886,486 [1910 census], Hungary was left with only 7,615,117.) Of the persons of Magyar tongue, no fewer than 3,200,000 became the subjects of Romania, Czechoslovakia, Yugoslavia, and Austria" (Deák, 1965, 372). Many of them, especially those who had been in the Hungarian military or civil service, fled to the now truncated Trianon Hungary and provided a strong stimulus to the formation of the Szeged fascist movement. The later loss of Hungarian territory to the westward-bound Soviet army in mid-1944 would act as a spur to the abandonment of Horthy's newly declared neutrality in the war, and the ascension of the Arrow Cross government on October 16, 1944 (Nagy-Talavera, 2001, 321).

Romania in 1940 lost Bessarabia and northern Bukovina to the Soviet Union in June, northern Transylvania to Hungary in August, and southern Dobrudja to Bulgaria in September (Jelavich, 1983b, 226). These territories were substantial in size, equaling roughly one-third of Romania at that time. The particular reasons for these territorial transfers do not concern us here; the consequences, however, were immense. These losses, especially the loss of Transylvania, were felt deeply by most Romanians, leading to an immediate increase in popularity of the Iron Guard and its entry into the government shortly thereafter.

Italy did not experience any direct territorial loss from its boundaries of 1914. However, territory promised to Italy in the Treaty of London of 1915 was not forthcoming at Versailles. Accordingly, northern Dalmatia, not including Fiume (today's Rijeka), was to join Italy after the war, but even after a plebiscite in Fiume requesting that outcome, neither territory was granted to Italy at Versailles. So incensed was the nationalist Gabriele D'Annunzio, speaking of the "mutilated victory" (Knox, 1996, 123), that he and his followers entered that city with the intent of ultimately forcing its annexation. And as we saw earlier, D'Annunzio's activities in Fiume were to provide a model for Mussolini's incipient fascist movement. This irredentism was to be intensified by the catastrophic military loss by Italy at Caporetto in October 1917, with German forces advancing to territory just north of Venice. A total of 294,000 soldiers having been captured, this was by far the most serious defeat that newly independent and unified Italy had ever experienced (Knox, 1996, 120). Thus, territory promised but not delivered would be seen as more of an insult and humiliation than would otherwise have been the case.

Gain and Earlier Subordination

After examining the most recent territorial contractions or expansions in our extremist cases prior to their losses noted earlier, in all instances these losses were found to be preceded by gains, and still earlier, by subordination to other political entities—the ephemeral gain. Unifications of Germany and Italy in themselves were giant leaps in the expansions of authority space, after the earlier limitations on their authority as the result of foreign occupation and/or small state factionalism. The rate of German economic growth was outstanding after unification in 1871, bested only by the United States in this time period. Between 1871 and 1890, Otto von Bismarck, the German Chancellor, was at the heart of European diplomatic activity, serving as the "honest broker" at the crucial (for Southeastern Europe) Congress of Berlin in 1878. Afterward, Germany continued in its central role within European diplomatic activity (Albrecht-Carrié, 1958). Italy, after unification in 1870, also progressed very rapidly both economically and politically, and now was counted among the great powers of Europe for the first time since the height of Venetian power in the fourteenth- to sixteenth centuries (Braudel, 1984, 124–138).

Contrasting Germany's sudden collapse in 1918 with France's *levée en masse* in response to French defeat by the Prussians at Sedan in 1870, Schivelbusch suggests that:

> The most important difference between the two was that the collapse of 1870 did not leave France in a free fall. France's safety net was its sense of national pride, which had developed over the course of two centuries of European hegemony. The vanquished Germans of 1918 lacked any comparable heritage. The memories of centuries of national inferiority, supposedly relegated to the past by the victory of 1870–71, by the founding of the empire, and by forty years of power politics, now reappeared like an unwelcome guest on Germany's doorstep.
>
> The burden of the past helps to explain the response to the news of German defeat. People reacted not with manly composure, as the heroic vision would have it, but with everything from bewilderment to literal paralysis and nervous breakdown. (Schivelbusch, 2003, 196–197)

Hungary prior to World War I, and Romania after that war boasted substantial gains. After subordination to Austria, in 1867 Hungary was admitted formally to equal participation with Austria in establishing the Austro-Hungarian (Dual) Monarchy, also one of the European great powers. Hungarian territory now included portions of Croatia, Slovenia, Slovakia, Transylvania, and Bukovina (Nagy-Talavera, 2001, 85). Interestingly, one of the states to gain most from the post–World War I dismemberment of the Dual Monarchy was Romania. As of 1920, the territory of Romania doubled, absorbing Transylvania, Bessarabia, Bukovinia, and Crişana (Jelavich, 1983b, 122–124). Prior to 1861, Romania was part of the Ottoman Empire (Jelavich, 1983a, 288).

Proto-Fascism in Russia and France

Similarities in the origins of Russian and French proto-fascism now occupy our attention.

Russia

Certainly, paramilitarism as one of the behavioral attributes of fascism existed in Russia in the form of the Black Hundreds, as well as willingness to kill. An etiology deriving from origins in war and contraction of authority space after the Russo-Japanese War also are characteristic of this instance. As the first European great power to be defeated by a non-European one in the modern period and with the loss of territory to Japan (southern half of Sakhalin Island and the Liaotung Peninsula [Mazour, 1962, 338]), Russia felt humiliated. The extent of that humiliation can be gauged by Stalin's victory address on the occasion of Japan's unconditional surrender on September 2, 1945:

> The defeat of the Russian troops in 1904 in the period of the Russo-Japanese War left grave memories in the minds of our peoples. It was a dark stain on our country. Our people trusted and awaited the day when Japan would be routed and the stain wiped out. For forty years have we, men of the older generation, waited for this day. And now this day has come. (Quoted in Wolfe, 1984, 279)

And this defeat came after the earlier gains of the 1877–1878 Russo-Turkish War in which territory was gained from the defeated Ottomans: southern Bessarabia, Kars, Ardahan, and Batum (as a free port; Mazour, 1962, 303).[9] Earlier still, Russia's performance in the Crimean War (1853–1856) against Britain and France and leading to an imposed peace settlement entailing the loss of the mouth of the Danube River, southern Bessarabia, and the demilitarization of the Black Sea, highlighted her backwardness relative to the other states of Europe (Mazour, 1962, 251). Further, prior to their victory, the Japanese apparently had financially assisted various revolutionary forces in the Russian empire, in the interests of its weakening. Jewish revolutionaries *and* capitalists, both representing elements of modernity, were to be blamed by the emerging rightist movements for these presumed accelerants of the Russian defeat (Wolfe, 1984, 280).

This defeat and the succeeding revolution were to be firmly linked in the public mind. On December 20, 1904, Port Arthur fell to the Japanese after a long siege. This was to be followed almost immediately on January 9 by Bloody Sunday in which the czar's troops fired on a peaceful crowd of demonstrators approaching the Winter Palace (Rawson, 1995, 10–11). It was this event that most clearly indicated the state insecurity pervading the czarist government at that time; it was also the event that was to signal the start of revolution in earnest to be followed by the rightist reaction.

In the spring and summer of 1905 there appeared a "veritable mushroom growth of right-wing groups in dozens of towns all over the country" (Rogger, 1965, 483). When the czar issued his October 17 manifesto granting civil liberties and an elected assembly in order to stem the tide of revolution (Rogger, 1965, 483), the counter-revolutionary Black Hundreds, blaming the Jews for this "liberal declaration," initiated a series of disturbances during the week of October 18–25, with Jews as the primary targets. About 50 pogroms were enacted against Jewish communities throughout Russia including those in Kiev, Odessa, and Kishinev (Dubnov, 1973, 739). Of the Odessa pogrom it was described by Hans Rogger (1965, 492) as committed by "yellow-shirted bands that terrorized the entire city of Odessa for three days" (Rogger, 1965, 492).

Most important among the Black Hundreds was the "Union of the Russian People" (URP) founded on October 22 to establish a firm political base for the violent counter-revolutionary activity (Rogger, 1964b, 402). Among the organizers of the URP at that time and later were a Dr. A. I. Dobrovin, N. E. Markov, and V. M. Purishkevich. When the organization broke up in 1909, it was Purishkevich, probably the most violent of the lot, who was to found the Union of the Archangel Michael as a successor organization (Rawson, 1995, 230). Note the similarity of this organizational title with the later Romanian fascist Legion of the Archangel Michael (Iron Guard). And as Purishkevich (quoted in Rogger, 1965, 494) exclaimed concerning his political participation in the Duma (the newly established Russian national legislature): "To the right of me there is only the wall." He also was prone to the outbursts and theatricality that we now associate with fascism (Rogger, 1965, 494).

On December 23, Czar Nicholas II accepted a medal from the URP and wished it "total success" in its efforts to unify the Russian people (Rawson, 1995, 143). Many Orthodox clerics joined the Union, or as in the case of one distinguished priest, Father Ioann of Kronstadt, dean of St Andrew's Cathedral at that important naval base near St. Petersburg, accepted honorary membership in the Union.

Thus, indicative of the anti-liberal purposes of the URP as the largest organization associated with the Black Hundreds is the affiliation of like-minded organizations such as "The White Flag," "People's Union,"

"League of Struggle against Sedition," "Autocracy and Church," and "For Tsar and Order" (Rogger, 1964a, 78). Because of these more traditional associations, the URP has not been considered by many to be a true fascist organization (e.g., Rogger, 1964b). Yet even Rogger (1964b, 404) admits that "paramilitary organizations (such as the 'Yellow shirts' [sic] in Odessa and secret combat groups, the *druzhiny*) . . . are reminiscent of the *fasci di combattimento*."

Perhaps the most accurate assessment of these organizations, especially their leaders, Markov and Purishkevich, is that they can be considered to be "proto-fascist" (Rawson, 1995, 230). This is especially the case in light of the apparent influence on the Romanian Iron Guard, and the fact that many of the Black Hundreds later escaped the Bolshevik Revolution of 1917 by fleeing to Germany, particularly Bavaria, where they were to be deeply involved in the Nazi cause (Malia, 1999, 351). It is this ability to exert influence in democratic Germany more than in increasingly autocratic Russia (but traditionally so) that suggests the importance of Juan Linz's (1980) concept of a political space in which fascists or their prototypes can maneuver to gain political influence.

The surprise associated with a lost war and territorial contraction in contrast to earlier gains, and evoking still earlier subordination to the West, spurred the rapid development of proto-fascism and later fascism during the interwar period. War here was an accelerator of the extremist response.

France

In the Action Française, we have another movement that Eugen Weber (1965a, 125) calls "proto-fascist"; Ernst Nolte (1966, 26) agrees: "The practice of the Action Française anticipates, in the clear simplicity of the rudimentary, the characteristic traits of the infinitely cruder and more wholesale methods used in Italy and Germany."

Like the Russian (URP) case, Action Française, under the leadership of Charles Maurras, was rigorously monarchist and prone to street violence. As a nationalist French movement it was anti-Dreyfusard[10] and anti-German. Maurras' early ideas very possibly were influenced by the French defeat in the Franco-Prussian War when he was roughly two and a half years of age. He described Prussians as "wicked men, barbarians wearing spiked helmets" (Nolte, 1966, 59).

When France was defeated in May 1940 in stark contrast to its victory in 1918 but consistent with the humiliation of 1870, and the independent Vichy regime under Maréchal Pétain was established only in the two-fifths of France not occupied by Germany, Maurras and Action

Française became even more extreme. After the first Vichy anti-Semitic legislation was passed in October 1940, Maurras remarked that an opportunity had now arrived to rid France of its "Jewish scourge" (Nolte, 1966, 82). Even into late 1944, he refused to countenance any effort to save the East European Jews in France, or even French-Jewish citizens that were continually under threat of deportation, yielding a total of approximately 72,500 Jewish dead (Marrus & Paxton, 1995, 343). This, despite his opposition in principle to German occupation.

And like the czar in relation to the URP, Pétain called Maurras "le plus français des Française" (Nolte, 1965, 80). Maurras reciprocated in his complete support for Pétain and the Vichy regime as the apotheosis of monarchism in the twentieth century. Nolte (1966, 26) concludes: "The Action Française was the first political grouping of any influence or intellectual status to bear unmistakably fascist traits."[11]

Apparent Exceptions

Austria did not experience a homegrown governmental fascism as did Italy and especially Germany. Why not? After all, Austrian losses after World War I would appear to be even greater than those of Germany, yet an overtly fascist party did not gain political power until after the *Anschluss* of 1938, accomplished by a German military invasion. What did happen in Austria was quite different from events in Germany. After a political crisis led to the resignation of the Austrian parliamentary leaders in March 1933, the Christian Social leader, Engelbert Dollfuss, assumed full power, establishing a dictatorship based on his own party and the *Heimwehr* [(home guard), a rough equivalent of the paramilitary *Freikorps*, a major source of Nazi recruits in Germany; Payne (1995, 248)]. However,

> Though both Dollfuss and the Heimwehr leader Starhemberg had promised Mussolini late in 1933 that they would move toward "fascism" the Austrian regime developed a different profile.... This represented among other things an attempt to realize the Catholic ideals of the recent papal encyclical *Quadragesimo Anno* (1931), which endorsed corporative forms of organization and representation for Catholic society. (Payne, 1995, 249)

Or as Mann (2004, 209) describes the Austrian dictatorship: "Though it drew some doctrines from Italian fascism, it most resembled the Franco [Spain] and Salazar [Portugal] regimes."

The major difference in etiology between the Austrian and German variants is to be found in the general absence of gain for Austrian society prior to World War I, especially in comparison with Germany. Instead of the unification of Germany and its triumphal march to continental European leadership, or Hungary's joining Austria in the Dual Monarchy and governing an empire of its own, Austria had to relinquish power to the Hungarians, thereby experiencing a vastly truncated authority space. Even the one territorial gain prior to World War I, that of Bosnia-Herzegovina in 1908, came not as a result of victory in war as did virtually all others in Europe, but as a consequence of a diplomatic *fait accompli*. And that territory then had to be shared with the Hungarians in a Common Ministry of Finance (Malcolm, 2002, 137). Certainly, the exacerbation of Serb nationalism as the result of this annexation and then Austro-Hungarian participation in World War I, were widely viewed in Austria as a catastrophe. Thus, when the Austro-Hungarian Empire was dismantled after World War I there was widespread sentiment for an *Anschluss* with Germany even at that time. Surprise, vividness, and the urge to act quickly in order to restore the status quo ante were decidedly absent.

Initially, few German speakers within the territory soon to be the Republic of Austria wanted to have a separate republic. Indeed, article 2 of the 1918 constitution stated explicitly that German Austria is part of the German republic. "This declaration of loyalty to a German identity and to the union with the German republic was common to all political persuasions" (Fellner, 1981, 9). But the Allies at Versailles sought to limit German expansion, not endorse it, and so they insisted on the permanence of the Austrian state despite the wishes of the majority of its population.

It is the experience of earlier loss, not gain during this period prior to World War I, even to the extent of advocating state extinction upon further loss after World War I, which strongly distinguishes Austria from the extremist cases.

Greece did not develop a fascist regime despite its 1922 loss of Anatolian territory in the Greco-Turkish War. At most, Greece suffered the dictatorial rule of General Ioannis Metaxas starting in 1936. It was a military dictatorship like that of Franco's Spain. Indeed, during the period of governance by Metaxas, there was never any sign of his abandoning the traditional Greek alliance with Britain in favor of the fascist powers (Clogg, 1992, 119–120).

As the result of the Treaty of Neuilly in 1919 (Jelavich, 1983b, 123, 125), Greece gained western Thrace from Bulgaria, thereby not only adding territory but providing a territorial buffer, hence enhanced state security, vis-à-vis Turkey. Additionally, earlier as a consequence of the Balkan Wars

(1912–1913), Greece expanded greatly. The acquisition of most of Macedonia, Crete, southern Epirus, and many Aegean islands led to a 68 percent increase of Greek territory and a population increase from 2.7 to 4.4 million people (Couloumbis et al., 1976, 35). But after the Greek invasion of Anatolia in 1919 (advancing more rapidly in 1921–1922) and its decisive defeat in the summer of 1922, a massive loss was incurred (Smith, 1998, 181). A consequence of that defeat was the expulsion of Anatolian Greeks leading to the resettlement of approximately 1 million of their number in Greece, and the 1923 Treaty of Lausanne that stipulated a population exchange resulting in approximately 350,000 Muslims from Greek territory and 200,000 additional Anatolian and Thracian ethnic Greeks to be resettled respectively in Turkey and Greece (Hirschon, 2003, 14).

The "Great Idea" of incorporating portions of western Anatolia with its large ethnic Greek population into greater Greece had driven Greek foreign policy for decades (Clogg, 1992, 97–99). It was now dead. Instead, a large Greek army, defeated and dispirited, returned to Greece along with the 1.2 million (total) ethnic Greek refugees. Yet, despite this similarity, there are two fundamental distinctions between the Greek illustration and our cases of extremism. First, the earlier period prior to the successes of the Balkan Wars was also replete with territorial increase as the result of a steady expansion. Greece achieved independence from the Ottoman Empire in 1829 (Jelavich & Jelavich, 1977, 50), earlier than any of the other cases analyzed here, indeed close to the start of the period of measurement, 1800. Thus, the period of subordination was shorter and in the more distant past, hence less salient than in our cases of extremism. Second, important for the failure of loss to generate the anger necessary for the urgent irredentist impulse was the simultaneous gain that accrued to Greece. While refugees typically constitute a burden on both the economy and society, in this instance they actually served a positive function for the Greek state.

A consequence of the earlier territorial gains at the end of the Balkan Wars and in 1919 was an insecurely held Macedonia and western Thrace populated by heavily Slavophone and Muslim populations. Bulgaria and Yugoslavia after World War I could have forcefully laid claim to these territories. Indeed, there were such disputes, especially with Bulgaria (Veremis, 2003, 61). By resettling most of the ethnic Greek refugees in Macedonia and western Thrace, the new territory, heretofore vulnerable to Slavophone expansion could be rendered safe and secure for the Greek state. Here is the mitigation of loss in the form of significant loss compensation. Security of the Greek state was enhanced by the addition of these refugees. While not fulfilling the "Great Idea," nevertheless the ingathering of this Greek diaspora, homogenizing the population of Greece through the forced emigration of its Muslim population from western Thrace, and securing the earlier expanded state boundaries was increasingly recognized as a salutary, if painful, outcome of the defeat of 1922 (Kontogiorgi, 2003, 65).

Bulgaria also experienced loss after World War I, specifically western Thrace to Greece and small border corrections to Serbia, at this time in Yugoslavia (Jelavich, 1983, 123).[12] But this loss occurred within the context of an earlier loss (not gain) in the Second Balkan War of June-August 1913 in which Bulgaria lost significant territories in Macedonia gained in the First Balkan War, and southern Dobrudja (October 1912–May 1913: Jelavich, 1983, 99, 166; Shaw & Shaw, 1977, 297).

Interestingly, in his exhaustive survey of fascism worldwide, Stanley Payne appears to have expected that the defeats and territorial losses of Greece (in 1922) and Bulgaria would have led to the mobilization of at least one significant fascist movement. Accordingly,

> Bulgaria, like Greece ... seemed to possess a number of the prerequisites for significant fascist mobilization. As the so-called Prussia of the Balkans, it had been at war almost continuously between 1912 and 1918, suffering great social and economic stress as well as loss of life. Defeated twice within five years, it was despoiled of territory after both the Second Balkan War of 1913 and World War I. Yet the only mass movement to emerge in post-war Bulgaria was the Agrarian Union—a peace movement par excellence. (Payne, 1995, 326)

What Payne did not recognize was the importance of these losses within an earlier context of gains and still earlier subordination in order to yield the surprise, vividness, and emotional intensity that would lead to a call for urgent action in a Bulgarian fascist mass movement, which, of course, did not eventuate.

Conclusion

European governmental fascism and proto-fascism can be understood as immediate consequences of war, and emotional responses to the experience of loss within an earlier context of gains and still earlier subordination—the ephemeral gain. Surprise, vividness, and a resulting urge to action are characteristic of the etiology of these movements. The will to power emerges from the strong incentives to reverse the recent losses, or at least to compensate for them in some form of overt action.

Yet there are ways to blunt or even obviate the consequences of an ephemeral gain. As the case of Greece after 1923 attests, loss compensation can serve to mitigate the impact of loss so that a peaceful and constructive outcome can be achieved. Failing such compensation, however, the analysis here yields the capacity to recognize the characteristics and etiology of embryonic extremist groups before the initiation of mass murder. If such recognition occurs early enough, then some loss compensation might even be initiated by interested countries or international organizations in order to deflect the homicidal impulse.

Undoubtedly there are additional sources of political extremism not explored here; this analysis has identified an etiology rooted in warfare and the loss embedded within an ephemeral gain that can serve as a basis for future research. Indeed, one can use this framework to explain the origins of contemporary radical Islamism.

War in Afghanistan established the bonding and élan among al Qaeda fighters that later was exported to the West. The gain provided by the victory in Afghanistan over the Soviets after a long period of humiliation and defeat proved to be ephemeral after the losses indicated both by the "occupation" of Saudi Arabia by Christian and Jewish American troops and the defeat of Saddam in the 1991 Gulf War. Additionally, according to Olivier Roy (2004, 43), "The real genesis of Al Qaeda violence has more to do with a Western tradition of individual and pessimistic revolt for an elusive ideal world than with the Koranic conception of martyrdom." To varying extents, much the same can be said about other instances of extremism. In South Asia, it is not the Muslim community of India that is principally responsible for terror in that region, but the mostly Hindu LTTE in Sri Lanka, whose origins are found to conform to the ephemeral gain.

Beyond radical Islamism and Sri Lankan terror, one can use this analytic approach to understand the accession to power of Hutu extremists in Rwanda, and their genocidal behavior (and that of the paramilitary *interahamwe*) in 1994, after significant territorial losses to the Rwandese Patriotic Front (Midlarsky, 2005b).

Despite the inability to capture the reigns of government in Russia after 1905, proto-fascism in Russia provided a sufficiently strong precedent to influence by example and migration the later Romanian and German fascist movements. This is another lesson stemming from understanding the origins of fascism. Existing extremist movements are seldom confined in their influence to one time or one place. Even after their formal dissolution, there is no guarantee that they cannot still derail the liberal trajectories of democratic regimes. And whereas members of al Qaeda could not successfully maneuver within the confines of their autocratic

Arab countries of origin, they nevertheless could find the necessary political space first by dominating the government of a neighboring weak state, Afghanistan, and then by exporting radical Islamism to liberal Western shores. Like the earlier proto-typical migration of the Black Hundreds to Germany, al Qaeda could export its influence to more liberal political climes in Western Europe and ultimately, on 9/11, to the U.S.

The process of globalization now has proceeded well beyond that of the early twentieth century, which makes the potential flourishing of extremist groups an even greater threat to contemporary liberal societies. Hopefully, the Iraq war and its opportunities for radical Islamism will not provide the nesting ground for even more extremism, as did the Russo-Japanese War, World War I, and the war in Afghanistan, all with extraordinary consequences for the international system. However, as of this writing, the Iraq war may be one such candidate; a U.S. intelligence assessment already "cites the Iraq war as a reason for the diffusion of jihad (sic) ideology" (Mazetti, 2006, N1).

Political violence and associated territorial losses (uncompensated), especially if contrasted with earlier gains and a still earlier subordination, are likely a necessary condition for the emergence of political extremism. Further theoretical and empirical developments of these ideas, including an expanded historical trajectory and applications to communism, radical Islamism, rampant militarism, and extreme nationalism are found in Midlarsky (forthcoming, 2011).

An unexpected outcome of this analysis is the finding of Russia's central role in the early development of political extremism of all types. From the first modern autocratic tendencies of tsarist Russia after the Decembrist uprising of 1825 until the emergence of authoritarian Bolshevism under Lenin and the first proto-fascists beginning in 1905, Russia had become a fertile source of political extremism. Whether Russia has abandoned that role for good is still an open question.[13]

The centrality of loss, made more vivid by the contrast with earlier gains and evoking still earlier subordination, yields a common purpose among the cases of fascism and proto-fascism, but absent from the instances where political extremism did not take root. This is the overarching goal of restoration, whether it be a latter day Roman Empire in the Mediterranean region under Mussolini's tutelage, an Ottonian-like Germany spread through Central and Eastern Europe, Hungary with restored boundaries including all ethnic Magyars, Romania with its Eastern Orthodoxy restored to prominence throughout all of its lost territories, Russia with its czar once again in full control, or France headed by leadership that was a modern version of late-seventeenth-century French absolutism.[14] The restoration of the Caliphate as a goal of al Qaeda also illustrates this form of "history seeking." None of the three cases of loss without extremism gave evidence of this purpose. Etiology therefore, can reveal an ultimate political program, even when it is not signaled in the early stages of extremist rule.

Finally, one can ask why Germany after 1945 and Russia after 1991 did not develop successful extremist movements upon experiencing substantial territorial losses. The same answer applies in both cases: the importance of international constraints and opportunities. At the end of World War II, Germany found itself occupied by victorious powers that certainly would not allow the formation of extremist movements. After that occupation ended, NATO and the European Union (and its predecessors) effectively cosseted Germany within much larger military and economic frameworks that would have reacted strongly to the rise of German political extremism. Similarly, the Russian Federation after 1991 found itself militarily weakened and economically dependent on the West, largely because of the failure of communism to reap its promised economic rewards. The economic and political support of newly unified Germany and the United States were required to receive needed capital, and most importantly to allow Russia access to the global economy, of course absent during the Cold War period. Permitting an extremist like Vladimir Zhirinovsky to attain political power would have undermined that necessary international support. Thus, international constraints, inducements, and cooperation can thwart the political extremism that is so intimately tied to the territorial losses incurred as the result of interstate conflict.

Notes

1. For reviews of these diverse approaches, see Gregor (1979, 1999, 2005) and Payne (1995, 441–495).

2. Several days after the invasion and the almost immediate realization that the loss of Sicily was a near certainty, for the first time, Mussolini granted Germany's request for the deportation of Jews from Italian occupied France (Zuccotti, 2000, 132).

3. For an important fascist movement with religious trappings that did not attain political power, see Brustein (1988).

4. An earlier regime with fascist leanings was formed in December 1937 (lasting only until February 1938) by a mentor of Codreanu, Alexander Cuza, and Octavian Goga of the National Christian Defense Party. But Cuza disapproved of illegality and violence (Weber, 1965b, 526), and the party ultimately did not achieve the mass base of the Iron Guard (Jelavich, 1983b, 206).

5. An example is found in Hitler's response to the signing of the concordat with the Vatican in 1933 that it would be "especially significant in the urgent struggle against international Jewry" (quoted in Midlarsky, 2005b, 223).

6. The importance of territory as an explanatory variable is found in Huth (1996), Diehl (1999), Vasquez (2000), and Walter (2003).

7. I concentrate on interstate war because here one finds most clearly the coercion by an external foe and consequent humiliation associated with territorial loss, in the midst of war or at its end. The Polish–Soviet War of 1919–1920 led to territorial loss for the Soviets, but was excluded from the cases in this study because at the time of this loss, Soviet extremism was already well established, thereby denying the opportunity for fascist mobilization. High-intensity civil wars involving territorial loss—those with many casualties—also could be included because they are emotionally laden, but were not found in Europe during this time period. Ottoman losses are not counted because of the status of the Ottoman Empire as principally a Middle Eastern state, with Anatolia and the Arab provinces (until 1919) comprising the vast majority of Ottoman territory.

8. This period extends from the beginning of the twentieth century until the close of World War II. After 1945, the grip of Soviet-style extremism had enveloped countries such as Poland that had or was about to experience territorial loss, but without the opportunity to initiate fascism because of the Soviet presence. Finland lost the Winter War of 1939–1940 with the Soviet Union, but almost immediately regained its lost territories in the Continuation War of 1941–1944. The Soviet presence, of course, also applies to the Finnish case after 1945.

9. Although the Congress of Berlin in 1878 frustrated the major Russian political goal of massive Bulgarian expansion at Ottoman expense, the territories conquered by Russia remained almost entirely intact (only Batum became a free port; Mazour, 1962, 303). Afterward, as Bulgaria drifted steadily out of the Russian orbit ultimately siding with the Central Powers during World War I, the "loss" of territory by Bulgaria was seen by Russian policy makers as a salutary consequence of the Congress of Berlin.

10. A Jewish officer on the French General Staff, Alfred Dreyfus, was falsely accused of treason and imprisoned until ultimately exonerated. Anti-Dreyfusards were those who opposed that process of exoneration.

11. Also quoted in Payne (1995, 47).

12. The loss here is that experienced at the end of World War I not that of the Second Balkan War just prior to World War I. Fascism must have an opportunity to take hold after a territorial loss and this was not possible during the enormous societal strains of World War I. Only an extremist movement already established well before the war could have initiated an extremist government, much as the Bolsheviks were able to do toward the end of that war, having been organizationally established even before 1905, and then only able to make the revolution because of German help in getting Lenin and his colleagues across Germany to Russia from Switzerland in 1917 (Pipes 1990, 390–392).

13. The restoration to a prominent public space from a "monster's graveyard" of the statue of Feliks Dzerzhinsky, the founder of the Cheka, forerunner of the KGB, and mass murderer, does not bode especially well for the future (Randolph, 2005).

14. In 1685, Louis XIV revoked the Edict of Nantes that earlier had granted civil liberties to the French Protestants (Huguenots) thereby opening the path to their slaughter and expulsion. In a striking historical parallel, Pétain's government

revoked Jewish civil liberties in the autumn of 1940, facilitating the later deportations to the Nazi death camps (Marrus and Paxton, 1995, 3).

References

Albrecht-Carrié, R. (1958). *A diplomatic history of Europe since the Congress of Vienna*. New York: Harper.
Anderson, B. (1991). *Imagined communities: Reflections on the origin and spread of nationalism*. London: Verso.
Ben-Ghiat, R. (2001). *Fascist modernities: Italy, 1922–1945*. Berkeley: University of California Press.
Berkowitz, L. (2003). Affect, aggression, and antisocial behavior. In R. J. Davidson, K. R. Scherer & H. H. Goldsmith (Eds.), *Handbook of affective sciences*. Oxford: Oxford University Press, 804–823.
Bodenhausen, G. V., Sheppard, L. A., & Kramer, G. P. (1994). Negative affect and social judgment: The differential impact of anger and sadness. *European Journal of Social Psychology* 24 (1), 45–62.
Bosworth, R. J. B. (2002). *Mussolini*. London: Arnold.
Braham, R. L. (2000). *The politics of genocide: The Holocaust in Hungary*. Detroit, MI: Wayne State University Press.
Braudel, F. (1984). *The perspective of the world*. Vol. 3 of *Civilization and capitalism, 15th–18th century*, (S. Reynolds, Trans.). New York: Harper & Row.
Browning, C. R. (2004). *The origins of the final solution: The evolution of Nazi Jewish policy, September 1939–March 1942*. Jerusalem: Yad Vashem, and Lincoln: University of Nebraska Press.
Brustein, W. (1988). The political geography of Belgian fascism: The case of Rexism. *American Sociological Review* 53 (February), 69–80.
Brustein, W. (1991). The "red menace" and the rise of Italian fascism. *American Sociological Review* 56 (October), 652–664.
Brustein, W. (1996). *The logic of evil: The social origins of the Nazi party, 1925–1933*. New Haven, CT: Yale University Press.
Clogg, R. (1992). *A concise history of Greece*. Cambridge: Cambridge University Press.
Couloumbis, T. A., Petropulos, J. A., & Psomiades, H. J. (1976). *Foreign interference in Greek politics: An historical perspective*. New York: Pella.
Deák, I. (1965). Hungary. In H. Rogger & E. Weber (Eds.), *The European right: A historical profile*. Berkeley: University of California Press, 364–407.
DeSteno, D. N., Dassgupta, N. M., Bartlett, Y., & Cajddric, A. (2004). Prejudice from thin air: The effect of emotion on automatic intergroup attitudes. *Psychological Science* 15 (5), 319–324.
Diehl, P. F. (Ed.). (1999). *The road map to war: Territorial dimensions of international conflict*. Nashville, TN: Vanderbilt University Press.

Dubnov, S. (1973). *History of the Jews: From the congress of Vienna to the emergence of Hitler* (Vol. V) (M. Spiegel, Trans.). New York: Thomas Yoseloff.
Elster, J. (2004). Emotion and action. In R. C. Solomon (Ed.), *Thinking about feeling: Contemporary philosophers on emotions*. Oxford: Oxford University Press, 151–162.
Evans, R. J. (2004). *The coming of the Third Reich*. New York: Penguin Books.
Fellner, F. (1981). Introduction: The genesis of the Austrian Republic. In K. Steiner, F. Fellner & H. Feichtlbauer (Eds.), *Modern Austria*. Palo Alto, CA: Society for the Promotion of Science and Scholarship, 1–20.
Frijda, N. H. (1986). *The emotions*. Cambridge: Cambridge University Press.
Frijda, N. H. (1994). The lex talionis: On vengeance. In S. H. M. Van Goozen, N. E. Van De Poll & J. A. Sergeant (Eds.), *Emotions: Essays on emotion theory*. Hillsdale, NJ: Lawrence Erlbaum, 263–289.
Goertz, G., & Diehl, P. (1992). *Territorial changes and international conflict*. London: Routledge.
Gregor, A. J. (1979). *Young Mussolini and the intellectual origins of fascism*. Berkeley: University of California Press.
Gregor, A. J. (1999). *Phoenix: Fascism in our time*. New Brunswick, NJ: Transaction.
Gregor, A. J. (2005). *Mussolini's intellectuals: Fascist social and political thought*. Princeton, NJ: Princeton University Press.
Haidt, J. (2003). The moral emotions. In R. J. Davidson, K. R. Scherer & H. H. Goldsmith (Eds.), *Handbook of affective sciences*. Oxford: Oxford University Press, 852–870.
Herz, J. H. (1957). Rise and demise of the territorial state. *World Politics* 9 (July), 473–493.
Hilberg, R. (2003). *The destruction of the European Jews* (3rd ed.). New Haven, CT: Yale University Press.
Hirschon, R. (2003). The consequences of the Lausanne convention: An overview. In Renée Hirschon (Ed.), *Crossing the Aegean: An appraisal of the 1923 compulsory population exchange between Greece and Turkey*. Oxford: Berghahn Books, 13–20.
Huth, P. K. (1996). *Standing your ground: Territorial disputes and international conflict*. Ann Arbor: University of Michigan Press.
Ioanid, R. (2000). *The Holocaust in Romania: The destruction of Jews and gypsies under the Antonescu regime, 1940–1944*. Chicago: Ivan R. Dee.
Jelavich, B. (1983a). *History of the Balkans* (Vol. I). Cambridge: Cambridge University Press.
Jelavich, B. (1983b). *History of the Balkans* (Vol. II). Cambridge: Cambridge University Press.
Jelavich, C., & Jelavich, B. (1977). *The establishment of the Balkan national states, 1804–1920*. Seattle: University of Washington Press.
Kahneman, D., & Tversky, A. (1979). Prospect theory: An analysis of decision under risk. *Econometrica* 47 (2), 263–292.

Kahneman, D., & Tversky, A., (Eds.). (2000). *Choices, values, and frames.* Cambridge: Cambridge University Press.

Knox, M. (1996). Expansionist zeal, fighting power, and staying power in the Italian and German dictatorships. In R. Bessel (Ed.), *Fascist Italy and Nazi Germany: Comparisons and contrasts.* Cambridge: Cambridge University Press, 113–133.

Kontogiorgi, E. (2003). Economic consequences following refugee settlement in Greek Macedonia, 1923–1932. In R. Hirschon (Ed.), *Crossing the Aegean: An appraisal of the 1923 compulsory population exchange between Greece and Turkey.* Oxford: Berghahn Books, 63–77.

Laqueur, W. (1996). *Fascism: Past, present, future.* New York: Oxford University Press.

Levy, J. S. (2000). Loss aversion, framing effects, and international conflict: Perspectives from prospect theory. In M. I. Midlarsky (Ed.), *Handbook of war studies II.* Ann Arbor: University of Michigan Press, 193–221.

Linz, J. J. (1980). Political space and fascism as a late-comer. In S. U. Larsen, B. Hagtvet & J. P. Myklebust (Eds.), *Who were the fascists?: Social roots of European Fascism.* Oslo: Universitetsforlaget, 153–189.

Lyttelton, A. (1996). The "crisis of bourgeois society" and the origins of fascism. In R. Bessel (Ed.), *Fascist Italy and Nazi Germany: Comparisons and contrasts.* Cambridge: Cambridge University Press, 12–22.

Malcolm, N. (2002). *Bosnia: A short history.* London: Pan Macmillan.

Malia, M. (1999). *Russia under western eyes: From the bronze horseman to the Lenin mausoleum.* Cambridge, MA: Harvard University Press.

Mann, M. (2004). *Fascists.* New York: Cambridge University Press.

Marcus, G. E., Neuman, R., & MacKuen, M. (2000). *Affective intelligence and political judgment.* Chicago: University of Chicago Press.

Marrus, M. R., & Paxton, R. O. (1995). *Vichy France and the Jews.* Stanford, CA: Stanford University Press.

McDermott, R. (2004). The feeling of rationality: The meaning of neuroscientific advances for political science. *Perspectives on Politics* 2 (December), 691–706.

Mele, A. R. (2003). Emotion and desire in self-deception. In A. Hatzimoysis (Ed.), *Philosophy and the emotions.* Cambridge: Cambridge University Press, 163–179.

Midlarsky, M. I. (2005a). The demographics of genocide: Refugees and territorial loss in the mass murder of European Jewry. *Journal of Peace Research* 42 (July), 375–391.

Midlarsky, M. I. (2005b). *The killing trap: Genocide in the twentieth century.* Cambridge: Cambridge University Press.

Midlarsky, M. I. (forthcoming, 2011). *Origins of political extremism: Mass violence in the 20th century and beyond.* Cambridge: Cambridge University Press.

Nagy-Talavera, N. (2001). *The green shirts and the others: A history of Fascism in Hungary and Romania.* Iaşi: Center for Romanian Studies.

Nisbett, R. E., & Cohen, D. (1996). *Culture of honor: The psychology of violence in the south.* Boulder, CO: Westview Press.

Nolte, E. (1966). *Three faces of fascism: Action Française, Italian Fascism, National Socialism*, (L. Vennewitz, Trans.). New York: Holt, Rinehart and Winston.
Paxton, R. O. (2004). *The anatomy of fascism*. New York: Vintage.
Payne, S. G. (1995). *A history of fascism, 1914–1945*. Madison: University of Wisconsin Press.
Pipes, R. (1990). *The Russian revolution*. New York: Knopf.
Randolph, E. (2005). Ultimate Soviet henchman returns to his pedestal. *New York Times*. November 20, wk 11.
Rawson, D. C. (1995). *Russian rightists and the revolution of 1905*. Cambridge: Cambridge University Press.
Rogger, H. (1964a). The formation of the Russian right, 1900–1906. In N. V. Riasanovsky & G. Struve (Eds.), *California Slavic studies* (vol. III). Berkeley: University of California Press, 66–94.
Rogger, H. (1964b). Was there a Russian fascism? The union of Russian people. *Journal of Modern History* 36 (December), 398–415.
Rogger, H. (1965). Russia. In H. Rogger & E. Weber (Eds.), *The European right: A historical profile*. Berkeley: University of California Press, 443–500.
Roy, O. (2004). *Globalized Islam: The search for a new ummah*. New York: Columbia University Press.
Schivelbusch, W. (2003). *The culture of defeat: On national trauma, mourning, and recovery*, (J. Chase, Trans.). New York: Metropolitan Books.
Shaw, S. J., & Shaw, E. K. (1977). *History of the Ottoman Empire and modern Turkey* (Vol. II), *Reform, revolution, and republic: The rise of modern Turkey, 1808–1975*. New York: Cambridge University Press.
Smith, M. L. (1998). *Ionian vision: Greece in Asia Minor, 1919–1922*. Ann Arbor: University of Michigan Press.
Stein, N., Trabasso, T., & Liwag, M. (1993). The representation and organization of emotional experience: Unfolding the emotion episode. In M. Lewis & J. M. Haviland (Eds.), *Handbook of emotions*. New York: Guilford Press, 279–300.
Steinberg, J. (1990). *All or nothing: The Axis and the Holocaust, 1941–1943*. London: Routledge.
Sternhell, Z. (1994). *The birth of fascist ideology: From cultural rebellion to political revolution*, (D. Maisel, Trans.). Princeton, NJ: Princeton University Press.
Toft, M. D. (2003). *The geography of ethnic violence: Identity, interests, and the indivisibility of territory*. Princeton, NJ: Princeton University Press.
Vasquez, J. (2000). Reexamining the steps to war: New evidence and theoretical insights. In M. I. Midlarsky (Ed.), *Handbook of war studies II*. Ann Arbor: University of Michigan Press, 371–406.
Veremis, T. (2003). 1922: Political continuations and realignments in the Greek State. In R. Hirschon (Ed.), *Crossing the Aegean: An appraisal of the 1923 compulsory population exchange between Greece and Turkey*. Oxford, UK: Berghahn Books, 53–62.
Walter, B. F. (2003). Explaining the intractability of territorial conflict. *International Studies Review* 5 (4), 137–153.

Weber, E. (1964). *Varieties of fascism: Doctrines of revolution in the twentieth century*. New York: Van Nostrand Reinhold.

Weber, E. (1965a). France. In H. Rogger & E. Weber (Eds.), *The European right: A historical profile*. Berkeley: University of California Press, 71–127.

Weber, E. (1965b). Romania. In H. Rogger & E. Weber (Eds.), *The European right: A historical profile*. Berkeley: University of California Press, 501–574.

Wellhofer, E. S. (2003). Democracy and fascism: Class, civil society, and rational choice in Italy. *American Political Science Review* 97 (February), 91, 106.

Westen, D., Blagov, P. S., Harenski, K., Kilts C., & Hamann, S. (2006). *An fMRI study of motivated reasoning: Partisan political reasoning in the U.S. presidential election*. Atlanta, GA: Emory University, Psychology Department.

Wolfe, B. (1984). *Three who made a revolution: A biographical history*. New York: Stein & Day.

Chapter 3

The Technology of Terror
Accounting for the Strategic Use of Terrorism

Christopher K. Butler and Scott Gates

The most disadvantageous peace is better than the most just war.
—Erasmus: Adagia, 1508

A bad peace is even worse than war.
—Tacitus: Annals, iii, ca. 110

Introduction

As the dust settled from the First Gulf War, American troops remained stationed in Saudi Arabia. Osama bin Laden—already exiled for his outspoken dissent regarding the stationing of American troops on Saudi soil even to defend the country against the possibility of Iraqi invasion—decided that he would take on the military might of the United States. Obviously, guerrilla tactics—of which terrorism is a part—would be required. Bin Laden had seen the success of such tactics against the Soviet army in Afghanistan. In fact, bin Laden largely achieved his immediate objective when the United States relocated the bulk of its Arabian Peninsula forces to Qatar in 2003. Confidence built on success should not to be overestimated.[1]

Given Osama bin Laden's motivation, experience, and resources, it seems patently obvious that he would follow through on his intent. Although many question the moral and ethical justification behind al Qaeda's war against the United States, we turn our attention to the flip side of the question. Why is it that all discontented groups with some ability to hurt their enemies *do not* turn to guerrilla tactics? For a group faced with certain (if eventual) defeat in a conventional war, their leaders must weigh the options of enduring peace on disadvantageous terms and of prosecuting an unconventional war.

In war, the more powerful do not always win. Sometimes the weaker party defeats the side with the bigger and better equipped army. History tells of many cases of Davids defeating Goliaths; in the later half of the twentieth century alone, a number of wars stand out: Indonesian Independence (1946–1954), Indochina (1947–1949), Algeria (1954–1962), Vietnam (1965–1975), Afghanistan (1978–1989), First Chechen (1994–1996) (Mack, 1975; Paul, 1994; Arreguín-Toft, 2001). Military strategists explain this phenomenon by focusing on the strategic adoption of unconventional tactics and strategies by the weaker side so as to put the conflict on a more even footing. In fact, systematic analysis of wars over time demonstrates that strategic factors play a significant role in determining victory in battle (Stam, 1996; Arreguín-Toft, 2001; Rotte & Schmidt, 2003).

Choices in the Face of Asymmetry

Guerrilla warfare and terrorism are common methods of overcoming superior troop strength and technology. In this chapter we discuss how terrorism addresses this asymmetry and, more importantly, what the limits of terrorism as an effective strategy may be. We confront this problem in terms of strategic choices in which there are at least three actors: a weak insurgent group fighting for some political purpose, a population that the group is fighting for, and a superior force that the group is fighting against. As we are trying to figure out the choices of the insurgent group, we confine our discussion of the population and the superior force to choices made in reaction to the choices of the insurgent group. These choices, in turn, affect the decision calculus of the insurgent group.

Unconventional warfare takes place when a vastly inferior force compensates for its relative weakness by engaging the superior power in such a way as to minimize the differences in capability. However, the choice to engage in unconventional warfare when the tables are so stacked against the inferior force is but one of many that the insurgent group could take. We simplify the choice set of the weak group to three classes of alternatives: suffering a disadvantageous peace, engaging in unconventional warfare (including terrorism and guerrilla warfare), or engaging in conventional warfare. These alternatives will guide the rest of the discussion of this chapter. Before delving into them, however, we first discuss the other actors and their choices.

Any insurgent organization fights for and to a large extent derives power from a complicit public. The population the insurgent group is fighting for is presumed to be a heterogeneous group of individuals from which the weak group is comprised. The population is important to the weak group for recruits, material support, and shelter, and immaterial legitimacy and public opinion. The choices of individuals within this population with respect to each of these things affect the strength of the group in absolute terms and, indirectly, in relative terms as well. We presume that the weak group is primarily made up of recruits from the heterogeneous population who feel most strongly that peace is disadvantageous and that the leadership of the group has the most intense feelings of all.[1] We also assume that recruits can desert the ranks of the insurgent group as perceptions of the group change within the population.

The superior force, which is often a state, is depicted by at least some in the population as an oppressor imposing a disadvantageous peace. The superior force is not likely to share this perception itself. Instead, it is likely to perceive itself as the sole legitimate political actor in a territory that is merely trying to govern the best that it can. How the superior force governs affects the opinion of the population toward it. Among the other choices of the superior force is the suppression of rebellion targeted at the insurgent group. The members of the insurgent group know who they are and the individuals of the public have relatively reliable information regarding who are members of the insurgent group, but the superior force is hindered in its suppression efforts by having high uncertainty about who are members and who are not.

As the concept of a disadvantageous peace is central to our argument, we turn now to a discussion of that. "Unfair" distributions of resources, or at least allocations that are perceived to be unfair across groups, often serve as the basis for conflict. Disparity between groups, or horizontal inequality, in fact, underlies many civil wars (Østby, 2005; Murshed & Gates, 2005).[2] If the superior force knowingly extracts an unfair allocation, one might argue that it should expect resistance. However, what constitutes fair and unfair is a question open to interpretation. Inequitable distribution of resources does not deterministically lead to armed civil conflict. As Butler, Gates, and Leiby (2005) argue, there may be any number of reasons for collective income being divided unequally *without* conflict. Proportional divisions are often regarded as the "fairest" outcome. "Indeed, this notion is the fundamental principle underlying proportionally representative political systems" (Butler et al., 2005:4).

Another feature of "unfairness" is less tangible and relies on in-group/out-group psychology. The greater the degree of dissimilarity between groups, the easier it is for insurgent leaders to appeal to the complicit public for support (Gates, 2002). This type of ethnic or ideological proximity makes it easier for insurgent leaders to demonize the superior force regarding even small injustices.

Logic and Limitations of Unconventional Warfare

In choosing between a disadvantageous peace and unconventional warfare, we assume that the option of prosecuting a conventional war has already been set aside. This may be due to an inherent inability to engage a significantly superior enemy or due to reverses in a conventional war that make continuing with conventional tactics unreasonable. There are important differences between conventional and unconventional war that highlight the disadvantages of guerrilla tactics.

In conventional war, each side has discernable territory and tactics involve extending one's own territory at the expense of one's enemy. This also implies, however, that each side can provide a degree of defense to its civilians. The absence of territorial demarcation within unconventional warfare implies both that the stronger side cannot guarantee the safety of its civilians and that the guerrillas cannot guarantee the safety of their compatriots. In fact, the superior force can do much to support peace by guaranteeing personal security for the general citizenry even if other aspects of the peace are biased (Gartner & Regan, 1996). It is no accident of history that the Basque in Spain were content to be ruled from Madrid prior to Franco's repression following the Spanish Civil War.

This lack of any provision of defense is a serious drawback to unconventional warfare when compared to conventional warfare and to a disadvantageous peace. In turn, it also affects recruiting and calculating the cost of war. Recruiting is affected in that potential guerrillas must recognize that their families will have an increased risk of harm if they join the war. In a conventional war, potential recruits can be sold on the notion that they are, in fact, defending their families by joining the war effort. By preventing an enemy from invading, one's family is generally spared the direct deprivations of war. In guerrilla war, however, a recruit's family may be intentionally targeted because of his involvement against the superior force. To the extent that the stronger side is indiscriminate in its violence against sympathetic civilians, the recruit is not significantly increasing the odds of harm befalling them. This may make it easier for the weaker side to recruit (Gartner & Regan, 1996; Kalyvas, 2003; Kalyvas, 2006). The more discriminating the stronger side, however, the larger this factor weighs on potential recruits.

There is a critical interaction between perceived inequalities, the actions of the insurgent group, and the reactions of the state. If the inequality is sustained by the state, especially if it is maintained by violence, the job of insurgent leaders is made even easier. "The danger is that itchy generals tire of talking and revert to seeking military solutions, becoming once again the [insurgents'] best recruiting sergeant" (*Economist* 2007, 54). Because the superior force has difficulty in ascertaining members of the insurgent group from the general public, it may target innocent civilians—inadvertently or intentionally—in its effort to suppress the rebellion. This may have an effect of increasing sympathy for the insurgent group (Gartner & Regan, 1996).

The use of violence against the civilian population is also an essential element of guerrilla warfare. The insurgent leaders target those within the civilian population who are sympathetic to the government side. A village in the proverbial guerrilla combat zone is controlled by government soldiers during the day and by insurgents at night. Nonuniformed and loosely organized, insurgents typically embed themselves in the civilian population, which serves to both sustain their activities as well as make it difficult for them to be detected. Unable to control territory outright (or at least where control of territory is fragmented), the state and insurgent group utilize violence directed at the civilian population. The state engages in violence directed at the civilian population believed to be harboring the insurgents. "Armed groups target civilians as they organize their militaries, solicit resources to sustain the fighting, build bases of popular support, and weaken the support networks of opposing groups" (Weinstein, 2007, 198). On top of such directed violence, civil war is also associated with episodes of opportunistic violence, in which private revenge, blood feuds, as well as violent criminal activity such as robbery thrive in an environment of widespread violence (Kalyvas, 2003; King, 2004; Kalyvas, 2006; Weinstein, 2007). Instead of assuring the security of the civilians, violence against civilians becomes an inherent element of the conflict between the insurgents and the state.

The calculations of the cost of war are also affected by this lack of human security. The toll on civilian lives can be expected to be significantly greater for both sides when employing guerrilla tactics as compared to either conventional war or a disadvantageous peace.[3] To the extent that leaders care about this factor as opposed to their own agenda, a disadvantageous peace may be the lesser of two evils.

Another difference between conventional and unconventional war is the nature of the chain of command. Command and control is fairly rigid in conventional war. When shifting to guerrilla tactics, however, the chain of command weakens to a point where leaders may not have any real influence over their operational commanders. Although the leaders may support a guerrilla war of hit-and-run tactics against explicitly military targets, the operational commanders may decide on their own to attack softer civilian targets. Such an attack is safer and easier to execute, but it has the potential drawback of reducing the legitimacy of the overall movement. Indeed, this type of reasoning may have been central to General Lee's decision not to have his troops disperse into the mountains at the end of the American Civil War (Winik, 2001).[4]

Unconventional war does have the benefit of being able to hurt the superior force perceived as imposing a disadvantageous peace. This approach appeals to the notions of justice and revenge. To the extent that individuals can get away with even small hurting actions without costs to themselves or their families, we should expect to observe them (Scott, 1976; 1985).[5] This then creates an opportunity for recruitment of such individuals into an organized opposition (Popkin, 1979; Lichbach, 1994).

The existence of an organized opposition usually implies motivations beyond hurting a common enemy. Leaders of such groups often have an ambition of taking over the state in its entirety or the secession of some distinct part of the country. Short of such goals, these groups may demand certain policy concessions that enhance their prestige and authority. As leaders of an armed group engaged in a violent struggle against the state, their primary problem is to recruit enough men to guarantee the viability of the group and to help ensure the security of the leaders. To do this, leaders must convince people to join as well to remain within the groups. Through a mix of pecuniary and nonpecuniary incentives and punishment schemes, this can be achieved (Gates, 2002). Nonpecuniary rewards, such as ideology or notions of religious solidarity or common kinship serve as especially power motivations. The nature of this mix will depend largely on the resource endowment of the group (Weinstein, 2007).

Violence against the civilian population plays a critical role in recruitment. Because the insurgent members are often embedded within the civilian population, they possess an information advantage vis-à-vis the state. Given this condition of asymmetric information, one strategy often employed by insurgency groups is to provoke the government's army to engage in indiscriminate violence. The insurgent group can hence appeal to the resultant sense of a transgression of justice and recruit those now charged with a desire to seek revenge. The information asymmetry further plays to the advantage of the insurgent group who are able to target their punishment to individual collaborators rather than engaging in indiscriminate violence.

Choices within Unconventional Warfare

Kiras (2007, 166–167) argues that a critical difference between guerrilla warfare and terrorism is the ability to win militarily. Although both are irregular tactics, guerrillas have sufficient strength that they can win the war outright if they win a pivotal battle or take a significant strategic location. Terrorists, in this argument, can never win their war.

We suggest that a more dynamic approach has to be considered before dismissing the terrorists' chances of winning so quickly. In particular, early local victories for guerrilla forces alter the pattern of recruitment. The side that employed guerrilla tactics and won in prominent wars—the American Revolution, Vietnam, the Cuban Revolution, and the Communist takeover of China in 1949 all come to mind—was a substantially enhanced side at war's end compared to their force strength at the beginning of the war. Indeed, in some of these cases, the war was eventually won on conventional terms. This suggests that insurgent leaders alter their decision regarding warfare strategy as circumstances change.

Terrorist groups that have made headway in their conflicts are, likewise, strengthened by their efforts. The other side of this distinction is what constitutes winning. Terrorist groups can get some of their smaller demands met, without formal bargaining with the target country. Ransoms are often paid, prisoners are sometimes exchanged, and—though rarely—superpowers remove their troops from holy territory. In such protracted conflicts, it is not clear that either side has the capability to completely subdue the other. This feature of warfare works between two territorial states, each of which must administer their territory to maintain their sovereign status. Irregulars of either type are not exercising sovereignty; hence, it cannot be taken away.

In some cases, groups that engage primarily in terrorist tactics can achieve victory. This is especially the case of an insurgency group engaged in conflict where media coverage is open. The British gave up authority of Palestine partly in response to the terrorist violence of such groups as the Zionist Stern Gang. The British government at the time was not prepared to engage in ongoing conflict with the Jewish population of Palestine, especially in the wake of the Holocaust. In this regard, the insurgency group raised the ante, which the occupying power was unwilling to match. Similarly, the British left Cyprus as a result of the EOKA guerrilla activity. Terrorist violence also can be effective more indirectly by maintaining visibility of the cause in the media through the employment of violence. The Provisional Irish Republican Army is not sitting in government in Northern Ireland directly because of their terrorist violence, but the violence kept their issues in the media and high on the policy-making agenda, which eventually led to the present state of affairs.

This discussion suggests that the time horizons of insurgent leaders affect their strategic choice of warfare, though how exactly is less than clear. One could argue that General Lee had a long time horizon when he made his decision to surrender his army to General Grant, but Lee also placed great weight on future Southern lives that would be lost by continued fighting. Another general may have had an equally long time horizon but placed great weight on winning eventually. Insurgent leaders with short time horizons, however, are likely to see any costs and any delays in reaching objectives as equally bad. Such "leaders" are less likely to pursue a long-term ideological struggle and more likely to be criminals pursuing easily attained economic gains. Even this type of leader, however, would seek the advantages of clothing his activities in political terms. This requires that the population perceives their situation as disadvantageous vis-à-vis the state and that they attribute legitimacy to the insurgent "leader." Given such a Robin Hood effect, the leader may well start out a thief but becomes a hero. If that "hero" eventually wins, however, the public may find that they have helped set up a kleptocracy.

Logic and Limitations of Terrorism

This section defines terrorism, identifies differences and similarities between terrorist and guerrilla strategies, evaluates limitations of terrorism as an unconventional strategy, and discusses the effect of asymmetric access to military technology on terrorist activity.

Defining Terrorism

Terrorism, like murder, is a word laden with extreme pejorative connotations and, hence, is prone to rhetorical abuse. But at least with the case of murder, we can use the more neutral term, homicide—we don't talk about *justifiable murder*, instead we use the term, *justifiable homicide*. Unfortunately, we lack a more neutral term for terrorism. To avoid the tendency for one side's terrorist to be another's freedom fighter and to engage in an analytical discourse about the phenomenon, we must clearly define the term in neutral language. Given the lack of a universally accepted definition of terrorism, we employ the following definition: *Terrorism is a strategy designed to further a political agenda by a system of violence perpetrated by a nonstate actor against noncombatant targets thereby instilling fear and intimidation among a wider audience.*

A number of assumptions underlie this definition. First as a strategy, terrorism is viewed to be an act based inherently on intentional choices, subject to the principles of utility maximization. In other words, terrorism is a rational choice. Furthermore, as a strategy, "the ability of one participant to gain his ends is dependent to an important degree on the choices or decisions that the other participant will make" (Schelling, 1960, 5).[6] Accounting for such strategic interaction is the fundamental element of game theory—the method of analysis that lies behind the arguments made in this chapter.[7] Military historian, Liddell Hart's definition of military strategy follows in this line, "the art of distributing and applying military means to fulfill the ends of policy" (Reiter, 1999, 367).

Second, the underlying motivation is political. We thereby rule out sadistically killing people "just for the fun of it." Ideological and religious motivations are subsumed as being fundamentally political. Fundamentally, terrorism is a strategy of coercion. Violence and the threat of violence are employed to coerce political change.

Third, noncombatants are the immediate target. Attacks on military personnel such as al Qaeda's attack on the USS *Cole* in 2000 or the Hezbollah attacks on the U.S. Marines and French paratroopers in Lebanon in 1983 are not terrorist attacks. The fact that the same groups target vulnerable military targets as well as softer civilian ones is merely indicative of their overall unconventional strategy. However, this distinction in targeting is one that we return to later.

Fourth, a broader audience serves as the ultimate target of terrorism than just the complicit public. This notion of a broader audience presumes a causal logic underlying the motivation, such that the terrorist *act* aimed at the immediate target leads to an *effect* of terrorizing a broader population, ultimately inducing political *change*. By creating a broad psychology of fear, the coercive threat of terrorist violence is made much more effective. In fact, the widespread environment of fear—the *effect* of terrorism—is much more of a threat to a state than the actual costs of the actual terrorist *act*.[8] Indeed, this larger effect belies the central logic of terrorism.[9]

By and large, these assumptions will not attract too much controversy. What is divisive is the one point remaining in our definition. That is, who is the perpetrator of terrorism? Our definition identifies the actor, as a nonstate actor. This is consistent with the mass media and general public use of the term; terrorism is an action committed by a nonstate actor with an intention of altering the status quo. In terms of criminal law, the legal definition of terrorism is also typically restricted to nonstate actors only.[10]

There is some irony to this convention. In its original usage, terrorism explicitly referred to the actions taken by the state.[11] Etymologically the term derives from the French word, *terrorisme*, regarding the Reign of Terror in Revolutionary France (Harper, 2001).[12] Terror as justified by Robespierre and applied by the Jacobins was used to destroy the old system as an inextricable aspect of the revolution, through which terror and virtue were coupled (Rapoport, 1982, xiii–xiv; Hoffman, 1998). "*Terrorist* in the modern sense dates to 1947, especially in reference to Jewish tactics against the British in Palestine—earlier it was used of extremist revolutionaries in Russia in 1866" (Harper, 2001).[13]

Given our definition of terrorism, a terrorist group is thus an organization that engages in terrorist activities against a state or several nation-states. Hence, a terrorist organization is an insurgency group engaged in civil conflict, but distinguished by its use of terrorism. Indeed, many insurgent armies engage in terrorism as one of many strategies and techniques of violence. In this regard, terrorism is not treated as a separate phenomenon or a distinct form of organized violence, but rather as a particular strategy of insurgency, a strategy designed to overcome asymmetry.

Differences and Similarities between Terrorist and Guerrilla Strategies

Etymologically, guerrilla derives from the Spanish term *guerra* (or war) with the diminutive *-illa* ending, which can be translated as "small war" (and directly translates to Clausewitz's *kleinkrieg*). "The actual word 'guerrilla' came from the Spanish insurgency against France in the early 1800s" (Winik, 2001, 149). We define guerrilla warfare as follows: *a method of unconventional warfare by which small groups of combatants employ mobile and surprise tactics, such as ambushes, raids, sabotage, and so forth in an effort to cripple the state, particularly the military capacity of the state.*

Both terrorism and guerrilla warfare constitute two different strategic alternatives of unconventional warfare. Both aim to alter the political order. In its purest forms, terrorism would affect change indirectly through the creation of a state of fear among the general populace. Guerrilla tactics, in contrast, focus more directly on the infrastructure and agents of the state.

Theories of guerrilla warfare have been developed by many different military theorists and revolutionaries over the centuries, though the dominant philosophy has been Maoist. The three phases involve: first, gain support of the population through propaganda and attacks on the state; second, escalate violence, particularly aiming at the state's military capabilities; third, shift to conventional warfare and capture the cities with the goal of seizing control of the country (Mao, 1937). This strategy has been widely adopted. Giap led the Viet Minh army in the Indo-china War against the French following Mao's strategy almost completely; it has also been employed by the Nepalese Maoists, Shining Path in Peru, FARC in Colombia, among others, have all explicitly followed Mao's strategic approach to guerrilla war. Other groups, such as the Naxalites in India present a Maoist political ideology, but have not explicitly followed a Maoist military strategy.

Terror plays a role in guerrilla warfare, but the focus of the strategy is primarily to weaken the capacity of the state. This is the principal difference between a pure terrorist line of attack and a guerrilla strategy. In general the demand on a group's resources will be higher with guerrilla warfare than with a pure terrorist strategy. Guerrilla movements, in general, require more manpower (more recruits), more money and more weapons (and weapons of greater degrees of technical sophistication). Terrorism requires much less.

Limitations of Terrorism as an Unconventional Strategy

According to Richard Betts, "Terrorism is the premier form of asymmetric warfare" (2003, 341). Asymmetry can stem from *unequal access to resources* with which to devote to the conflict and *unequal military technology*. We apply both forms of asymmetry to our analysis.

Insurgent organizations engaged in guerrilla warfare or terrorism fight on behalf of and for the favor of a broad or narrow public. A group may claim to represent their ethnic kin, or fellow believers, or the poor and downtrodden in general. These complicit publics, whose support (tacit as well as active) is critical to the success of their military strategy, play an important role in civil conflict. Insurgencies are played out in the broader context of how different groups in a society interact and how resources are distributed between respective groups.

Most analyses of terrorism focus on the decision to employ this tactic. Yet, to comprehend why a group would intentionally target civilians, we need to understand why some groups do not. The following case is exemplary. From 1963 to 1970 a radical Quebec nationalist group, *Front de Libération du Québec* (FLQ), began a campaign of blowing up Canadian public mailboxes. Colored red and decked with the crown of the Canadian Post Office Department, they served as good symbols of Anglo-Canada and thus constituted a good target. Other symbolic targets were also bombed, for example, anglo-phone McGill and Loyola Universities and the Canadian Army Recruitment Centre in Montreal. The campaign was reasonably popular. In 1970 the FLQ decided to get more violent. They kidnapped James Cross (British High Commissioner in Montreal) and Pierre Laporte (Minister of Labour), who had been negotiating with the FLQ. Laporte was murdered, which resulted in the imposition of the War Measures Act. Rather than rallying in support of the FLQ, the general public approved of the enhanced security measures (Gurr & Ross, 1989; Tetley, 2006). The events of October 1970 led to spectacular loss of public support for the FLQ, which had received reasonably popular in Quebec for nearly 10 years. Henceforth, public opinion shifted away from violent action and toward efforts for attaining independence through nonviolent political means, mainly involving support for the secessionist *Parti Québécois*. This case demonstrates the critical role played by a complicit public. They supported what many of them regarded as an unfair peace over a violent conflict. Given widespread support by the Quebecois, the government successfully arrested and imprisoned most of the leadership of the FLQ and the group faded away. So it was not the mere fact that FLQ did not get public support that they stopped. The key shift was away from the terrorist group and to the government.[14]

All other things being equal, a group "representing" a sizable or distinct minority and receiving support from this group will be able to sustain terrorist activities even in the face of tremendous military disadvantage. If such a group loses support from its complicit public at the expense of the state, it will lose any advantage that it possessed. Moreover, the more a group is nonproportionally disadvantaged with access to resources, the stronger the support the group will receive. The more indiscriminate violence used by the state, the more support will go to the insurgent group.

Asymmetric Access to Military Technology

Another important element of asymmetric conflict is unequal access to military technology. As a country becomes more economically developed, the state will possess increasingly sophisticated military technology. Coinciding with this advancement in military technology is an increasing asymmetry between the state and any potential insurgent group. Thus we should expect to see insurgent groups in more industrialized societies to not possess the capacity to even wage a guerrilla war against the state, let alone engage in conventional war. Terrorism may be the only military option available to an insurgent group if it should decide to take up arms against the state.

Grossman and Kim (1995) featured the relative advantage of offense and defense.[15] In the normal state of affairs for a rich industrialized society, the military asymmetry between the state and a latent insurgent group using conventional military technologies is so strong that the state can defend against guerrilla tactics. Terrorism, however, alters this equation. As noted by Richard Betts (2003), terrorism offers a way for an insurgent group to deliver the greatest military effect for the least expenditure. This is particularly evident when considering the magnifying role of the attack created by the ensuing terror. By directing attacks against noncombatants, it erases this asymmetric advantage.[16]

Guerrilla warfare is a technological response to asymmetric military technology given the group's incapability to engage the state in conventional war with large standing armies. An insurgent group relies on guerrilla tactics as a means of maximizing military effectiveness vis-à-vis the state. Similarly, terrorism is a strategic response to the state's ability to defend or deter guerrilla attacks.

A good example of this is seen in the activities of the Provisional Irish Republican Army. Initially the IRA targeted military targets in Northern Ireland. Such activities strictly speaking were guerrilla. But after the British began to better defend their military installations, the IRA began to target civilians "in Britain, and then to high value commercial targets in the City of London" (Dunne et al., 2006). Such strategic adaptation of terrorist tactics is also evident in Afghanistan and Iraq the 2000s. Regarding the Taliban's resurgence that began in 2006, Jason Burke reports:

> The new Taliban . . . is no longer the parochial, traditional militia that seized Kabul almost exactly 10 years ago and was ousted by the American-led coalition in 2001. Tactics, ideology, equipment and organization have all moved on. The use of suicide bombings, roadside bombs and targeted assassinations of those cooperating with Western forces are methods copied from Iraqi insurgents . . . More than 70 suicide bombings, four times as many as last year, have together killed scores of civilians. In 2001 the tactic was almost unknown among Afghans.

In terms of assuring damage and casualties, suicide bombing has been remarkably effective (Pape, 2003). This effectiveness has not gone unnoticed by insurgency groups. More and more groups have adopted the tactic. The path of diffusion of this particular type of terrorist technique can be traced, starting with Amal in Lebanon (1981), to Hezbollah (1983), to other Lebanese organizations, to the LTTE in Sri Lanka (1987), to

Hamas in Israel (1993), the PKK in Turkey (1996), al Qaeda in Kenya and Tanzania (1998), Lashkar-e-Toiba in Kashmir, India (1999), Chechens in Chechnya, Russia (2001), DHKP in Turkey (2001), Jama'ah Islamiyya in Indonesia (2002), and to Ansar al-Islam in Iraq (2003) (Gambetta, 2005, 288). Other organizations have followed suit in Iraq and now the Taliban have employed this technique in Afghanistan. Given the level of efficiency of this strategy, the diffusion of suicide bombing is not too surprising. Such diffusion also demonstrates the adaptability of different groups as they fight against a far stronger opponent.

Conclusion

War is the quintessential strategic activity. It is curious that strategic adaptation is so often missing from rational choice explanations of civil conflict. In the dominant explanation of civil war, Fearon and Laitin (2003) argue that the critical factor is state capacity. Hence, civil war occurs in weak and failed states. Their explanation, however, fails to explain civil wars in the United Kingdom (Northern Ireland), Spain (the Basque Country), and Israel (Palestine). Ironic, given their rational choice orientation, is that Fearon and Laitin neglect the role of strategy, especially in its use to overcome asymmetry.

The presumption by many rational choice theorists is that for war to be rational, both sides must presume that they have a chance of winning due to incomplete information or commitment problems (Fearon, 1995; Reed, 2003). It thus follows that both sides must be fairly well balanced. Otherwise, at least one of the parties will determine that the costs of war exceed the gains, and will conclude that there is no point in going to war, either having been deterred from initiating armed conflict or capitulating to demands without going to war. Following this reasoning, we should not expect to see unbalanced dyads, yet we often do.

The problem with these analyses is that the strategic question facing the weaker side is not between losing the war and capitulation, but between the options of enduring peace on disadvantageous terms and of prosecuting an unconventional war. In addition, the strategic dilemma for the superior force is twofold. First, as long as there are disgruntled populations investing in different kinds of military technology merely shifts the strategic response of any insurgent group that seeks to represent this complicit public. Second, making disgruntled populations satisfied may be more difficult and politically costly than prosecuting a "war on terror."

Latent insurgent groups are, by definition, dissatisfied with the existing peace. They perceive that the status quo is disadvantageous to them and their complicit public. Under such a condition, engaging in war against a superior force can be supported by strategic logic as long as the cost of war to the insurgent group is low enough (Butler, 2007). The insurgent group's choice of warfare makes the cost of war endogenous. Given asymmetry, the cost of conventional warfare is too high for that option to make sense but the cost of guerrilla warfare may not be. Given extreme asymmetry, the cost of guerrilla warfare may also be too high. The use of terrorist warfare, however, may well make the cost low enough.

This focus on asymmetry and endogenous cost of war for the insurgent group makes the problem of preventing terrorism all the more pernicious for the state. By investing in greater defensive technology, the state is merely making the asymmetry more severe and altering the strategic calculus of the insurgent group (Rosendorff & Sandler, 2005). This shifts the nature of the violence perpetrated by the insurgent group rather than eliminating it.

Given that the logic of insurgent violence is supported by their perception of a disadvantageous peace, it may seem easy for the superior force to quell dissent merely by "being fair." Although this may well help (and is a component of counterinsurgency strategies), a number of factors prevent such simple advice from having its intended effect. First, the actions of the state are filtered by the existing perceptions of the public. If the prevailing sentiment of injustice is strong, equally strong actions will be required to overcome such opinions (Kydd, 2005, chap. 7). Such actions are costly for the state and it may reason that suppressing rebellion is the cheaper option.

Second, the insurgent group—harboring the most intense feelings of disadvantage—will require much more costly actions to be reassured of the intentions of the state and will try to counteract any state generosity perceived by its complicit public. Thus, although the state may be able to placate most of the public with some initial reassuring action, placating the insurgent leaders is usually too costly. To the extent that the state placates most of the public, the recruiting base of the insurgent group shrinks. This spurs the insurgent group to take action that makes the state look disingenuous. The combined actions of the Israeli government in the summer of 2005 may well have been of this nature. By forcing settlers to vacate the Gaza Strip, Israel was making a costly political statement (Lynfield, 2004; *NPR*, 2005). But by continuing with "targeted killings" of Palestinian leaders—that the Palestinians called assassinations—the Israelis lost whatever goodwill may have been engendered (*NPR*, 2005).

However, persistent goodwill may eventually pay off for the state as it becomes harder for the insurgent group to paint the state as ingenuous. The core members of ETA remain committed to an independent Basque country, but they have largely lost the support of their public. Similarly, persistent goodwill may alter the calculus of opposition leaders such that a disadvantageous peace is no longer seen as disadvantageous. There is now peace in Northern Ireland as Gerry Adams, leader of the political party Sinn Fein, in 2007, called on allied republican groups to cease engaging in violent activity. Sensing that his goal of a unified Ireland was then possible through peaceful means, he added, "I do not want to see any other people killed or imprisoned as a result of their activities" (*Reuters*, 2007). By altering the frame of peace sufficiently, the cost of any mode of warfare may be too high to support violence.

Notes

1. This project has been funded by the Research Council of Norway, an EU 7th Framework grant. We thank Daniel Arce, Martin Austvoll, Morten Bergsmo, Joakim Hammerlin, Pat James, and Todd Sandler for their valuable input.

2. Volunteer recruits would have the strong feelings assumed above. Forced recruits may well be conscripts of convenience who do not (initially) sympathize with group goals (Gates, 2002).

3. Many studies have attempted to estimate the link between inequality and civil conflict, but have failed to find robust statistical evidence of any relationship. The problem is that inequality in these studies is operationalized at the level of the individual, but insurgency is organized at the level of the group not the individual. Studies of horizontal inequality, in contrast, have found much stronger and robust relationship between this form of inequality and civil conflict.

4. Although it should be noted that in the case of conventional war involving the use of aerial bombardment, control of territory alone cannot guarantee security for the citizens. In fact, examining all wars since 1900, the war with the greatest number of battle casualties is the Second World War, followed by the Great War (World War I). Well below these two wars come the Vietnam War, Korean War, and Chinese Civil War. All involved extensive aerial bombardment. The number of casualties increases dramatically for a number of civil wars, if indirect casualties are included, but such indirect figures are largely guess work (Lacina & Gleditsch, 2005; Lacina et al., 2006).

5. The decision by Lee can be appreciated even more, if one keeps in mind that guerrilla warfare had been raging in some theaters, such as in Missouri, throughout the war. To be sure, the atrocities committed in Missouri and Kansas still horrify, and the distinction between terrorist and guerrilla blurs. Indeed, after the raid on Lawrence in which all the men of the town were killed, Kansans began to refer to Quantrill's Bushwackers as "Quantrill's Guerrillas." William T. Anderson, who had been a lieutenant of Quantrill, later formed his own gang, notorious for mutilating their victims (i.e., slicing off male organs and stuffing them in the mouths of those murdered) (Stiles, 2003). Although these guerrilla bands occasionally attacked Union troops, they mostly preyed on civilians who sympathized with the Union.

6. The problem with James Scott and others who adopt the moral economy perspective is that they fail to account for the organization of rebellion. Indeed, they fail to account for how a group of peasants overcome fundamental collective action problems. Without accounting for the fundamental institution for organizing human activity in rebellion (the insurgency group), it is no wonder that Scott fails to account for strategic behavior.

7. As a strategy, terrorism is more than a tactic. The specific method in which an act of terrorism is carried out is a tactic. An example of a terrorist tactic would be the taking control of a fully fueled passenger airplane and flying it into a building. Conventional military tactics include frontal assaults, flanking maneuvers, encirclement, use of overwhelming force, trench warfare, ambushes, and myriad others.

8. See Sandler and Arce (2003) for an overview of the applications of game theory to terrorism.

9. We are indebted to Morten Bergsmo for drawing our attention to the distinction between terrorist *acts* and the *effects* of terrorism.

10. Kalyvas (2004) distinguishes between indiscriminate and discriminate violence; we do not disagree with the importance of this distinction, but argue that what is important is not the actual act of violence, but the effect. And if the effect of a discriminate form of violence is to create terror in general, the effect is indistinguishable from indiscriminate violence, which also leads to a general state of terror.

11. Then again, three defendants in the Nuremberg trials were found guilty of terrorism perpetrated by the Nazi state (Greve, 2003, 82). In fact, in contrast to a neutral definition that we seek to develop for analytical purposes, laws are inherently normative and are designed with the purpose of protecting interests—the political order, the integrity of the state, or the innocent, and so forth.

12. Of course, states commit acts of terror regularly. In fact, states are more likely to be the perpetrators of violence against civilians than any other political organization. In the twentieth century more people have died at the hands of their own government than have died from attacks from enemy governments (i.e., interstate war) or from terrorism committed by nonstate actors (Rummel, 2005).

13. The first use of the word "terrorist" in English is most likely in Edmund Burke's *Reflections on the Revolution in France* (1795/1955).

14. Indeed, the Zionist Stern Gang referred to themselves as "terrorists" much in the way Russian anarchists had done in the late 1800s (Nunberg, 2004).

15. Of course, if a group does not care about public opinion, or if it thinks they suffer from "false consciousness," then a complicit public will play no role in the decision to engage in terrorism. But such groups as the Baader Meinhof Gang and the Red Brigade never received widespread public support and had a more difficult time avoiding police detection than a group such as the IRA, which always maintained high public support.

16. Quite a lively debate centers on whether offensive or defensive strategies dominate. The problem is that the concept is quite slippery (Levy, 1984) and difficult to operationalize.

17. See Sandler and Enders (2004), Sandler and Arce (2003), and Dunne et al. (2006) for theoretical analyses of the effectiveness of antiterrorism policies and

the strategic interaction played out between a terrorist group and a government. See Enders and Sandler (1993) for an empirical analysis of the effectiveness of antiterrorism policies.

References

Arreguín-Toft, I. (2001). How the weak win wars: A theory of asymmetric conflict. *International Security* 26 (1), 93–128.
Betts, R. K. (2003). The soft underbelly of American primacy: Tactical advantages of terror. In R. D. Howard & R. L. Sawyer (Eds.), *Terrorism and counterterrorism: Understanding the new security environment* (pp. 338–353). Guilford, CT: McGraw-Hill-Dushkin.
Burke, J. (2006, October 29, Sunday). Taliban plan to fight through winter to throttle Kabul. *The Observer.* http://observer.guardian.co.uk/world/story/0,,1934251,00.html
Butler, C. K. (2007). Prospect theory and coercive bargaining. *Journal of Conflict Resolution* 51 (2).
Butler, C. K., Gates, S., & Leiby, M. (2005). To fight or not to fight: Contest functions and civil conflict. Paper presented at the annual meeting of the American Political Science Association, September 1–4, 2005, Washington, DC.
Crenshaw, M. (1998). The logic of terrorism: Terrorist behavior as a product of strategic choice. In R. D. Howard & R. L. Sawyer (Eds.), *Terrorism and counterterrorism. Understanding the new security environment* (pp. 55–67). Guilford, CT: McGraw-Hill-Dushkin.
Dunne, J. P., García-Alonso, M. D. C., Levine, P., & Smith, R. P. (2006). Managing asymmetric conflict. *Oxford Economic Papers* 58 (2), 183–208.
Economist. (2007). In need of help to douse the flames. 382 (8516) (February 17, 2007), 53–54.
Enders, W., & Sandler, T. (1993). The effectiveness of anti-terrorism policies: Vector-Autoregression-Intervention analysis. *American Political Science Review* 87 (4), 829–844.
Fearon, J., & Laitin, D. (1996). Explaining interethnic cooperation. *American Political Science Review* 90 (4), 715–735.
Fearon, J. (1995). Rationalist explanations for war. *International Organization* 49 (3), 379–414.
Gambetta, D. (2005). Can we make sense of suicide missions? In D. Gambetta (Ed.), *Making sense of suicide missions* (pp. 259–300). Oxford: Oxford University Press.
Garfinkel, M., & Skaperdas, S. (2000). Conflict without misperceptions or incomplete information. *Journal of Conflict Resolution* 44 (6), 793–808.
Gartner, S. S., & Regan, P. M. (1996). Threat and repression: The non-linear relationship between government and opposition violence. *Journal of Peace Research* 33 (3), 273–287.

Gates, S. (2002). Recruitment and allegiance: The microfoundations of rebellion. *Journal of Conflict Resolution* 46 (1), 111–130.
Greve, H. S. (2003). Acts of terrorism and crimes within the jurisdiction of the international criminal court. In M. Bergsmo (Ed.), *Human rights and criminal justice for the downtrodden: Essays in honour of Asbjørn Eide* (pp. 75–110). Leiden: Marinus Nijhoff.
Grossman, H. I., & Minseong, K. (1995). Swords or plowshares? A theory of the security of claims to property. *Journal of Political Economy* 103 (6), 1275–1288.
Gurr, T. R., & Ross, J. I. (1989). Why terrorism subsides: A comparative study of Canada and the United States. *Comparative Politics* 21 (4), 405–426.
Harper, D. (2001). *Online etymology dictionary*. Retrieved March 16, 2006, from http://www.etymonline.com/
Hoffman, B. (1998). *Inside terrorism*. New York: Columbia University Press.
Kalyvas, S. (2003). The ontology of "political violence." *Perspectives on Politics* 1 (3), 475–494.
Kalyvas, S. (2004). The paradox of terrorism in civil war. *The Journal of Ethics* 8 (1), 97–138.
Kalyvas, S. (2006). *The logic of violence in civil war*. Cambridge: Cambridge University Press.
King, C. (2004). The micropolitics of social violence. *World Politics* 56 (April), 431–455.
Kiras, J. D. (2007). Irregular warfare: Terrorism and insurgency. In J. Baylis, J. Wirtz, C. S. Gray & E. Cohen (Eds.), *Strategy in the contemporary world* (2nd ed.) (pp. 163–191). Oxford: Oxford University Press.
Kydd, A. H. (2005). *Trust and mistrust in international relations*. Princeton, NJ: Princeton University Press.
Lacina, B. A., & Gleditsch, N. P. (2005). Monitoring trends in global combat: A new dataset of battle deaths. *European Journal of Population* 21 (2–3), 145–165.
Lacina, B. A., Gleditsch, N. P., & Russett, B. M. (2006). The declining risk of death in battle. *International Studies Quarterly* 50 (3), 673–680.
Levy, J. S. (1984). The offensive/defensive balance of military technology: A theoretical and historical analysis. *International Studies Quarterly* 28 (2), 219–238.
Lichbach, I. M. (1994). *The rebels dilemma*. Ann Arbor: University of Michigan Press.
Lynfield, B. (2004, September 22). Gaza settlers weigh price of withdrawal. *Christian Science Monitor*. Retrieved March 13, 2007, from http://www.csmonitor.com/2004/0922/p06s03-wome.html
Mack, A. (1975). Why big nations lose small wars: The politics of asymmetric conflict. *World Politics* 27 (2), 175–200.
Mao T. (1992 [1937]). *On guerrilla warfare*. 2nd ed. (Brig. Gen. Samuel B. Griffith II, Trans.). Baltimore: Nautical & Aviation.
Murshed, S. M., & Gates, S. (2005). Spatial-horizontal inequality and the Maoist insurgency in Nepal. *Review of Development Economics* 9 (1), 121–134.

National Public Radio. (2005). Profile: Increased violence could disrupt Israel's withdrawal [sic] from Gaza. (July 17, 2005). Retrieved March 13, 2007, from http://www.npr.org/programs/atc/transcripts/ 2005/ jul/ 050717 gradstein.html

Nunberg, G. (2004, July 11). The –ism schism: How much wallop can a simple word pack? *New York Times*. Retrieved February 27, 2007, from http://www.ischool.berkeley.edu/~nunberg/terror.html

Østby, G. (2005). *Horizontal inequalities and civil conflict*. Paper presented at the 46th Annual Convention of the International Studies Association, 1–5 March, Honolulu, HI.

Pape, R. A. (2003). The strategic logic of suicide terrorism. *American Political Science Review* 97 (3), 343–361.

Paul, T. V. (1994). *Asymmetric conflicts: War initiation by weaker powers*. Cambridge: Cambridge University Press.

Popkin, S. (1979). *The rational peasant: The political economy of rural society in Vietnam*. Berkeley: University of California Press.

Powell, R. (2005). The inefficient use of power: Costly conflict with complete information. *American Political Science Review* 98 (2), 231–241.

Rapoport, D. C. (1982). Introduction. In D. C. Rapoport & Y. Alexander (Eds.), *The morality of terrorism. Religious and secular justifications*. Oxford: Pergamon Press.

Reed, W. (2003). Information, power and war. *American Political Science Review* 97 (4), 633–641.

Reiter, D. (1999). Military strategy and the outbreak of international conflict: Quantitative empirical tests, 1903–1992. *Journal of Conflict Resolution* 43 (3), 366–387.

Reuters. (2007, January 18). Sinn Fein calls on dissidents to end violence.

Rosendorff, B. P., & Sandler, T. (2005). Too much of a good thing: Proactive response dilemma. *Journal of Conflict Resolution* 48 (5), 657–671.

Rotte, R., & Schmidt, C. (2003). On the production of victory: Empirical determinants of battlefield success in modern war. *Defence and Peace Economics* 14 (3), 175–192.

Rummel, R. (2005). *Never again: Ending war, democide, & famine through democratic freedom*. Retrieved February 27, 2007, from http://www.hawaii.edu/powerkills/NH.HTM#SUPPLEMENT

Sandler, T., & Arce, D. G. M. (2003). Terrorism and game theory. *Simulation & Gaming* 34 (3), 319–337.

Sandler, T., & Enders, W. (2004). An economic perspective on transnational terrorism. *European Journal of Political Economy* 20 (2), 301–316.

Schelling, T. (1960). *The strategy of conflict*. Oxford: Oxford University Press.

Scott, J. C. (1976). *The moral economy of the peasant: Rebellion and subsistence in Southeast Asia*. New Haven, CT: Yale University Press.

Scott, J. C. (1985). *Weapons of the weak. Everyday forms of peasant resistance*. New Haven, CT: Yale University Press.

Slantchev, B. L. (2003). The power to hurt: Costly conflict with completely informed states. *American Political Science Review* 97 (1), 123–133.

Stam, A. C. III. (1996). *Win, lose, or draw: Domestic politics and the crucible of war*. Ann Arbor: University of Michigan Press.
Stiles, T. J. (2003). *Jesse James: Last rebel of the Civil War*. New York: Vintage Books.
Tetely, W. (2006). *The October crisis, 1970: An insider's view*. Montreal: McGill-Queen's University Press.
Wagner, R. H. (2000). Bargaining and war. *American Journal of Political Science* 44 (3), 469–484.
Weinstein, J. M. (2007). *Inside rebellion. The politics of insurgent violence*. Cambridge: Cambridge University Press.
Werner, S. (1998). Negotiating the terms of settlement: War aims and bargaining leverage. *Journal of Conflict Resolution* 42 (3), 321–343.
Winik, J. (2001). *April 1865: The month that saved America*. New York: HarperCollins.

Chapter 4

How to Win Enemies and Influence Terrorism

State Repression in Chechnya

Rhonda L. Callaway and Julie Harrelson-Stephens

> There was one nation which would not give in, would not acquire the mental habits of submission—and not just individual rebels among them, but the whole nation to a man. These were the Chechens. . . . I would say that of all the special settlers, the Chechens alone showed themselves unbroken in spirit.
>
> —Alexsander Solzhenitsyn

Introduction

Anecdotal evidence has increasingly linked poverty, human rights, and quality of life issues to terrorist activity. For example, Han Seung-Soo (BBC, 2002), president of the UN General Assembly, referred to the poorest countries as "the breeding ground for violence and despair." We posit a theory of terrorism examining conditions within the state, particularly human rights conditions, as well as systemic factors that contribute to terrorist activity. While the traditional approach to studying terrorism has focused on the individual level of analysis and typologies of terrorists and terrorist activity (Rubenstein, 1974; Schultz, 1990; Sederberg, 1994; Laqueuer, 1999, 2001), we contend that a lack of human security increases the likelihood of terrorist activity. In our recent research, we conclude that security rights violations amount to a necessary condition for widespread support for terrorist activity (Callaway & Harrelson-Stephens, 2006). We again find that the denial of each type of human right, together, creates a climate that is conducive to terrorism. Moreover, this research represents the next step in the refinement of our theory, as the internationalization of the Chechen struggle fundamentally alters the Chechen terrorist movement and indicates the significant difference between modern and traditional terrorism.

In order to explore the relationship between human rights violations and terrorism, we examine the case of Chechnya, whose independence movement began again in earnest in the early 1990s and quickly spawned a terrorist movement. While the Chechen case is extremely complicated, we outline the emergence and growth of the terrorist movement, and its relationship to human rights violations. The Chechen historical memory of repression and deportation is reinforced by renewed Russian policies of repression.[1] Terrorism in Chechnya emerges after a long period of oppression and exclusion from the political processes, in particular, in the aftermath of the destruction of Grozny, the imposition of *zachistas*, the burning of villages, as well as state policies of torture and disappearances.

Theoretical Considerations

In order to develop a theory of terrorism, we first address the problematic nature of defining the term. The controversy and lack of consensus regarding how we define terrorism (Rubenstein, 1974; Crenshaw, 1995; Cooper, 2001; Laqueur, 2001; Combs, 2003) has resulted in a field of study that is not only "descriptive, prescriptive and obliquely emotive in form" (Schultz, 1990, 49), but one that has precluded empirical analysis (O'Brien, 1998). This problem is exacerbated by states that use the term politically to caste their enemies in a negative light. This is particularly true in the Chechen case where anti-Chechen attitudes have consistently been described as xenophobic and Russian leaders regularly refer to Chechens as "bandit, thieves, and murderers," as well as terrorists. The anti-Chechen rhetoric promulgated by the Russian Federation, many argue, is used to divert attention away from Russia's own economic and political troubles (see Russell, 2005; Souleimanov, 2006).

The emotive nature of many terrorists' definitions renders the term problematic. However, we argue that terrorism can, in fact, be measured in an empirically neutral way if we focus on the target. Although any move toward an agreement on the definition of terrorism will no doubt be controversial, it is warranted for two reasons. First, although terrorism is a difficult concept to define, this is hardly a unique problem in the social sciences. Concepts like power and war, which are critical to the study of international relations, are difficult to define and measure and continue to be debated among political scientists. Yet these concepts are defined and measured and as more political scientists join the debate, the concepts continue to be refined. Second, if we conclude terrorism is indefinable and therefore immeasurable, then the study of terrorism will be doomed to the descriptive stage, precluding prediction. The globalization of terrorism, internationalization of terrorist networks, and the U.S. War on Terror, all make the explanation and prediction of terrorism critical. Thus, we employ Bueno de Mesquita's (2000, 339) definition, which describes terrorism as "any act of violence undertaken for the purpose of altering a government's political policies or actions that targets those who do not actually have the personal authority to alter governmental policy." Rather than relying on the researcher to make a normative assessment, the researcher must ascertain whether the target is civilian in nature. We further argue that terrorists are nongovernmental actors and thus terrorism is conceptually different from state terror or repression. Accordingly, terrorism involves nongovernmental actors who target civilians in order to pressure governments to change their policies.

In terms of human rights, we rely on a general definition posited by Donnelly (1989, 1998) that human rights are rights that one possesses simply because they are human. However, in order to adequately test our hypotheses, we examine three types of rights that are more readily quantifiable. Here, we use the term human security to encompass three classes of human rights: political rights, subsistence rights, and security rights. Political rights are those that allow citizens to actively participate in government. Citizens who regularly enjoy their political rights are able to vote, protest, assemble, and oppose the government in power. Security rights are those rights that protect the individual's person or integrity. Violations of security rights include torture, state murder, and extrajudicial killings, as well as disappearances. Lastly, subsistence rights are a subset of human rights that include issues pertaining to quality of life such as nutrition, employment, and education. These types of rights differ from the previous two categories in that the violation of subsistence rights generally stem from state neglect. However, it should be stressed that this neglect can be intentional, such as depriving citizens from food at international food aid sites or, in the Chechen case, in terms of deportations. Either way the state's inability or reluctance to address these types of issues can breed discontent among the populace. Additionally, external factors, such as international influences and colonial histories impact domestic conditions.

In order to systematically explore the relationship between human security and terrorist activity, we examine the realization of three distinct classes of human rights: political rights, security rights, and subsistence rights. We hypothesize that there is a linear relationship between political rights and terrorist activity; specifically, states with low levels of political openness are associated with higher levels of terrorism. In states with higher levels of political rights, generally democracies, citizens have effective and numerous methods of engaging in the political process. Democracies, by definition, are more open, transparent, and willing to accept political opposition (Hamilton, 1978; Gurr, 1979; Turk, 1982; Ross, 1993; Eubank & Weinberg, 1994). Conversely, the less open the political system, the more likely citizens are to operate outside the norms of the political process. Thus, in order to affect change, citizens in politically closed states are more likely to feel justified working outside the system to achieve their political goals. Moreover, the denial of political rights can be exacerbated in situations where the state promises increased political rights only to later deny the citizenry those same rights, which intensifies the atmosphere of injustice.

The lack of subsistence rights or basic human needs further creates conditions conducive to terrorism. We contend that the relationship between subsistence and terrorism resembles an inverted U, where citizens in states at both extremes are less likely to engage in terrorist activity. Essentially, the poorest citizens are struggling to survive while the wealthiest are generally satisfied. It is those citizens living in the middle of the subsistence spectrum who have been exposed to greater levels of basic needs and have rising expectations, who are more likely to engage in and support terrorist activity, particularly when their expectations rise faster than their economic well-being.[2] An early example is provided by de Tocqueville (1850) in his description of the French Revolution. He argues that it was those who were part of the emerging middle class that demanded more rights, not the poorest in French society. Further, we suggest that levels of subsistence are inextricably linked to a nation's or people's identity, one that is created over years, decades, and even centuries. In societies where there is widespread support for terrorism, there is also often an identity of marginalization whereby the excluded group feels systematically discriminated against by the state. The lack of subsistence becomes associated with other forms of state discrimination as part of an institutionalized policy of exclusion. Groups with economic standing that are relatively poorer than other groups within that society are likely to hold the state accountable for those discrepancies. If the economic division of society appears to be tacitly or explicitly supported by the state, then groups are more likely to feel warranted working outside of state sanctioned processes to attempt to redress those discrepancies. Thus, at the upper and lower margins of the realization of basic human needs, we expect less terrorist activity and we expect a greater likelihood of terrorism within states that fall in the middle of the subsistence spectrum.

We contend that even when political and subsistence rights are accounted for, the violation of security rights has an independent effect on the likelihood of terrorist activity. State repression engenders a like response from the oppressed group, as those groups feel justified in responding to arbitrary state violence with arbitrary violence in-kind. In addition, it is likely that state repression is felt not only by the actual victims, but by the populace at large, creating an atmosphere of fear shared by all of society. However, this relationship is nonlinear, since in the most repressive regimes, as in totalitarian states, the leadership is quite effective in dealing with domestic opposition and unrest. It is in the regimes that regularly abuse its citizens, short of the most repressive regimes, where we expect to see the greatest level of terrorist activity. More specifically, we suggest that gross security rights violations are a necessary condition for widespread support for terrorist activity.

Many international factors are at play in state relations, but we focus on two major factors in our model of terrorist activity: the historical development of the state with particular attention to colonial influence, and current international influences. Oftentimes these two factors are inextricably related. We hypothesize that states with a more brutal colonial history are more likely to experience terrorist activity. This argument is predicated on the idea that the political and economic realities of many states are a function of their colonial heritage and the resulting institutional development. For example, Poe, Tate, and Keith (1999) find that security rights in former British colonies are far better than in non-British colonies. In a similar vein, Moon (1991) finds that the British were better able to impart greater levels of basic human needs than the French, Portuguese, or Belgians. In fact, decolonization in the regions colonized by the latter proved far more brutal and violent than that experienced by the former British colonies. To some extent, the current state of human rights conditions, both in the political and economic realm, can be traced to the colonial experience.

The second international factor considered here is the relationship the state has to other states and nonstate actors within the international system. Specifically, we hypothesize that weaker states or nations in the international system are more likely to engender terrorist activity. This is derived from the reality that powerful states are more capable of expressing their policy objectives within the norms of the system; whereas, in weaker states, the citizenry have a greater sense of marginalization. In addition, like-minded groups outside the state can often feel a sense of kinship, either real or perceived, with the oppressed group and choose to support that group. Support can manifest itself in a variety of ways including money, armaments, tactics, and increasingly, fighters.

In sum, we theorize that states that systematically deny political rights as well as fail to provide adequate levels of subsistence create a breeding ground for terrorism to foment. Often, the denial of these rights over a long period of time helps create an identity of marginalization, which may serve as a key element in the formation of terrorist activity. In addition, a variety of international influences help create an environment conducive to terrorism. Ultimately, we argue that it is the violation of security rights, or severe acts of state repression, that provides the necessary condition for terrorist activity to receive widespread support in a society. Thus, in the case of Chechnya, we expect to see terrorism in instances where political rights are low, subsistence rights are short of the lowest levels, and security rights violations are high, but fall short of total repression.

Human Rights in Chechnya

> For a Chechen, to be a man is to remember the names of seven generations of paternal ancestors . . . and not only their names, but the circumstances of their deaths and the places of their tombstones. This constitutes an enormous depth of historic memory, and in many cases the remembered deaths occurred at the hands of Russian soldiers—under Catherine the Great, under Nicholas the First, under Stalin.
>
> —Sergei Arutiunov (in Dunlop, 1998, 211)

The history of Chechnya and the Chechen people is concomitantly linked to the history of Russia and stretches back over many centuries. Although terrorism in Chechnya is relatively new, the factors that contribute to the current level of terrorist activity have been fomenting for decades, if not centuries. In fact, Gammer (2002, 122) notes that over the last 300 years there have been four periods of genocide, nine revolts, and, in between these revolts, "low-intensity resistance never stopped." Historically, the Chechens lived in the mountainous region of the Caucasus and based their society on clan relations. This provided for a unique system of equality where members of the clan were considered free and equal in both the economic and political sphere (Dunlop, 1998). In this clan-based society, family and legacy were critical social units and political units were inconsequential, resulting in clans serving "as the collective repository of reputation that plays a key role in structuring the social interactions and creating trust among the people" (Derluguian, 2003, 11). It is within this context that the Chechens resisted the Czar and later Soviet and Russian states.

The Chechens were initially successful at warding off invasions, including that of Peter the Great, until 1818 and the efforts of Russian General Alexander Yermolov. In a fashion similar to that of General Sherman during the American Civil War, Yermolov embarked on a massive slash and burn approach to deal with the Chechen "savages," leveling villages and killing their inhabitants. Russia's Chechen policy further focused on destroying the Chechens economic way of life, as General Vel'yaminov (Yermolov's chief of staff) argued that "the enemy is absolutely dependent on his crops for the means of sustaining life. Let the standing corn be destroyed each autumn as it ripens, and in five years they would be starved into submission" (Dunlop, 1998, 15; see also Seely, 2001; Derluguian, 2003). This was merely the beginning of the brutal treatment levied against the Chechen people, one that would come to be characterized by starvation, exile, and massacres, all of which contributed to the collective memory of the Chechens.

In spite of Chechen resistance under the legendary leader, Imam Shamil, Russia finally conquered that area in 1859 resulting in the incorporation of Chechnya into the Russian Empire. The result of the annexation was devastating to Chechens.

> During the nineteenth century Caucasus War, the Chechens lost close to half of their population and saw their economy uprooted and destroyed. They were incorporated against their will and by naked force into the Russian Empire. Despite pledges made to them by Emperor Alexander II and by other high-ranking Russian officials following the surrender of Shamil' in 1859, they did not come to receive equal treatment with other peoples of the Empire but were instead reduced to a condition of harsh poverty and of "land hunger" and, in contrast with ethnic Russians, saw justice meted out to them by military rather than civilian courts. (Dunlop, 1998, 35)

This was also the time of the first deportations of Chechens to Siberia, a practice that would be repeated and proved to the Chechens that the Russian state could not be trusted. The actions of the czarist leadership produced the opposite effect than was intended. Rather than fully conquering and subjugating the Chechens, the abusive treatment actually led to the consolidation of traditionally warring clans against a common enemy (Dunlop, 1998).

After being subjugated in the czarist empire, the Bolshevik revolution initially provided a glimmer of hope for the Chechens and a possible respite from Russian domination and persecution. Chechens initially fought for the Bolshevik cause in part due to the promises made by Lenin and Stalin "to restore land to the peasants and liberate the oppressed colonial peoples" (Derluguian, 2003, 14). The establishment of the Chechen Ingush Autonomous Soviet Socialist Republic (ASSR) by the Soviets led to the development of some Chechen political institutions as well as societal ones such as universities and theaters (Derluguian, 2003; German, 2003). These institutions were also accompanied by improvements in many social services, particularly in the areas of health care and education (Derluguian, 2003). However, the promise of economic and social equality and autonomy was quickly replaced with political repression and the collectivization programs initiated between 1929 and 1932. Like other peasant groups, the Chechens resisted (including the revolt of 1929–1930), with little success.

During World War II many Chechens fought in the Soviet army; however, others deserted and fought for the Nazis. The Soviet response toward the end of the war was the final deportation of the Chechens to Siberia and Kazakhstan. Over half a million Chechens, Ingush, and other neighboring ethnic groups were ultimately uprooted from their homeland, losing not only their homes, but their land and livelihood (Gall & de Waal, 1998; Seely, 2001; Tishkov, 2004; Gammer, 2006). Approximately one-fourth to one-half died en route and others were summarily shot and burned during the expulsion process (Mikhailov, 2005, 49). In other cases, the Chechens were simply wiped out in Soviet purges, as happened in the village of Khaibakh where more than 700 people were burned alive (Dunlop, 1998). Undoubtedly, the policy of deportations was "the defining factor in their history and, to Chechens, carries the same significance as the Holocaust does to Jews" (Seely, 2001, 9). Although the struggle against what Chechens' perceived as Russian occupation began a century earlier, it is the deportation that convinced Chechnya that no matter their sacrifice, Russian promises could not be trusted.

During their exile, "the Chechens more than other repressed peoples managed to 'preserve their culture, language, identity and especially spirit of independence' in a 'deeply impressive' way" (Gammer, 2006, 178). Many of the leaders of modern Chechnya were either born or were children during this deportation, and it fundamentally shaped their view of the Russians. For example, Shamil Basayev, who would later lead the Chechen resistance, explained that "when Stalin deported us, the Russians took over our empty houses and they ripped the stones of our graveyards, then they used them to make roads, bridges, [and] pigsties" (Gammer, 2006, 183).

Upon return from exile, many Chechens were not allowed to resettle in the place of their choosing; rather they were directed to certain areas of economic production (Tishkov, 2004; Gammer, 2006). This was particularly true for those Chechens who were originally from more mountainous regions. The central government in Moscow not only wanted to use Chechen labor in the industrial areas of the region, but the Soviets also wanted to keep returning Chechens "away from the mountains, where topography complicated control and anti-Soviet bands were still active" (Gammer, 2006, 187). Overall, the Russian plan was to resist reconstituting any traditional ethnic influence within the region, save that of Russian nationals. Thus, ethnic Russians were given preferential treatment in jobs, salaries, and housing in comparison to the returning Chechens (Seely, 2001; Gammer, 2006). In essence, a dual economy developed within the region: a Russian economy based on oil extraction and other heavy industry and a national economy based upon traditional modes of production including seasonal work (Tishkov, 2004).

The effect of this dual economy is seen in the unemployment figures for the region and illustrates the level of economic disparity suffered by ethnic Chechens. In 1980, unemployment in the Russian dominated economic sector was 4.9 percent, whereas in the more traditional economic areas the unemployment rate was 14.3 percent. By 1990, unemployment had dropped to 2.2 percent in the former sector, while unemployment in the Chechen dominated areas rose to 16.1 percent. In other words, chronic unemployment was rampant in areas that depended on traditional methods of subsistence. According to Tishkov (2004, 41) there was eventually a labor surplus of 20 percent to 30 percent, or 100,000 to 200,000, and "these people became the main reserve of the armed struggle." Beyond employment opportunities, the Chechen population had higher mortality rates, inferior health care systems, were paid lower wages, experienced higher levels of poverty and lower levels of education compared to Russians living in the territory (German, 2003). Given these differences, "one can see that there were indeed powerful social, demographic, and economic factors underlying the 1991 Chechen Revolution" (Dunlop, 1998, 88).

The latest phase of the Russo-Chechen case begins with Mikhail Gorbachev's policies of glasnost and perestroika in the mid-1980s, and his announcement that more autonomy would be allowed throughout the Soviet Empire. By 1991, we see the dissolution of the Soviet Union as other autonomous regions begin declaring independence. The Chechen declaration of independence was met with resistance from the Russian government, even as it was collapsing from within. However, the Russian response reveals significant internal divisions within the now crumbling empire. Boris Yeltsin refused to recognize Chechnya's independence and immediately sent Russian troops to the area to impose martial law and remove Dzhokhar Dudayev, the recently elected leader of Chechnya. When the troops arrived in Grozny, in November 1991, they were met with "the largest demonstrations in Grozny since the Bolshevik coup in 1917" (Seely, 2001, 109). Although Gorbachev ordered the troops to stand down, the effect, mobilization of the Chechen population, had already occurred. The political situation in Chechnya quickly dissolved into a violent cycle of rebellion and repression.

Even then, though, it is fair to say that support for terrorism and even full independence within Chechnya was limited. Chechens wanted some degree of autonomy but many Chechens, particularly those within urban areas, felt the fight for independence would push the Russians too far. This division was mirrored in the growing opposition to Dudayev's regime. In fact, Dudayev's hold on power was always more anti-Russian than pro-Dudayev. The decision by Yeltsin to use force in Chechnya reflects, in part, Yeltsin's consolidation of power within Russia and the resolution by early 1994 of the other independence movements, notably Tartarstan. Chechnya remained the last holdout within the Russia Federation.

Terrorist acts at this point were not receiving widespread support within Chechnya. That changed with the attack on Grozny beginning in late 1994, followed shortly by the invasion of Chechnya. The destruction of Grozny is perhaps as important as the Soviet deportations a half a century earlier. The "means used were so vastly disproportionate to the scale of the problem" that any sane person "was inclined to say, 'if this is Russia's solution, I would prefer the problem' " (de Waal, 2005, 182). The Russian forces relied initially on aerial attacks, followed by ground forces, which moved slowly from outlying villages into the center of Grozny. These troops, operating with impunity, were often poorly trained, undisciplined, drunk, and failed to distinguish between civilians and Chechen fighters. After facing significant resistance in late 1994 and again on January 1, 1995, the Russian army regroups, sends reinforcements, and destroys the capital of Chechnya.

Civilian casualties in Grozny were high. Human rights activist Sergei Kovalyov estimated casualties at about 24,000, most of whom where ethnically Russian (Seely, 2001). Grozny was home mostly to ethnic Russians and professional Chechens. The cost of razing the capital "was therefore physically to destroy and drive out the very constituency of Chechnya's residents who were most sympathetic to political accommodation and who also were agents of modernization inside society" (de Waal, 2005, 183; see also Gakaev, 2005). The utter annihilation of the city became a new symbol of the repressive nature of the Russian government, one that was readily tied to their past. Moreover, the destruction of the city was accompanied by the destruction of important cultural symbols including the deportation monument, the Central State Archives, the university, and museum which Chechens felt "was not merely one of the effects of the bombing but a deliberate attempt to complete the task, begun by Stalin, of wiping out all traces of the Chechens (Gammer, 2002, 132). Thus, where Stalin attempted to complete Yermolov's policy, we see Yeltsin attempting to complete Stalin's policy of cultural genocide. The destruction of Grozny would also mark a fundamental change in the Chechen strategy. From this point forward, we see dramatic increases in the use of terrorism and in particular the use of suicide bombing.

As the Russian military continued its advance through the cities and villages of Chechnya, its military tactics continued to rely on repression and, in many cases, actual formalized repression as part of the standard procedures. According to Lieven (1998), atrocities by Russian troops took three forms. One was the direct bombardment of civilian targets either in the course of military operations (as in Grozny) or to punish villagers who supported the separatists (as in Novogroznenski where 40 percent of houses were destroyed).[3] A second form involved the direct massacre of civilians (as in Samashki where more than 100 civilians were killed in an apparently officially sanctioned operation).[4] This included brutalization of civilians at checkpoints, house searches, torture, and rape. A third form of repression involved the widespread torture and murder of prisoners of war. In addition, the Russian government used clean up operations, or *zachistas,* which have been detailed by Anna Politkosvskaya (2003). In a *zachistas,* the military would issue an ultimatum to the villagers to "give up the fighters and weapons" (though any peace agreement was rarely respected), bomb the village, beat the women, shoot at the inhabitants, set up a humanitarian corridor and charge the villagers a fee to leave, often shooting at them as they fled, and caused males over 12 years of age to disappear (Doctors without Borders, 1996; see also Human Rights Watch, 1996; Lagnado, 2003). Although Grozny is symbolic, these Russian tactics were repeated in village after village until "out of 428 villages, 380 were bombed, 70 percent of houses were destroyed . . . 30,000 hectares of agricultural land were contaminated by explosives" (Gakaev, 2005, 40).

The effects of the Russian military campaign were directly felt by every Chechen. Undoubtedly, the egregious violations of security rights committed by Russian soldiers led many individuals to become terrorist fighters in Chechnya. For example, Shamil Basayev, the leader of the Chechen resistance suggests that he decided to take the war to Russian territory after Russians razed the village of Vedeno, killing 11 of his relatives (Bivens, 2002). Similarly, so-called black widows, who had lost their husbands to Russian military action, would become frontline suicide bombers. Thus, it is after the Russian invasion of Chechnya that we see the birth of a solidified terrorist movement. During the first Russo-Chechen war we see a significant number of terrorist actions, including the delivery of radio-active waste to Moscow, the attack of Budennovsk's hospital that killed more than 100 civilians, and a bomb on a Moscow subway, to name a few.

The period between the wars, Chechnya was a virtual wasteland and lawlessness reigned. The first Chechen War devastated an already precarious economy. In essence, "nobody was paid" during the period between the two wars (Nivat, 2003, 19; see also German, 2003), nor was any international economic assistance forthcoming (de Waal, 2003). Walker (1998, 10) indicates that the first Chechen war all but destroyed the economic infrastructure of Grozny; "unemployment is estimated by the government to be over 90%; better educated Chechens have mostly fled; the Chechen authorities are unable to secure internal order; and revenues from the oil pipeline running through the region will be modest under the best circumstances." At this point, those that could leave did so.

Also during this period, foreign fighters begin arriving from Afghanistan to join what they perceived as a jihad (Vidino, 2006). By 1999, *sharia* law was adopted in Chechnya and by the second Chechen war, the movement was co-opted by international actors, in particular Wahhabists. The second Chechen war was marked by "indiscriminate attacks by the Russians [that] are countered by guerrilla warfare and terrorist strikes. Thus far, the second Chechen war has been characterized by greater reliance on terrorist tactics previously unseen in the conflict and clearly imported by the foreign mujahideen" as well as the use of female suicide bombers or so called 'black widows' " (Vidino, 2006, 204). What is striking about the international hijacking of the movement and its subsequent radicalization is that many Chechens continued to resist these new interlopers and only around one-tenth of the population is sympathetic to them (de Waal, 2003). We now examine the Chechen case in light of our theoretical expectations.

Theoretical Connections

We argue that the denial of political rights and the denial of subsistence rights, when accompanied by gross security rights violations, create the conditions most conducive to the genesis and growth of terrorism. The denial of human security is further exacerbated by certain international influences, including colonial histories and marginalization within the current international system which further increase the likelihood of terrorism. Thus, we examine the Chechen case in light of each of these aspects of human security.

Political Rights

> The injustice of violence, its heavy burden over my soul and the soul of my people came to my mind when I grew up in an earth house in Siberia experiencing hunger, poverty, repression. None of those [things] could scare me—neither hunger, nor cold and poverty. The most scary feeling was the absolute absence of rights and protection by neither the law nor the state.
>
> —Dzhokhar Dudayev

For a people whose traditional political identity was one of individual freedom, subjugation to Russian rule all but eliminated these freedoms. As discussed in the case study, during the czarist period the Chechens were politically marginalized and subjected to a different legal standard. Political conditions do not improve during the Soviet era, when the Bolsheviks, and later Stalin, reneged on their political promises. An appeal was made, signed by both Lenin and Stalin to "All Muslims Toilers of Russia and the East" on December 3, 1917:

> Muslims of Russia! Tatars of the Volga and the Crimea! Kyrgyz and Sarts of Siberia and of Turkestan! Turks and Tatars of Trans-Caucasus! Chechens and mountain people of the Caucasus! All you whose mosques and prayer houses used to be destroyed, and whose beliefs and customs were trodden underfoot by the Tzars and oppressors of Russia! From today, your beliefs and your customs and your national and cultural institutions, are free and inviolate. Organize your national life freely and without hindrance. You are entitled to this . . . Comrades! Brothers! Let us march towards an honest and democratic peace. On our banners is inscribed the freedom of oppressed peoples. (Gall & de Waal, 2003, 52)

These political promises were quickly broken and replaced with collectivization programs, along with a lack of representation in Chechen political institutions. The deportations that followed World War II violated the entire spectrum of human security, including political rights. For returning Chechens, the so-called rehabilitation period was characterized by the continued lack of political representation in their own autonomous region. Like most other ethnic groups in Russia, the Chechens were denied their basic political rights throughout the Soviet era. Chechens were prevented from holding political offices during Soviet times (Dunlop, 1998; Seely, 2001; Gall & de Waal, 2003), and they were significantly underrepresented in the communist *nomenklatura* (Gakaev, 2005), while Russians in Chechnya were given preferential treatment.

With the collapse of the Soviet Union, more political promises were made. Some progress was achieved as Chechnya elected their first ethnic representative, Doku Zavgaev, as first party secretary in 1989 (Dunlop, 1998). The call for independence, from the Chechens' perspective, was given the green light from Moscow. Almost as soon as Gorbachev, and later Yeltsin, promised greater autonomy, the Chechens demanded SSR status (Gammer, 2006), that is status equal to Russia. The Russian denial of this political right to self-determination was followed by three years of Russian inertia with the Chechens attempting self-governance. The invasion in December 1994, much like the deportations half a century earlier, effectively denied Chechens any human security.

The current crisis in Chechnya began, quite simply, with a demand for political equality. In the Chechen case, the fall of the Soviet Union offered them an opportunity to actually work within the system to affect political change. The shutting of that political door by the Russians changed the dynamic. The taste of political freedom and then the denial laid the groundwork for terrorist activity to follow. In examining the political rights of Chechens, two things are clear. First, equal political rights are fundamental to Chechens. It is the promise of equality that leads the Chechens to initially support the Bolshevik revolution and it is the demand for political equality that leads to the first Russo-Chechen war. Second, the Chechens' political rights have been almost wholly denied since they were conquered by the Russians. The denial of political rights alone is not enough to produce support for terrorism. It is only when that denial is accompanied by the denial of security rights that we see the development of terrorism in Chechnya.

Subsistence Rights

> After Stalin's death, we returned to our home not as masters of that land, but as mere inhabitants, tenants. Other people took our jobs in our factories. We hardly had the right to work or educate ourselves.
>
> —Usup Soslambekov, Chechen nationalist (Seely, 2001, 88)

In this section we examine whether the lack of subsistence rights or basic human needs contributed to the development of terrorist activity in

Chechnya. Although the early Chechen history is one of relative deprivation, the economy of Chechnya was fundamentally changed between the first and second Chechen war, with Chechens now virtually destitute. In fact, the economic bleeding began before the first war when "overall production in the republic fell by 60 per cent in 1992 as the already high level of unemployment rose dramatically" (German, 2003, 61). This drastic downturn, in an otherwise promising economy (supported by oil and manufacturing industries), can be traced to the actions by leaders in Moscow. The end of the Soviet Union also meant the end of the socialist economic system, one that supported all of the regions, albeit not equally. In addition, the call for Chechen independence further severed many remaining economic ties. In essence, a form of economic warfare began before any Russian troops made their way into the Chechen capital. Figures reported by *Nezavisimaya Gazeta* in 1993 and cited in German (2003, 61) indicate that "gross national income was down by 67.8 per cent in comparison with 1991, real per capita income had declined by 75 per cent, total profits in the republic had fallen by 72 per cent and trade turnover by 68 per cent." Naturally, this devolution of the economy resulted in high unemployment, a precarious situation in a region that is traditionally well-armed, uneducated, and hostile toward Moscow (German, 2003).

Although it is difficult to draw a straight line from subsistence rights abuses to terrorist activity, we posit that support for terrorism is more likely to arise in areas of relative deprivation. In others words, it is when expectations of subsistence rise faster than the level of actual benefit (which contributes to an identity of marginalization) that individuals are more likely to pursue terrorists actions. In the Chechen case, traditional modes of production were systemically destroyed under Yermolov and later Stalin. Revenues from oil extraction and production were also expropriated by the Russians, particularly after the final Chechen deportation following World War II. Subsequent economic conditions developed in a two-track fashion, with ethnic Russians receiving better jobs, education, and health care within the region. The economic subjugation of ethnic Chechens, in their own homeland, contributed to an identity of marginalization. Chechen support for terrorism emerged in a period when the economic standing was relatively low. However, in the years after the first Chechen war, with the economy in ruins, popular support for terrorism dissipated. Many Chechens at this point desired peace and reconciliation with Russia. We find general support for our hypothesis that it is in states with medium levels of subsistence where we find conditions conducive to terrorism. The rise of terrorism after Chechens fell below a decent level of subsistence runs counter to our theory. This is due to the hijacking of this struggle by foreign fighters who continued to pursue terrorist tactics.

Security Rights Violations

> Nobody really knows what the raids are for, and the effect is counterproductive: very zatchiska adds to the numbers of the resistance! The will to fight, to kill and avenge the blood of our fathers and mothers and sisters increases all the time. Those who until a short time ago were still loyal to Russia now see the true face of the enemy, and understand that Chechnya can never be subject to Russia again. We have nothing in common. After the shameful barbarism that we've witnessed, what human relationship could we conceivably have?
>
> —Aslan Maskhadov (Nivet, 2002, 18)

In the Chechen case, security violations reach back for centuries. Chechnya's resistance of Russian occupation was strong from the beginning, but it is the forced deportation of Chechens following World War II that most vividly defines their historical memory. Stalin's regime, however, was one of the most repressive regimes in recent history. Thus, it is not surprising that we see little formal resistance during Stalin's regime, as his near complete repression would have effectively suppressed Chechen resistance. During the post-Stalin Soviet era, repression decreased significantly across the Soviet Union, including in Chechnya.

It is only beginning with Gorbachev and the elusive promise of autonomy that the stage is set for a new round of repression and resistance. The celerity of the Chechen independence movement, in the face of the crumbling Soviet empire, is a testament to the latent but unbroken Chechen desire for independence that Solzhenitsyn refers to decades earlier. Gorbachev's promise of greater degrees of autonomy throughout the empire was quickly followed by a Chechen declaration of independence in 1991. Within a month, Yeltsin declared a state of emergency and sent troops to Chechnya and we immediately see our first act of terrorism when Chechens hijacked a Russian passenger plane. Although the Russian troops stood down, as Yeltsin and Gorbachev vied for power within Russia, the Chechen population was effectively mobilized. It is clear had Yeltsin not been challenged by Gorbachev, Russian troops would have been used to squelch the Chechen independence movement. It is also clear to the Chechens that internal Russian problems created an opportunity to achieve some degree of independence.

Between 1991 and the beginning of the first Chechen war, there was sporadic insurgent activity, although it mostly involved holding hostages for ransom. We do not see a surge of terrorist activity until after the razing of Grozny and the utter destruction and repression of the first war. During this period, terrorism emerges almost overnight. The growth of the terrorist movement after the invasion and *zachistas* seems to indicate support for our hypothesis that state terror helps to justify an in-kind response. Paradoxically, as the repression and standard of living situation in Chechnya worsens, certainly between the wars, support for terrorism wanes. The overall effect of the invasion of Chechnya and the destruction of most of its villages is the demarcation from a rebellion to a more militant, terrorist movement, albeit led by a small faction within the Chechen population. However, the denial of human security in Chechnya quickly becomes overshadowed by the internationalization of the conflict.

International Influences

> The real problem in Chechnya is not the Arab fighters—it's Russia's wildly brutal rule. The Russian military has reduced this patch of the Caucasus to the sort of Hobbesian hell we associate with . . . well, like Afghanistan. Groups like al-Qaida thrive in such places. They arrive when things are bad, and make them worse; village-by-village "cleansings" only swell their ranks. (Bivens, 2000)

Terrorist activity in Chechnya can be connected to international factors in several ways. First, the political and economic development of the region was severely maligned by interference from successive Russian governments. Initial efforts to subdue the Chechen population were primarily carried out by destroying the farming and agricultural abilities of the Chechens, followed by a series of deportations. The state, whether Czarist, Soviet, or Russian, continually made promises of equality and rights and later reneged on those promises. Soviet policies of Russification and deportation were specifically designed to subjugate the Chechen people and destroy Chechen culture. Overall, Russian colonization stunted the development of institutions and prevented the emergence of political elites that may have helped to secure greater political rights today. These actions support our first hypothesis that brutal colonization may create conditions conducive to terrorism today. More importantly, though, is the effect of the colonial experience on the Chechens historical memory. The cycle of broken promises, and institutionalized policies of discrimination, including, in the extreme, mass deportations and state sponsored massacres, helped form a climate of distrust of the Russians in general. This long historical memory further created an identity of marginalization that continues today.

We hypothesize that, in addition to the historical colonial effects, external international factors can play an important contemporary role in creating a climate of support for terrorism. One important international factor is the distribution of power within the international system and how the state, or in this case the nation, fits within the international system.

Groups that perceive themselves as marginalized from the international community will feel less bound by international rules of the game and be more willing to pursue unconventional means to redress their grievances, including terrorist tactics. In terms of the Chechens, they clearly perceive themselves as alienated within the international community. Russia was able to define its policies in Chechnya in the early 1990s with only muted objection from the international community (de Waal, 2003; Russell, 2005). Indeed, Russia was granted admission to the Council of Europe while it simultaneously waged its war on Chechnya. In general, the West, including Europe and the United States, officially condemned Russian repression in Chechnya while making clear that they would not intervene in Russian affairs. Perhaps capitulation to Russian policy by the West reflected the very real goal in the post-Soviet environment to secure Russia as an ally. In either case, both the Chechens and the Russians would have correctly perceived the international response to Russian military involvement in Chechnya as tacit acceptance. After September 11th, even that early objection seemed to be silenced, as Russia justified the razing of Grozny and subsequent bombings under the umbrella of the War on Terror.

One of the most significant effects of the perceived marginalization of the Chechens within the international community is the involvement by like-minded actors who sympathize with the Chechen cause. The result is the cooption of the struggle by jihadists such as al Qaeda and former Afghani soldiers. Indeed, "By the late 1990s, no other major conflict involved Muslims, adding to Chechnya's attractiveness to hundreds of jihadists seeking the battlefield" (Vidino, 2006, 205). In particular, the Dayton Peace Accords brought an end to major conflict in Bosnia while simultaneously freeing up jihad-fighters who then moved into Chechnya (Williams, 2005). These fighters, led by Amir Khattab, began to take up the Chechen cause, even as many Chechens had abandoned it. According to one analyst, "It was this alliance between the 'Second Shamil' . . . and a Saudi holy warrior who saw himself as something of an Islamic 'Che Guevera' that was to have such negative consequences for hundreds of thousands of innocent Chechens who simply dreamed of rebuilding their lives following Russia's defeat in the 1994–96 Russo-Chechen War" (Williams, 2005, 100). In addition to fighters, Chechens also received money from international sources including Saudi Arabia and al Qaeda (see, for example, Bowers et al., 2004; Radu, 2004; Gakaev, 2005). In addition, LaFraniere (2003) estimates that 500,000 to 1,000,000 dollars a month arrives in Chechnya from al Qaeda. Both the money and the fighters began to dominate the Chechen movement.

This radical cooption served as a pretext for even greater Russian repression, now with at least implicit international acceptance, under the guise of fighting an international war on terror. However, the majority of Chechens remained skeptical of the jihadists' movement and tactics. The jihadists were "hated by many average Chechens, who saw them as foreign trouble-makers who gave Russia a pretext to reinvade their lands" (Williams, 2005, 100; see also de Waal, 2003; Bowers et al., 2004). The Russian response eventually resulted in the 1999 reinvasion of Chechnya. This drove many moderates, who may have supported the expulsion of the jihadis, into an alliance with Khattab (Williams, 2005).

This internationalization of terrorist movements has fundamentally changed the nature of modern terrorism. Unlike earlier terrorist's movements where guns and tactics were shared to aid disparate movements, the Chechen case reveals a new trend, whereby international actors enter the conflict zone and appropriate the movement for their own goals. As in the case of Chechnya, these goals may be incompatible and even contrary to the original revolution. Furthermore, most Chechens who shared the Sunni faith with many of the foreign fighters, rejected their radical Wahabbism. A Chechen doctor, Khassan Biaev, sums up the tension between these ideologies.

> We are grateful for humanitarian aid from Middle Eastern countries, but most Chechens have rebuffed the efforts of the Wahabbi to introduce extremist ideology into Chechnya's way of life. We are a very independent people. For hundreds of years we have fought again the Russians telling us what to do. We don't welcome other nations telling us how to behave, even if we share the same faith. The Wahabbis tried to seduce our young people with money, and it is true that some men joined them to support their families. But our elders constantly spoke out against the presence of these troublemakers and asked them to leave the villages. (Biaev, 2002)

Thus, while international factors clearly play a decisive role in the formation and growth of terrorism in Chechnya, the Chechen case serves as an important indicator of how international actors may fundamentally alter the nature of such movements.

Conclusion

We argue that terrorism occurs where human security is denied. We contend that states that deny citizens political rights, fail to provide adequate levels of subsistence, and repress their citizens provide the environment where terrorism is most likely to develop. When all of these conditions exist concomitantly, we are most likely to see the genesis and growth of terrorism. Moreover, it is security rights violations, in particular, that are necessary conditions for the growth of terrorism. Indeed, we see that it is only when we have each of these conditions in tandem, following the repression of the first Russian invasion, that we get substantial Chechen support for terrorism. When the repression is near complete (under Stalin) or the level of subsistence is inadequate (after the first Russo-Chechen war), support for terrorism dissipates. This case further illustrates that international factors, particularly colonial experience and international marginalization, continue to play a role in the growth of terrorism. Even as Chechens called for independence, their rhetoric referenced the deportation a half a century earlier. More importantly, though, this case indicates the critical role the internationalization of a particular terrorist movement can play. In this case, Chechnya's struggle for independence is overshadowed by foreign fighters whose goals are not always identical.

Notes

1. While all groups have some degree of historical memory, the clan-based nature of Chechen society makes such a memory critical to their identity. It should be noted that every historical account of Chechnya emphasizes the vital role of the collective memory in Chechnya (e.g., Seely, 2001; Gall & de Waal, 1998; Dunlop, 1998; Gammer, 2003, 2006).
2. This argument is informed by Fein's (1995) more murder in the middle thesis.
3. See also Felgenhauer (2003) regarding the Russian strategy of bombardment and other military tactics.
4. Human Rights Watch World Report (1996) provides a detailed description of this massacre.

References

BBC. (2002). Poverty fueling terrorism. http://news.bbc.co.uk/2/hi/1886617.stm
Baiev, K. (2002, November 9). Stop heinous acts by Russians and Chechens. *Boston Globe.*
Bivens, M. (2002, November 1). Chechnya war making not breaking terrorism. *Moscow Times.*
Bowers, S. R., Akhmadov, Y., & Derrick, A. A. (2004). Islam in Ingushetia and Chechnya. *The Journal of Social, Political and Economic Studies* 29 (4), 395–407.

Callaway, R. L., & Harrelson-Stephens, J. (2006). Toward a theory of terrorism: Human security as a determinant of terrorism. *Studies in Conflict and Terrorism* 29, 773–796.

de Waal, T. (2003). The Chechen conflict and the outside world. In *Chechnya: The world looks away*, edited by the Crimes of War Project (pp. 10–13). www.crimesofwar.org

de Waal, T. (2005). Chechnya: The breaking point. In R. Sakwa (Ed.), *Chechnya: From past to future* (pp. 181–198). London: Anthem Press.

Derluguian, G. M. (2003). Forward. In *A Small corner of hell: Dispatches from Chechnya*, by Anna Politkovskaya (pp. 1–25). Chicago: University of Chicago Press.

Doctors without Borders. (1996). Civilians targeted—Humanitarian law flouted in Chechnya. Available at www.doctorswithoutborders.org/publications/reports/before1999/chechnya 1996.cfm

Dunlop, J. B. (1998). *Russia confronts Chechnya: Roots of a separatist conflict.* Cambridge: Cambridge University Press.

Felgenhaur, P. (2003). The Russian army in Chechnya. In *Chechnya: The world looks away*, edited by the Crimes of War Project (pp. 6–9). www.crimesofwar.org

Gakaev, D. (2005). Chechnya in Russia and Russia in Chechnya. In Richard Sakwa (Ed.), *Chechnya: From past to future* (pp. 21–42). London: Anthem Press.

Gall, C., & de Waal, T. (1998). *Chechnya: A calamity in the Caucasus.* New York and London: New York University Press.

Gammer, M. (2002). Nationalism and history: Rewriting the Chechen national past. In B. Coppieters & M. Huyssune (Eds.), *Secession, history and the social sciences*. Brussels: Brussels University Press.

Gammer, M. (2006). *The lone wolf and the bear: Three centuries of Chechen defiance of Russian rule.* Pittsburgh, PA: University of Pittsburgh Press.

German, T. C. (2003). *Russia's Chechen war.* London: RoutledgeCurzon.

Krag, H. (2003). Chechnya and the Caucasus. In S. Troebst & F. Daftary (Eds.), *Radical ethnic movements in contemporary Europe* (pp. 71–83). Canada: Berghahn Books.

LaFraniere, S. (2003, April 26). How jihad made its way to Chechnya. *Washington Post.*

Lagnado, A. (2003). An interview with Oleg Orlov. In *Chechnya: The world looks away*, edited by the Crimes of War Project (pp. 14–17). www.crimesofwar.org

Lieven, A. (1998). *Chechnya: Tombstone of Russian power.* New Haven, CT: Yale University Press.

Mikhailov, V. (2005). Chechnya and Tartastan: Differences in search of an explanation. In Richard Sakwa (Ed.), *Chechnya: From past to future* (pp. 43–66). London: Anthem Press.

Nivat, A. (2003). Brutality and indifference. In *Chechnya: The world looks away*, edited by the Crimes of War Project (pp. 18–19). www.crimesofwar.org

Politkovskaya, A. (2003). *A small corner of hell: Dispatches from Chechnya.* Chicago: University of Chicago Press.
Radu, M. (2004, November/December). Russia's problems: The Chechens or Islamic terrorists? *Society*, 10–11.
Russell, J. (2005). Terrorists, bandits, spooks and thieves: Russian demonisation of the Chechens before and since 9/11. *Third World Quarterly* 26 (1), 101–116.
Sakwa, R. (2005). *Chechnya: From past to future.* London: Anthem Press.
Seely, R. (2001). *Russo-Chechen conflict, 1800–2000: A deadly embrace.* London: Frank Cass.
Smith, S. (1998). *Allah's mountains: Politics and war in the Russian Caucasus.* London and New York: I.B. Tauris.
Souleimanov, E. (2006). Caucasian and Chechen phobias within Russian society. *Prague Watchdog.* Available at http://www.watchdog.cz/ index.php?show=000000–000015–000006–000014&lang=1
Tishkov, V. (2004). *Chechnya: Life in a war-torn society.* Berkeley: University of California Press.
Vidino, L. (2005, Summer). How Chechnya became a breeding ground for terror. *Middle East Quarterly*, 57–66.
Vidino, L. (2006). *Al Qaeda in Europe.* New York: Prometheus Books.
Wetherall, B. (2004). Chechen terrorism: Old world motive, new world method? *YaleGlobal Online.*

Reports

Human Rights Watch. (2000). *Welcome to hell: Arbitrary detention, torture, and extortion in Chechnya.*
Human Rights Watch. (1996). *World Report.*

Chapter 5

Democratic Pieces
Democratization and the Origins of Terrorism

Erica Chenoweth

Introduction

Why are terrorist groups more prevalent in democracies than in nondemocracies? Why do individuals and groups resort to terrorist violence rather than using legal channels through which to express their grievances? Two different theoretical arguments in the literature argue different interactions between democracy and terrorism. One theoretical perspective argues that democracy will reduce terrorism as a phenomenon because democracies offer avenues for interest articulation among citizens and endorse nonviolent resolutions of conflicts. Because of the increased ability to express grievances, individuals and groups will pursue nonviolent alternatives to terrorism.

The second argument, on the other hand, expects the opposite effect. Some argue that political and civil liberties are positively correlated with terrorism because of the increased opportunity and permissiveness of democratic systems. The freedoms of movement and association enjoyed within democracies provide opportunities for terrorist groups to take root in societies and perform actions against either their own governments or foreign governments abroad. Parceling out the effects of democratic participation and constraints on executive power, still others have argued that different elements of democracy have competing effects on terrorist incidents.

This chapter contributes to this debate by exploring the causal processes linking democracies to terrorist group activity. I argue that terrorist activities proliferate in democratic countries for two related reasons. First, democracies provide the permissive environment, or opportunity structure, where terrorist groups can flourish. Second, the motivation for terrorist groups to escalate in democracies can be explained by inter-group dynamics, with terrorist groups of various ideologies competing with one another for limited agenda space. In order to test my hypotheses, I conduct a cross-national, longitudinal analysis of 119 countries for the period 1975 to 1997, using agenda competitiveness as the key independent variable and the number of new terrorist groups as the dependent variable.

This research is significant for several reasons. First, this project contributes to the debate concerning the relationship between democracies and terrorism. Few studies have investigated the dynamics existing between groups or the significance of such dynamics in explaining the relationship between democracy and terrorism. Therefore, this research is critical and progressive in developing both testable hypotheses regarding terrorism and recommendations concerning potential policy responses. A further goal is to contribute to the growing policy literature endorsing democracy as a way to eradicate terrorism. This project is a critique of the latter perspective, offering some considerations for scholars and policy makers who advocate democratization without taking into account all of its potential ramifications. Improved knowledge about the origins and development of terrorist groups—and the conditions that enhance them—is necessary in order for policy makers to make informed choices in foreign policy, especially in light of the current emphasis on terrorism and its potential impacts on U.S. security.

Political Opportunities for Terrorist Activity

There are two primary theoretical arguments concerning the relationship between democracy and terrorism.[1] First, some have argued that the lack of opportunities for expression of political grievances motivates terrorism (Crenshaw, 1981). In democratic societies, where freedom of expression is encouraged, dissenters are less likely to resort to terrorist violence in expressing their grievances (Schmid, 1992). Members of any class are able to join political parties, affect public policy, cast votes, and protest through peaceful means. In essence, democracy lowers the opportunity cost of achieving ones' political goals through legal means, thereby making terrorism less attractive to would-be perpetrators (Ross, 1993; Eyerman, 1998; Li, 2005).

Since democratic participation through elections improves the responsiveness of the government, those residing within democracies may be less likely to resort to terrorism. In addition, the presence of civil liberties may generate a mitigating effect on terrorism, because those who reside in countries with abundant political freedoms may be less likely to resort to terrorist violence as a form of political expression. Civil liberties may accompany democratic processes, and therefore reduce terrorist violence in democracies in addition to providing a permissive factor (Li, 2005). In general then, opportunities for political expression diminish the root causes of terrorism because citizens in democratic countries are more likely to be satisfied in the first place.

The second line of argumentation expects the opposite effects, arguing that democracy will encourage terrorism. First, Gurr (1990) argues that terrorism in democracies occurs in the context of a wider violent conflict. Ostensibly democratic transitions are particularly vulnerable events, as the fragile country attempts to overcome the potential backlash of internal and external actors opposing the transition or its implications. Indeed, some scholars have found that new democracies are particularly prone to internal conflict (Gleditsch et al., 2002; Mansfield & Snyder, 2005).

Furthermore, most scholars in this camp have suggested that democracy provides a permissive environment for terrorist growth because of the necessity of adherence to certain civil liberties (Schmid, 1992; Eubank & Weinberg, 1994, 1998, 2001; Ross, 1993; Eyerman, 1998). This perspective is much in line with the political opportunity literature prevalent in sociology (see, for instance, Oberschall, 1973. Also, see McAdam et al., 2001). Democratic guarantees such as freedom of assembly reduce the costs of conducting terrorist activities. Moreover, legal systems are less able to quickly pursue and prosecute potential terrorists because of the constraints placed on them by civil rights. Political leaders in the United States, for instance, have expressed frustration about the constraining effects of civil liberties in conducting the war on terrorism: "the spirited defense of civil liberties is a 'tactic that aids terrorists ... erodes our national unity ... diminishes our resolve [and] gives ammunition to America's enemies' " (Attorney General John Ashcroft in Crank & Gregor, 2005, 158).

Moreover, the specific civil liberty of press freedom may also have a positive effect on terrorism through two distinct processes. First, and most bothersome to researchers, is the problem of reporting bias across different regime types. Autocracies have less incentive to report the existence of oppositional groups or oppositional violence, and therefore restrict the material printed by their media. With a democracy, however, the free media has an incentive to report not only transparently, but also sensationally (Nacos, 2002). Furthermore, the democratic government places fewer restrictions on media content (Li, 2005). Therefore, terrorist incidents are less likely to be reported in autocratic countries than in democratic ones. Reporting bias, then, may lead researchers to the erroneous conclusion that civil liberties actually contribute to terrorist violence in the long run.

Press freedom may have an additional causal effect on terrorism, however. Without media coverage, terrorist groups are essentially obsolete. Widespread fear and panic are fundamental elements of terrorist strategy. Without the aftermath of a terrorist attack, the terrorist attack has not expressed itself fully. To be sure, Margaret Thatcher called the press the "oxygen" for terrorists (British Prime Minister Margaret Thatcher in Apple, 1985). Because of the existence of free press in most democracies, terrorists have increased incentives to grow in, move to, and conduct their violence within such countries. Sensational media coverage also serves the terrorists in recruiting, teaching, and training techniques. The press, therefore, is inadvertently complicit in fulfilling terrorists' objectives. This particular effect of the press may have a positive effect on terrorist activities.

However, Li suggests that the positive effect of civil liberties and press freedom may be epiphenomenal of a crucial aspect of democratic governance, which is the degree of institutional constraining power on the decision-making power of the government. Whereas the freedom of action in a nondemocracy is contingent on support from the members of the elite, the democratic government is held accountable to other branches of government as well as to the domestic electorate. In other words, as Li (2005) argues, "there are more veto players over government policy in democracy than in autocracy. Such political constraints prevent the democratic government from encroaching on civil liberties." The effect of civil liberties, therefore, is epiphenomenal of the constraints on the executive because the extent of civil liberties is largely determined by the strength of these constraints (Li, 2005).

Even more important, however, is that institutional constraints weaken the government's ability to fight terrorism. Checks and balances force the democratic government to be more accountable to a broader range of domestic interests. The democratic government is unlikely to engage in counterterrorist activities that could be perceived as undermining core democratic values, due to electoral incentives as well as norms of fair play. Authoritarian regimes, on the other hand, are less constrained and more able to find and crush terrorist organizations (Crenshaw, 1981). Democratic countries, therefore, are less likely to adopt counterterrorist strategies that are as strict as those enacted by nondemocratic regimes (Wilkinson, 2001).

A final consideration is that institutional constraints may actually strengthen the terrorists' strategic interactions with the government (Li, 2005). Because of institutional checks and balances, the democratic government must answer to a number of domestic interests. Providing a general sense of security is of paramount importance to democracies. The cost of generating a general terrorist threat is low because of the multitude of available targets that may be considered valuable by the democratic government. In autocracies, on the other hand, terrorists need only target those among the ruling elite. Because a small number of individuals is much easier to protect than a wide array, the costs of planning and launching an attack against a small elite group would be much higher than in a democracy. The greatest strength of democracy—governance by the people—thus becomes its greatest weakness vis-à-vis the terrorist threat. There is not only a higher degree of opportunity, but also a higher degree of vulnerability in democratic countries.[2]

Some scholars have also found a relationship between the form of democracy and the incidence of terrorism. Huber and Powell have found differing effects of majoritarian and proportional representation on the congruence between citizen preferences and public policies. On the whole, Huber and Powell found that the proportional representation system generates closer alignment of citizen self-placement and the estimated positions of governments on either majoritarian or mixed systems (Huber & Powell, 1994; Li, 2005, 284). Unsurprisingly, then, Marta Reynal-Querol has found that proportional representation also reduces the probability that groups will rebel within a state (Reynal-Querol, 2002). In effect, proportional representation systems are less likely to experience civil wars than majoritarian or mixed systems, since the opportunity costs of engaging in conflict are higher in a proportional representation system than any of the others. In a recent analysis, Li has found a negative correlation between proportional representation and terrorist incidents, following Reynal-Querol's findings (Li, 2005).

To summarize, democracy has been found to both encourage and reduce terrorist incidents, albeit through different causal mechanisms. That is, democratic participation reduces transnational incidents in ways indicated by Crenshaw and Schmid. It "increases satisfaction and political efficacy of citizens, reduces their grievances, thwarts terrorist recruitment, and raises public tolerance of counterterrorist policies" (Li, 2005, 294). However, the institutional constraints on the government actually exacerbate terrorism by imposing upon the government the "tough task of protecting the general citizenry against terrorist attacks" and weakening the government's strategic balance vis-à-vis the terrorists—essentially providing the opportunity structure in which terrorism can thrive (Li, 2005, 294). However, it seems that restricting freedom of movement, press, and association does not decrease the number of terrorist incidents. Instead, we observe a "substitution effect" in which terrorists merely replace their tactics with those that can continue in light of the government's new restrictions (Enders & Sandler, 2002).

Instead of focusing on purely linear correlations, Abadie (2006) suggests that perhaps political freedom, poverty, and terrorism have a curvilinear relationship. That is, it is neither the freest nor the most repressive states, but rather the intermediate states that experience terrorism most adversely. Using data from the World Market Research Center's "Global Terrorism Risk" index for 2003 and 2004, Abadie suggests that these nonmonotonic relationships show that terrorism is more likely in countries undergoing a democratic transition. However, Abadie gives no theoretical explanation for this seeming relationship, and he also fails to account for the temporal component of the relationship to establish causality.

Despite these important findings, the literature stops short of explaining why terrorist groups would prefer democratic, open societies to weak or failed autocracies. Why would terrorist groups prefer an open society with avenues of interest articulation to a closed society with a weak government enforcing it? In other words, is it truly the nature of democracies that attracts terrorist groups, or is it the opportunity structure alone? If it is only the opportunity structure, then terrorist groups would be similarly attracted to states that cannot control their own territories, conventionally referred to as "weak" states.

Interestingly, there are a number of these so-called "weak" states that do not contain or endorse substate terrorist groups, whereas almost every democratic country in the world has confronted terrorism during its history. Moreover, despite Li's argument that constraints on the executive prevent democracies from adopting strict counterterrorism policies, there are many cases in which democratic executives have circumvented these constraints in order to adopt such strategies. Therefore, it seems that the opportunity structure alone is insufficient to explain the proliferation of terrorist groups in democracies. There must be some other intervening factor(s) that affect the growth of terrorism as well.[3]

The Motivation for Terrorist Group Activity in Democracies

I argue that the pivotal dimension of the relationship between democracy and terrorist group emergence is that inter-group dynamics differ in democracies and nondemocracies.[4] The main difference is that in democracies, terrorist groups tend to compete against one another, whereas in nondemocracies, they tend to cooperate.

First, in democracies interest groups compete for space on the public agenda, which is dominated by numerous issues. The public agenda is comprised of "those political controversies the polity deems worthy of attention." (Flemming et al., 1999, 77)[5] Importantly, however, both institutional and systemic agendas are susceptible to crowding effects, which result in different interest groups competing to maintain their positions on the agenda to the exclusion of other issues, especially those in ideological opposition to the given issue (Lowrey & Gray, 1995). Because the agenda-setting process is highly competitive, various political organizations or interest groups are pitted against one another, even if they have similar interests at stake. Often, these groups are in direct conflict with one another and may even be hostile at times.[6]

Like more conventional conceptions of interest groups, the main object of a terrorist group is either to preserve the status quo of politics, or to bring about political change. According to the logic of terrorists (Group A, for instance), adroit articulations of violence may bring their grievances to the awareness of the public and succeed in putting issues of political salience on the agenda. Congleton (2002) writes:

> Both terrorist networks and ordinary political interest groups attempt to influence controversial public policies in a manner disproportionate to their votes. The probability and extent of the success of their efforts increase as the resources devoted to exerting "influence" expand, and decline with opponent efforts to resist their aims, other things begin equal. To the extent that participants are rational, institutional arrangements that change the probability of success among alternative methods of influence affect the level and allocation of group efforts across these methods. Terror is, analytically, simply another *method* that groups may use to influence decisions reached by government. In all these respects, terrorism is simply another form of interest-group politics. (Congleton, 2002, 48)

However, terrorist groups are distinct from normal interest groups in several important ways. First, whereas conventional interest groups use inducements through positive sanctions (such as financial rewards, campaign support) to influence legislative voting on the agenda, terrorist groups use negative sanctions (violence) to influence policy. Second, whereas conventional interest groups participate in the political process through generally accepted means of public discourse, terrorist violence is always perceived as illegitimate and outside the range of acceptable by democratic societies. Thus, while normal interest groups may eventually gain access to the political process, terrorist groups are perceived as perpetual outsiders unless they denounce violence and become legally recognized political parties (as with Sinn Fein).

To illustrate, let us consider a hypothetical situation between two potential terrorist groups—Group A and Group B. Group A may be the result of a social interaction between two aggrieved individuals within a democratic society. In their view, these individuals have exhausted conventional means of expressing their political preferences to no avail. Perhaps they subscribe to a similar ideology but perceive themselves to be isolated from mainstream political discourse. Ultimately, given a crisis of legitimacy and confidence in their government, these individuals may resort to terrorist violence in order to express their grievances (Sprinzak, 1990). The new group may be able to achieve through collective action what they had difficulty achieving separately due to limited resources. This particular process does not differ across democracies and nondemocracies.

Among other potential groups (Group B, for one), several processes may occur as a reaction to Group A's initial violent action. First, because of the competitive nature of the agenda-setting process in democracies, Group B may find Group A's violent expression as threatening to Group B's ability to add its own interests to the agenda. Second, if Group A is a right-wing terrorist group, a left-wing group has an even greater incentive to adopt violent strategies. Ideological opposition becomes especially salient in this dynamic, because the interests of the respective groups may be so incompatible that there is no possibility of satisfaction should one's opponent successfully gain space on the public agenda. In other words, paying attention to Group A necessarily diverts the audience's attention away from Group B. Beginning in 1969, for example, right-wing terrorist groups in Italy promoted the so-called "strategy of tension" in order to prevent the Italian public and government from succumbing to the Red Brigades' left-wing terrorist influences. Moreover, in the conflict in Northern Ireland, reactionary groups such as the Ulster Defense Force have arisen in response to the Irish Republican Army as a way to abet the possible effects of Northern Irish violence on British policies in the region.

Furthermore, democracies permit terrorist groups to pay attention to the effectiveness of certain tactics and the futility of others. Midlarsky, Crenshaw, and Yoshida have referred to the "contagion effect" of terrorist tactics in which groups emulate each other's effective organizational and attack strategies primarily by monitoring the media (Midlarsky et al., 1980). Because of the existence of widespread publicity on terrorist activities in democracies, groups within democracies are aware of one another's actions, therefore motivating them to act themselves. Again, this may be especially true in cases in which terrorist groups contain directly opposing viewpoints, such as the dual existence of both radical left-wing terrorists and neo-Nazi skinhead terrorists within the same democracy. In fact, we see this "action—reaction" relationship in many democracies. Throughout the West, for instance, the left-wing terrorists of the 1960s and 1970s had their counterparts in neo-fascist terrorist groups—in Italy, the Red Brigades rivaled with Prima Linae, for instance. As a further example, the IRA has its counterparts in the Ulster Freedom Fighters and Ulster Voluntary Force. Indeed, these groups have experienced such a high intensity of issue incompatibility and competition that they have frequently attacked one another.

Most research on terrorism acknowledges the fact that through their actions, terrorists speak to media, governments, and civilians as primary audiences. However, I wish to argue that in addition to these conventionally explored audiences, *terrorist groups are talking to each other*, a claim seldom made in the existing literature. In democracies, which I have already claimed to be permissive in terms of ideological pluralism, assembly, and press freedom, terrorist groups are able to monitor the existence and actions of rival groups that are competing for issue recognition.

An alternative expectation may be that agenda competitiveness actually diminishes the motivation for terrorism for two reasons. First, because of a plurality of ideas represented in the legislature, potential terrorist groups may actually find violence unnecessary because the likelihood of their viewpoints represented will increase. Second, there may be more citizen satisfaction due to the openness of the agenda, diminishing the underlying causes of terrorism in general (Crenshaw, 1981).

To summarize, the cherished elements of democracy—competitiveness, freedom of association, freedom of press, freedom of speech, responsive government, and a plurality of ideas—may also have dark sides. These features of governance, while desirable, inadvertently lead to contagion effects among terrorist groups, which perceive the effectiveness of terrorist tactics in overwhelming the population, monitor other groups' efforts at recognition, and struggle to organize themselves to compete for agenda space.

Empirical Analysis

In order to test my argument, I conduct a cross-national, longitudinal study of the emergence of terrorist groups in 119 countries (democracies and nondemocracies) for the period 1975–1997. The unit of analysis is the country year, and the dependent variable is the number of new terrorist groups that emerged in that country in that year, led ahead of the independent variables as suggested by Quan Li. Thus, since terrorist attacks may affect some of the independent variables (such as gross domestic product, GDP), all independent variables are lagged one year behind the dependent variable. The data for the dependent variable is taken from the RAND-MIPT and *Encyclopedia of World Terrorism*, each of which includes country and group profiles that indicate the date of group formation (Shanty et al., 2003; RAND-MIPT Terrorism Knowledge Base).[7] Because the dependent variable is an event count, I use negative binomial regression analysis.

Both RAND-MIPT and the *Encyclopedia of World Terrorism* include profiles in which they designate the date of group formation and (where applicable) group demise. This method includes obvious reliability concerns on several counts. First, it runs the risk of omitting terrorist groups that were in existence and active but unknown to the country and therefore unreported. This is a difficult and obvious problem that all terrorism researchers face, and I will not claim to solve it here. However, I am aware that this reporting bias exists and I try to account for it by determining whether press freedom has a positive and significant effect on terrorist group emergence independent of the other regressors.

The second caveat is that not all formation and ending dates were available or known. When formation and ending dates were unclear, I used the dates of the first attack and last attack claimed by that group as the respective formation and ending dates. The profiles included in the RAND-MIPT and *Encyclopedia of World Terrorism* are explicit about presumptions of inactivity. That is, if a group is claimed to be "inactive," I simply use the date of its last attack as the ending point of its existence. This eliminates the need for fear of mistakenly including the group in the total number of groups active in the country during a given year when it was actually out of operation. For the purposes of this study, however, I am limiting these claims to the number of new groups.

My independent variables are *Compindx* and *Participation competition*. First, I have generated a novel index measure, *Compindx*, which identifies the degree of ideological heterogeneity among terrorist groups within a given country during that year. The information on the terrorist groups was taken from the RAND-MIPT database and the *Encyclopedia of World Terrorism*. For instance, many groups are described as "leftist," "communist/socialist," "nationalist/separatist," "religious," "right-wing reactionary," or "racist." Since such categories are simplistic, however, I was able to discriminate between the ideologies of these groups when they were distinct from one another. For example, the category "religious" is used to describe groups such as Japan's Aum Shinrikyo as well as Christian groups such as the Covenant, Sword, and Arm of the Lord, and Islamic groups such as al Qaeda. In such cases, these groups were coded as having separate ideologies, since their ideologies are obviously distinct from one another.

Moreover, some groups possess more than one of these ideological descriptions, such as the Popular Front for the Liberation of Palestine (PFLP), which contains both a communist/socialist and a nationalist/separatist ideology. Similarly, Hamas possesses a nationalist/separatist and a religious (Islamic) ideology. In such cases, though their strategic objectives may occasionally coincide, these groups are coded as ideologically distinct.

In order to create the measure, I first counted the number of distinct ideologies operating among terrorist groups within the country in the year under inquiry. Therefore, the diversity within the United States yields a large number of ideologies with a broad range of interests represented: black separatist groups, right-wing militia groups, neo-Nazi groups, Islamic groups, leftist groups, environmental groups, and so forth. However, in recent years Greece has contained an ostensibly large number of terrorist groups, but most of them are anarchist groups. Therefore, despite its high numbers of groups, Greece contains a relatively low number of competing ideologies due to the homogeneity of the groups' ideologies.

Then I created the ideological heterogeneity/homogeneity index (called *Compindx*) measure among groups by dividing the number of ideologies by the number of the groups. The resulting measure is a continuous measure on a scale of 0–1, with 0 indicating total homogeneity among groups, and 1 indicating complete heterogeneity among groups.

An important caveat to this measure is that I omitted cases in which only one group is present to avoid coding this as a case of absolute homogeneity and therefore biasing the results, as a score of 1 indicates total heterogeneity (and therefore increased competition). Instead, in cases where only one group is present, I coded the index measure as a 0, indicating absolute ideological homogeneity. Also, even if there is more than one group, if the number of groups existing share a common ideology (such as revisionist Islam), the value of the index likewise equals 0 (meaning that no matter how many groups exist, they all contain the same ideology). For instance, if there are two groups with two different/competing ideologies, then the resulting proportion is 2/2 = 1 (absolute heterogeneity). This indicates a situation in which groups should compete (or escalate), whereas a proportion of 0 would indicate that the groups are more likely to cooperate. In the latter situation, we should see fewer attacks and fewer new groups emerging.[8]

The second independent variable is *Participation competition*, which measures the relative degree of agenda openness in each country. Taken from the POLITY IV dataset, Participation competition is on a 6–point scale, with 0 meaning nonexistent agenda openness, and 5 meaning a high degree of agenda openness.[9] This index measure demonstrates the ability of citizens to influence the government, thereby adequately capturing the sense of agenda openness for my purposes. Li suggests that this variable be centered to avoid collinearity (Li, 2005, following Aiken & West, 1991). According to the argument hypothesized above, the more competitive a polity, the more terrorist activity will take place. Thus participation competition should have a positive effect on terrorist group emergence.[10]

Hence, the model I describe results in the following estimate:

$$Y_i \text{ (number of new groups)} = a_i + \beta_1 X_1(compindx)$$
$$+ \beta_2 X_2(parcomp) + \varsigma_i + t_i + e_i$$

Where a_i = the intercept, ς_i = control variables, t_i = country fixed effects and panel corrected standard errors, and e_i = the residual error.

I also introduce several control variables. First, as I have mentioned, *Press freedom* is based on Van Belle's measure of descriptive summaries of the International Press Institute's annual reports, country reports by experts, and country-specific historical documents (Van Belle, 1997, compiled by Li, 2005). Van Belle codes levels of press freedom into five classifications: nonexistent press, free press, imperfectly free press (due to corruption or unofficial influence), restricted press, and government-controlled press. Press freedom is coded 1 if a country's press is clearly free and 0 otherwise. Li finds that without confounding variables such as democratic participation and institutional constraints, press freedom has a positive, statistically significant relationship to terrorist groups. Therefore, I expect the relationship between press freedom and terrorist group emergence to be positive as well.

I also control for *GDP* through a measure of real GDP per capita adjusted for purchasing power parity and logged (following Heston et al., 2002, compiled by Li, 2005) GDP per capita is expected to have a negative effect because the higher the economic development, the less likely the country is to have terrorism (Li & Schaub, 2004). I also control for *income inequality*, which includes a gini measure ranging from 0 to 100, 0 indicating less inequality, and 100 indicating the highest level of inequality.[11] Income inequality is expected to have a positive effect on terrorist group emergence, following the relative deprivation hypothesis.

Next, *regime durability* measures the number of years since the most recent regime change (Marshall & Jaggers, 2000).[12] Regime durability is expected to have a negative effect. I also control for size, which measures the total population, logged, from World Bank data (*poplog*) (World Bank, 2002). Size should have a positive effect on terrorist group emergence, since more populous nations have a higher probability of producing terrorist groups. *Government capability* is also expected to have a negative effect on terrorist group emergence, since the less able governments are more likely to experience widespread internal turmoil (Gleditsch et al., 2002). This measure is the logged annual composite percentage index of a state's share of the world's total population, GDP per capita, GDP per unit of energy, military manpower, and military expenditures. I also include dummies for type of democracy—specifically variables called *proportional*, *majority*, and *mixed*, all of which are coded 1 if they contain that type of system and 0 otherwise, exclusively in democracies.[13]

History of attacks is the average annual number of transnational terrorist incidents that have occurred in a country since 1968. This variable was computed by Li using the ITERATE data, and it is expected to have a positive effect due to the contagion effects of terrorism (Crenshaw et al., 1980; Mickolus et al., 2003; Li, 2005). I also control for *conflict*, which is coded 1 if a state is engaged in interstate military conflict or war, and 0 otherwise. This measure comes from Gleditsch, et al., and I expect it to have a positive effect (Gleditsch et al., 2002).

Finally, there are several dummy variables worth mentioning. The *region* dummies are Europe, Africa, Asia, and the Americas, relative to the Middle East, which has the highest number of terrorist incidents. I also include a *Post–Cold War* dummy, coded 1 since 1991 and 0 otherwise, since terrorist attacks have decreased dramatically since the end of the Cold War due to the end of Soviet funding of left-wing groups (Enders & Sandler, 1999). This dummy is expected to have a negative effect on terrorist attacks. Together with the *History of attacks* variable, I thus control for intertemporal effects.

In separate models, I evaluate the utility of Li's claims about the opposing effects of democratic participation and institutional constraints for explaining new group formation (see Table 5.2). *Democratic participation*, taken from Li (2005), combines the electoral participation variable in Vanhanen's Polyarchy dataset with a dichotomous indicator of democracy from POLITY IV (Vanhanen, 2000; Marshall & Jaggers, 2000). Vanhanen's democratic participation index measures the percentage of the population that voted in general elections. Democratic participation is coded as equal to Vanhanen's index if the country is a democracy (a polity score of 6 or higher), and 0 if the country is not a democracy (lower than a 6 on the polity score). This removes the threat of including high voter turnout that may result from forced voting in autocracies. On the other hand, in order to mitigate the possible confounding effects of low voter turnout due to overall satisfaction with the government, real GDP is also included in the model as previously mentioned. According to Li's argument, *Democratic participation* should have a negative effect on terrorist incidents.

The final indicator of democracy is *Institutional constraints*, which is based on the executive constraints variable in the POLITY IV dataset. This variable features a scale of 1 to 7, with 1 indicating that the executive has unlimited authority, and a value of 7 indicating executive parity or subordination. We can expect institutional constraints to have a positive effect on terrorist incidents, as an executive with a higher number of checks and balances is less likely to enforce stiff counterterrorist policies.

Following Abadie, in a separate model I use two measures called *Participation competition squared* and *compindx squared* (see Table 5.3)

(Abadie, 2006). These independent variables follow from the hypothesis that it is neither the freest nor the most repressive regimes that contain the highest number of terrorist groups, but rather the intermediate cases. I generate these variables by simply squaring *Participation competition* and *compindx*, with the anticipation that these variables will be positively correlated with the dependent variable.

Because the hypotheses are directional, one-tailed tests are applied. I also include robust standards errors clustered by country to produce standard errors that are robust to both heteroskedasticity and serial correlation within the cross-sectional unit (Li, 2005, 286).

The results appear in Table 5.1.

In Model 1, I conduct a negative binomial regression with robust standard errors, dispersed around the constant and clustered around country. This model tests the hypothesis that agenda competition and the competition index will have positive effects on terrorist group emergence. As anticipated, both variables have positive and significant effects on the emergence of new terrorist groups.

Government capability has a negative and insignificant relationship with terrorist group emergence, meaning that governments with a declining resource base will have a more difficult time preventing terrorist groups from arising within their borders. The population log variable is positive and significant, indicating that the higher a population, the more likely is terrorist group emergence.

The gini index measure of inequality has a positive but insignificant effect. This means that higher degrees of inequality within a country are associated with more terrorist events. Societies that experience more social and economic cleavages are therefore more likely to experience terrorist attacks. Real GDP per capita also has a negative but insignificant effect, suggesting that the more economically deprived nations are more likely to produce terrorist groups. However, both relationships are weak and require further investigation. The conflict dummy has a positive and significant effect on terrorist group emergence, meaning that states that are involved in international conflicts with other states are generally more likely to experience a proliferation of terrorist groups. This may be the case because international conflicts require a large degree of agenda space and create the crowing effects to which terrorists react. Finally, durability has a positive but insignificant effect, indicating that regimes that maintain power longer are more likely to inadvertently develop new terrorist groups.

As expected, there are some temporal effects as evidenced by the negative yet insignificant effects of the Cold War dummy variable and the positive and significant effects of the history of attacks. During the Cold War, therefore, less terrorist groups emerged. However, states with a history

Table 5.1. The Relationship Between Competition and Terrorist Group Emergence

Ind./Model Var.	1	2	3	4	5	6	7	8
Parcomp	.343*** (.081)				.280** (.117)	.368** (.154)	.317*** (.084)	.310** (.123)
Compindx	.652*** (.239)		.689*** (.222)		.683*** (.231)	.490* (.299)	.606*** (.225)	.335 (.263)
PR				.223 (.26)	.020 (.37)			
Maj.				.717** (.306)	.306* (.344)			
Mixed				.246 (.276)	.125 (.354)			
Press Freedom		.139 (.227)						
Gov't capability	-.086 (.239)	.063 (.295)	-.071 (.240)	.079 (.232)	-.049 (.221)	-.372 (.405)	.078 (.227)	-.237 (.261)
Conflict	.608** (.157)	.557*** (.204)	.600*** (.168)	.601*** (.157)	.591*** (.147)	.475** (.216)	.503*** (.148)	.786*** (.279)
Gini	.0002 (.025)	.002 (.024)	-.005 (.025)	.008 (.025)	.017 (.027)	.019 (.026)	.005 (.023)	-.034 (.031)

continued on next page

Table 5.1. (*Continued*)

Ind./Model Var.	1	2	3	4	5	6	7	8
Population (log)	.173** (.078)	.210** (.083)	.169** (.078)	.195** (.079)	.111 (.077)	2.26*** (.748)	.193*** (.074)	.188** (.088)
Post–Cold War	−.203 (.164)	−.317 (.193)	−.127 (.158)	.008 (.158)	−.162 (.161)	−.672*** (.204)	−.824* (.453)	−.408** (.199)
Europe	−.350 (.337)	−.424 (.328)	.018 (.358)	−.315 (.339)	−.200 (.333)	−5.37 (7.97)	−.250 (.319)	−.739* (.380)
Africa	−.107 (.441)	−.478 (.515)	−.071 (.450)	−.407 (.483)	−.210 (.417)	8.92 (541.88)	.024 (405)	−.633* (.523)
Asia	−.709** (.333)	−.554* (.308)	−.463 (.320)	−.798** (.317)	−.787 (.336)	**5.15 (161.22)	−.625 (.318)**	−1.18*** (.450)
Americas	−.305 (.240)	−.521** (.261)	−.082 (.254)	−.643** (.292)	−.339 (.239)	8.62 (277.95)	−.275 (.243)	−.555* (.293)
Real GDP (log)	−.238 (.176)	−.128 (.176)	−.013 (.175)	−.133 (.173)	−.203 (.178)	−.193 (.572)	−.266 (.171)	−.280 (.226)
History of attacks (lagged)	.211** (.088)	.646*** (.100)	.255*** (.086)	.564*** (.100)	.191** (.097)	−.536** (.253)	.248*** (.086)	.210** (.105)
Regime durability	.009 (.086)	.025 (.117)	.028 (.089)	−.033 (.070)	−.009 (.078)	.107 (.133)	−.0001 (.084)	−.038 (.089)

Constant	−2.41 (2.47)	−5.05* (3.01)	−4.19 (2.53)	−2.65 (3.03)	−3.53 (2.40)	−29.36 (12.73)	−3.09 (2.38)	.529 (3.38)
N	1016	1897	1016	2148	1016	918	1016	771
Wald chi2	244.11	297.38	128.67	348.13	274.50	38.07	631.74	84.08
Prob > chi2	.0000	.0000	.0000	.0000	.0000	.0005	.0000	.0000

Note: ***p < .01; **p < .05; *p < .1

of terrorist attacks are more likely to produce new groups. This finding is consistent with the explanation that terrorist violence is competitive: the more attacks perpetrated by Group A, the higher Group B's incentive to escalate its own activities. This competition results in more new groups. Moreover, Asia, Africa, Europe, and the Americas experience fewer new terrorist groups than the Middle East.

Next, I ran a series of diagnostics to test the robustness of my findings over several alternative specifications. Model 2 estimates a negative binomial regression that tests the effects of press freedom on terrorist group emergence in order to account for any potential reporting bias. The effect of press freedom is positive, but insignificant. I therefore proceeded without including press freedom in my analysis because press freedom is statistically insignificant and does not significantly change the results recorded in Model 1.

Model 3 estimates a negative binomial time-series regression assessing the independent effect of terrorist group competitiveness on the number of new groups emerging within a country. As expected, the effect is positive and significant. The more ideologies that exist in conflict with one another, the more groups will develop in that country.

In Model 4, I investigate the effects of the type of democracy on terrorist group emergence. As expected, majoritarian systems are more conducive to group emergence than either proportional representation or mixed systems. This finding is consistent with Li and Reynal-Querol's earlier findings (Reynal-Querol, 2002; Li, 2005). Model 5 estimates the effects of type of democracy when combined with the main regressors of participation competition and terrorist group competition. All of the variables maintain their direction and significance.

Model 6 estimates the original model with fixed effects diagnostics clustered around country code. This regression tests whether the relationship between events and participation competition holds up when I account for country dummies. As evidenced in Table 5.1, there is no significant change except for the change in direction of the region dummies, which likely occurred due to multicollinearity. Model 7 tests a negative binomial time-series regression accounting for time effects and displays no major changes to Model 1. Finally, Model 8 tests the model for autocorrelation effects, estimating the model with panel-corrected standard errors. In this model, I test to see whether the relationship between events and participation competition remains robust when controlling for possible autocorrelation. The index for terrorist groups competition drops out in terms of significance, but the participation competition variable retains its significance; thus the results do not change significantly.

The following table provides a test of the relative explanatory power of my model vis-à-vis Quan Li's explanation. In Table 5.2, I estimate

Table 5.2. Effects on Executive Constraints on Terrorist Group Emergence

Ind./Model Vars.	9	10	11
Parcomp		.385**	.362**
		(.166)	(.166)
Compindx		.634***	.645***
		(241)	(.240)
Xconst	.086*	−.004	−.012
	(.051)	(.087)	(.094)
Partdem	−.009	−.012	
	(.006)	(.008)	
Gov't capability	.030	−.113	−.085
	(.241)	(.236)	(.240)
Conflict	.616***	−.604***	.609***
	(.161)	(.152)	(.156)
Gini	−.003	.002	.0006
	(.022)	(.025)	(.026)
Population (log)	.223***	.155**	.174**
	(.076)	(.079)	(.080)
Post–Cold War	−.058	−.245	−.202
	(.158)	(.175)	(.164)
Europe	−.286	−.247	−.358
	(.371)	(.331)	(.313)
Africa	−.287	−.073	−.097
	(.466)	(.445)	(.461)
Asia	−.688**	−.677**	−.701**
	(.315)	(.340)	(.346)
Americas	−.612**	−.391	−.310
	(.279)	(.257)	(.238)
Real GDP (log)	−.102	−.179	−.242
	(.178)	(.171)	(.175)
History of attacks (lagged)	.603***	.222***	.214**
	(.096)	(.095)	(.096)
Regime durability	−.010	.021	.012
	(.072)	(.079)	(.083)
Constant	−4.93*	−2.51	−2.42
	(2.99)	(2.43)	(2.48)
N	2147	1016	1016
Wald chi2	372.21	265.82	249.58
Prob > chi2	.0000	.0000	.0000

Note: ***$p < .01$; **$p < .05$; *$p < .1$

three models assessing the likelihood of an alternative explanation, which is that constraints on the executive allow for terrorist groups to emerge. Model 9 utilizes a negative binomial regression to test whether the relationship between group emergence and democracy is better explained in the institutional constraints and degree of democratic participation, as suggested by (Li, 2005). Although executive constraints do have a positive and significant statistical effect on terrorist group emergence, the coefficient value shows that there is little substantive effect when compared to participation competition. There is little change in the remaining control variables. Model 10 estimates the original model, accounting for the possible effects of executive constraints and democratic participation. However, whereas participation competition and group competition maintain their positive and significant effects, both executive constraints and democratic participation drop out. This is most likely due to high correlation (approximately .75) between the two POLITY IV variables. Model 11 tests the relationship omitting democratic participation, and the findings are similar to those in Model 10.

Finally, Table 5.3 identifies the possibility of a nonlinear relationship between participation competition, group competition, and the number of terrorist groups that emerge within a polity.

Model 12 estimates a negative binomial regression that tests for curvilinear effects of participation competition on group emergence, with group competition having a linear effect. Whereas the participation competition value is positive and significant, the interaction variable is negative and insignificant. Next, Model 13 tests whether group competition has a curvilinear effect, while holding participation competition at a linear estimator. In this model, group competition is positive, and its interaction term is negative. This suggests that it is the situations in which there is no competition and extremely high competition in which terrorist groups emerge. Intermediate levels of competition are more "stable" in terms of the number of terrorist groups. This may be due to the "balancing effect" of two different terrorist groups who oppose one another—such as the Red Brigades versus Prima Linae in Italy in the 1970s and early 1980s.

Finally, Model 14 tests whether there are joint curvilinear effects of participation competition and group competition. The results suggest that the curvilinear effects of group competition are robust to two alternative specifications, whereas the curvilinear effects of participation competition are positive but less explicit. However, the lack of statistical evidence indicating a curvilinear relationship between participation competition and terrorist group emergence may exist due to the collinearity of the interaction variable and the original regressor. Therefore, preliminary evidence suggests that it is neither the most restrictive nor the most competitive

Table 5.3. Nonlinear Effect of Competitive Terrorist Group Emergence

Ind./Model Vars.	12	13	14
Parcomp	.350*** (.084)	.327*** (.076)	.318*** (.076)
Parcomp^2	−.019 (.075)		.027 (.072)
Compindx	.662*** (.242)	4.17*** (.817)	4.21*** (.827)
Compindx^2		−3.35*** (.798)	−3.40*** (.823)
Gov't capability	−.092 (.247)	−.175 (.246)	−.165 (.254)
Conflict	.606*** (.157)	.643*** (.144)	.646*** (.143)
Gini	−.002 (.027)	.002 (.023)	.005 (.024)
Population (log)	.171** (.081)	.175** (.080)	.178** (.084)
Post–Cold War	−.215 (.168)	−.305* (.169)	−.289* (.169)
Europe	−.334 (.331)	−.130 (.336)	−.151 (.336)
Africa	−.070 (.425)	.101 (.386)	.058 (.377)
Asia	−.719** (.335)	−.567 (.310)	−.551* (.319)
Americas	−.300 (.240)	−.023 (.246)	−.027 (.251)
Real GDP (log)	−.225 (.186)	−.093 (.171)	−.111 (.179)
History of attacks (lagged)	.212** (.088)	.051 (.095)	.048 (.097)
Regime durability	−.014 (.090)	−.043 (.083)	−.051 (.089)
Constant	−2.35 (2.54)	−3.57 (2.38)	−3.65 (2.46)
N	1016	1016	1016
Wald chi2	241.50	209.72	211.87
Prob > chi2	.0000	.0000	.0000

Note: ***p < .01; **p < .05; *p < .1

regimes that experience the largest number of terrorist incidents, but rather the intermediate cases.

Summary

These findings suggest that a theory of competition among terrorist groups has some preliminary support. In fact, on its own, this explanation has just as much support as structural theories, which offer less explanatory power. However, at this point, it is difficult to say which theory holds up best under different cases. For further research, therefore, scholars should consider examining case studies to test whether structural or inter-group approaches contain the most explanatory power. My future research will attempt to do so. Additionally, deriving more reliable measures of inter-group competition would greatly benefit the field of terrorism studies, as well as counterterrorism efforts. According to the analysis conducted here, inter-group competitiveness is a fairly good predictor of whether terrorist groups will form in competitive democracies. Finally, additional consideration should be given to the proposition that the relationships between terrorist events and various independent factors may in fact be curvilinear—a notion that is both theoretically and empirically undeveloped, but that receives some initial support here.

Conclusion

The empirical analysis in this chapter provides preliminary confirmation of the argument that structural explanations of democratic terrorism are incomplete. A more complete explanation concerns the incentives that motivate terrorist groups to escalate their activities, such as competitiveness. As violent forms of more conventional interest groups, different terrorist groups compete for space on the public agenda. Because such competition results in crowding effects, the groups then perceive a need to "out-do" one another for influence thereby resulting in an overall escalation of violent incidents. Terrorists do not hate freedom, as is commonly touted in political rhetoric. On the contrary, they seem to thrive on and exploit it. This seems to be especially true in cases of democratic transitions, during which competition for agenda primacy is most fearsome.

Most structural studies that establish a positive relationship between terrorism and democracy find themselves in awkward positions because of the implications of their results—namely, that undermining democracy may also undermine terrorism. Some scholars are obliged to admit that their results suggest that either democracies should forego their institutional constraints in this policy arena and restrict civil liberties, or that terrorism is something that contemporary democracies must learn to live with. The implications of group-level analyses are more hopeful than structural explanations, because they suggest that terrorist motivations may actually be more dynamic than suggested by solely structural hypotheses.

Moreover, just as structural explanations of terrorism are incomplete, so are structural approaches to counterterrorism. The most obvious implication is that governments cannot eradicate terrorist groups by simply implementing democracy. Democracy is permissive to and inadvertently encourages terrorist activity. Moreover, the most vulnerable time for the emerging democracy may be its period of transition—an expectation confirmed by the experiences in Iraq and Afghanistan.

However, even if democracies attempted to reduce civil liberties and crush terrorists within their borders, the competitive nature of inter-group dynamics within democracies remains beyond anyone's control. Furthermore, the alternative to democracy may be normatively unacceptable, so governments must seek ways to disrupt the inter-group dynamics that cause terrorist groups to constantly escalate their activities. One possibility is to focus counterterrorism efforts on covert infiltration of terrorist groups in an effort to dismantle the groups from the inside out. Promoting group schisms may contribute to the downfall of these groups.[14] Although this strategy is supported by governments internationally, intelligence agencies have not yet obtained the resources required to be successful.

Indeed, there may be no single international strategy that will effectively win the fight with terrorism. Officials must take into account local environments—including both structural and group-level conditions—in order to derive effective counterterrorism policies. The best bet, however, is for governments to increase their efforts at preventing inter-group competitiveness while promoting new and innovative ways to infiltrate groups to contribute to their self-destruction.

Notes

Some of the material in this chapter also appears in the author's article in the January 2010 issue of the *Journal of Politics*.

1. To be sure, there are many important questions to answer regarding the nature of democracy and terrorism, the internal features of democracy and how they give rise to groups, and the consequences of foreign and domestic policies on terrorist groups. Because of time and resource constraints, I will not be able to

analyze each of these important issues in this particular chapter. However, future research will investigate the impacts of "social climates" within both democracies and autocracies on terrorism as data becomes more readily available.

2. Whereas in a democracy, the institutional constraints may depend on the number of veto players involved in decisions, nondemocracies may face other constraints—namely, the lack of control over their own populations due to limited resources. Therefore, the causal processes differ slightly between democracies and nondemocracies. When terrorist groups arise out of nondemocracies, then, there are two possible explanations: resource constraints, or willing support of the groups by state agencies.

3. Some arguments are that most terrorist groups are inherently hostile toward Western democracy, because of its secularism, its hedonism, or its market strategies. Those who subscribe to the belief that terrorism is primarily an ideological phenomenon use suicide bombing as evidence to support their claims—that the "martyr culture" of Islam, for instance, endorses the use of suicide violence against Western enemies. This argument is further substantiated by examining texts of Islamic terrorist leaders, who denounce the West—particularly the United States—as "the Great Satan" (bin Laden, 2004). This evidence, unfortunately, does not explain suicide terrorism or the grievances that have arisen. First, they still do not explain why some Islamic individuals become terrorists and some do not. Second, it forces researchers and policy makers to ignore the great abundance of non-Islamic terrorists (including, for instance, the Christian Patriots, ETA, and the IRA). Moreover, Islamic terrorists are not the sole proprietors of suicide terrorism. Indeed, it has been used as a purely secular phenomenon, as the Tamil Tigers began to use it as a successful tactic in the 1990s. Some Islamic groups have used the Tigers' success as a justification for using it against perceived occupiers in the Middle East. Islamic terrorists have then scrambled for justification in the Quran, but many influential Islamic clerics have since denounced suicide terrorism as violating religious laws within Islam (Bloom, 2005; CNN.com, 2005).

4. Most terrorist groups—regardless of the regime type in their place of origin—claim that they suffer oppression from the government. Although the purpose of this study is not to examine the validity of their claims, I wish to argue that there are nevertheless certain distinct characteristics of democracies that inadvertently encourage groups to form, regardless of the factual or realistic bases of the groups' grievances and perceptions.

5. Whereas the institutional agenda includes "the specific, concrete issues being attended to by the government," the systemic agenda refers more broadly to the general concerns of the public.

6. Mia Bloom (2005) has argued that the competition between terrorist groups for recruits and resources has caused them to escalate their tactics to suicide bombing. However, few have examined the competitive pressures that persuade groups to choose terrorism over peaceful forms of political discourse.

7. ITERATE (International Terrorism: Attributes of Terrorist Events) is one commonly used events dataset, but it records only transnational terrorist incidents and is therefore inappropriate for this study. ITERATE is an events dataset based on international newspaper headlines describing terrorist attacks.

8. One important exception to this expectation is when terrorist attacks escalate as a result of protest against a nondemocratic domestic government that all of the groups oppose. This may indicate that the terrorists are pooling their resources toward one goal. In this case, however, we should see less inter-group rivalry.

9. Missing values (coded in POLITY IV as -44, -88, etc.) were dropped from the analysis.

10. I use participation competition rather than executive competition because the legislature is the most deliberative body of influence in governments.

11. Missing values were filled in by Li, 2005, following Feng and Zak, 1999; Li and Reuveny, 2003; and Deininger and Squire, 1996.

12. This variable will be logged following Li, 2005.

13. These data come from Golder (2005), and were compiled by Li (2005).

14. Rex Hudson (1999) makes a similar argument in *Who Becomes a Terrorist and Why*.

References

Abadie, A. (2004). Poverty, political freedom, and the roots of terrorism. *American Economic Review* 96, 159–177.

Aiken, L., & West, S. G. (1991). *Multiple regression: Testing and interpreting interactions*. Newbury Park: Sage.

Apple, R. W. (1985, July 18). Meese suggests press code on terrorism. *New York Times*.

bin Laden, O. (2004). Declaration of war against the Americans occupying the land of the two holy places. In W. Laqueur (Ed.), *Voices of terror* (pp. 410–412). New York: Reed.

Bloom, M. (2005). *Dying to kill: The allure of suicide terror*. New York: Columbia University Press.

CNN.com. (2005). Spanish clerics issue fatwa against bin Laden. Last accessed 9/14/05.

Congelton, R. D. (2002). Terrorism, interest-group politics, and public policy: Curtailing criminal modes of political speech. *Independent Review* 3, 47–67.

Crank, J. P., & Gregor, P. (2005). *Counterterrorism after 9/11: Justice, security, and ethics reconsidered*. Cincinnati, OH: Lexis-Nexis.

Crenshaw, M. (1981). The causes of terrorism. *Comparative Politics* 13, 379–399.

Deininger, K., & Squire, L. (1996). A new dataset measuring income inequality. *World Bank Economic Review* 10, 565–591.

Enders, W., & Sandler, T. (1999). Transnational terrorism in the post-cold war era. *International Studies Quarterly* 43 (1), 145–167.

Enders, W., & Sandler, T. (2002). Patterns of transnational terrorism 1970–99: Alternative time series estimates. *International Studies Quarterly* 46 (2), 145–165.

Eubank, W. L., & Weinberg, L. (1994). Does democracy encourage terrorism? *Terrorism and Political Violence* 6 (4), 417–463.

Eubank, W. L., & Weinberg, L. (1998). Terrorism and democracy: What recent events disclose. *Terrorism and Political Violence* 10 (1), 108–118.

Eubank & Weinberg. (2001). Terrorism and democracy: Perpetrators and victims. *Terrorism and Political Violence* 13 (1), 155–164.

Eyerman, J. (1998). Terrorism and democratic states: Soft targets or accessible systems. *International Interactions* 24 (2), 151–170.

Feng, Y., & Zak, P. (1999). The determinants of democratic transitions. *Journal of Conflict Resolution* 43 (2), 162–177.

Flemming, R. B., Wood, B. D., & Bohte, J. (1999). Attention to issues in a system of separated powers: The macrodynamics of American policy agendas. *Journal of Politics* 61 (1), 76–108.

Gleditsch, N. P., Walkensteen P., et al. (2002). Armed conflict 1946–2001: A new dataset. *Journal of Peace Research* 39 (5), 615–637.

Golder, M. (2005). Democratic electoral systems around the world, 1946–2000. *Electoral Studies* 24 (1), 103–121.

Gurr, T. R. (1990). Terrorism in democracies: Its social and political bases. In W. Reich (Ed.), *Origins of terrorism* (pp. 86–102). Washington, DC: Woodrow Wilson.

Heston, A., Robert, S., & Aten, B. (2002). *Penn world table version 6.1*. Philadelphia: Center for International Comparisons at the University of Pennsylvania (CICUP).

Huber, J. D., & Powell Jr., G. B. (1994). Congruence between citizens and policymakers in two visions of liberal democracy. *World Politics* 46 (3), 291–326.

Hudson, R. (1999). *Who becomes a terrorist and why*. Washington, DC: Lyons Press.

Li, Q., & Reuveny, R. (2003). Economic globalization and democracy: An empirical analysis. *British Journal of Political Science* 33 (1), 29–54.

Li, Q., & Schaub, D. (2004). Economic globalization and transnational terrorist incidents: A pooled time series analysis. *Journal of Conflict Resolution* 48 (2), 230–58.

Li, Q. (2005). Does democracy promote or reduce transnational terrorist incidents? *Journal of Conflict Resolution* 49 (2), 278–297.

Lowrey, D. C., & Gray, V. (1995). The population ecology of Gucci Gulch, or the natural regulation of interest group numbers in the American states. *American Journal of Political Science* 39 (1), 1–29.

Mansfield, E., & Snyder, J. (2005). *Electing to fight: Why emerging democracies go to war*. Cambridge: BCSIA.

Marshall, M. G., & Jaggers, K. (2000). Polity IV project: Political regime characteristics and transitions, 1800–2000. Dataset User's Manual. Available at http://www.bsos.umd.edu/cidcm/inscr/polity/index.htm#data/

McAdam, D., Charles T., & Tarrow, S. (2001). *Dynamics of contention*. Cambridge: Cambridge University Press.

Mickolus, E., et al. (2003). *International terrorism: Attributes of terrorist events, 1968–2001*. Dunn Loring, VA: Vinyard Software.
Midlarsky, M., Crenshaw, M., & Yoshida, F. (1980). Why violence spreads: The contagion of international terrorism. *International Studies Quarterly* 24 (2), 262–298.
Nacos, B. (2002). *Mass-mediated terrorism: The central role of the media in terrorism and counterterrorism*. Boulder: Rowman-Littlefield.
Oberschall, A. (1973). *Social conflict and social movements*. New York: Prentice-Hall.
RAND-MIPT Terrorism Knowledge Base. http://www.tkb.org
Reynal-Querol, M. (2002). Political systems, stability, and civil wars. *Defence and Peace Economics* 13 (6), 465–483.
Ross, J. I. (1993). Structural causes of oppositional terrorism: Towards a causal model. *Journal of Peace Research* 30 (3), 317–329.
Schmid, A. (1992). Terrorism and democracy. *Terrorism and Political Violence* 4 (4), 14–25.
Shanty, F., & Picquet, R. (2003). *Encyclopedia of world terrorism*. Armonk: Sharpe.
Sprinzak, E. (1990). The pscyhopolitical formation of extreme left terrorism in a democracy: The case of the weathermen. In W. Reich (Ed.), *The Origins of Terrorism* (pp. 65–85). Washington, DC: Woodrow Wilson.
Van Belle, D. (1997). Press freedom and the democratic peace. *Journal of Peace Research* 34 (4), 405–414.
Vanhanen, T. (2000). The polyarchy dataset: Vanhanen's index of democracy. Available at http://www.svt.ntnu.no/iss/data/vanhanen
Wilkinson, P. (2001). *Terrorism versus democracy: The liberal state response*. London: Frank Cass.
World Bank. (2002). *The 2002 world development indicators CD-Rom*. Washington, DC: World Bank.

Part Two

Escalation and Expansion

Chapter 6

Internationalizing Domestic Conflict
From Local and Political Insurgency Toward Global Terrorism. The Colombian Case

Sandra Borda

Introduction

The attacks of September 11th and the consequent beginning of the U.S. war against terror have created a new political context full of opportunities for the Colombian government and its long-lasting fight against insurgent movements. These events have facilitated the continuation and intensification of a calculated and explicitly articulated strategy of *internationalization* of the local struggle, advanced by the Colombian government. This strategy has substantially strengthened and expanded the U.S. support to the Colombian government in its war against insurgencies, and it has transformed the Colombian war into another front of the U.S. international war on terror. To be sure, this new strategy has resulted in an increasing military involvement of the U.S. not only in the now old war against drugs, but more importantly, in the war against the guerrillas in the South American country.

Even though the process has been so clearly planned by the Colombian government and has successfully resonated with the Bush Administration's foreign policy, most of the literature treats the *internationalization* of the conflict in Colombia as a matter of course (Carvajal & Pardo, 2002; Gaitán et al., 2002; Rojas, 2006). Internationalization is implicitly defined as a process in which the conflict has crossed, almost unintentionally, a certain threshold marked by Colombian state boundaries. My question in this chapter takes as a matter of inquiry what others treat as an assumption:

I explore if, when, how, and why the Colombian government *decided* that its domestic conflict should "go international." Even though I focus specifically on the way Colombia conceived its most recent strategy of internationalization after September 11th, I explain how this strategy finds its origins before the attacks.

Generally speaking, actors capable of making the decision of internationalizing the Colombian conflict might be *external*, in other words, international organizations, superpowers, neighboring states, or *internal*; that is, any of the parties to the conflict. In the *external* realm, for instance, the literature on the U.S. foreign policy toward Colombia is extensive (Randall, 1992; Tokatlian, 1995, 1998, 2000; Comisión, 1997; Bagley, 2000; Matthiessen, 2000; Tickner, 2002; Coy, 2003). Perspectives on the role the United Nations or the Organization of American States have played in Colombia also abound (García & Londoño, 2002; Tirado Mejía, 1995; Tirado Mejía, 1998). For various reasons, however, little effort has been devoted to analyzing why or how the Colombian state has willfully internationalized its own struggle. One of the strongest reasons for this might have to do with the perception in academic and official positions in Colombia, that their relationship with the U.S. is, in most if not all cases, characterized by U.S. demands and impositions and a constant undermining of Colombia's autonomy.

On the contrary, I argue that the Colombian state has a great deal more space for autonomous decision making than the relevant literature has acknowledged and, therefore, that its active role in the internationalization of the local conflict warrants extensive discussion (Borda, 2002). This chapter provides a framework for this discussion, and begins to lay out the terms and stakes of Colombia's active role in its own destiny. More generally, through the study of the Colombian state's decision to further internationalize its war after 9/11, I observe and explain both how the international system has constituted a crucial constraint, and how it has also provided the Colombian state with opportunities that have facilitated its efforts to internationalize the conflict. Both constraints and opportunities are important for understanding Colombia's strategies in its armed conflict. This in turn presupposes that even though international forces shape and somehow limit the decision the Colombian state makes, it still has the ability and the space to make the decision of shaping the involvement of the U.S. or any other international actor in its domestic struggle. Colombia's decision to internationalize is *conditioned* and/or *transformed* by the international system but not *determined* by it. As any other state, it has a substantial amount of autonomy to decide whether international actors should (or should not) eventually participate in its conflict and under what conditions.

However, it is necessary to point out that the extent of this autonomy, states' interests, external actors' motivations, the nature of the relationship between the former and the latter, and other important factors vary across cases. In Latin America, it is possible to find domestic conflicts in which the process of internationalization has varied in interesting ways. In El Salvador, for instance, the participation of the United States and the United Nations was intense during the armed conflict (the U.S.) and also during the negotiation process (the United Nations). In Guatemala, the internationalization of the conflict happened only at the last stage of the negotiation process. Both the conflict and its resolution remained relatively isolated from international actors for the most part. Finally, the U.S. official involvement in Colombia was limited by the confines of the war against illegal drugs until very recently. However, by 2002, "the pretense that U.S. guns and training were restricted to the drug war was obliterated, as President Bush signed a war on terror funding bill that allowed all past and present aid to support a 'unified campaign' against both drugs and Colombian groups on the U.S. list of terrorist organizations" (Isacson, 2004, 246).

In this chapter, I attempt to account for this recent form of internationalization of the Colombian conflict. I explore why the Colombian state further internationalized its conflict when it did and why 9/11 provided excellent conditions for this decision and its implementation. I argue that the Colombian government's attempt to turn the fight against the subversion into a crucial component of the U.S. post-9/11 war on terror has been a successful strategy designed and implemented by the Colombian government: a strategy of internationalization of the conflict that has strengthened its own military position vis-à-vis insurgent organizations. In other words, this calculated and voluntary process of internationalization follows a purely domestic equation: bringing Colombia to the fore of the Bush administration's war on terror would help the Colombian government to obtain more resources from the U.S. for its war against guerrillas.

In order to develop this argument I first describe exactly what I mean by "internationalization" and explain why this concept, defined in this way, is crucial to understand the specific manner in which the Colombian government has attempted to include the domestic conflict into the current U.S. war against terror. Then, I describe how the Colombian government developed a strategy over time—facilitated also by changes in U.S. foreign policy—in which the war against illegal drugs and the war against guerrillas was successfully framed as a single, relatively undifferentiated battle. At the end of the chapter, I evaluate how the strategy has worked and how it has resulted in a closer alliance between the U.S. and Colombia (obviously, with costs), and in an increasing military involvement of the U.S. in Colombia's domestic struggle.

On Internationalization

The concept of internationalization needs to be more specifically defined to be made useful in the context of this chapter. Internationalization, defined in a general way, is the process through which a *conscious* and *explicit decision* is made: the *decision* to involve international actors in any phase—during hostilities or negotiation—of a domestic conflict. The alternative strategy is to "stay domestic" or isolate the domestic conflict by consciously excluding international actors.

The word "internationalization" has been loosely used, though. Like "globalization," internationalization is a word that seems to imply a fuzzy intersection between the domestic and the international realms and efforts to define it more precisely are rare. In order to make even more visible and tangible the conceptual boundaries of this definition, it is also necessary to identify what lies outside of those boundaries or, more simply, to describe the sort of phenomena that I *do not* include in the definition of internationalization. For the purposes of this chapter, internationalization *is not* a process through which international cultural and socioeconomic divisions are broken up—or at least reformulated—producing new patterns of politics and substantially changing the nature of international governance (Kaldor, 1999, 70). In this sense, internationalization is *not* a loose synonym of globalization. It is *not* a cosmopolitan politicization that could be located within transnational NGOs or social movements, and within international institutions, as well as among individuals, around a commitment to human values and to the notion of transnational civil society (Kaldor, 1999, 76). It is *not,* then, cosmopolitanism from above or from below or a loose new form of global governance. In fact, internationalization is not a structural phenomenon. On the contrary, it is a decision-making process through which specific agents with specific goals and interests in mind formulate and enact specific kinds of policies.

The concept of internationalization *does not* refer either to the widely analyzed impact of globalization on the structure of the nation-state and its political survival; it is *not* then about how globalization renders territorial sovereignty no longer possible. Internationalization *does not* describe either how violence has spread to the international system; it does not address the problem of how difficult it is to contain the condition of war both in space and in time and how this local problematic remains a source of international instability after the end of the Cold War (Brzezinski, 1989/90; Mearsheimer, 1990; Snyder, 1990; Jervis, 1991/92). Internationalization is not a synonym of *spillover* or *contagion* effects. It is not a synonym either of collateral damages or externalities that result from internal conflicts (Murdoch & Sandler, 2001). First, states are still crucial actors because they do make the decision to participate or to invite actors to participate in a domestic conflict. Clearly, they are not the only actors, but they are some of the most relevant agents that make the engine of internationalization work. Hence, internationalization does not necessarily undermine states' sovereignty; it is often the result of their own choice. Second, internationalization is not inadvertent or unintentional. This is why the metaphors of spillover, contagion and collateral damage are inappropriate. Internationalization is, on the contrary, a *conscious* and *explicit* set of policies that results from a rational decision-making process. As I define it, internationalization is clearly intentional and calculated.

One can better grapple with the concept of internationalization if the sort of actors that could eventually be involved and the mechanisms through which this process is advanced are defined more clearly. First, state actors might (or might not) participate in domestic struggles. Usually, neighbor states that somehow have been or will be affected by the conflict or regional hegemonic states are part of this process. The latter is precisely the case of the type of internationalization I analyze in this chapter. These states might participate in the conflict either unilaterally or through multilateral means (mainly international or regional organizations). Second, multilateral organizations could be directly involved. These organizations could participate independently or with specific instructions from states (Barnett & Finnemore, 2004). Third, nonstate actors such as nongovernmental organizations, international foundations, international political party associations, and religious groups, among others might (or might not) be engaged and committed to domestic conflicts. These three types of involvement might play a crucial role in the conflict through myriad mechanisms that I identify in Table 6.1 (next page). These mechanisms include military or economic assistance, mediation, verification, and observation, among others. Additionally, international actors might exercise pressure in order to persuade or coerce the parties to comply with certain sets of international norms such as the laws of war or human rights law.

Any of these actors can participate either in the context of an overt and highly militarized war or during negotiations; they can participate either at the beginning of the conflict or at its end. These actors can take part through different *degrees* of internationalization (high or low depending on the amount of aid given); and they can also participate through different forms of internationalization, such as military aid, humanitarian relief, and mediation. As I have already suggested, these actors can also make the alternative choice: to decide *explicitly* and *consciously* to avoid the participation of international actors in their conflict.

In this chapter, I analyze a process of internationalization, which in Table 6.1 denominates *States* internationalization (second column). It is a

Table 6.1. Internationalization

International Organizations	States	NGOs and other nonstate actors
Economic aid	Diplomatic support and recognition	Generation of credible information quickly and move it where it will have more impact
Military intervention	Economic aid	Call on symbols, actions, or stories to make sense of the conflict
Mediation	Military intervention	Call on powerful actors to affect a conflict
Humanitarian assistance	Shipping arms and supplies to insurgent groups	To hold powerful actors to their previously stated policies or principles*
Fact finding	Humanitarian relief	Verification, mediation
Confidence-building measures	Confidence-building measures	Judicial enforcement measures
Traditional and multifunctional peacekeeping operations	Arms embargoes	Remittances by diasporas living abroad
Arms embargoes	Economic sanctions and economic inducements	
Economic sanctions and economic inducements	Judicial enforcement measures	
Judicial enforcement measures		

Note: *For these tasks, see the introduction chapter in Keck and Sikkink (1998).

process of internationalization designed and advanced by the Colombian state and explicitly directed toward the United States government. It is a policy of internationalization with important historical antecedents in Colombia, but clearly facilitated by the abrupt changes in U.S. foreign policy after the 9/11 attacks. In this chapter, I explore these antecedents and also describe how exactly changes in U.S. policy facilitated an increasing internationalization of the Colombian conflict. Internationalization in this case, as I point out, has taken the shape of military aid, it has ostensibly increased over time, and it has contributed to the strengthening of the Colombian state's military position vis-à-vis insurgent groups.

From the War on Drugs to the War on Terror

The emergence of Colombia's current war against insurgent movements, mainly against the FARC (Revolutionary Armed Forces of Colombia) and the ELN (National Liberation Army), took place in the 1960s. During the 1980s and the 1990s the war continued and intensified because of "the lack of political spaces that characterize Colombian political history" (Murillo, 2004, 45). The FARC, specifically, were born in the communist-influenced area of Sumapáz and Southern Tolima. Initially, the FARC established organized communities of military self-defense, communities that later become known as Independent Republics. The government, as a response to the increasing economic and political independence of these territories and pressured by landowners, organized a U.S.-supported counterguerrilla operation of vast proportions against these armed holdouts.

In February 1962, a U.S. mission led by General William Yarborough evaluated the situation in Colombia and suggested to assign five battalions of Special Forces, each one composed of 12 men with the objective of directing and coordinating the Colombian Counter-Insurgency Brigades and providing military and logistic advice to the army. This was the seed of a new security strategy denominated Plan Lazo, probably the first predecessor of the current Plan Colombia. Plan Lazo is defined for many analysts as the beginning of the modern war between the Colombian state and the FARC. Doug Stokes summarizes its impact in an eloquent way:

> Plan Lazo and its largest strategic deployment in Marquetalia was a success in so far as the geographical areas of the independent republics were placed under Colombian military control. However, the majority of the armed peasantry that made up the independent republics escaped and formed a collective self-defense organization called the "bloc of the South" in 1964. At a later conference in 1966, the Revolutionary Armed Forces of Colombia (FARC) were formed from this embryonic structure, and took their inspiration from the Cuban revolution. (Stokes, 2005, 73)

About 30 years later, the government again asked the U.S. for help in its war against the same guerrilla group. This time around, the strategy was denominated Plan Colombia and it was promoted by Andrés Pastrana, a president who came to power under the promise of peace dialogues and the political end of the conflict with the guerrillas. In 1999, while peace talks were being held with the government, the final version of the Plan was made public and it was presented as a strategy that would help Colombia find real solutions to the internal armed conflict and the illegal drug business (Rojas, 2007, 15). President Pastrana later affirmed that Plan Colombia was the main foundation of subsequent president Uribe's policy of *democratic security*: "Uribe received from me, the most powerful war machinery of our history, ready to face the eventuality of the peace dialogue failure. The military component of Plan Colombia wan an essential part of our Plan B, which has found its clearer expression in president Uribe's policy." (Semana, 2007). Figure 6.1 shows how U.S. participation through military and socioeconomic spending increased clearly with the initiation of Plan Colombia and during the following years.

On February 20 2002, almost at the end of Pastrana's administration (1998–2002), peace talks with the FARC (Fuerzas Armadas Revolucionarias de Colombia) ended with no concrete results. The same day, President Pastrana declared: "no one can doubt that, between politics and terrorism, the FARC has chosen terrorism. We Colombians offered an open hand to the FARC and they have responded to us with a slap in

Figure 6.1. U.S. Aid to Colombia Since 1997

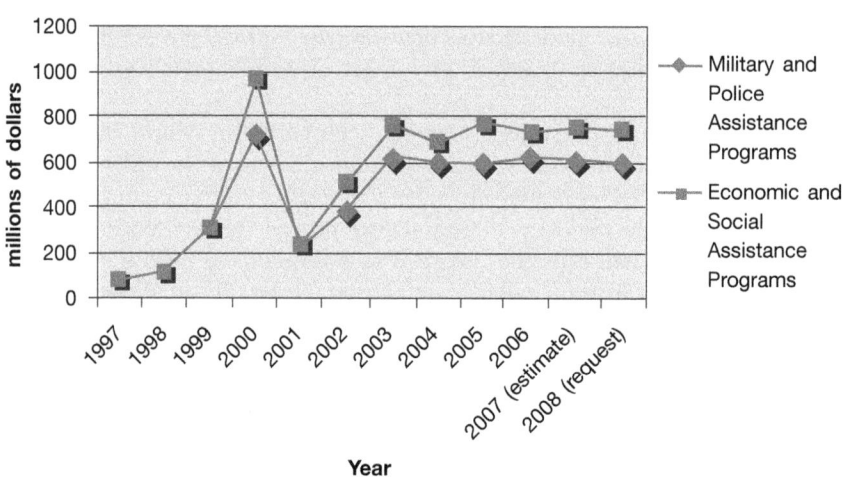

Note: For the source of these data, see Center for International Policy (2006).

the face" (Isacson, 2003, 3). This public definition of FARC members as *terrorists* marked a change in strategy long known by Colombians: when the government, in the process of advancing peace dialogues, explicitly or implicitly recognizes these groups as illegally armed actors with political agendas. However, when the predominant strategy is a military one and peace talks are not contemplated by the government, *terrorists* and, more often, *narco-terrorist* are the labels members of the government prefer to use to refer to these groups in public settings. By defining guerrilla movements as terrorists instead of combatants, the government removes the political and social content of the insurgents' agenda; it undermines the principle under which these groups fight in the name of marginalized sectors of the population and, by contrast, it portrays their activities as hostile to this same population and to the whole country. This strategy also contributes to legitimizing and justifying the use of military force against them and the complete elimination of an eventual political solution to the conflict. And finally, this perspective "leaves no room for the application of international humanitarian law with regard to them. This position recalls the classification by the U.S. administration of all suspected terrorists captured following the military campaign in Afghanistan as "unprivileged combatants" (Sossai, 2005, 260–261).

But aside from the end of peace talks in 2002, two more issues helped Pastrana´s government switch from the anti-insurgency to the anti-terrorist rhetoric. The first issue is related to the increasingly clear link between guerrilla movements and the production and traffic of illegal drugs. Linking drugs with guerrillas was a strategy that started long before the Pastrana administration though. I briefly examine the process in the next paragraph. The second issue is related to how the strategy of labeling these groups as *terrorists* has a different meaning after 9/11: it easily resonates now more than ever, with Washington and its new international war on terror. Pastrana's administration, and especially current president Uribe, have understood well how these two issues create opportunities for a new and more effective strategy of internationalization of the domestic struggle.

The first issue, the link between guerrilla movements and illegal narcotics trafficking, has been the subject of a long debate in Colombia.[1] The level of insurgency's involvement in the business has not been clearly determined though. Suffice to say that most of the coca crops are located in the southern part of the country, a clear stronghold of guerrilla groups. Hence, "guerrilla and paramilitary groups substitute for the state in imposing a very authoritarian regime, defining and applying iron laws and regulations, and providing education, police, and civil justice to solve conflicts among the population. In exchange, these groups charge coca production and cocaine export taxes" (Thoumi, 2002, 106). As Thoumi suggests, "the collapse of the iron curtain weakened the FARC guerrillas who sought alternative funding in the illegal industry" (Thoumi, 2002, 106).

The existence of this linkage has facilitated the emergence of the governmental argument (in times of open military confrontations) according to which these groups have degenerated into mere criminal organizations only interested in the economic profits that result from illegal drug trade. Their objective is no longer a revolutionary one. Nor is it the political and economic inclusion of marginalized Colombians. Instead, so the argument goes, their purpose is to make a growing illegal industry stronger and to accumulate profit from narcotics trade. They are narco-bandits and, for them, ill-gotten earnings have turned into ends in themselves. This argument matches almost perfectly the other component of the governmental rhetoric in times of war, according to which these groups are transnational crime networks, *terrorists* who attempt to destroy the legitimately constituted Colombian state and constantly threaten a legitimate and democratically constituted institutional order.

This association between guerrillas and illegal drug trafficking has an additional implication. The U.S. government has avoided its direct participation in the Colombian conflict and therefore has always insisted that U.S. aid to help Colombia fight its war against drugs must not be used by the government in its war against the FARC and other insurgent groups. Among many reasons, this U.S. self-imposed restriction to its interference in Colombia's domestic affairs was the result of the need to limit bureaucratic focus and capacity in Washington: officials working on Latin America were bogged down with Central America during most of the Cold War. Colombia's size, its degree of independence from foreign states, and its civil tradition were factors that also deterred further U.S. involvement (Guáqueta, 2005, 34). For obvious reasons, once guerrillas started to participate in the production of illegal narcotics, this condition imposed by Washington turned out to be difficult to implement in the field. Additionally, the participation of the U.S. in Colombia's justice sector reform, the enhancement of interdiction measures, and the adoption of systematic eradication campaigns "provided the U.S. crucial and long-term points of entry into Colombian domestic politics, and interdiction and eradication opened the door to greater U.S. military participation in the war against drugs" (Guáqueta, 2005, 37).

As a consequence, as early as 1994–1998, the Samper administration initiated efforts to make these restrictions more flexible. But before the end of the 1990s, "despite the gradual relaxation of norms on the U.S. military's role in Colombia, both sides still showed some restraint and neither Colombia nor the United States had an explicit policy on narco-guerrillas or narco-paramilitary as such" (Guaqueta, 2005, 41). Only until December 1998, under the presidency of Andrés Pastrana, both governments "(lay) the groundwork for the expansion of U.S.–Colombian military cooperation. (. . .) The proposed new aid would intensify all (antinarcotics) efforts, with the largest set of initiatives—categorized as 'the push into Southern Colombia coca-growing areas'—designed to prepare the U.S.—created army battalions to operate in a known guerrilla stronghold" (Isacson, 2000, 1). By March 1999, the U.S. government issued new guidelines that, according to Isacson, allowed sharing of intelligence about guerrilla activity in Colombia's southern drug-producing region, even if the information was not directly linked to any sort of anti-narcotics operation. The new framework of cooperation was denominated Plan Colombia and it consolidated an already existing trend of adding counterinsurgency goals to the old war against illegal drugs in Colombia. As it was mentioned earlier, president Pastrana later acknowledged that the Plan Colombia was a mechanism designed to debilitate the guerrillas and to push them to negotiate at the beginning of his term.

The area of overlap between U.S. aid for counter-narcotics and counterinsurgency operations grew dramatically. First, the location of the new U.S.-aided counter-narcotic battalions coincided with guerrilla-controlled territory. In fact, as Isacson observes, "the first counter-narcotics battalion's base at Tres Esquinas is within a 100-mile radius of some of the Colombian Army's most notorious defeats at the hands of the FARC. This highly strategic location makes the unit's performance—and Washington's contribution—a central part of the Colombian military's war effort, the drug war notwithstanding" (Isacson, 2000, 7). Secondly, the military training that the U.S. was providing could easily be applied to counterguerrilla operations since "both drug traffickers and guerrillas are well-armed enemies who (were) confronted using irregular combat techniques in difficult terrain" (Isacson, 2000, 7). And finally, for the first time, in 1998, the U.S. decided to fund alternative development projects and assigned $500, 000 to the Colombian PLANTE Program. This constituted Washington's open acknowledgement of the existence of "an important number of (. . .) rural communities and connected them to the flourishing of illegal armed groups. Thus, based on traditional security reasoning, some U.S. officials saw the need to work on alternative development as a way to undermine narco-guerrillas and narcoparamilitary" (Guáqueta, 2005, 48).

But the full and explicit institutionalization of the U.S. participation in Colombia's war was not achieved until later. As I mentioned, by February 2002 another round of peace talks had ended and presidential elections were rapidly approaching. After numerous failed attempts to find a peaceful resolution to the conflict, Colombians decided to elect (on the first round in a two-round system) the candidate who offered a "strong hand" approach for dealing with guerrilla groups. Álvaro Uribe personified the frustration most Colombians felt with what appeared to be the insurgency's lack of commitment with peace. Hence, his political campaign insisted on the inadequacy of a political resolution to the conflict. Uribe's argument was simple and clear: these groups did not have a political agenda; they were threatening the democratic institutions and did not have popular support. On the contrary, they were constantly attacking civilians in their war against a legitimate state. Consequently, a military response was the only possible way to end the war and to end what was denominated a terrorist threat.

The audience in the United States could not have been more receptive to this approach. The 9/11 attacks marked the emergence of new parameters in U.S. foreign policy that were, almost coincidentally, strikingly compatible with Colombia's government new militaristic approach to its domestic war. The FARC, ELN, and the paramilitary were already added to the U.S. list of international terrorists in October 2001. Subsequently, by May 2002 and just months before president Uribe took office, Colombia's Ambassador in Washington articulated the connection in an even clearer way:

> While the United States' attention is fixed on fighting terrorism in Afghanistan, the Middle East and Asia, a grave threat lurks in the Americas. Colombia is the leading theater of operations for terrorists in the Western Hemisphere. Under the false pretense of a civil war, Colombian guerrilla groups have ravaged the nation with violence financed by cocaine consumers in the United States. The Bush administration, appropriately, is pushing in Congress to have anti-narcotics aid expanded to strengthen Colombia's ability to defeat terrorists.

And to reinforce the construction of the already recognized association between insurgency and illegal drugs, he asserted:

> Drugs are the root of almost all violence in Colombia. It is simple: everywhere there are poppies or coca in Colombia, there are guerrillas and paramilitaries. The Pastrana administration has moved aggressively to sever ties between the armed forces and the paramilitary group called the United Self-Defense Forces of Colombia, which is itself involved in the drug trade; in 2001 government forces, including police, captured 992 paramilitaries

and killed 116. Where there are guerrillas and paramilitaries, there are terror and violence against civilians. While they may hide behind a Marxist ideology, Colombia's leftist guerrillas have ceased to be a political insurgency. They have traded their ideals for drug profits. (Moreno, 2002)

Some might think that guerrilla leaders in the mountains of Colombia have little to do with Osama bin Laden and his followers (Sossai, 2005, 206). However, and not surprisingly, given the atmosphere of fear resulting from the newborn war against terrorism, the Colombian government was successful in including Colombia as part of the U.S. international war on terrorism. To confirm Colombia's attempt to join the U.S. in its new enterprise, President Uribe traveled to Washington two months before taking office. Among other things, he insisted on the need to reorient Plan Colombia resources (Semana, 2002).

Signs of a mutual understanding between Washington and Bogotá, an understanding that conceived the Colombian conflict as a chapter of the U.S. new war on terror, emerged soon. At the end of 2002, the U.S. Attorney General, John Ashcroft, formally accused two FARC commanders (Mono Jojoy and Romaña) of different crimes, among them, the kidnapping (1999) and murder (1999) of three American New Tribes Missionaries—Dave Mankins, Rick Tenenoff, and Mark Rich. Ashcroft also accused them of illegal traffic of drugs and weapons.

But the FARC were not helping their case. In February 2003, they killed an American citizen and kidnapped three more when they were on an intelligence mission in the Colombian province of Caquetá. This served the Colombian government in its attempt to escalate the U.S. presence in Colombia: 49 soldiers, FBI and forensic specialist personnel arrived to support the search of these American citizens: "with these special forces, plus 100 soldiers that arrive as part of the Plan Colombia package, the number of American military personnel ascends to 411" (Semana*a*, 2003). They still remained kidnapped by the FARC (until mid-2008).

The final consolidation of this internationalization strategy probably took place in August 2003 when Secretary of Defense, Donald Rumsfeld, and General Richard Myers, Chairman of the Joint Chiefs of Staff, visited Colombia. Their message was clear and substantially different from Washington's usual stance on the war on drugs: if there is aid for Colombia in its war against drug trafficking, it is only because that is the oxygen of terrorism. Rumsfeld insisted that drug trafficking was not a danger in and of itself, on the contrary, it was a danger because "it feeds terrorism and terrorist networks and this is something that people who think alike, should work together to confront" (Semana*b*, 2003). Six months later, the Bush administration presented to the Congress the second version of Plan Colombia (entitled Plan Colombia II) in order to get approval for the 2005 aid package for the afflicted South American country.

In the field, the U.S. involvement in counterinsurgency operations became public. In May 2004 U.S. ambassador in Colombia, William Wood, declared that there was American equipment and military training involved in the capture of alias Sonia, one of the FARC head commanders. He confirmed that the U.S. gave military advice to Colombian generals in the planning, logistics, and tactics of this important operation: "We lend Plan Patriota more than 100 hours of helicopters' air time . . . we transported more than 1.000 soldiers and 58.000 pounds of equipment . . . but pilots were Colombian. We did not participate in combat." (Semana*a*, 2004). He later insisted on the content of his country's position vis-à-vis the FARC: "They are not political actors anymore. They are kidnappers, murderers, drug traffickers" (Semana*b*, 2004).

But Uribe's internationalization strategy had a boomerang effect that seriously affected its peace process with the paramilitary organization AUC (Autodefensas Unidas de Colombia, United Self-Defense of Colombia). Paramilitary groups emerged in Colombia in 1981 as an additional and illegal option to combat rebel groups. Their links with the military, the private sector, multinational companies, and Colombia's political class have been demonstrated in many occasions. Their violations of human rights have also been documented numerous times by local and international NGOs. President Uribe initiated a peace process with one of the paramilitary groups, the AUC. But his position in this dialogue has been harshly criticized for being too close to the paramilitaries. Some sectors of Colombian public opinion and media have insisted that the president has been too lenient, to the point that has allowed most of paramilitaries' serious crimes to remain unpunished. In this context and when the process was at a critical stage, U.S. Attorney David Kelly from New York's Southern District, asked the Colombian government to extradite alias Don Berna, one of the heads of the AUC, on the account of trafficking several tons of cocaine to the United States. The United States concern with its war against illegal drugs was trumping its support to the Colombian government in its attempt to end paramilitary groups. In 2008, when detained paramilitary leaders denounced the participation of key governmental allies in their illicit activities and threatened to directly denounce Uribe himself, they were extradited to the United States where they still wait to be judged for their participation in illegal drug trafficking.[2] That ended the shadow of conflict between Washington and Bogotá.

Additionally, U.S. Senators Edward Kennedy, Christopher Dodd, Barack Obama, Russel Feingold, Joseph Biden, and Patrick Leahy sent a strong letter to President Uribe expressing their concerns about the negotiation process with the AUC. This trend was accompanied by Human Rights Watch's constant criticism of the government soft treatment and prosecution of paramilitaries. The strength of these criticisms forced the government to send a high-profile mission to the U.S., which attempted to explain the nature of negotiations.

This trip and the constant lobbying were not enough though. In 2006 the U.S. Congress lowered the amount of money allotted to demobilization of paramilitaries to $20 million (from the $80 million the Bush administration initially suggested) and conditioned this part of the aid package to a state department's certification on Colombia's cooperation with the extradition of leaders and members of terrorist organizations required by the U.S. justice. Of $734 million given to Andean countries, Colombia received almost $600 million and even though there was no clear satisfaction with the way the Colombian government was dealing with paramilitaries, the U.S. Congress softened its conditions in terms of human rights (Semana, 2005).

The Bush Administration's request for 2006 had anticipated providing $331,850,000 to the Colombian military and police through the ACI-Andean Counterdrug Initiative, and it had provided $324.6 million in such aid under this rubric in 2004. However, on June 30, 2005, the Senate Appropriations Committee met to "mark up" the Senate's version of the 2006 foreign aid bill. This bill fully funds the Andean Counterdrug Initiative (ACI) request for $734.5 million in military and economic aid for Colombia and six of its neighbors. However, according to the Colombian Program of the Center for International Policy, the bill language seeks a better balance between military and economic aid for Colombia. It puts a "ceiling" on the amount of ACI aid that can go to Colombia's military: "not more than $278,450,000 shall be made available for assistance for the Colombian Armed Forces and National Police." If the Senate language passes, 2006 military and police aid to Colombia through the ACI account could total $53.4 million less than what the Bush Administration had requested (http://ciponline.org/colombja/aidO6.htm). Hence, trends in terms of the nature and volume of U.S. aid toward Colombia might experience important changes in the next years. The eventual transformation of the relationship between the U.S. Congress and the president, and the arrival of the Democratic Party to the White House, might be crucial factors affecting the U.S. support to Colombia.

It is clear then that by linking issues—drugs/insurgence, terrorism/insurgence—the Colombian government turned a situation that under different circumstances would not have meant much for the U.S. into one of the U.S. priorities in terms of military aid. The persistence of a

Marxist rebel group in a third-world country after the end of the Cold War could have been interpreted by Washington as a purely local matter with no international or regional implications. However, by actively attempting to include the Colombian conflict first in the war against drugs and then in the war against terror, the Colombian government did not allow for the construction or interpretation of the struggle as a purely domestic event.

In 2002, after the failed attempt of President Pastrana to provide a peaceful and negotiated solution to the conflict, current President Uribe was elected with an absolute majority of votes and came to power promising a strong military stance against insurgency.[3] To be sure, "a majority of Colombians from all social sectors were willing to try the iron fist that only Uribe offered among the candidates for President" (Dugas, 2003, 1134). Uribe has been, so far, the strongest advocate of the form of internationalization I have described in this chapter (Tickner & Pardo, 2002/03). The new world order has allowed his administration to define the Colombian conflict in terms of the war on terrorism (as it has been done many times before) but more importantly, it made possible for President Uribe first, to demand "more funds and privileged treatment (from the U.S.) (today, both governments are deeply convinced that they are dealing with 'narcoterrorists'); second, to ask for a further relaxation of human rights standards to more easily confront the terrorist threat; and third, though in a rather oblique manner, to invite deeper intervention by the U.S. Thus, the conflict is used to suggest that guerrillas threaten vital U.S. interests" (Gutiérrez, 2003, 148). The war on terror has finally landed in Colombian territory. Then Secretary of Defense, Donald Rumsfeld, made it official in the U.S.: "What we are doing—as a partner, and anxious to be as cooperative as possible—is working, military-to-military, to see what are the kinds of things we can do as the Colombian war on terror migrates into a somewhat later stage, as is now happening" (Defense, 2003).

Conclusion

I have shown that in the case of the Colombian domestic struggle, the picture of a coerced U.S. imposition of the war on terror on a reluctant and powerless Colombian government does violence to reality. The internationalization of the domestic conflict in Colombia is often seen either as the result of an inevitable U.S. hegemony or an uncontrollable process of conflict "spill-over." However, more attention needs to be paid to the part of internationalization that is calculated, voluntary, and the result of explicit decisions from governmental officials. This is the realm of internationalization that I explored in this chapter.

The field of international relations does provide mechanisms to understand these phenomena; scholars dedicated to the study of alliance formation pointed out, long ago, that not only international but also domestic factors are crucial to understand when states decide to ally and what sort of states or other international actors they prefer to ally with. Barnett and Levy, for instance, suggested that internal threats to government rule produce incentives for state leaders to seek an external alliance. In this sense,

> while the process of developing and producing resources within a threatened state can be slow and difficult, alliance formation can bring a rapid infusion of funds and other resources, including military expertise and equipment. These external resources can in turn either benefit the economy as a whole, or certain supporters of the regime in power and can be used for internal as well as external security purposes. If a regime allies with a military powerful or ideologically respected state, the benefits can also include prestige. (Barnett & Levy, 1991, 374)

Consequently and of crucial relevance to the study of the Colombian case, these alliances are stronger in third-world countries since the "sense of threat and insecurity from which (those) states suffer emanates to a substantial degree from within their boundaries rather than from outside" (Ayoob, 1991, 263; David, 1991) and because they have limited capabilities to extract resources from society. In Barnett and Levy's words,

> although many Third World governments would like to develop an independent arms production capacity and thereby preserve their autonomy, this goal is constrained by an insufficient industrial base, an inability to achieve the desired economies of scale, and a lack of appropriate technology, all in an age in which military technology has become increasingly sophisticated and expensive. (Barnett & Levy, 1991, 377)

These economic and political constraints on the state's mobilization of societal resources are, according to the authors, a powerful incentive to make alignment concessions to others in return for military support to deal with external threats to security and for economic support to deal with threats to the domestic political economy. Hence, third-world leaders might prefer alliances over internal extraction because "political leaders are often tempted to try to secure the material resources necessary to deal with (internal) threats (by placating disgruntled social groups or by other means) through external alliance formation rather than through internal extraction from a society that is already economically stretched and politically alienated. That is, Third World states often form external alliances as a means of confronting internal threats" (Barnett & Levy, 1991, 378).

International relations' rationalist analyses partially tell us what factors explain whether states would be interested in internationalizing their struggle and what sort of international support they would favor. But they do not help us explain which sort of international actors would states invite to participate and why they would eventually privilege some actors over others. In other words, why did the Colombian government prioritize the U.S. over other states (i.e., European states) that would be willing to provide help? How can we explain this decision? In fact, when a state attempts to find assistance of any type, it knows that help rarely comes without trade-offs or commitments of different sorts. In Barnett and Levy's words, "alliances involve potential costs in terms of security and autonomy. The risks include abandonment by an ally that fails to fulfill its commitment, entrapments in a war involving the ally's interests rather than one's own, and a general loss of autonomy or freedom to maneuver" (Barnett & Levy, 1991, 374). Thus, states try to find help not only from international actors that can provide it, but also from international actors that somehow "sympathize" with them, and therefore would not impose additional costs on the domestic party that has asked for assistance. This is why the high level of compatibility between President Uribe's militaristic approach against the guerrillas and President Bush's war on terror is so important to understand the incorporation of Colombia's war into the international war on terror.

But even in this almost perfect scenario, a state *cannot fully control the effects of it own decision to internationalize and it is very frequently, the subject of entrapment.* The Colombian case is clear in this respect. Recent presidential administrations in Colombia invited the U.S. to participate by requiring and obtaining military assistance during the current military stage of the conflict. But the conditions of this assistance might, in the future, hinder the position of the Colombian state in an eventual transition to a negotiated or political resolution of the conflict. This was already the case in the negotiations with paramilitary groups that the Uribe administration advanced during the last two years: the AUC (Autodefensas Unidas de Colombia) is included in the U.S. Department of State's list of terrorist groups and this was a constant issue in the negotiation table since the U.S. is still requiring the extradition of paramilitary leaders because of their participation in the illegal drug business. Additionally, the U.S. government has constantly observed the penetration of organized crime into politics as part of its effort to help strengthen Colombia's old but fragile democracy. This is not out of altruism though. Washington knows that a strong and legitimate state would be more effective in its war against illegal drug trafficking and/or terrorism. In sum, even though the state plays an important role in deciding when and under what conditions the internationalization process starts, it may lose control over how the participation of international actors unfolds.

In this chapter I have tried to work with a particular definition of internationalization that I explained at length in the second section. Why is it so important to talk about internationalization and its nature the way I recommend here? As I suggested at the beginning of the chapter, previous approaches to the study of U.S.-Colombia relations have emphasized so much the power of U.S. hegemony and the weakness of the Colombian state, that they have left no room for the study of Colombia's still significant autonomy and space for deliberation. Consequently, by ignoring Colombia's intentionality they have rendered the Colombian government immune from political criticism. The government is portrayed as fighting both drugs and insurgency on behalf of a powerful patron state. On this account, Colombia is a mere client state, a pawn in the war on drugs and the war on terror. This double insulation precludes political engagements with the sites of power in Colombia and this situation is dangerously convenient for Colombian governmental officials. Hence, an important step forward in attempting to create a space for political discussion and accountability in Colombia is to recognize internationalization as an explicit and voluntary decision-making process that, in this case, involves the active and calculated construction of a strategy by the Colombian government.

Notes

1. For an extensive account of this debate in Colombia and in the U.S. see Tickner, 2003.

2. The government argued that they were extradited because they did not stop their illegal activities from jail but that it will make sure they will be judged also for their crimes against humanity and their multiple violations to human rights.

3. President Uribe was reelected, again, with a majority of votes in the first round, by using a similar agenda. Colombian media have already started to discuss the solid chances for a third mandate. It is crucial to say that the Colombian Constitution did not permit the reelection of presidents until his arrival to the

Casa de Nariño. Soon after he started his first term, Uribe initiated a national campaign to change the Constitution and allow reelection. In December 2004, the Colombian Congress agreed to reform the Constitution to allow this possibility and, in October 2005, the Colombian Constitutional Court ruled in favor of the reform. As a result and for the first time in Colombian history, presidential reelection is today permitted.

References

Ayoob, M. (1991). The security problematic in the third world. *World Politics* 43 (2), 257–283.

Bagley, B. (2000). Narcotráfico, violencia política y política exterior de Estados Unidos hacia Colombia en los noventa. *Colombia Internacional* (49/50), 5–38.

Barnett, M., & Finnemore, M. (2004). *Rules of the world: International organizations and global politics.* Ithaca, NY: Cornell University Press.

Barnett, M., & Levy, J. S. (1991). Domestic sources of alliances and alignments: The case of Egypt, 1962–1973. *International Organization* 45 (3), 369–395.

Borda, S. (2002). La política exterior Colombiana antidrogas o cómo se reproduce el ritual realista desde el tercer mundo. In A. B. Tickner, M. Ardila & D. Cardona (Eds.), *Prioridades y desafíos de la política exterior Colombiana.* Bogota: Fundación Hanns Seidel Stiftung, Friedrich Ebert Stiftung en Colombia—FESCOL.

Brzezinski, Z. (1989/90). Post-communist nationalism. *Foreign Affairs.* wwwstage.foreignaffairs.org

Carpenter, T. G. (2005, January 4). Drug prohibition is a terrorist's best friend. *National Post.*

Carvajal, L., & Pardo, R. (2002). La internacionalización del conflicto doméstico y los procesos de paz. Historia reciente y principales desafíos. In M. Ardila, D. Cardona & A. Tickner (Eds.), *Prioridades y desafíos de la política exterior Colombiana.* Bogota: FESCOL, Harms Seidel Stiftung.

Center for International Policy. (2006). *U.S. aid to Colombia since 1997: Summary tables,* Center for International Policy's Colombia Program.

Comisión de Análisis y recomendaciones sobre las relaciones entre Colombia y Estados. (1997). Colombia: Una Nueva Sociedad en Un Mundo Nuevo. *Análisis Político* Edición Especial.

Coy, F. (2003). Injerencia reciente y desnarcotización fallida: Las relaciones Colombia—Estados Unidos desde el fin dela guerra frIa. *Desafios* 9, 165–192.

David, S. R. (1991). Explaining third world alignment. *World Politics* 43 (2), 233–256.

Dugas, J. C. (2003). The emergence of neopopulism in Colombia? The case of Alvaro Uribe. *Third World Quarterly* 24 (6), 1117–1136.

Gaitán, P., Pardo R., & Osorio, J. M. (2002). *Comunidad internacional, conflicto armado y perspectivas de paz en Colombia, libros de Cambio.* Bogota: Alfaomega.

Garcia, A., & Londoño, P. (2002). La política multilateral de Colombia y Colombia en la nueva agenda multilateral. In A. B. Tickner, M. Ardila, & D. Cardona (Eds.), *Prioridades y desafíos de la política exterior Colombiana*. Bogota: Fundación Hanns Seidel Stiftung, Friedrich Ebert Stiftung en Colombia—FESCOL.
Guáqueta, A. (2005). Change and continuity in U.S.-Colombian relations and the war against drugs. *Journal of Drug Issues* 35 (1), 27–56.
Gutiérrez, F. (2003). Institutionalizing global wars: State transformations in Colombia, 1978-2002. *Journal of International Affairs* 57 (1), 135–152.
Isacson, A. (2000). Getting in deeper. The United States' growing involvement in Colombia's conflict. *International Policy Report* February.
Isacson, A. (2003). Was failure avoidable? Learning from Colombia's 1998–2002 peace process. In *The Dante B. Fascell North-South Center University of Miami Working Paper Series*. Miami, Florida.
Isacson, A. (2004). Optimism, pessimism, and terrorism: The United States and Colombia in 2003. *Brown Journal of World Affairs* X (2), 245–252.
Jervis, R. (1991/92). The future of world politics: Will it resemble the past? *International Security* 16 (3), 39–73.
Kaldor, M. (1999). *New and old wars. Organized violence in a global era*. Stanford, CA: Stanford University Press.
Keck, M. E., & Sikkink, K. (1998). *Activist beyond borders*. Ithaca and London: Cornell University Press.
Matthiessen, T. (2000). *El arte político de conciliar: El tema de las drogas en las relaciones entre Colombia y Estados Unidos, 1986–1994*. Bogota: Fundación Friedrich Ebert de Colombia—FESCOL, Centro de Estudios de la Realidad Colombiana—CEREC, Fedesarrollo.
Mearsheimer, J. J. (1990). Back to the future. Instability in Europe after the cold war. *International Security* 15 (1), 141–192.
Moreno, L. A. (2002, March 3). Aiding Colombia's war on terrorism. *New York Times*.
Murdoch, J. C., & Sandler, T. (2001). Economic growth, civil wars, and spatial spillovers. In *Development Research Group of the World Bank*.
Murillo, M. A. (2004). *Colombia and the United States. War, unrest and destabilization*. New York: Seven Stories Press.
Randall, S. J. (1992). *Aliados y distantes*. Bogota: Tercer Mundo Editores, Ediciones Uniandes, CEI.
Rojas, D. M. (2006). La internacionalización de la guerra. Estados Unidos y la guerra en Colombia. In *Nuestra guerra sin nombre. Transformaciones del conflicto en Colombia*, edited by Instituto de Estudios Políticos y Relaciones Internacionales IEPRI. Bogotá: Grupo Editorial Norma.
Rojas, D. M. (2007). Plan Colombia II: More of the same? *Colombia Internacional* 65, 14–37
Semana. (2002). La nueva agenda. *Revista Semana* 1051, June 24.
Semana*a*. (2003). Gringos al rescate. *Revista Semana* 1087. March 3.
Semana*b*. (2003). ¿Giro radical?. *Revista Semana* 1112. August 25.
Semana*a*. (2004). Los paras perdieron su disfraz. *Revista Semana* 1149. May 10.

Semana*b*. (2004). Las AUC no son un actor político. *Revista Semana* 1171. October 11.
Semana. (2005). Por ahora, todo bien. *Revista Semana* 1227. November 7.
Semana. (2007). El Gobierno está legalizando a los narcos. *Revista Semana* 1325, September 22.
Snyder, J. (1990). Averting anarchy in the new Europe *International Security* 14 (4), 5–41.
Sossai, M. (2005). The internal conflict in Colombia and the fight against terrorism. *Journal of International Criminal Justice* 3, 253–267.
Stokes, D. (2005). *America's other war. Terrorizing Colombia*. London: Zed Books.
Thoumi, F. (2002). Illegal drugs in Colombia: From illegal economic boom to social crisis. *The ANNALS of the American Academy of Political and Social Science* 582 (l), 102–116.
Tickner, A. B. (2002). Colombia es lo que los actores estatales hacen de ella: Una (re)lectura de la política exterior Colombiana hacia los Estados Unidos. In A. B. Tickner, M. Ardila & D. Cardona (Eds.), *Prioridades y desafíos de la política exterior Colombiana*. Bogota: Fundación Hanns Seidel Stiftung, Friedrich Ebert Stiftung en Colombia—FESCOL.
Tickner, A. B. (2003). Colombia and the United States: From counternarcotics to counterterrorism. *Current History* 102 (661).
Tickner, A. B., & Pardo, R. (2002/03). En busca de aliados para ta "seguridad democrática": La politica exterior del primer año de la administración Uribe. *Colombia Internacional* 56–57, 64–80.
Tirado Mejía, Á. (1995). *Colombia en la ONU: 1945–1995*. Bogota: Goldstar.
Tirado Mejía, Á. (Ed.). (1998). *Visiones de la OEA~50 años, 1948–1998*. Bogota: Ministerio de Relaciones Exteriores.
Tokatlian, J. G. (1995). *Drogas, dilemas y dogmas*. Bogota: Tercer Mundo Editores, Ediciones Uniandes, CEI.
Tokatlian, J. G. (1998). *Colombia y Estados Unidos: Problemas y perspectivas*. Bogota: Tercer Mundo, IEPRI, Colciencias.
Tokatlian, J. G. (2000). *Globalización, narcotráfico y violencia: Siete ensayos sobre Colombia*. Bogota: Editorial Norma.
United States Department of Defense. (2003). Secretary Rumsfeld Joint Press Conference with the Colombian Minister of Defense. Washington, DC: Department of Defense.

Chapter 7

Unspoken Reciprocity
The Effect of Major Shifts in Israeli Policy on International Terrorism

David Sobek and Alex Braithwaite

Introduction

The prevention of international terrorism—with a focus on policies of counterterrorism—has emerged as perhaps the primary stated security goal of the majority of *status quo*[1] states globally. In order for governments to be successful in limiting the actions of terrorist organizations, it becomes crucial for them to gain a greater understanding of the motivations underlying these actions, of the types of organizations posing a threat, and of the range of goals that they are seeking to satisfy using this tool. Underlying each of these aims is the need to establish whether terrorists can be considered rational, or at least, if they are actors who have a definable set of goals that they wish to accomplish via their tactic of terror. The responses that we give to these points have crucial implications for both our understanding of the phenomenon and toward our development of methods for mitigating its occurrence.

Toward these ends, this chapter characterizes terrorists into two broad types: moderate (goal-seeking) and extreme (dedicated/ideological).[2] In general, moderate terrorists have a set of goals that they are attempting to achieve and will end their attacks once an acceptable level of these are accomplished. Extreme terrorists, however, either simply garner utility from terrorism and have no set goals outside of the perpetration of more terrorism or have established such incredible goals and demands for revision of the status quo that we might never expect these to be achieved via government concession. An example of the former might be the Irish Republican Army's (IRA's) demands for the cessation of British rule in Northern Ireland; whereas, a possible example of the latter is al Qaeda's goal of forming a fundamentalist Islamic state that absorbs the sovereignty of a majority of Islamic Middle Eastern states.

Differentiating between moderate and extreme terrorists is critical because it directly relates to the choice of counterterrorism strategy that a government employs. Previous empirical works on international terrorism have implicitly assumed all actors to be extremists (apparently more dedicated to the act of terror than to the pursuit of particular political goals) and subsequently have tended to look only at the impact of retaliatory policies. Although it is important to understand the effect of such actions, doing so ignores a great many possible responses to moderate terrorism. Specifically, this project attempts to assess the impact of Israel's ratification of the Camp David Accords and their invasion of southern Lebanon on levels of international terrorism, or more generally speaking, it examines the differing affects of concessionary and retaliatory government policy choices.

At this first step, this chapter looks at the Israeli case in relative isolation. Focusing on a single case has some shortfalls—most notably that it restricts the generalizability of any findings. On the other hand, there are two reasons to suspect that this particular case allows for an important first cut at our research questions. First, terrorism directed against Israel and Israelis has a long and well-documented history. In this sense, understanding this case sheds light on the processes underlying a significant portion of terrorist acts in the modern era. Second, the issues that motivate international terrorism against Israel are relatively easily identified—this is important because the ease of identifying and referring to the notion of ideal points and of aggregating goals and actions is crucial to tackling our research questions.

In order to empirically test the effect of policy orientation on terrorist activity, this project employs a negative binomial regression model on the number of international attacks against the Israeli state and Israelis between 1968 and 1997. The tests consistently find that when the Israeli Government moves toward the Palestinian/Arab ideal point (as exemplified by their participation in the Camp David Accords) they experience a decrease in the amount of terrorism, while movements away from that point (as epitomized by Israel's invasion of Lebanon) increase anti-Israel terrorist activity.

As will be discussed at greater length later, these results have two important implications for the broader study of terrorism and for future appraisals of counterterrorism strategies. First, some terrorist groups are moderate in respect to the goals they wish to achieve and can thus be tempered in their use of terrorism by means other than strategies of deterrence. Second, and more specifically, it appears as though a large proportion of those terrorists targeting Israel are goal-seeking and responsive to credible Israeli concessions. The implication of this is that a comprehensive Middle East peace plan might feasibly mitigate the level of international terrorist activity against Israel.

In the next section, we briefly identify and comment on some of the key extant efforts at characterizing the relationship between terrorism and counterterrorism. In doing so we endeavor to identify the notable shortcoming of the literature on the prevention of international terrorism: that there is no systematic appraisal of the benefits of accommodation over deterrence outside of the analogous study of domestic terrorism. We then outline a theory that differentiates the motivations of moderate and extremist terrorist organizations in highlighting the potential success of a counter policy of accommodation. Next we introduce a research design centering on the negative binomial regression model in which we identify attacks against Israeli interests as a function of Israel's position of power in the Middle East and their policy orientation in regard to their dealings with their internal and external Arab counterparts. Finally we describe some of the possible substantive implications of our empirical findings.

Countering the Threat of International Terrorism

A variety of studies have addressed the oft-observed interdependence of levels of terrorism and government counterterrorist responses. At the domestic level, such studies have addressed the impact of both retaliatory and concessionary government responses to terrorism upon subsequent levels (e.g., Bueno de Mesquita, 2005; Darby, 2000; and Kydd & Walter, 2002). At the international level, however, the focus has been placed squarely and solely upon the employment of retaliatory tools (e.g., Enders & Sandler, 1993; Brophy-Baermann & Conybeare, 1994). In this section, we briefly outline some of the major arguments regarding both concession and retaliation at both domestic and international levels. It is our expectation that this provides a strong background ahead of the introduction of our theory and propositions and justifies our attempt to remedy the extant gap in the literature relating to the impact of concessionary policies upon levels of international terrorism.

Describing the intersection of government policy choices and domestic terrorist attacks, Bueno de Mesquita argues that

> when governments make concessions, only moderate terrorists accept, leaving extremists in control. Nonetheless, the *ex ante* expected level of terror decreases following concessions because

the government's probability of eradicating terror improves as a result of a decrease in active terrorist cells and the collusion of former terrorists. However, should governments counter-terror fail, the increased radicalization leads to an *ex post* increase in violence. This suggests that the empirical observation that concessions lead to more violence is the spurious result of selection bias caused by focusing on those cases where terror continued, and thus counter-terror failed. (2003, iii)

Bueno de Mesquita supports this thesis by using case study evidence from government policies in Spain (countering the activities of ETA), Israel (countering the activities of a number of Palestinian groups), the United Kingdom (countering activities of the IRA), and Canada (countering the activities of the FLQ). The empirical record offered confirms that where conciliation efforts were successful, levels of terrorism were seen to have dropped if the resources of the terrorist movement dwindled. If, however, either the counterterror policies were unsuccessful or the resources lay in the hands of the extremists among the group, levels of terrorism in fact increased in the aftermath of concessionary efforts.

Such observations of increasing terror in the wake of government concessions are more broadly acknowledged in the extant literature. Studies of the effectiveness of policies aimed at reducing levels of anti-state terrorism tend to observe an increase in levels of terrorism in response to government concessions. A variety of stories for this observation are offered. Ross and Gurr (1989) argue that concessions may be identified by terrorists as containing an indirect threat to the terrorist organizations carrying out attacks. Darby (2000) additionally suggests two potential explanations for the observation that numbers of attacks increase during negotiations: (1) fear of the inevitable need to reduce attacks in the near future; (2) a reduction in security forces devoted to countering terrorism. Moreover, if we accept that the perception held by the terrorist organization of the strength of the government will have a bearing on their preference toward the employment of terrorism, it is logical that concession might well be viewed as a sign of government weakness (Bueno de Mesquita, 2005). Finally, Kydd and Walker (2002) suggest that terror may be seen as increasing at such times because terrorists endeavor to undermine the negotiations by causing the government to question the decision to address the issue at negotiations (i.e., cause government to react using force and undermine democracy!).

From an alternative perspective, Bueno de Mesquita (2003) invokes DeNardo's theory of social movement activity in arguing that it is just as feasible that a government concession would be expected to lead to a reduction in levels of terrorism because it brings about a division between extremists and moderates. This notion underlies Bueno de Mesquita's central contention (as detailed earlier) that, when satisfied, moderates will cease to employ the tools of terror. This attention to concessions represents a surprising novelty in a literature that has otherwise tended to focus on the notion of countering terrorism by restricting the terrorist's ability to function (via deterrence or policy designed to inhibit communications and minimize available resources). We maintain that this shortfall is even greater in respect to the impact of such policies on levels of international terrorism.

The works of Enders and Sandler (1993, 2002) and Enders, Sandler, and Cauley (1990) are exemplary of both the strength of empirical studies addressing the interplay of levels of international terrorism and retaliatory government policies and of the shortfall in failing to address the concomitant impact of concessionary acts. In the most recent of these studies, Enders and Sandler posit that terrorist organizations have to choose between the employment of legal actions and terrorist events when trying to maximize their utility during the process of political communication. In the process of maximizing their utility, the terrorists must determine how best to allocate their available resources. Within this model, the government is introduced as the authority figure attempting to curtail terrorist activity by decreasing the resources available to the terrorist group.

In examining the impact of retaliatory/restrictive government policies, Enders and Sandler operationalize a time series of deaths from international terrorist events (also taken from the ITERATE data) and explore the impact on this series of a range of U.S. government policy changes—including the introduction of metal detectors at airports, increases in spending on security for embassies, and the retaliatory raids on Libya in 1986. The authors posit—and offer support for—a twofold result of such endeavors. On the one hand, such policy interventions appear to reduce the overall level of observed international terrorism. At the same time, however, they note that the introduction of specific remedies precedes an evolution in terrorist tactics. For example, following the introduction of metal detectors in U.S. airports in 1973, they identify a decline in levels of hijackings but increases in levels of nonaviation-based events. What they do not address within their study is the impact on levels of terrorism that is witnessed following government attempts at concession.

The brief overview offered earlier has highlighted a key gap in the terrorism literature that provides significant motivation for the study that we are conducting. Assessment of concessionary as well as retaliatory counterterrorism policies is common among studies of the dynamics between government policy and terrorist responses. In the study of the dynamics between government policy and international terrorism, however, the focus hitherto has been placed squarely on the use and effect of retaliatory policy, thus leaving the effect of concessions largely unaccounted for. In the sections that follow, therefore, we place a great deal of focus on an exploratory assessment of the dynamics between concessionary government policies and subsequent levels of international terrorism against Israeli interests.

Accommodation and Deterrence: Tools for Countering Moderate and Extremist Terrorists

In this study we assume that the international system contains a range of terrorist organizations that resemble one or both of the two types described in the introduction: moderates and extremists. The utility of such a typology is manifold. For this chapter, it simply enables us to arrange our thoughts as to what responses we ought to expect to witness in the aftermath of significant government policy changes. Elsewhere, classification of individual organizations into these two types enables a "thicker description" of the dynamics between terrorism and counterterrorism in particular cases (Bueno de Mesquita, 2003, 2004).[3]

In the sections that follow, we argue that a state can limit terrorist attacks via two main policy tools: retaliation and concession. Retaliation involves the use of the resources of the state to hinder a group's ability to perform new acts of terror.[4] Concessions alter the political and/or social environment toward the terrorist's ideal point in order to limit a group's desire to utilize further acts of terror. For moderate organizations we might expect that both sets of actions would decrease their use of terrorism. Concessions will tend to satisfy some minimal set of goals, thus reducing the number of active terrorists, while retaliation will restrict the ability of some number of groups to utilize available resources. For extreme organizations, however, we expect a positive mitigating effect from retaliation but little impact from concession. For these groups, no amount of reasonable concession (short of meeting their extremist goals) will change their desire to utilize terrorism. This occurs simply because they largely commit terror for terror's sake, recognizing the massive incongruence of their preferences from those of the status quo states. Governments that encounter these groups are thus forced to limit their actions toward retaliation.[5]

In respect to international terrorist attacks, however, there are important reasons to believe that retaliatory policies will tend to bare fewer fruits in regard to reducing levels of attacks than is the case with domestic attacks. If we follow the logic of Enders and Sandler (2002), one clear priority of counterterrorism policies is to attempt to reduce terrorists' levels of resources, or simply to restrict their access to these resources. If, however, these resources tend to come from or be located overseas—as is the suggestion when the attacks themselves are defined as being international in nature—the opportunity for and ability of the government to affect these resources are drastically reduced. Moreover, whereas domestic terrorists are by definition located within a single state (that of the government), international terrorists may have a range of host nations. As such, any retaliatory policy designed to counter the threat of terror from a particular country (e.g., the invasion of southern Lebanon in 1982) may witness an improvement in regard to levels of terror originating from that host, yet may simultaneously fuel the activity of terrorists based elsewhere. Although we cannot directly test this proposition for individual incidents, it does lead—via the notion of aggregation—to the general expectation that retaliatory policies will not have the desired effect of reducing international terrorist attacks, but, in fact, will be shown to have provoked increases in levels of terrorism. This leads directly to our first research hypothesis:

H1: Levels of international terrorism increase in response to Israel's employment of retaliatory policies.

Contrastingly, when judging potential changes to aggregate levels of international terrorism in the wake of concessionary actions by the government, it seems logical to forecast a decline that falls short of eradication. As stated earlier, such policy shifts ought to be expected to appease the moderate contingents but not the extremists. As such, we ought to expect a net decline in levels of international terrorism—with little change from extreme sources and a reduction in activity conducted by the moderates. This leads to the statement of our second research hypothesis:

H2: Levels of international terrorism decrease in response to Israel's employment of concessionary policies.

Our theory linking dominance and international terrorism has been detailed elsewhere (Sobek & Braithwaite, 2005). For now a brief summary will suffice. The inability to alter or expect an alteration of the status quo via politico-military methods provokes revisionist and revolutionary actors to employ alternative methods—in the most extreme circumstance, terrorism (Carr, 1997). In particular, dominance is the ability, or inability, of actors in the international system to alter (through politico-military actions) another state's policies or position. It reflects both the desire (preferences) and ability (capabilities) to alter another state's policies. According to this story, when Israel is dominant in the Middle East, there are fewer conventional means by which revisionist claims can be voiced and acted upon successfully, that is, revisionist states are few or weak, or both. Thus any revisionist substate actors overseas (think about the likes of Hezbollah) observe a reduction in the number and/or abilities of potential state-level opponents to Israel. Thus they recognize the need for themselves to carry the burden of revisionism if their goals are to be met. This implies that when the likely effectiveness of political-military strategies (i.e., the actions conducted by revisionist states) remains low, terrorism becomes increasingly likely. Employing the same logic, it thus follows that a reduction in levels of international terrorism ought to be observed when Israel's dominance of the Middle East declines. This leads directly to our third research hypothesis:

> H3: Levels of international terrorism increase as Israel's dominance of the Middle East increases.

The next section details our strategies for empirically testing the three hypotheses detailed above. Following this description, we outline the concomitant results and offer some discussion as to how we might interpret our results with a view to offering insight to the policy community.

Research Design

This chapter examines international terrorist attacks against Israel in a 29-year period (between 1968 and 1997) both at the yearly and quarterly level of aggregation. Because the dependent variable is an event count (taking on non-negative integer values), a negative binomial regression is used.[6] As our brief review of the literature suggests, a great many studies addressing annual and quarterly levels of terrorism tend to view these dynamics as a time-series process. Although we believe that both methods are appropriate, we favor the event count approach because it is more easily converted into the cross-sectional framework should this be necessary in future studies and also because it is more easily translated into a multivariate model—as is required in this study. Many of the studies to which we referred that employ time series tend to do so from a largely univariate standpoint—addressing the impact of particular intervention variables upon the dynamics of a single series of data. The choice between time-series models and a negative binomial is characterized by a variety of costs and benefits. Given our question, however, the negative binomial seems most appropriate.

The negative binomial model builds on the Poisson by allowing practitioners to specify a gamma distributed parameter in the place of the mean value of the Poisson distribution. This additional parameter permits the specification of a model with an expectation that the data are over-dispersed. Adopting the notation of Long (1997), we can identify the following expectation of the dependent variable according to the Poisson model:

$$E(y_1 / x_1) = \exp(x_1\beta) = \mu_1$$

and

$$\Pr(y_1 / x_1) = \frac{\exp(-\mu_1)\mu_1^{y_1}}{y_1!}$$

We can then replace the mean term, μ_r, with a random variable, $\tilde{\mu}_r$ with a gamma distribution and we have the negative binomial distribution for which:

$$E(y_1 / x_1) = \tilde{\mu}_1 = \exp(x_1\beta + \epsilon_1) = \exp(x_1\beta)\exp(\epsilon_1) = \mu_1\exp(\epsilon_1) = \mu_1\delta_1$$

where, $E(\delta_1) = 1$.
Therefore, $E(\tilde{\mu}_1) = E(\mu_1\delta_1) = \mu_1 E(\delta_1) = \mu_1$.
Thus, the distribution of our observations given the values of x_r and δ_r is a Poisson distribution with a gamma distributed random variable in the place of its mean:

$$\Pr(y_1 / x_1, \delta_1) = \frac{\exp(-\tilde{\mu}_1)\tilde{\mu}_1^{y_1}}{y_1!} = \frac{\exp(-\mu_1\delta_1)\mu_1\delta_1^{y_1}}{y_1!}$$

Dependent Variable: Terrorist Attacks

The data for our dependent variable are drawn from the *International Terrorism Attributes of Terrorist Events* (ITERATE) dataset (Mickolus, 1982; Mickolus et al., 1989; Mickolus et al., 1993). Specifically, we operationalize our dependent variable as the count of international attacks listed as occurring within the borders of the Israeli state or that incur casualties or deaths among the Israeli population around the world in a given quarter or year. Excluded from this collection, therefore, are state-sponsored actions and Palestinian acts in Israel (unless they injure or kill foreigners). One key advantage of these data is that they were collected with the express purpose of maximizing coverage of international events worldwide. For this study we have simply aggregated all international attacks that took place within Israel and were known to have been perpetrated by foreign nationals and those that caused harm to Israeli nationals overseas. Our aggregations were conducted at both the quarterly and yearly level.

Previous studies that have used the ITERATE data (see Enders & Sandler, 2003, as an example) have utilized the number of deaths as the dependent variable. Although this may be appropriate for the study of certain question, we feel it is not best for this analysis. This project is interested in the use of terror as a tool to affect change. This implies that the number of attacks matter. The level of casualties, while related to the number of attacks, is also dependent upon their relative success. Using the number of deaths from attacks as the dependent variable would thus conflate the correlates of terrorist acts with the correlates of their success.

Independent Variables

This project controls for two main types of nonpolicy variables: Israeli regional dominance and Israeli power. The power measure for Israel is simply its Composite Index of National Capabilities (CINC) score as coded by the Correlates of War project (COW). This variable is introduced to reflect Israel's baseline ability to deter foreign attacks (both terrorist and conventional).[7] The CINC score is composed of six different components that account for a states short (military personnel and military spending), medium (energy use per capita and iron/steel production), and long (urban population and total population) term power attributes/capabilities.

Our second measure, dominance, examines not only the power or capabilities at Israel's disposal, but also its diplomatic influence in the Middle East.[8] The measure assumes that Israel is most dominant when there is no strong challenger to its policies in the Middle East.[9] To capture policy congruence this project uses the Affinity score that examines similar voting patterns in the United Nations general assembly (Gartzke, 1998). Those states that have similar voting records have scores that approach 1 and those with opposite records have scores approaching −1. Simply relying on this measure for dominance fails, however, to capture the effect of military capacity. For a state to truly challenge Israel it would require both differing policies and the military capacity to affect change. This implies that strong challengers would have both a highly negative affinity and a highly positive CINC score. Interacting these two factors produces a rough measure of a state's willingness and ability to challenge Israel in the Middle East.

This measure can be calculated for each state in the Middle East. In other words, we have a measure for the ability and willingness for each state in the Middle East to challenge Israel. Thus, when Israel is most dominant, her closest rival has a highly negative product because either its policies do not differ from Israel, or it does not have the power to affect change in Israel's policies. Thus, our operationalization of Israeli dominance is simply the lowest product from among the numerous states in the Middle East.

As the dominance measure becomes more negative it implies that a more powerful state more strongly disagrees with Israel, that is, Israel is no longer as dominant. A less negative (closer to zero) value for dominance means that less powerful states have fewer disagreements with Israel, implying a period of relative dominance.

On examination of data on the dependent variable (see Figure 7.1.), we additionally felt it prudent to introduce a dummy variable for the year 1972, which represents a massive outlier in the data set. In 1972 Israel experienced a tremendous jump in attacks associated with their athletes' participation in the Munich Olympics. To control for this, a dichotomous variable was created and code 1 for 1972, and 0 otherwise.

Policy Variables

This project uses three measures of Israeli policy and its congruence with the interests of other states in the Middle East. The first variable again uses the Affinity score developed by comparing U.N. voting records. *Policy congruence in Middle East* is simply the average dyadic affinity score. In other words, this measure averages the affinity between Israel and every other state in the Middle East. As Israel's policies more closely match those of other Middle Eastern states this variable becomes more positive. Thus we would expect a negative between relationship policy congruence in the Middle East and terrorist attacks.

Two dichotomous policy change variables are also included in the models: *Camp David Accords* and *Invasion of Lebanon*. Both of these events represent critical changes in Israel's relationship with other Middle Eastern states, and should have drastic impacts on international terrorism. These variables are designed to examine our central hypotheses regarding the impact of concessionary and retaliatory policy shifts on levels of international terrorism. These variables are coded as 1 in the year (or quarter) in which they occurred and in all subsequent following years (quarters), and zero otherwise. In particular, Camp David is coded as having an effect from the third quarter of 1978 onward, and the invasion of Lebanon from the second quarter of 1982.

Results

Figure 7.1 presents a general view of the number of attacks against Israel. Note the spike that occurs in 1972—linked to the attacks against Israel during the Olympics. Outside of that outlier the data appears fairly smooth, although some trends do appear. After 1978 (Camp David Accords), one finds two straight years of declines (from 25 to 17 and then 10) and a third year of relatively few attacks (13). In fact after 1978, only 3 years out of 20 have more than 25 attacks none of which occur before the invasion of Lebanon. In 1982 one finds another spike in the data of 27 attacks. In addition, the years following the invasion only have 3 occasions where fewer than 13 attacks occurred (the 1981 value) all of which appear in the nineties. While the figure is not conclusive it provides a hint of the effect of the major shifts of Israeli policy on international terrorism.

Tables 7.1 and 7.2 examine the effect of regional and policy variables on levels of terrorist attacks against Israel. The models consistently support the contention that major Israeli policy shifts that attempt to resolve the underlying grievances lead to a decrease in the number of attacks. In addition, policies that aggravate the underlying issues of contention relate to increases in the number of attacks. In accordance with our expectations, therefore, it appears as though concessionary actions mitigate levels of terrorism, whereas retaliatory actions provoke these levels.

Table 7.1 examines annual numbers of international attacks against Israel. Note in the first model, which solely looks at the continuous variables, that only Israeli power has a statistically significant effect. The

Figure 7.1. Number of International Terrorist Attacks Against Israel (1968–1998)

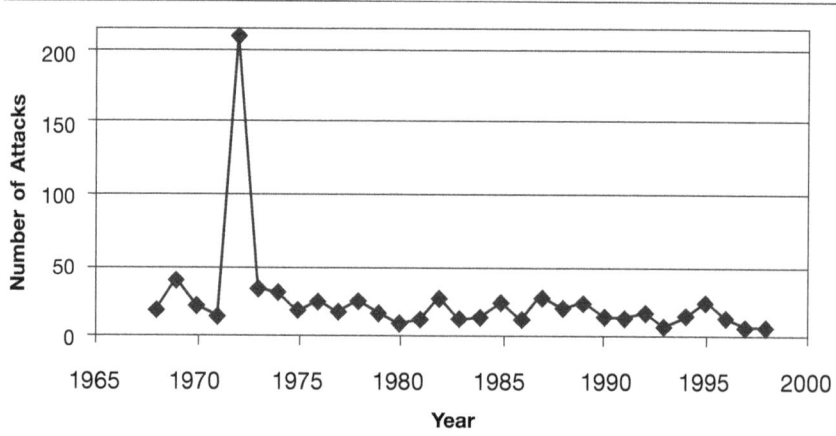

Table 7.1. Negative Binomial Regressions of Yearly Attacks on Israel

Variable	Model 1 (System)	Model 2 (Policy)	Model 3 (Combined)
Israeli Dominance in Middle East	40.45 (1.27)	— —	76.27 (4.01)***
Israeli Power	–54.43 (–1.66)	— —	–61.63 (–1.86)*
Policy Congruence in Middle East	–0.27 (–0.47)	— —	–0.57 (–0.98)
Post–Camp David Accord	— —	–0.46 (–2.21)**	–0.43 (–1.89)*
Post–Invasion of Lebanon	— —	0.04 (0.19)	0.58 (2.57)***
Dummy of 1972	2.11 (16.03)***	2.11 (19.35)***	2.02 (12.72)***
Constant	3.65 (9.44)***	3.2 (29.81)***	4.05 (14.38)***
Alpha	0.06	0.08	0.03
Log Likelihood	–99.52	–105.17	–96.14
Number of Observations	30	31	30
Psuedo R-Squared	0.21	0.19	0.23

Note: T-Scores are in Parentheses
*p-value < 0.10; **p-value < 0.05; ***p-value < 0.01 (all are two tailed-tests)

negative coefficient implies a deterrent effect where increases in power decrease the expected number of attacks. Model 2—examining the impact of the dummy variables for policy choices—finds that only the Camp David Accords having a statistically significant effect on the amount of terrorism. Specifically, this model offers early evidence that concessionary actions have encouraged a decline in levels. The more fully specified third model, in turn, provides a clearer picture of the interactive relationships between policy, dominance, and levels of international terrorism.

In particular, the fully specified model indicates that both the Camp David Accords and the invasion of Lebanon have statistically significant effects in the expected directions. Moreover, a number of the control variables exert an important influence. As also seen in Model 1 Israeli power has a statistically significant deterrent effect on terrorism. Israeli dominance, which examines Israel's relationship within the Middle East, however, also has a positive effect. Thus, as Israel becomes more dominant relative to the other states in the Middle East, the number of attacks against its interests actually increases.

The findings provide some evidence that policy changes influence the decision to engage in terrorism, but the aggregation at the yearly level limits the sample size under investigation. Thus, Table 7.2 highlights modeling that aggregates the data at the quarterly level, which in essence quadruples the sample size. Notice that the results differ only slightly when looking at the quarter. The only key difference is the statistical insignificance of Israeli power in the fully specified model.

Table 7.2. Negative Binomial Regressions of Quarterly Attacks on Israel

Variable	Model 4 (System)	Model 5a (Policy)	Model 6 (Combined)
Israeli Dominance in Middle East	41.11 (1.49)	— —	72.86 (2.56)***
Israeli Power	−54.39 (−1.82)*	— —	−57.05 (−1.76)*
Policy Congruence in Middle East	−0.28 (−0.52)	— —	−0.89 (−1.53)
Post–Camp David Accord	— —	−0.59 (4.95)***	−0.62 (−3.29)***
Post–Invasion of Lebanon	— —	0.15 (0.98)	0.54 (1.92)*
Dummy of 1972	2.11 (4.88)***	2.09 (4.95)***	2.09 (4.77)***
Constant	2.27 (6.86)***	1.88 (21.43)***	2.74 (8.45)***
Alpha	0.31	0.32	0.29
Log Likelihood	−312.12	−320.61	−308.74
Number of Observations	120	124	120
Psuedo R–Squared	0.12	0.12	0.13

Note: T-Scores are in Parentheses
*p-value < 0.10; **p-value < 0.05; ***p-value < 0.01 (all are two tailed-tests)

Interestingly policy congruence has no statistically significant affect on the amount of terrorism, although it comes close in Model 6 (Table 7.2). This implies that marginal changes in policies between Israel and other members of the Middle East have no effect; rather, it appears that the major events captured by the Camp David Accords and the Invasion of Lebanon are more significant in causing terrorists to change their behavior.

Although the policy variables have the statistically significant effects that we expected, perhaps the more important question is the substantive impact they have on terrorism. Figure 7.2 looks at the effect of Israeli dominance in three separate time periods: before the Camp David Accords, between Camp David and the Invasion of Lebanon, and after the invasion of Lebanon. In addition, the values of Israeli power and policy congruence are set to their means.

Figure 7.2 clearly shows the effects of changes in Israeli dominance as movement from the minimum to maximum values almost quintuple the expected number of attacks. More importantly, however, are the effects of changes in Israeli policy. The most dangerous period for Israel, regardless of its dominance, was before the Camp David Accords. With the signing of those accords, however, attacks are virtually halved. The invasion of

Figure 7.2. The Effect of Israeli Dominance and Policy on Quarterly Terrorist Attacks

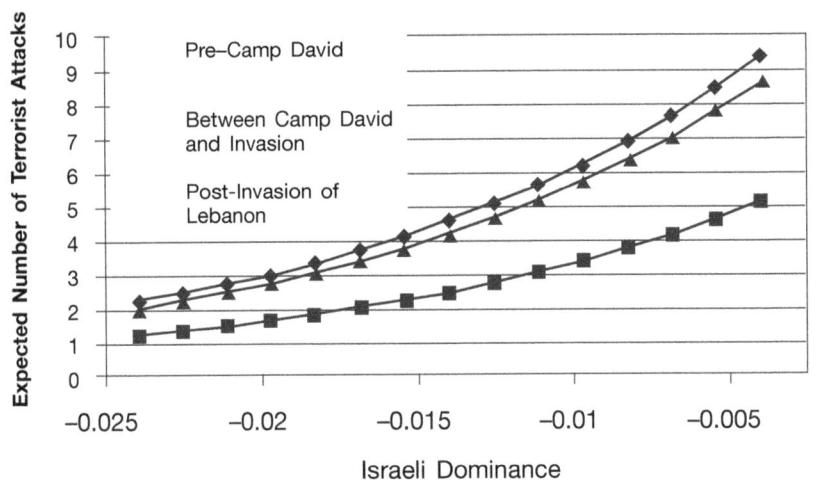

Lebanon, as expected, increases the expected number of attacks to a level close to that in the period prior to the Camp David Accords.

In general, changes in Israeli policy have a significant and substantive impact on the amount of international terrorism that it experiences. Actions taken that exacerbate the tension between Israel and the Palestinians or other Arab states statistically and significantly increase the amount of terrorism. At the same time, however, these levels appear to be mitigated by attempts at more concessionary policy choices.

Conclusion

Previous studies have generally shown how changes in the way states defend against terrorism can alter its patterns (Enders & Sandler, 2002). Yet terrorists may respond to more than variations in the obstacles set before them. If one assumes that terrorists have a set of political objectives that they wish to accomplish, then movements by the government toward or away from those goals should alter the behavior of terrorists.

This chapter examines this claim in the Israeli case. This provides a plausible test case because changes in policies toward the Arabs and/or Palestinians are clearly made and publicized. In particular, the analyses examine the impact of the Camp David Accords and the invasion of Lebanon on the number of international terrorist attacks that Israel experienced between 1968 and 1996. The results generally show that Israeli actions that move toward the Palestinian and/or Arab positions (i.e., Camp David) decreases the levels of international terrorism directed against their interests. This finding is important because it is counter to that observed in the dynamics between concessionary policies and levels of domestic terrorism, where a subsequent increase in terror levels is most commonly witnessed. In some sense, however, testing on the Israeli case does not provide the strongest support for this contention and does not immediately offer opportunities for generalization even given the importance of international terrorism directed against Israel. What the support does indicate, however, is the need for further investigation into this matter at the international level. In particular, two avenues of future research may shed light on this question.

First, scholars need to more explicitly deal with the preferences of international terrorists and how they differ from those of their targets. This analysis shows that anti-Israeli terrorists are generally goal-seeking in that they have a set goal that they attempt to accomplish through a given tactic (terrorism). This implies that movements toward their goals should decrease the incentive for terrorism. The analyses bear out this implication, but the interaction between state and international terrorist preferences needs further elaboration.

Second and certainly related to the first, there is a great need for additional data collection to fully and properly examine the nature and reasoning behind terrorism. Current data resources do not provide information as to why terrorists attack only how and how often. Scholars need to develop a method to both categorize terrorist actors and measure their preferences and/or goals. Although certainly a monumental task, only after this information is available can we more confidently hope to understand why terror happens.

The presence of international terrorism will plague status quo powers for the foreseeable future. Simply because the tactic of terrorism has pejorative connotations does not mean, however, that all terrorists are irrational and solely dedicated to political violence. Understanding of when and why these actors choose this method has critical implications for policy makers. The existence of moderate (goal-seeking) international terrorists implies that sole reliance on deterrence policy may not succeed. As seen in the Israeli case, movements toward concessionary solutions can and do lead to a drop in levels of attacks.

Notes

1. This concept—*status quo*—is subject to great definitional debate. Here we refer to the global status quo, in other words, the system maintained by the U.S. and her allies, which at present prioritizes the war against terrorism.

2. Bueno de Mesquita (2003, 2004, 2005) utilizes a similar typology of actors employing terrorism.

3. Ideally, scholars and policy makers alike will increasingly utilize such a spectrum of typologies when classifying terrorist organizations and attempting to gain a greater understanding of their individual goals and motivations.

4. Retaliation can be similar to the notion of deterrence. The latter, more typically employed before the counterpart has acted, also aims at limiting the ability of groups to utilize available resources toward their preferred goal. In this chapter we tend to employ the term *retaliation* because most government actions would appear to be taken subsequent to the outset of some terrorist campaign.

5. At this point it is prudent to offer a disclaimer in respect to the theory being outlined. The quasi-dichotomous categorization that has been discussed thus far is aimed in this chapter at merely offering a means by which to arrange arguments and expectations about levels of terrorism that could be expected to result in response to government policy choices. As such, we will not be attempting to identify specific groups according to this categorization. Rather, we will instead use this framework to make references regarding the likely aggregate outcomes of these groups predicted responses to policy-making choices. For example, although

it would be tempting to directly identify moderate and extreme terrorists and then to test variations in their respective levels of activity in the aftermath of government policy shifts, such an endeavor is not facilitated by available data resources. What is possible, however, is to use this categorization to inform our hypotheses regarding aggregate levels of international terrorism that ought to be expected under varying policy-making environments; this will be the task of forthcoming sections.

6. Although this is the appropriate method for this type of dependent variable, it does not directly account for temporal trends and effects in the dependent variable Thus we chose to run the model both with and without a lag of the dependent variable as an explanatory variable. The results of these two methods were virtually identical; except that the coefficient on Camp David Accord dropped to insignificance at both levels of aggregation. We have additionally run a number of time-series models on the quarterly data and have found similar results.

7. This is distinct from any measure of overt policy shift that is designed in retaliation to terrorism.

8. For a discussion of the concept of dominance see Sobek and Braithwaite (2005).

9. The states that are coded as belonging to the Middle East are Morocco, Algeria, Tunisia, Libya, Sudan, Iran, Turkey, Iraq, Egypt, Syria, Lebanon, Jordan, Saudi Arabia, Yemen Arab Republic, Yemen, Yemen People's Republic, Kuwait, Bahrain, Qatar, United Arab Emirates, and Oman.

References

Brophy-Baermann, B., & Conybeare, J.A.C. (1994). Retaliating against terrorism: Rational expectations and the optimality of rules versus discretion. *American Journal of Political Science* 38, 196–210.

Bueno de Mesquita, E. (2003). An adverse selection model of terrorism: Theory and evidence. In *Essays in Comparative Political Institutions*. PhD Dissertation, Harvard University.

Bueno de Mesquita, E. (2004). Conciliation, counter-terrorism, and patterns of terrorist violence: A comparative study of four cases. Working Paper. St. Louis: Washington University.

Bueno de Mesquita, E. (2005). Conciliation, counterterrorism, and patterns of terrorist violence. *International Organization* 59, 145–176.

Carr, C. (1997, January). Terrorism as warfare: The lessons of military history. *World Policy Journal* 31, 1–8.

Darby, J. (2000). The effect of violence on peace processes. In M. Cox, A. Guelke & F. Stephens (Eds.), *Farewell to Arms?* London: Macmillan.

DeNardo, J. (1985). *Power in numbers: The political strategy of protest and rebellion*. Princeton, NJ: Princeton University Press.

Enders, W., & Sandler, T. (1993). The effectiveness of anti-terrorism policies: Vector-autoregression-intervention analysis. *American Political Science Review* 87, 829–844.

Enders, W., & Sandler, T. (2002). Patterns of transnational terrorism, 1970–1999: Alternative time-series estimates. *International Studies Quarterly* 46 (2), 145–165.

Enders, W., Sandler, T., & Cauley, J. (1990). Assessing the impact of terrorist-thwarting policies: An intervention time series approach. *Defense Economics* 2, 1–18.

Kydd, A., & Walter, B. (2002). Sabotaging peace: The politics of extremist violence. *International Organization* 56, 263–296.

Long, J. S. (1997). *Regression models for categorical and limited dependent variables*. Thousand Oaks, CA: Sage.

Mickolus, E. (1982). *International terrorism attributes of terrorist events* (ITERATE 2). Ann Arbor, MI: Inter-University Consortium for Political and Social Research.

Mickolus, E., Sandler, T., Murdock, J., & Fleming, P. (1989). *International terrorism attributes of terrorist events 1978–1987* (ITERATE 3). Dunn Loring, VA: Vinyard Software.

Mickolus, E., Sandler, T., Murdock, J., & Fleming, P. (1993). *International terrorism attributes of terrorist events 1978–1987* (ITERATE 4). Dunn Loring, VA: Vinyard Software.

Ross, J., & Gurr, T. (1989). Why terrorism subsides: A comparative study of Canada and the United States. *Comparative Politics* 21, 405–426.

Singer, J., Bremer, S., & Stuckey, J. (1972). Capability distribution, uncertainty, and major power war, 1820–1965. In B. Russett (Ed.), *Peace, war, and numbers* (pp. 19–48). Beverly Hills: Sage.

Sobek, D., & Braithwaite, A. (2005). Victim of success: American dominance and international terrorism. *Conflict Management and Peace Science*, 22, 135–148.

Chapter 8

Unholy Alliances
How Trans-State Terrorism and International Crime Make Common Cause

Lyubov G. Mincheva and Ted Robert Gurr

Introduction

Trans-state political terrorism is a strategy used in pursuit of ethnonational, religious, or revolutionary objectives. International organized crime, in contrast, seeks material gain by smuggling weapons, drugs, consumer goods, and humans as well as by illegal fund transfers. How do these two types of "global bads" make common cause? Under what conditions do politically motivated terrorists cooperate with international criminal cartels and networks, and vice versa? A major challenge in the building of such an explanatory model is its complex dependent variable demanding explanation for the *interaction* of two conceptually distinct motives for joint action.

We sketch a typology and theoretical framework that incorporate perspectives from social movement theory, conflict analysis, and criminology. Three major factors are proposed to condition such interactions. A strongly disposing condition for alliances of the political and the criminal is the existence of trans-state nationalist, ethnic, and religious movements. They provide settings conducive to collaboration between terrorists and criminals based on shared values and mutual trust. A second condition is the occurrence of armed conflict, which provides incentives and opportunities for interdependence. Third are the constraints that facilitate or impede complex transnational exchanges of illegal commodities, exchanges that frequently involve third- and fourth-party intermediaries and corruptible internal security forces.

The proposed model is illustrated using evidence from the Albanian ethno-territorial separatist movement. This was activated in the early 1990s and, over the last decade, has evolved into a political-criminal syndicate. We suggest that the varying intensity of the ethnic Albanians' separatist conflicts has shaped different patterns of terrorist-criminal collaboration. The conclusion identifies other instances of political-criminal syndicates in the Balkans and in other world regions.

Power, Profits, and Violence: The Complex Dependent Variable

A major challenge in this chapter is defining and describing a complex dependent variable, the *interaction* between two distinct motives. We do so by focusing on actors: the actors whose behavior and driving motivations we want to explain are criminalized rebels who cooperate in or conduct illegal enterprises in pursuit of radical political goals.

Our assumption that the violent pursuit of power (terrorism for short) and illicit material gain (criminal enterprise) are different purposes may seem obvious. It is not just a definitional point but a difference that helps explain actors' choices of strategies and their organizational structures. However, international conventions conflate crime and terrorism: from a legal perspective, terrorism *is* criminal behavior. Both revolutionary and criminal enterprises engage in illegal violence whether in pursuit of power or profit (van Duyne, 2003). The United Nations Secretariat has characterized terrorism as the most visible and openly aggressive form of transnational organized crime (see Mueller, 1998, cited in Stanislawski & Hermann, 2004).

Martin and Romano, following other writers, have introduced the general concept of *multinational systemic crime* (1992) to denote the "collective behavior" of groups engaged in terrorism, espionage, and trafficking in drug and arms (1992, 14–15). A fashionable economic theory of rebellion deals with political motivations by ignoring them. Collier and Hoeffler posit that rebellion is "an industry that generates profits from looting.... Such rebellions are motivated by greed...." (Collier et al., 2005, 3).

If we accepted these premises as a beginning point, we would have little to explain: social movement and conflict theories would be irrelevant, or at best secondary, to the explanation of linkages between terrorism and crime. The essential differences are these. Profit maximization and risk reduction are the motives that shape the behavior of international criminal groups. In contrast, ideologically driven pursuit of social and political goals motivates political terrorist groups. They seek to influence political processes and the exercise of state power. Strategically, criminal groups use violence to establish and maintain control over the supply, shipment, and marketing of illicit goods. Political terrorists, by contrast, use violence mainly to publicize their objectives and to demonstrate the weakness of their opponents—usually the state, sometimes rival groups. Organizational differences follow. International criminal enterprises need regular access to suppliers, transit routes, and markets, implying a relatively high degree of organizational structure and coordination. Their profits are usually large and can be used to buy immunity from security and judicial officials. Terrorist organizations, by contrast, are more likely to function as cells or networks, capable of carrying out episodic attacks on political targets but otherwise flexible and mutable. Their survival depends on evading and deterring security forces, not on buying them off (Curtis & Karacin, 2002).

This dualistic approach to analyzing terrorism and crime is affirmed in different contexts. European experts point to "symbiotic partners from arms trades and narcotics" as a connection that straddles the schism between the two spheres (Curtis & Karacin, 2002, 1). "Narco-terrorism" is a term widely used to describe the activities of Latin American narcotics traffickers in collusion with revolutionary movements in Peru, Colombia, and elsewhere. The term can mask complex and mutable interactions among traffickers, revolutionaries, and security agencies, as it has in Peru (Magallanes, 2003), and Colombia (Holmes et al., 2004).

What brings these two types of actors together in "unholy alliances" and "marriages of convenience" are pragmatic considerations. Although political terrorism is often characterized as rebellion on the cheap, it does require resources for arms, logistics, and sustenance and shelter for militants. Consequently terrorist movements frequently engage in criminal activity to finance their activities, relying on robbery, kidnapping for ransom, extortion, and trafficking in drugs and humans. Joint action between terrorists and criminal enterprises potentially provides more opportunities for profit and political impact than either group enjoys when acting alone. But there are barriers to joint action. Cooperation depends on a common basis of trust. Ethnonational and sectarian identifications seem especially important to establishing trust that transcends international boundaries because they imply cultural cohesion, group loyalty, and shared antipathy toward states and other social actors (see von Lampe, 2003).

It has been proposed that terrorists gradually lose interest in establishing alliances with criminals as basic sources of funding. Where such alliances do exist they usually are transitory rather than basic for the economy of terrorism. The general pattern seems to be that successful terrorists become self-funded, at the risk of an agenda shift in which they evolve in the direction of "fighters turned felons" (Curtis & Karacin, 2002, 4; also see Adams, 1992, 244). Their chances for political survival and success increase as they run criminal enterprises themselves. In doing so their political agenda may remain central. Or they may shift away from political objectives to profit-seeking.

Terrorist groups have incentives to skip intermediaries in their business operations also because most lines of transborder exchange of illegal commodities become increasingly complex. Being driven by demand alone, narcotics and arms sales do not necessarily have a symbiotic relationship. However, conditions that promote one type of trafficking more often than not promote the other as well. Narcotics and arms thus often become items of exchange in a complex deal involving third and fourth parties. Within this setting few partners could expect to be "end recipients" of precisely what they were seeking from the market, with no collateral transactions (Curtis & Karacin, 2002, 21–23). And where the availability of arms for a terrorist group depends on the status of another transaction the arms customer may run into the need to make ad hoc decisions. This presents contemporary terrorists with the need to increasingly think as businessmen to whom profits will be available if they are pragmatic while lost will follow if they remain doctrinaire.

As this discussion suggests, the interaction of terrorist and criminal objectives can take various and mutable forms. We sketch below a typology of ways in which terrorists may operate or cooperate with illegal enterprises: *ideological, pragmatic, predatory,* and *opportunistic*. The fourth pattern, the opportunistic, comprises the actors whose behavior and driving motivations are central to our analysis—criminalized rebels who cooperate in or conduct illegal enterprises in pursuit of radical political goals. The central question is how the political and the economic—the terrorist and the criminal—become linked, and by what processes.

Four Patterns of Terrorism-Crime Linkages

Terrorism is often characterized as rebellion on the cheap. Nonetheless terrorists still need to acquire weapons and munitions, buy shelter and sustenance, maintain communications and travel—in other words they need money. To acquire money, terrorists are pressed either to seek connections with organized crime or to operate illicit enterprises. We posit four general types of terrorist-crime connections. These connections are based on the motivation and circumstances that drive terrorists' interests in illegal business, and the extent of agenda shifts by which terrorists become illegal entrepreneurs.

Ideological

Some terrorists give primacy to their ideological objectives without losing focus on politics. They undertake illicit economic activities to fund their political program. The Provisional IRA is an example. It was activated in 1969 by Irish nationalists who were provoked by violent Protestant paramilitary attacks on Catholics to resurrect their ancient and violent strategy to unify Ireland. At the outset the IRA's funding came in contributions from Americans of Irish descent channeled through the Irish Northern Aid organization—Noraid. By the late 1970s the IRA had become an effective terrorist group supported by homegrown private business. This successful transformation was due to a major change in organization's tactics, said to have been initiated by Gerry Adams—a senior member of the IRA high command and also leader of the Sinn Fein, the political party representing the IRA. The change was carried out by a new generation of militants who moved away from "simple bombing" and got themselves into organized crime projects (Adams, 1992, 167). Profitable illegal activities included smuggling of fuel and cigarettes; fraud on building sites; operating security firms and cab companies; and running nightclubs (Adams 1992, 167–179; Horgan & Taylor, 1999). The new IRA leaders sought a revolutionary change by means of armed struggle and economic subversion at once (Adams, 1992, 181). In the process the division between terrorism and pure crime was blurred, and IRA chief of staff Thomas Murphy ran a lucrative smuggling operation that continued until 2006 (Associated Press, 2006). But for the IRA high command political objectives remained paramount. In a parallel process the nationalists engaged ever more effectively in negotiations and conventional politics. And the money earned in illegal business was partly reinvested in democratic politics.

Pragmatic

The second pattern of terrorism-crime connections leads to a "pragmatic shift" in a terrorist organization's agenda. Although political goals are not abandoned altogether, material gain yet becomes a major objective. The Marxist Revolutionary Armed Forces of Colombia (FARC) seems to provide an example. FARC was established in 1966 as a leftist guerrilla movement whose overriding objective was to establish a Communist government in Colombia. The organization also supported peasant struggles aimed at winning social concessions (Ronderos, 2003, 224). Yet at the outset FARC was reportedly a poor organization with limited social support (Adams, 1992, 217). Finding money to finance its insurgency was imperative. By the late 1970s a solution had been found. FARC established collaborative relationships with drug producers and traffickers—well established by the late 1970s—who decided to locate processing facilities in FARC-controlled areas and relied on guerrillas to maintain order and security, in exchange paying protection taxes. Subsequently, though, as the "narcos" developed their own paramilitaries, this marriage of convenience broke down and in some areas paramilitaries fought with guerrillas for local control (Holmes et al., 2004).

It is worth noting that unlike the IRA, which directly involved itself in illegal business, FARC does not grow, process, or traffic in coca. It relies on kidnappings for ransom and continues to extract significant revenue in the form of production taxes on narcotics. FARC's financial drug dependence presumably has affected leaders' estimates of the costs and benefits of continuing their insurgency rather than accept the government's persistent peace initiatives that have brought other Colombian revolutionary groups into conventional politics. In a 2005 working paper Tore Bjørgo suggests as a general principle that "leaders or factions within the militant movement sometimes oppose political solutions to the conflict because it would undermine their vested 'business interests.' Why should the Colombian FARC guerrillas seriously support a peace solution when they run a highly successful ransom-for-money business and collect protection taxes from drug barons?" (cited in Gurr, 2006, 95).

Predatory

A third pattern is one in which political militants' agenda shifts entirely away from political objectives toward material gain. "Social bandits" are a recognized object of historical analysis—marginalized rural groups for whom banditry displaced explicit political objectives. The Sicilian Mafia, for example, originated in nineteenth-century political resistance to foreign rule (Hobsbawm, 1959). A contemporary example is provided by Algeria's Islamist insurgents. In Miriam Lowi's view "a politically motivated insurgency quickly turned into an instrument of predation." At the outset in 1992 the militants sought financing through raids and armed robberies but soon shifted to extortion and pillaging of commercial traffic, seizing property, and taxing local populations. Their next step was involvement in the parallel economy and illicit trade in hashish, vehicles, and food products. "As the violence became increasingly articulated with the micro-economy, the interest in capturing the state gave way to looting it and, eventually, to holding the state at bay so as to focus squarely on gaining and maintaining access to resources. Violence and the Islamist insurgency provided a cover for corruption and contraband" (Lowi, 2005, 232–233).

Opportunistic Interdependence

The fourth pattern of terrorism-crime connection, which is our main focus in the remainder of this chapter, is one of opportunism in which political goals and material gain coexist on an equal footing. Actors shift easily from one to another. Analysts call this pattern a political-criminal hybrid. What is distinctive about it is the indistinguishable pursuit of political and criminal objectives at once. The Balkans region provides examples of political-criminal hybrids including the Albanian case described later in this chapter. Analyst Vesna Ristanovic reports on another political-criminal hybrid, based on ethnic Serbs. It was activated at the time of the Bosnian war in the early 1990s and ever since has been a major factor in Serb politics. Ristanovic refers to it as an "unholy alliance" established between politicians and organized crime, and given organizational form in ethnically based paramilitary units. The troops consisted of gangsters from the underworld previously employed by Yugoslavia's secret services. They were largely responsible for the Bosnian ethnic cleansing and mass murder (Bovenkerk. 2003, 48), as well as for continuing interference in Serbia's politics. Like the ethnic Albanian nationalists, they, too, are terrorists who from the onset are themselves the criminal enterprise.

Opportunistic interdependence is engendered by transborder (transstate) identity movements that provide networks for collaboration between trans-state terrorists and organized crime. Such movements straddle interstate boundaries and make renewed claims for ethnonational liberation at times of nation-state building or boundary adjustments. Based on the Balkans evidence, we suggest that movements per se are not directly responsible for exporting terrorism or cooperating with criminal networks. Rather, the real political-criminal agents are the trans-state criminal paramilitary units (networks).

Analytical Framework:
When Terrorists Cooperate with Criminals

The four patterns discussed earlier illustrate different degrees of interdependence between terrorists' political and material objectives. They can be summarized as follows: First, the terrorists' main objective is pursuit of power, however, profit is also on their agenda. Power and profit are frequently mutable, with power taking the lead. Occasionally profit displaces political objectives. Second, terrorists involve themselves in criminal enterprises using either or both of two patterns. They can establish alliances of convenience with criminals. Alternatively, they can run illicit enterprises independently. Third, terrorist objectives cannot of themselves explain the choice or rejection of cooperation. To explain how the two types of "global bad" make common cause we need to develop a model on the *circumstances* conditioning terrorist-criminal interaction. Our model is two-sided. We first look at the circumstances conditioning terrorists' cooperation with criminals. Next, we examine circumstances conditioning criminals' cooperation with terrorists. Finally, we combine them in an analysis of the Albanian case.

Organized crime is a global phenomenon, terrorism usually is local. In order to connect themselves to the world of global crime networks and become a part of it, terrorists must accept the rules guiding criminal enterprise and comply with them. The analytical framework provided below introduces major factors conditioning successful criminal enterprise. We examine these factors from the perspective of terrorists' motivations for participating in them.

No generally accepted definition of organized crime exists. However, three approaches to criminal enterprise seem to have held sway over public and professional thinking for much of the past century. One is focused on activities. It is mostly concerned with racketeering and other predatory aspects of domestic criminal enterprise. The second focuses on criminal actors. The latter have been long perceived as centralized Mafia-type underworld power structures that exercise control over illegal domestic markets. This image of criminal actors has evolved into a conception of international criminal conspiracies as multiple, ethnically based crime cartels engaged in drug trafficking, money laundering, and related illegal activities.

Contemporary studies of organized crime integrate and simultaneously depart from previous traditions. Current criminology is less concerned with illegal business activities and their actors; instead it focuses on increased *opportunities* for illicit activities by rational actors, as well as on *crime networks* (see Klerks, 2003). Analyses of the new criminological orthodoxy thus build on the *criminal opportunity analytical framework* (see Ekblom, 2003) and on the fluid *criminal networks* that provide occasional "nodes" for successful operations (Klerks, 2003, 100–101).

We draw on criminology and organization theory for purposes of our analysis. A major element within our analytical framework is the interpretation of criminal enterprise as collective action (see Figure 8.1). We look at organized crime as profit-driven illegal "collective behavior"

Figure 8.1. Under What Conditions Do Terrorists Cooperate with Criminals?

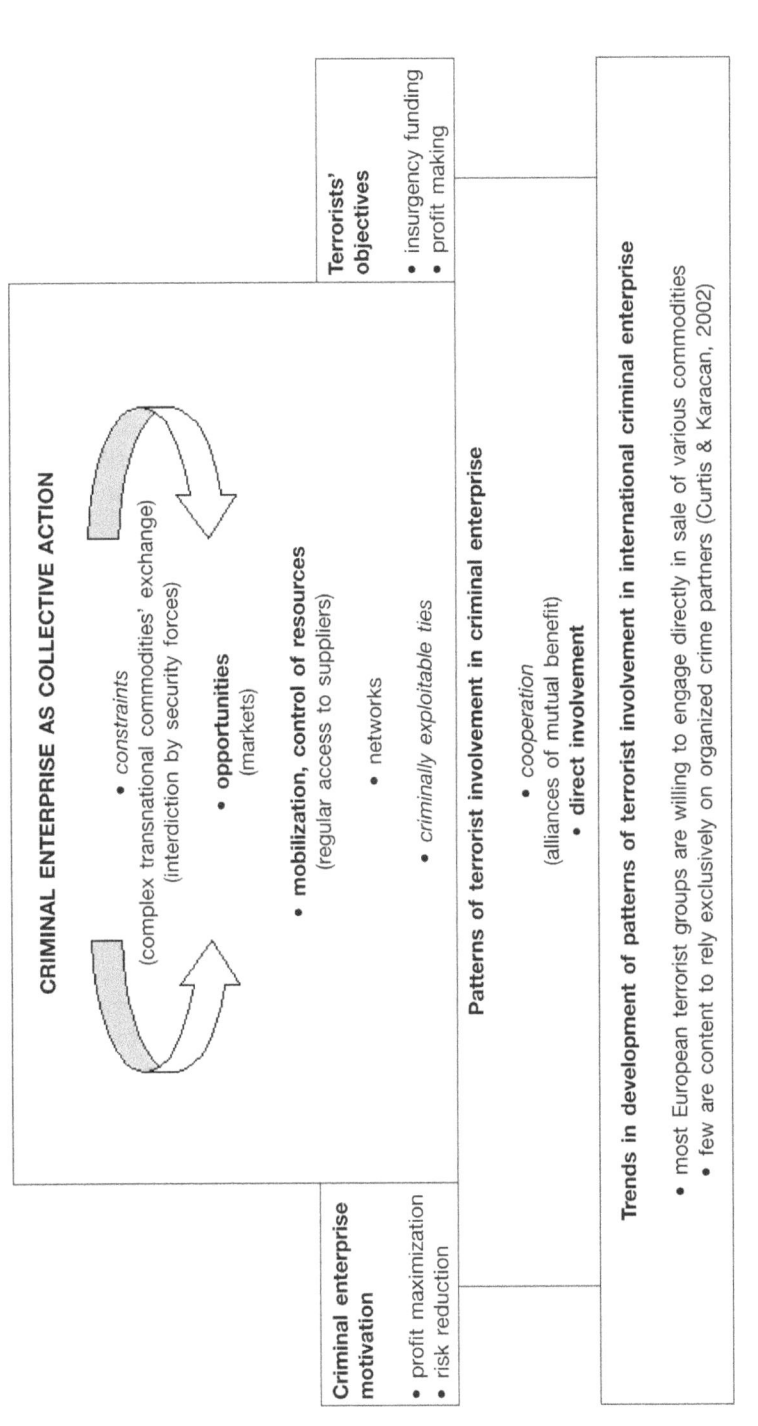

(Martin & Romano, 1992, 14) shaped by the interaction of the criminal market's opportunities and constraints, and performed within fluid criminal cooperatives (Klerks, 2003, 100–101). Four elements condition successful criminal enterprise. As commercial enterprise it is highly dependent on *criminal market opportunities and constraints*. Transnational crime expert Phil Williams identifies factors that expand opportunities. Among them is the process of globalization of financial, commercial, transportation, and communication networks. These factors help buyers and sellers locate each other, identify points of common interest, and establish cooperation. Next, the increasing number of states with "limited capacities for effective governance" also expands illicit business opportunities (Williams, 1999). Their economies are weak and their easily corruptible police and judicial systems lack the means and will to combat organized crime. Other contributing factors include lack of common international standards and cooperation in law enforcement. Not least, organized crime may profit—but it may lose as well—from the increasing complexity of transnational exchange of commodities. Exchanges of different illegal commodities usually involve third and fourth parties. In this transnational environment few partners become "end recipients" of what they seek from the market, with no collateral transactions (Curtis & Karacan, 2002, 21–23). Ad hoc interactions with third parties may lead to profit, as well as loss.

The second general element conditioning successful criminal enterprise is *mobilization and control of resources*. The latter vary. Analysts distinguish between legal goods and services provided by illegal production and distribution; and illegal goods and services offered for free market exchange between suppliers and willing customers (Naylor, 2003, 36). The first group, consisting of legal goods and services produced or distributed illegally, is mainly of interest for domestic profit-driven crime. The availability of those commodities and services should be sought in "the criminogenic properties of the industry and its regulatory environment," which create a "twilight zone where crime and business interact, often to their mutual benefit" (Naylor, 2003, 52). The second group of resources—illegal goods and services—is mostly of interest to international criminal enterprise. Production and distribution of illegal drugs by emerging crime cartels in the 1980s displaced "traditional organized crime." Illegal drug activities are indeed the "only one of several illegal activities that transcended national boundaries." However, these drug activities became the primary concern of U.S. policy makers and led to the opening of America's war on drugs. In either case, in order to control resources a criminal enterprise either must find the suppliers or establish itself as such, and protect itself against interdiction by authorities.

The third factor impacting on the success of criminal enterprise is the availability of efficient networks. Criminal networks are a relatively recent way of conceptualizing the units that run illicit business activities. Their predecessors—Mafia-type structures—were long perceived as the main actors in profit-driven crime. Currently, criminal enterprises are conceived as webs of "social networks" or "criminal cooperatives" where "social ties, much more than business relations of formal command structures form the basis for criminal cooperation" (Klerks, 2003, 101). Important for the analysis of criminal networks is the "overall network size" because it sets the limits for an undertaking. The locally centered networks are useful for domestic crime analysis. Cross-border and trans-state networks are, more often than not, embedded in trans-state identity groups or diasporas, locally and abroad. We argue that they are key factors of international organized crime. Also important for the analysis of criminal networks is "the relative position of particular actors within the network" (von Lampe, 2003, 14).

A fourth element within our framework of criminal enterprise as collective action consists of what Klaus von Lampe calls "criminally exploitable ties." They are the basic ingredient of any form of criminal cooperation and are defined by two main characteristics. First are similar or corresponding criminal dispositions, meaning that actors have similar criminal interests and preferences. They may include cigarette-, and liquor smuggling, drug trafficking, arms trafficking, or trafficking in women, and illegal transfers. Second is the availability of a common basis for trust whose basis could be kinship, ethnicity, childhood relations, or any other social affiliation. These affiliations help guarantee relative predictability of actors' behaviors and thus minimize the risks of discovery and betrayal. Research findings suggest that where strong social links exist, working criminal networks do not exist and criminal cooperation is ephemeral (see von Lampe, 2003, 12). Criminally exploitable ties are an important analytical category because they help establish niches in which criminal enterprise can flourish, and as we argue, they provide settings for cooperation between terrorists and criminals.

How do terrorists become linked with criminal enterprise? As suggested earlier, terrorists either establish alliances of convenience with criminals (under conditions shown in bold in Figure 8.1), or alternatively become directly involved in illicit activities (conditions shown in italics in Figure 8.1). Cooperative relations reduce constraints on criminal markets. Terrorists and criminals establish marriages of convenience to remove obstacles and expand the possibilities of both power- and profit-seeking. Next, criminally exploitable ties also strongly encourage cooperation. They increase the chances that partners (a) share common interest in business interactions; and (b) trust one other for their implementation. Alternatively, factors that discourage cooperation are market opportunities available to terrorists. Their direct access to markets promises profit making, so is unlikely to lead them to cooperate with criminals. Direct involvement will most likely be sought. The second factor conditioning terrorists' direct involvement in criminal business is low-cost control of resources and/or regular access to suppliers. These conditions are especially likely when terrorists operate in a socially supportive environment, for example in territories inhabited by kinsmen or co-religionists.

Analytic Framework: When Do International Crime Networks Cooperate with Trans-State Terrorists?

In pursuit of profit terrorists can choose to cooperate with criminals. Alternatively, they can choose to carry out criminal enterprises themselves. Criminals on their part have little choice but to cooperate. Being driven by profit maximization and risk reduction they can be expected to seek expanding commercial opportunities. A new rebellion provides plenty of them. Rebellion's export across international borders multiplies those opportunities. The analytical framework provided below introduces major factors conditioning successful cross-border insurgency, and discusses within them how they affect the interests and motivations of criminal enterprise.

Trans-state terrorism has become pervasive in the post–Cold War era. Examples can be found in the Balkans, Central and South Asia, Central America, the Caucasus, the Middle East, Central Africa, and elsewhere. Essential preconditions of trans-state terrorism are trans-state nationalist, ethnic, and religious movements. We integrate conflict theory and social movement theory for purposes of this analysis.

Trans-state identity movements emerge out of regionally concentrated cross-border and trans-state identity diasporas. When politicized these movements develop transnational networks and articulate mutable objectives. Cross-border movements are mostly concerned with territorial issues. As East European evidence suggests, they aim at boundary revisions and territorial adjustments. Depending on circumstances their objectives may range from autonomy, to secession, to unification with kindred across borders. Trans-state movements whose segments are not territorially adjacent may raise alternative claims such as power devolution, power sharing, regime change, or global revolution.

Cross-border or trans-state movements—just as domestic social movements—tend to be durable and adaptive. Key to understanding their robustness are their recurring contentious collective actions, which aggregate and diffuse across the border from more mobilized to less mobilized segment (see Tarrow, 1994, 96). Actions of these kinds recur as movement elites draw on trans-state identities and networks to pursue shifting objectives. We use trans-state contentious collective action as the analytical framework for understanding the economy of trans-state terrorism. Parallel to the preceding analysis, three elements shape the structure of collective action. Cross-border/trans-state identities and networks are key. The political strategies of elites shape the changing objectives of collective action. And changing opportunities determine strategies of collective action, transforming it from political into military, or the reverse (see Figure 8.2, next page).

Funding of (cross-border) insurgency is increasingly a business of criminal groups. Insurgencies provide opportunities for profit making and risk reduction at once. Arms supply is a highly profitable business, for example, and in times of political upheaval the transaction risks go down. Criminals thus have good reasons to cooperate with insurgents. Cross-border insurgencies increase potential profits and decrease risks even further. Demand for weapons and munitions increases as insurgency expands. And risk decreases as militants establish control along or close to border areas. The latter are known as "bandit countries" and havens for smugglers (see Adams, 1992, 156). Stanislawski and Hermann call them "criminal enclaves" or "black spots" (2004) and point to weak state structures and high levels of corruption as factors that sustain these sovereignty-free zones. Rebels and criminals equally benefit from them because they provide relatively secure bases and make it easy to move across international borders. Additionally, kindred group and network stretches across the border.

Clearly, cross-border/trans-state insurgency is an undertaking that makes it easy for terrorists and criminals to form strong alliances (see Figure 8.2). Next we examine the establishment of such alliances in the Balkans and their subsequent transformation into political criminal syndicates.

Unholy Alliances as Political-Criminal Syndicates: Evidence from the Balkans

The ethnic Albanian political criminal syndicate is a criminal paramilitary unit of the ethnic Albanian separatist movement. The latter bridges the

Figure 8.2. Under What Conditions Does International Crime Cooperate with Trans-State Terrorism?

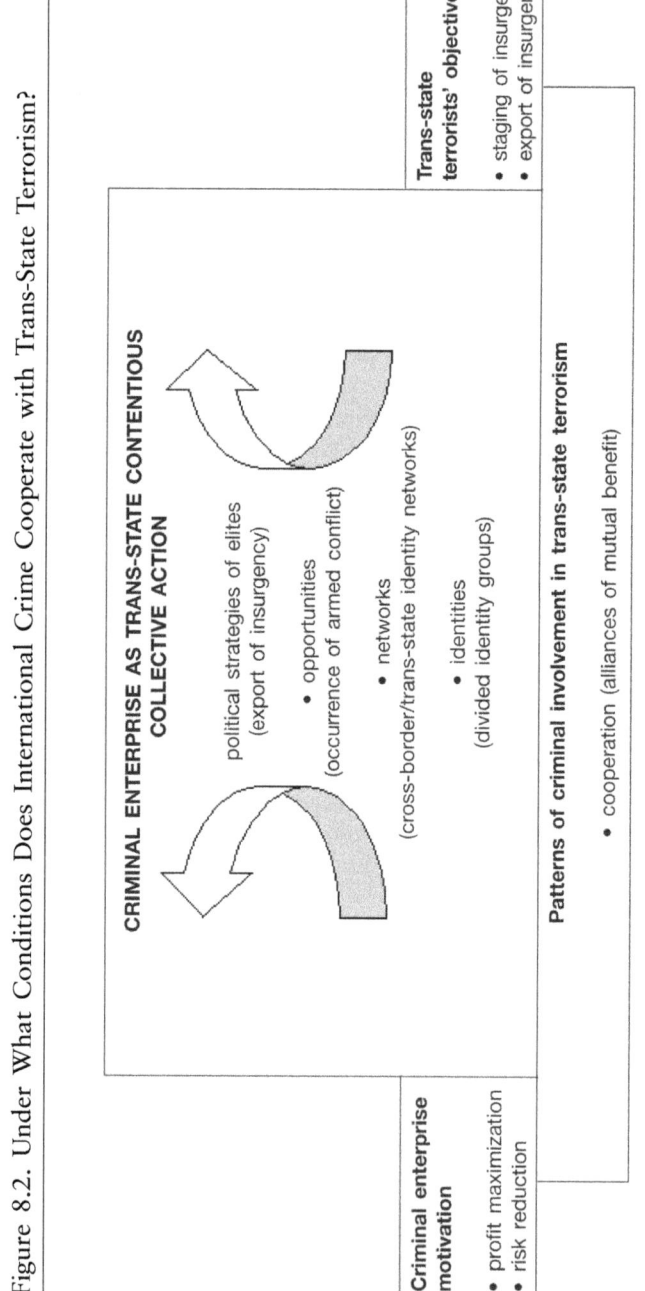

ethnic Albanian bisected diaspora populating Kosovo—a former autonomous province of Yugoslavia and currently a UN protectorate—as well as border areas of west Macedonia, south Serbia, and Montenegro. The movement activated in late 1960 when its most active segment—the Kosovar Albanians—began to raise claims for self-governance. They range from autonomy, to secession, to unification with mother state Albania, or at least with kindred groups across the (former) Yugoslav republican borders. Kindred groups echoed these claims.

The movement has been intensely active since early 1990s, when the Kosovo Albanians declared independence after the Yugoslav government, then dominated by Milosovec's Serbian nationalists, terminated Kosovo's status as an autonomous region. The first paramilitary unit of the ethnic Albanian separatist movement is usually said to be the Kosovo Liberation Army (KLA), which emerged in 1995. However it had a predecessor, the All Albanian Army, identified in 1993 as a clandestine paramilitary organization operating within the army of the Republic of Macedonia (RFE/RL, 1994).

The KLA was a paramilitary unit that operated a dispersed guerrilla movement. The political unit that funded KLA was the People's Movement of Kosovo (LPK), a rival underground movement to the legal Democratic League of Kosovo (LDK) (Wright, 1999, 17). The KLA's claims were equivocal. KLA's radical left and radical right wings argued "over whether to carry the fighting to the pockets of ethnic Albanians who live in Western Macedonia and neighboring Montenegro" (Hedges, 1999, 28). The wings agreed only "on the need to liberate Kosovo from Serbian rule," while all else was left to be decided later (Hedges, 1999, 28).

The army first appeared in 1995 when it launched a few attacks on Serbian police in Kosovo. One year later, in June of 1996, the KLA assumed responsibility for a series of acts of sabotage committed against police stations and policemen in Kosovo (Cordesman, 1999, 6). In 1997 the KLA benefited from the spring rising in Albania, following the collapse of the financial pyramid scheme, when large numbers of looted weapons found their way to Kosovo (Pettifer, 1999, 26). Information also suggests that al Qaeda provided financial aid and organized rival mujahideen from Islamic countries in Kosovo (BBC, 2005). In early 1998 KLA escalated its violent attacks on the Belgrade regime, prompting a campaign of ethnic cleansing carried out mainly by local Serbian militia. This led in 1999 to NATO air strikes against Yugoslavia and to the establishment of Kosovo as a NATO protectorate.

Nearly simultaneously a Balkan-wide network of Albanian criminal clans or *fares* was activated. These clans were able to flourish because of the decay of state power in neighboring Albania. As Cilluffo and

Salmoiraghi observe, "The *fares'* success illustrates the extent to which the state [Albania] has slipped into ungovernability" (1999, 24). Dispersed in Kosovo, Macedonia, and Albania, the *fares* smuggled arms and men across boundaries. They helped in founding the KLA as well as in the establishment of the KLA's bases in neighboring Albania and Macedonia.

The Albanian nationalist movement has evolved considerably since the establishment of Kosovo as a protectorate. Most important is the movement's radicalization and fractionalization. All fractions of the ethnic Albanian movement—the newly emerging included—are radical in their political objectives. However not all of them are extremist in their tactics. The emergence of ethnic Albanian extremism at the turn of the twenty-first century is a significant change within the movement's evolution and is now the most serious threat to interethnic peace and stability in Albanian-populated areas in the Balkans. During the last five years the KLA insurgency of 1995/1999 has evolved into campaigns of terrorism said to be aimed at the speedy attainment of Kosovo's independence and resolution of the all-ethnic-Albanian issue. The Kosovars now demand, at a minimum, independence for Kosovo and, at a maximum, incorporation of all Albanians in a single political entity. Violence aimed at ethnic cleansing of Serbs, Jews, Roma, and Muslims also has been reported since 2000. Most serious were riots in Mitrovica from 2000 and 2004. In 2004 interethnic tension in Mitrovica, initiated by ethnic Albanians against ethnic Serbs, resulted in 19 fatalities and 900 wounded. The pogrom was condemned by the NATO commander as "ethnic cleansing."

Kosovo terrorist attacks also recurrently challenge international attempts to help Kosovars build provisional institutions of self-government as defined within the April 2001 Constitutional Framework. Terrorist attacks increased in 2001 in protest against closer links established between NATO and Belgrade. From then to the present they have targeted peacekeeping units (*Washington Post*, 2005), the office of the Yugoslav government in Pristina (*Los Angeles Times*, 2001), and ethnic Serbs living in the province. Attacks intensified in the summer of 2005 as talks on Kosovo's status were to begin. Recent attacks have targeted the UN mission, the provincial parliament, the European Agency for Reconstruction and Development in Pristina, and OSCE headquarters.

Countering terrorism and criminality in the province is a challenge because of the linkages that exist between them and the newly established Kosovar institutions. The unit responsible for countering terrorism is the Kosovo Protection Corps (KPC). It is an outgrowth of the KLA, which was dissolved at the end of the Kosovo insurgency in 1998–1999. With the help of the UN and KFOR, the personnel of the KLA provided the basis for the KPC and the Kosovo Police Service. These units now are blamed for maintaining links with political violence, terrorism, and crime.

Kosovo terrorism is successfully exported across borders. Most prominent KLA commanders shifted to conventional politics. Hashim Thaci and Ramush Haradinaj are examples. Parts of KLA however gave birth to new paramilitary organizations outside Kosovo's borders. The first paramilitary off-shoot of "mother" KLA was the Liberation Army of Preshevo, Bujanovac, and Medvedja (UCPMB), which was activated in 2000. UCPMB militants used the NATO-established buffer zone around Kosovo as a base for exporting the Kosovo insurgency to the south Serbia municipalities of Preshevo, Bujanovac, and Medvedja—home of some 70,000 Albanians. Arms smuggling and cross-border incursions from Kosovo into Preshevo valley recurred throughout the year (*Financial Times*, 2000; *Daily Telegraph*, 2001). The political objective of ethnic Albanian leaders was to extend Kosovo's protectorate status to south Serbia (*Daily Telegraph*, 2001).

Cadres of the former KLA next moved to western Macedonia where a new paramilitary unit—the National Liberation Army (NLA)—was established. The NLA staged a rebellion against Macedonian authorities in early 2001. The conflict dynamics were clearly regional. Analysts suggest that the precipitant of the spread of armed conflict to that country was the ratification by the Macedonian parliament of a long-awaited border treaty with Serbia (*Financial Times*, 2001). There were reports of simultaneous fighting of ethnic Albanian insurgents against Yugoslav police in the Preshevo valley in south Serbia and against the Macedonian forces in Brest (*Washington Post*, 2001).

The NLA dissolved after the principal Macedonian parties signed the Ohrid Agreement, which ended the 2001 Macedonian spillover crisis. Before returning to Kosovo, however, the NLA paramilitary cadres established the Albanian National Army (ANA), which urged the creation of a Greater Albania (BBC, 2005). This came in conflict with provisional authorities in Kosovo who sought instead the establishment of an independent Kosovo. In the meantime the U.S. blacklisted the ANA while in 2003 the head of UNMIK, Michael Steine, branded it as a terrorist organization following a new wave of attacks in northern Kosovo, southern Serbia, and northern Macedonia.

Two new terrorist groups have recently emerged in Kosovo. One is the National Unification Front (NUF), which describes the UN mission in the Kosovo province as occupier (BBC, 2005). The Front demands immediate recognition of Kosovo's sovereignty and merging of south Serbia areas with independent Kosovo (Malic, 2005). Its counterpart in south Serbia is another newly emerged terrorist organization, called the Black Shadow.

In the meantime, the ethnic Albanian criminal clans have been intensely involved in drug trafficking. They acquire Afghan-cultivated heroin from Turkish (possibly Kurdish) criminal organizations and they are also involved in cocaine trafficking with some South American countries. The *fares* dominate local sales of drugs in Central and North Europe, and are highly competitive and aggressive. A Western intelligence official in Kosovo province observed that "The rebels in Macedonia, former KLA freedom fighters in Kosovo, and extremist Albanians in southern Serbia are all part of the network of Albanian and Kosovar Albanian families who [currently] control criminal networks [even] in Switzerland, Austria, Germany and elsewhere" (Free Republic, 2002).

Regular access to European markets in the Albanian case is complemented by regular access to suppliers. A recent report by Europol notes that Albanian production of marijuana is increasing and that the country is increasingly a trans-shipment site for various types of drugs (Europol, 2004, 2). The proceeds of drug trafficking are partly reinvested in weapons commerce aimed at arming KLA and its splinter terrorist groups.

The ethnic Albanian terrorist groups and the mafia are bound in an alliance of convenience. Analysts call such alliances political-criminal syndicates. Criminologist Xavier Raufer describes it as follows: "In the Albanian world—you have clans and in those clans you have a mix of young men fighting for the cause of national liberation, . . . belonging to the mafia, . . . driving their cousins . . . into prostitution. . . . It is . . . impossible to distinguish between them. . . . The guys are liberation fighters by day and sell heroin by night and vice versa" (Raufer cited in Bozinovich, 2004). Analyst Bozinovich adds further details: "Claims are made that 15 leading family clans in Albania *(fis)* . . . during the collapse of the Albanian state into anarchy in 1997 . . . established complete control over the criminal activity in Albania including arms smuggling." Motivated by fear of inter-*fis* blood feuds over the limited Balkan criminal turf, the 15 *fis* allegedly made a deal to accept a common paramilitary enforcement unit, the KLA, in order to incite violence in Kosovo with the dual objectives of making money by financing the war and to incorporate Albanian-inhabited areas of the Balkans (Bozinovich, 2004).

Conclusion

Note: The preceding discussion describes conditions in 2005. Since Kosovo's independence in 2009, terrorism has largely ceased and the Albanian clan's market share of the European drug trade has declined sharply. Government corruption remains a major problem.

This chapter proposes a typology of terrorist-criminal connections and has introduced two analytical frameworks aimed at identifying the conditions under which terrorist-criminal alliances are forged. One framework, summarized in Figure 8.1, identifies conditions motivating terrorists to cooperate with criminal enterprises. The second framework (Figure 8.2) examines the motivation of international criminal networks to cooperate with trans-state terrorist movements. The frameworks also specify conditions under which either group would prefer direct and exclusive involvement in criminal enterprise. In this conclusion we merge the two frameworks into a general model identifying the basic conditions of unholy alliances.

Terrorists cooperate with criminals because of interest and market constraints. International crime for its part seeks cooperation with trans-state terrorism because of interest in profits and trans-state identity networks. Accordingly, three major factors condition such interactions. First is the availability of trans-state nationalist, ethnic, and religious movements, which provide settings conductive to collaboration based on shared values and mutual trust. Second is common interest, or similar criminal dispositions. These increase with the onset of armed conflict. Third are the constraints imposed by markets and by security forces—whose role is not fully analyzed here.

Terrorists and criminals are motivated to cooperate. But how frequently do they so, and in what ways? Here we have focused on the Balkan trans-state ethnonational movements and on their cells, and discovered that terrorists and criminals in this region are increasingly indistinguishable. We anticipate that other networks of ethnic and religious movements around the globe are conducive to such a close collaboration and have also established political criminal syndicates. It appears that alliances bearing some resemblance to those in the Balkans have developed in Colombia, Peru, eastern Paraguay, Anatolia, Afghanistan, and adjoining parts of Central Asia, and the hinterlands of Burma and Thailand.

References

Adams, J. (1986). *The financing of terror.* New York: Simon & Schuster.
British Broadcasting Corporation, September 8, 2005; November 3, 2005.
Bovenkerk, F. (2003). Organized crime in the former Yugoslavia. In D. Siegel, H. van de Bunt & D. Zaitch (Eds.), *Global organized crime.* Dordrecht: Kluwer Academic Publishers.

Bozinovich, M. (2004). The new Islamic mafia. www.serbianna.com/columns/mb/028.shtml, September 10.
Cilluffo, F., & Salmoiraghi, G. (1999, Autumn). And the winner is . . . the Albanian mafia. *The Washington Quarterly.*
Collier, P., Hoeffler, A., & Sambanis, N. (2005). The Collier-Hoeffler model of civil war onset and the case study project research design. In P. Collier & N. Sambanis (Eds.), *Understanding civil war: Evidence and analysis, volume 2: Europe, Central Asia, and other Regimes.* Washington, DC: World Bank.
Cordesman, A. (1999). *Kosovo: Unpleasant questions, unpleasant answers.* Washington, DC: Center for Strategic and International Studies.
Curtis, G., & Karacan, T. (2002). *The nexus among terrorists, narcotics traffickers, weapons proliferators, and organized crime networks in Western Europe.* Washington, DC: Library of Congress. http://www.loc.gov/rr/frd/
Ekblom, P. (2003). Organized crime and the conjunction of criminal opportunity framework. In A. Edwards & P. Gill (Eds.), *Transnational organized crime: Perspectives on global security.* London & New York: Routledge.
Europol Annual Report. (2004). http://www.europol.eu.int/
Free Republic. (2002), February 17.
Gurr, T. R. (2006). Economic factors. In P. R. Neumann & L. Richardson (Eds.), *The roots of terrorism* (pp. 85–101). New York: Taylor & Francis.
Hedges, C. (1999, May–June). Kosovo's next masters? *Foreign Affairs.*
Hobsbawm, E. J. (1959). *Social bandits and primitive rebels: Studies of archaic forms of social movement in the 19th and 20th centuries.* New York: Free Press.
Holmes, J. S., Gutiérrez de Piñeres, S. A., & Curtin, K. M. (2004). A subnational study of insurgency: FARC violence in the 1990s. http://usregsec.sdsu.edu/docs/holmes3
Horgan, J., & Taylor, M. (1999). Playing the "green card"—Financing the provisional IRA: Part I. *Terrorism and Political Violence* 11 (2), 1–38.
Klerks, P. (2003). The network paradigm applied to criminal organizations: Theoretical nitpicking or a relevant doctrine for investigators? Recent developments in the Netherlands. In A. Edwards & P. Gill, *Transnational organized crime: Perspectives on global security.* London and New York: Routledge.
Lowi, M. R. (2005). Algeria, 1990–2002: Anatomy of a civil war. In P. Collier & N. Sambanis (Eds.), *Understanding civil war: Evidence and analysis, volume 1: Africa* (pp. 232–233). Washington, DC: World Bank.
Magallanes, J. (2003). The uses of social myth: Drug traffickers and terrorism in Peru. In E. C. Viano, J. Magallanes & L. Bridel (Eds.), *Transnational organized crime: Myth, power, and profit* (pp. 73–90). Durham, NC: Carolina Academic Press.
Malic, N. (2005). Toward the Kosovo "negotiations": Once more, with feelings. Internet publication. www.antiwar.com, November 2.
Martin, J., & Romano, A. (1992). *Multinational crime. Terrorism, espionage, drugs and arms trafficking.* Newbury Park, CA: Sage.

Naylor, R.T. (2003). Predators, parasites, or free-market pioneers: Reflections on the nature and analysis of profit-driven crime. In M. Beare (Ed.), *Critical reflections on transnational organized crime, money laundering and corruption*. Toronto: University of Toronto Press.
Pettifer, J. (1999). The Kosovo liberation army—The myth of origin. In K. Drezov, B. Gokay & D. Kostovicova (Eds.), *Kosovo: Myths, conflict and war*. Staffordshire, UK: Keele European Research Centre.
RFE/RL 3 (4) January 28, 1994.
Ronderos, J. (2003). The war on drugs and the military: The case of Colombia. In M. Beare (Ed.), *Critical reflections on transnational organized crime, money laundering and corruption*. Toronto: University of Toronto Press.
Tarrow, S. (1994). *Power in movement: Social movements, collective action and politics*. New York: Cambridge University Press.
The Daily Telegraph (February 28, 2001, March, 2, 2001, March 6, 2001).
The Financial Times (March 2, 2001).
The Los Angeles Times (April 19, 2001).
The Washington Post (March 10, 2001, April 12, 2001).
Stanislawski, B., & Hermann, M. (2004). Transnational organized crime, terrorism, and WMD. Discussion paper prepared for the Conference on Non-State Actors, Terrorism, and Weapons of Mass Destruction. Center for International Development and Conflict Management, University of Maryland, October 15.
Van Duyne, P. (2003). Medieval thinking and organized crime economy. In E. C. Viano, J. Magallanes & L. Bridel (Eds.), *Transnational organized crime: Myth, power, and profit* (pp. 23–44). Durham, NC: Carolina Academic Press.
Von Lampe, K. (2003). Criminally exploitable ties: A network approach to organized crime. In E. C. Viano, J. Magallanes & L. Bridel (Eds.), *Transnational organized crime: Myth, power, and profit* (pp. 9–22). Durham, NC: Carolina Academic Press.
Wright, E. (1999, April 9). A Balkan version of the IRA. *New Statesman*.

Part Three

Counter Strategies

Chapter 9

Rational Counterterrorism Strategy in Asymmetric Protracted Conflicts and Its Discontents
The Israeli-Palestinian Case

Gil Friedman

Introduction

Counterterrorism/insurgency strategy in cases of asymmetric protracted conflict is in need of further theoretical elaboration. Scholarly literature on protracted conflict that emphasizes nonrealistic causes of violence—the leader who deliberately foments hatred and visceral fear of the rival group as a means to his or her personal interests, (for example, Posen, 1993; Kaufmann, 1996, 141, 142, fn. 20, 143, 144, 150, 156, 173–174; Snyder & Jervis, 1999, 23, 25; Brown, 2001, 9–10, 14, 19–20; Lake & Rothchild, 2001, 126, 129, 138–139; Van Evera, 2001, 51–54)[1] long-standing histories of intergroup brutality and hatred and deep primordial divisions more generally, (for example, Kaplan, 1991, 93–104; Kaplan, 1993, 1, 30–32; Brown, 2001, 20–23; Lake & Rothchild, 2001, 140; Kaufmann, 1996, 140–145)[2] often characterized by horrific episodes of violence between individual members of groups who reside in close proximity to one another[3]—precludes such analysis from the start. Scholarly literature that does model violent behavior in "asymmetric" conflicts from a rationalist perspective does not, for one, focus on various nuances of asymmetric protracted conflict (Mack, 1975; Arreguín-Toft, 2001). Myriad interviews of public officials in the Israeli media during the al-Aqsa intifada suggest striking limitedness and gaps in the thinking of Israeli security officials as well as party leaders on the strategic costs and benefits of particular Israeli counterterrorism/insurgency policies and actions.

This study develops a model of the strategic costs and benefits of dominant rival counterterrorism/insurgency strategies in cases of asymmetric protracted conflict. The study posits that competitions in resolve instigated by the subordinate, occupied rival are at the root of violence in such conflicts. It presumes that, on the most general level, once a violent episode has begun, the dominant rival should evaluate the effects of particular counterterrorism/insurgency strategies on both the capability and will of the subordinate rival to continue with the violence. The study proceeds to elaborate the model, by breaking down the general variable "will of the subordinate rival to conduct attacks" into its essential components, adding various variables that are integrally related to these components and to capability, and specifying relationships among the variables in the model. The discussion also indicates that particular types of counterterrorism/insurgency strategies inevitably have countervailing effects across the model, and identifies basic debates on the relative salience in counterterrorism strategy cost-benefit analysis of particular elements of the model.

The model might be viewed as a comprehensive, systematic, convincing explanation of terrorist action and thus of the full set of criteria along which to evaluate the utility of any given counterterrorism/insurgency action. Yet, as the study proceeds to demonstrate, it is basically not possible to estimate conclusively whether any given counterterrorism/insurgency strategy will reduce or increase the amount of terrorism overall; in other words, the competing claims of those who see any given counterterrorism/insurgency strategy as good or bad for overall security are nonfalsifiable. If the model is unable to predict with any consistency or reliability the effects of particular counterterrorism strategies on ultimate levels of violence, it does enable isolating the specific effects of particular strategies on particular elements of the occurrence of subordinate rival attacks and comparison of the relative effects of two or more particular counterterrorism strategies along the same set of criteria. We could treat the model as a basis for estimating and then trying to explain gaps and biases in the strategic thought of influential individuals and institutions.

Basic Principles of Asymmetric Protracted Conflict Strategy

This study takes "protracted conflict" to mean a particular form of conflict that occurs between *nations*. Leaving aside any specific conceptualization of "nation," the conceptualization of protracted conflict advanced here assumes that a nation has three interrelated needs that are basic in a Maslowian sense (Maslow, 1943): (1) control over symbols, traditions, and myths, integral to the maintenance of national identity; (2) material, geopolitical, and personal, security; and (3) political autonomy, or outright statehood. Sovereignty itself is both the ultimate affirmation of national identity and, perhaps by definition, an integral facet of national security (see also Azar, 1985, 60; Van Evera, 2001, 27). The relationship between these basic needs and essential stakes under contention, such as territory, control over religio-historical sites, formal political arrangements, and so forth, embodies the essence of protracted conflict. In protracted conflict, the bundle of essential stakes exerts a *substantial* impact on the *basic* needs of *both* of the protagonists. A substantial level of internation physical integration is the linchpin locking this severe conflict of interests into place. Both rivals deem the same territory as an integral part of their respective dominions, and the disputed territory contains members of each of the rival nations (see also Azar, 1990, 7). Asymmetric protracted conflict is a particular form of protracted conflict, distinguished by only one of the rivals enjoying full-fledged statehood. We assume that this asymmetry is correlated with two more causally proximate properties: (1) the rival with statehood enjoys a marked preponderance of power; and (2) by virtue of its superiority, the dominant rival is likely to monopolize the disposition of the essential stakes of the conflict. These properties entail an asymmetry in the sorts of concessions that the rivals can make to one another. The dominant rival has to give, share, or withhold some of the essential goods. The subordinate rival has to concede or withhold the use of force against the dominant rival and the normalization of relations (see Brynen, 1994, 38).

Violent competitions in resolve are natural to asymmetric protracted conflict. Mutually acceptable settlements of the disputed stakes are difficult to achieve. Concessions on even tiny increments of the essential stakes are of substantial significance to the rivals, both intrinsically, because the stakes are essential to the identity and viability of each collectivity, and because they affect the reputation and leverage of each rival in future rounds of bargaining. In the context of initial agreements in an extended peace process, the stingy competition over relatively small amounts of the stakes may well lead a nation to perceive that its rival is defecting. Ambiguity in the stipulations of an interim, partial agreement also allows for believing that the rival is not adhering to the agreement in good faith. Additionally, the very decision by the subordinate nation to sit down at the negotiating table, or to sign a partial, interim, agreement, may undermine the ripeness of conflict resolution (Zartman, 1989). The subordinate rival refraining from force is precisely the essential concession it has to make, and the dominant rival for its part is willing to make only the minimal amount of concessions along the essential issues needed to pacify its rival. Thus, the subordinate rival resorting to nonviolent diplomacy dissolves the willingness of the dominant rival to make further concessions that are painful to it but minimal for the subordinate rival. One could argue that key Israeli gains embodied in the Oslo accords, namely, an end to the *Intifada* that began in December 1987 and Palestinian security cooperation, took the steam out of Israel's willingness to make further, more vital, concessions on the essential stakes of the conflict. These considerations may make it expedient for the subordinate rival to amend its efforts at conciliation with confrontational or at least intransigent behavior,[4] in order to pressure the dominant rival to make more concessions in the concurrent conciliatory process, or to leave formal conciliation efforts aside and embark on a full-fledged limited war,[5] in order to signal its resolve, that is, its willingness to risk escalation and suffer the costs of war, and place costs on the dominant rival for its continued intransigence on contended stakes.

Competitions in resolve in cases of asymmetric protracted conflict have a quite natural mechanism of self-perpetuation. Once it has embarked on a policy of explicit confrontation, the subordinate rival will be unwilling to cease its violence in the absence of concessions on the essential stakes. This preference may be that much more entrenched if the violent competition was preceded by a partial, interim agreement, because, believing that it was already once taken advantage of in an interim agreement, the subordinate rival may not be willing to accept another such agreement. Once the subordinate rival has initiated an episode of violence, the dominant rival for its part is likely to be unwilling to make concessions on the essential stakes. The dominant rival will fear that making concessions under fire will be interpreted as a lack of resolve. Some members of the dominant rival may well become less willing to make major concessions on the essential stakes on the belief that doing so will enhance the subordinate rival's capability to make heady challenges thereafter. Under these conditions, how can we evaluate the possible utility of particular dominant rival efforts to minimize the amount and damage of subordinate rival violence?[6]

A Model of the Effects of Dominant Nation Repressive Counterterrorism Strategies

To address this question, this study develops a model accounting for subordinate rival violence. The model begins with the assumption that the security of the dominant nation is a function of the capability and willingness of the subordinate rival to attack its people (see Most & Starr, 1989).[7] The task becomes to specify the linkages between dominant nation counterterrorism/guerrilla strategy and the will and the capability of the subordinate nation to attack.

The Basic Model and Basic Debates on the Relative Salience of Its Elements

During episodes of violent competitions in resolve, the willingness of the subordinate rival to attack is based on three elements, its estimates of the costs of dominant nation repression, anger, and hatred toward the dominant nation, and resolve/morale (Morgenthau, 1949; Rosen, 1972). Estimates, however rough and intuitive, of the efficacy of violence in achieving the nation's political aspirations is a fundamental element of resolve/morale; without the sense that violence can succeed, the subordinate rival will not be willing to suffer the costs of repression. (Mack, 1975, 178; Pape, 1992, 424, 430).[8] Another basic element of resolve, the salience of the essential stakes of the conflict (see also Kecskmeti, 1958; Snyder & Diesing, 1978; Pape, 1992, 430), can be assumed to be constant during the episode of violent competition in resolve. Thus the model lumps views on the efficacy of violence with resolve/morale. See Figure 9.1, which presents a diagram of the basic model.

Figure 9.1. General Model of the Effects of Counterterrorism/Insurgency Repression

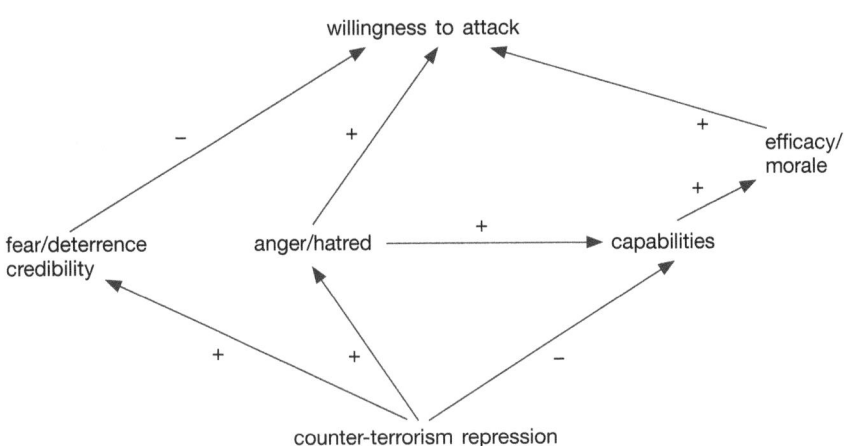

One self-evident prescription is for the dominant nation to use force in ways that cause the subordinate rival to fear punishment while minimizing its anger and hatred. In the words of Machiavelli, "The prince should ... make himself feared [rather than loved, but] in such a mode that if he does not acquire love, he escapes hatred ..." (Machiavelli, 1985, 67). Here we have a basic dilemma of counterterrorism/insurgency strategy. Let us first reformulate the "hatred" variable, though we will still use the label, into one that indeed includes hatred and rage but also value-rationality—that is, attacking as a matter of principle. The dilemma is that the same act of force that instills fear is likely also to increase negative affect and/or the value-rationality of violence, if only by a relatively small amount. This tendency is only reinforced by the ambiguity of the distinction between defensive and offensive repression. Guerrillas or terrorists and their capabilities are integrated into and concealed within and supported by civilian populations. Thus, it is difficult to conduct military operations targeting terrorists or guerrillas without harming civilians (see also Jervis, 1985 [1978], 87–88). The soldiers conducting those operations for that matter do not do so with love in their eyes. Thus, while the dominant rival may see its deliberate infliction of pain and damage on the subordinate population as strictly defensive strategically, the subordinate population, perhaps for that matter backed by international resolutions and foreign sympathizers, will view such acts as callously violent.

To get all of the most basic pieces of the puzzle in place, let's turn to the impact of counterterrorism strategy on the attack capabilities of the subordinate rival. Dominant rival counterterrorism/insurgency actions will, other things equal, directly reduce the weapons and other material that contribute to attacks, and, via killings or arrests, eliminate quality leaders and militants of the terrorist/guerrilla organization(s) and their knowledge on the nuts and bolts of violent operations, and reduce logistics opportunities, meaning primarily freedom of movement and communication and access to dominant rival targets.[9] Additionally, the dominant nation taking the battle hard to the subordinate nation's population centers and political institutions may cause the subordinate rival, if only for no longer than the duration of the dominant rival's onslaught, to focus on staving off the dominant nation's onslaught. At the same time, all other things equal, an increase in the negative affect of a guerrilla or terrorist organization's constituency and/or the civilian population increases the size and logistical support of the organization's forces.

It is plausible to assume that capability is positively related to feelings of efficacy. All other things equal, the subordinate rival will be less confident that a strategy of violence will achieve national goals the more it deems its capability limited.[10]

Perhaps most observers will agree with the general logic of the model so far, but they will exhibit disagreement about the relative salience of different relationships. Some will claim that an increase in subordinate rival anger and hatred is insignificant, because the level of animosity in the subordinate population is as high as it is that any increase in this level that would result from further repression is marginal. This claim is expressed in Panel A of Figure 9.2. Support for this proposition can be drawn from Machiavelli. Machiavelli states that the ruler will avoid hatred

> if he abstains from the property of his citizens and his subjects . . . ; and if he also needs to proceed against someone's life, he must do it when there is suitable justification and manifest cause for it. But above all, he must abstain from the property

Figure 9.2. Counterterrorism Repression, Anger, and Hatred, and Willingness to Attack

Panel A: Diminishing marginal increase in support for violence

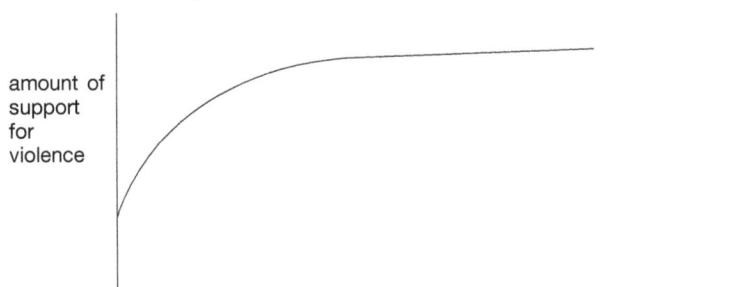

Panel B: The container metaphor of the relationships between anger, hatred and willingness to attack

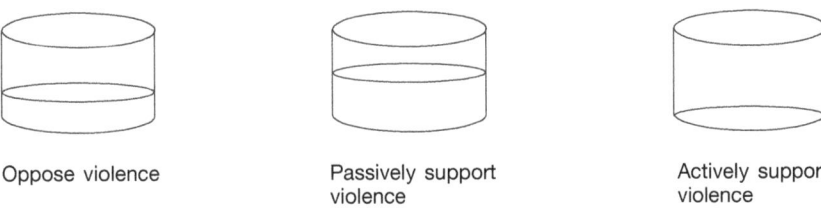

of others, because men forget the death of a father more quickly than the loss of a patrimony. (Machiavelli 1985:67. See also, Angelo M. Codevilla, Trans. and Ed., *The Prince*, at 70, 71–72, 74–75, and Mansfield & Tarcov, Trans., *Discourses on Livy*, at 156, 262, 263, 274, xxxx)

In asymmetric protracted conflict, however, indeed by definition, the dominant nation militarily controls territory that the subordinate nation deems its own patrimony.[11] This line of reasoning similarly implies skepticism that the dominant rival even strictly adhering to liberal idealist norms of *jus in bello* would prevent subordinate rival animosity. Above, we saw that the subordinate rival is likely to find the dominant rival's military as callously violent. Furthermore, one can emphasize that, by the very logic of the violent competition in resolve, the subordinate rival has an overall commitment to attack regardless of how much it might hate. We might elaborate the point by building on Michael Walzer's (1977) war metaphor of a bank robbery. Imagine the bank robber who comes to the bank in prim attire and tells the teller in the most civil of tones to kindly provide the cash, and who says thank you and farewell in the same tone as he or she leaves without having hurt a soul. The bank and its customers will nonetheless view the action as a crime to be terminated by resort to institutions packing coercive power.

Perhaps the most basic counterarguments are as follows. First, with a large population, even if the added segment of the subordinate population that comes to hate the dominant nation in the wake of repression is small relative to the size of the segment of the population already hating the dominant nation, it may be substantial in absolute terms. With a total population of one million people, for example, a one percent increase in haters means an additional 10,000 haters. Second, we can distinguish between different qualities of animosity. We can differentiate between those who do not hate the rival nation, those who do but not to the point of giving their lives to active participation in violence, and those who are personally devoted to fighting. As Panel B of Figure 9.2 illustrates, it is plausible to assume that, holding the deterrence variable constant, any dominant rival act of repression shifts the membership of some increment of people to a greater preference for violence.[12] Third, a meaningful increase in popular animosity within the subordinate nation will place pressure on the nation's elites to perform attacks or more intense forms of attacks than previously. One might point, to cite but one example, to Fatah's turn to attacks within the Green Line, after basically restraining itself to attacks within the disputed territories, in the wake of the Israeli assassination of Raed Karmi in January 2002. Fourth, the interaction opportunity is high such that absolute numbers of attack attempts may increase with an increase in negative affect even if organization leaders seek to restrain the amount or severity of attacks. Fifth, negative affect can only reinforce willingness to pay the costs of violence against the rival (Coser, 1956).

The dominant rival's estimate of the current ratio of the number of subordinate rival devoted militants to the amount and finiteness of its capabilities might also influence dominant rival estimates of the salience of further increases in subordinate rival willingness to attack. If the subordinate nation has a total of 5,000 bombs and 10,000 guns, and if concomitantly 150,000 of its members are committed to participating in the fighting, then an increase in the number of people in the subordinate nation committed to fight might not significantly increase the number of attacks. On the other side, if violent operations are relatively manpower-intensive and the opportunity for interaction with the target nation-state is high, then the proliferation of support for violent action within the population increases the vulnerability of the target nation-state. The desirable size of the pool of activists is a function as well of the policy preferences of the organization. If a terrorist or guerrilla organization has a strategy of limiting the amount and pace of violent attacks, then, if the organization has already amassed an adequate population of militants, the value-added to the organization, and the value-subtracted from the security of the targeted nation-state, resulting from increased popular support and recruits for the organization are marginal. In this scenario, the argument can be made that the increased discontent that arises from military repression of the subordinate population is outweighed by the corresponding reduction in the capabilities of the organization.[13]

Some will say that the model should include an arrow from deterrence to capabilities, to represent the idea that fear of repression discourages people from joining and logistically supporting the ranks of the fighters. Certainly this idea has a priori legitimacy, but two forces inherent in the structure of asymmetric protracted conflict reduce the ability of dominant rival repression to deter support for violence among members of the subordinate nation. First, deterrence is most effective when the potential fighters deem they will not pay a heavy price if they refrain from participating in violence. Yet, as subordinate rival violent resistance is dependent on the cooperation of myriad members of the broader society, and as the active militants operate under civilian guise, the dominant rival will resort inter alia to collective and less discriminating military operations. This undermines its ability to assure that those who do not participate in violence will not get harmed. Second, the dominant rival is restrained by its or powerful third party conscientious objection to egregious repression.

Andrew Mack (1975, 186–187) elaborates, "When the survival of the nation is not directly threatened, and when the obvious asymmetry in conventional military power bestows an underdog status on the insurgent side, the morality of the war is more easily questioned.... Moral outrage is in large part a function of the interests perceived to be at stake in the conflict."[14] The subordinate nation may be well aware that its rival is constrained from incurring markedly brutish punishment. Some members of the subordinate nation might even seek to insight large-scale dominant rival repression so as to garner greater sympathy and support around the world and from relevant powers in particular. As the subordinate rival is substantially dependent on outside power intervention to achieve adequate gains on the essential stakes of the conflict, dominant nation repression might even, by increasing foreign sympathy and support for the subordinate nation, enhance its feelings of efficacy. In conjunction with the high stakes of the conflict, constrained levels of repression of the subordinate rival will not suffice to overwhelm its commitment to violence if it deems violence may contribute to meaningful gains on the essential stakes.[15] Additionally, leaders may be desensitized to the costs of their nation's violence by a concern that shifting away from a strategy of violence will be interpreted domestically as an admission that the rebellion was a mistake and thus harm their domestic standing.

An Elaborated Model, with Subordinate Rival Political Disintegration, Economic Distress, Political Islam, and Estimates of the Prospects of Diplomacy

At least a few other intervening variables on the path from dominant rival counterterrorism actions and subordinate rival willingness and ability to attack the dominant nation deserve incorporation into the model, subordinate rival political institutional disintegration,[16] economic distress, political Islam, and estimates of the prospects of diplomacy. By political institutional disintegration we mean the unraveling of a coherent authority structure and institutional infrastructure, including the polity's security apparatus. In the Israeli-Palestinian case, to elaborate, Israel has assassinated and arrested many Palestinian political elites and fighters, has sabotaged the material infrastructure of the Palestinian Authority, including its Preventive Security Force (PSF), which was devoted during the interim period of the peace process to cracking down on militant opposition to Israel and the peace process, and has severely restricted Palestinian movement (see, e.g., Usher, 2003, 27–28). Inter-elite competition resulting from consequent disintegration may encourage, as a means to mobilizing domestic support, greater resort to external violence.[17] Political disintegration and also economic distress can also lead to feelings of frustration and anomie, which may in turn encourage an embracing of traditional religion.[18] They can also reduce the quality of education; existing research has demonstrated that low level of education is associated with support for political Islam. Support for political Islam in turn is associated with support for violence against Israel. Economic distress will also lead to greater discontent with the dominant nation, assuming that the subordinate rival blames the dominant nation for its economic ills.

Political disintegration can have an important countervailing effect by reducing the subordinate nation's morale. For one, feelings of efficacy are undermined by the passage of time over the course of the competition in resolve without any meaningful concessions or movement toward concessions by the dominant nation on the essential stakes of the conflict (Lewin, 1997 [1948], 93). The disintegration of subordinate nation political infrastructure in fact represents a regression in its slow crawl to statehood, one of its essential aspirations. Political disintegration can furthermore reduce the rationality of subordinate rival strategy and thus its morale.[19] Kurt Lewin (1997 [1948], 89) presents research suggesting "the importance of definite goals for group morale." He adds that "Group morale during a prolonged effort depends much on the degree to which the members keep clearly in view the total task and the final objective" (Lewin, 1997 [1948], 93). Some Palestinians have correspondingly argued that the al-Aqsa intifada's lack of a clear and coherent mission has caused disillusionment within the Palestinian public (Jarbawi, 2001; Jad, 2002. See also Barghouti, 2002). In analyzing Israel's military reoccupation and operations in the West Bank in March through June of 2002, during which Israel detained many middle-level Fatah activists, the core of Fatah's political and military leadership, Graham Usher (2003, 33–34) writes: "Their replacements were often young and inexperienced fighters, grouped in local AMB-like brigades whose loyalty was as much to the clan or locale or their own militia as to any central national leadership. The result was a movement dissolute and in disarray, with a widening gulf between its political and military wings."

A final variable is added to the model, the prospects of a negotiated settlement. It is reasonable to assume that, the more confident a member of the subordinate rival that the dominant rival is willing to make adequate concessions on the essential stakes of the conflict in the wake of a cessation of the violence, reestablishment of security cooperation, and subordinate rival normalization of relations,[20] the less willing the person to continue bearing the costs of war. Palestinian public opinion data have confirmed that skepticism about the prospects of peace may increase the willingness of the subordinate rival to resort to force. Political disintegration may have a few, countervailing effects on this variable. Sociologists of conflict have emphasized the importance of group level unity in the management and resolution of inter-group conflict. Within-nation unity allows the nation to formulate and commit to coherent and stable policy preferences (see Coser, 1956, 122–123). It also allows for consistent adherence to basic norms and rules for regulating the conflict and for control of dissenting and unruly group members (Coser, 1956, 129, 132–133, also 123–124; Dahrendorf, 1959, 226). So, for example, by virtue of destroying the PSF's capabilities, Israel reduced the ability of the PSF to crackdown in the future on militant opposition to Israel and to any peace process.[21] Additionally, by giving freer reign to local-level vigilante repression, political disintegration might make the dove activist more prone to excessive sanction. We can assume that the less the dominant rival believes its diplomatic counterparts can deliver a negotiated settlement, the less willing the dominant rival to make major concessions. On the other side, political disintegration may well entail the existence of at least one faction supportive of peace, which may constitute a shift from a previously monolithic support for violence; moreover, as a source of weakness, political disintegration might reduce the demands of the subordinate rival on essential stakes, thereby increasing the prospects of settlement. Figure 9.3 presents the elaborated model.

A basic puzzle connected to the prospects of settlement, though not included in the diagram, is the relationships between a shift in the subordinate rival's feelings of efficacy and the magnitude of its political

Figure 9.3. An Elaborated Model of the Effects of Counterterrorism/Insurgency Repression

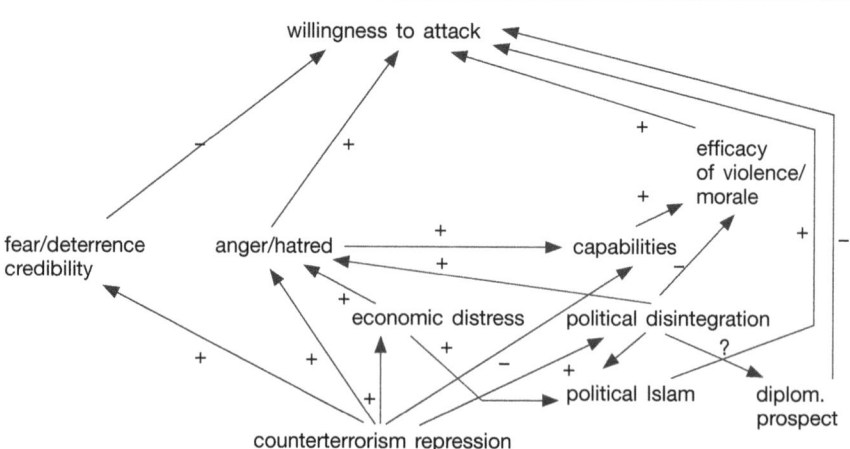

ambitions. The most basic expectation of Realism is that the subordinate nation coming to deem its resistance unsuccessful will encourage it to reduce its demands, because it amounts to the subordinate rival coming to believe that the dominant rival is willing to suffer the costs of not conceding to the subordinate rival's initial demands. Lewin (1997 [1948], 86) meanwhile posits that an individual unsuccessful in the pursuit of some endeavor can react in one of two ways, either by reducing his or her goal or in fact setting his goal "far above his ability." Anger and hatred, as well an Islamicization of Palestinian society, are factors in our model that might account for a nonrealistic shift to a focus on "liberating all of Palestine."[22] Since at least the late 1980s, the goal of a complete return to pre-June 1967 borders has had the status of consensus in Palestinian society. A shift to the view that violence is not efficacious can thus encourage a shift from the goal of the pre-June 1967 borders uncompromised to the goal of pre-June 1967 borders compromised, or to the goal of liberating all of Palestine.[23] Arguably, a Palestinian shift to a preference for a single, bi-national state solution may be realistic, that is, instrumentally rational, assuming that the person couples this shift with corresponding shifts to a very long-term time horizon and to a focus during this time on such strategies as building Palestinian society and cultivating foreign support. Yet, herein lies an important general point. We should not at all necessarily expect a positive relationship between the magnitude of demands on the essential stakes and preferred level of violence. As mentioned above, preference for a single, bi-national state is compatible with a moderation of means, at least in the short- and medium-terms. Conversely, Palestinians who seek a permanent two-state settlement may deem that continuing violence enhances their bargaining leverage. Some factions tend to see a two-state solution as a stage on the path to a "liberation" of all of British Mandate Palestine. A member of the subordinate rival also might come to deem the violent resistance ineffective at the present time, yet perhaps also that the subordinate nation will only become stronger relative to the rival over time, and thus not alter his or her positions on the essential stakes and come to support not diplomacy but strategic inaction, coupled perhaps with a focus on state-building and/or some form(s) of nonviolent nonengagement, with the intention of advancing the uncompromised national aspirations over the more distant future.[24]

The Nonfalsifiability of Competing Evaluations and the Utility of Rational Evaluation

Even if we were to agree that the study's model is compelling, it does not provide falsifiable estimates of whether any given counterterrorism strategy serves or harms the dominant rival overall. For one, as we have seen, people will disagree about the relative salience of different relationships in the model (and thus criteria in cost-benefit analysis). It is important to note that some members of the dominant rival may support continued occupation if not expanded control of disputed territory and thus may in fact be content with subordinate rival violence and a radicalization of the subordinate rival's politics, on the premise that these provide the dominant rival a premise for shunning undesired concessions on the essential stakes. As controversial as it might sound, some Israelis may deem relatively low-intensity levels of Palestinian violence and the radicalization of Palestinian politics less damaging to Israel's long-term national interests than a Palestinian shift to large-scale peaceful demonstrations or even to negotiations, because the latter shifts may reduce the legitimacy of an exclusive reliance on repression by Israel to quell the Palestinians, empower the Israeli left, garner the Palestinians greater international sympathy, and place greater pressure on Israel to make major permanent settlement concessions. Some Israelis might likewise find that suffering further casualties brings the payoff of legitimizing a policy of destroying the prospects for a viable Palestinian state (see Khalidi, 2002, 11).

Agreeing on the respective salience weights of the various variables in the model leaves various obstacles to conclusive estimation. Within reasonable limits, the respective security values of specific increments of different variables in the model, even if we agree to the relative salience of the criteria, defy quantitative comparison. How, for example, can we assess the relative value of the capture of 100 bombs of the terrorists or guerrillas and a dramatic increase in animosity among the families and friends of those killed in the operation? That distinct costs and benefits of any given counterterrorism/guerrilla policy unfold at different rates of time injects yet further complexity into policy evaluation. To illustrate, by what criteria can we rank the relative value of lives of our countryman saved today and a substantial increase in militancy and extremism over the course of a few years as the children experiencing frustration, anger, and/or hatred today come of age?

Any conceivable estimate of the strength of the impact of any given policy on any one variable in the model will be open to question. The model leaves out some forces that in specific cases if not generally will bias estimates of the effects of variables in the model. Just one of these is the level of sympathy of influential third parties deriving from dominant nation repression. The direct damage resulting from the implementation of any given counterterrorism policy is another variable that may influence the willingness and/or capability to attack; yet, the amount of damage of any actual policy can be known only probabilistically, and any estimation of this probability distribution will be open to question. A piece of anecdotal evidence may be enlightening. In August 2001, on the heels of Palestinian mortar shelling of a Jewish residential area in land captured by Israel in the June 1967 war (Gilo), the Israeli Defense Force conducted a military incursion into neighboring Bethlehem. From its inception, the operation was intended to last only a few days and to culminate with the withdrawal of the Israeli troops from the area. Israeli troops conducted the operation and withdrew as planned. Many Palestinians interpreted the Israeli withdrawal—which to repeat was from Israel's view the scheduled culmination of an Israeli offensive operation—as an Israeli retreat. Many would not have predicted such a result, and, of course, people would continue to make differing estimates about the impact of the operation on the distribution of feelings of efficacy across Palestinian society. Relatedly, a person can evaluate losses of any given resource in either individual, egoistic, terms or collective, altruistic, terms; he or she can evaluate national losses either in absolute terms or relative to the total amount of the resource that the nation has (Rosen 1972, 173). Estimates on the societal-level distribution of individual-level suffering at any given point in time or in the face of any given punishment will vary. Another dynamic external to the model is as follows: If the militants find themselves desperate in the face of a dominant rival onslaught, they may in the short-term in fact increase their violence in order to try to get the dominant nation to back off (see also Schelling 1966, 214). During the al-Aqsa intifada, certain Fatah leaders explicitly threatened Israel with greater violence if Israel did not stop its operations in Palestinian population centers and its assassinations of Palestinian militants. Furthermore, the respective independent effects of any single form of repression or conciliation on the elements of the model are difficult to tease out from the effects of other forms of repression and conciliation and structural constraints concomitantly operating on subordinate nation capabilities and incentives. Clearly, the variables in the model defy consistent measurement.

Compounding the problem of estimating the relative effects of different counterterrorism/insurgency strategies is that some forms of repression are discrete and short-lived, and others continuous and long-term. A military strike may come and go in a matter of hours or even minutes; a policy of restricting the movement of members of the rival nation and their goods may be imposed for months and even years.[25] Accordingly, the cumulative effects of different counterterrorism tactics may unfold over differing intervals of time.[26]

These problems undermine policy evaluation even if we assume the basic model (Figure 9.1); the elaborated model only complicates estimation. It follows from these considerations that basically any given counterterrorism strategy can be found to have either a net gain or a net loss on dominant nation security, and, conversely, that any terrorist or guerrilla act can be attributed to insufficient coercion or too much coercion (see also Lichbach 1987, 1995, 62).

The impossibility of conclusively proving the superiority or inferiority of any given counterterrorism strategy, however, does not annul the value of the dominant rival evaluating all of its strategic options squarely in terms of the elements of a sound model of subordinate rival will and capability to attack. The model of this study focuses evaluation and debate on a theoretically comprehensive set of essential factors. This is illustrated in Table 9.1, an evaluation matrix of distinct types of dominant rival counterterrorism strategies by the elements of the study's model. Although it is sensible to view as superior any policy option that performs better than another option on all elements of the model,[27] it is likely that each of various options performs better than the others on at least one element of the model. The evaluation matrix and the study's various propositions about the relative salience of these elements nonetheless help to focus policy judgments.

To illustrate, let's consider a first-cut comparison of the relative effects of arresting and assassinating militants of the subordinate rival. We might assume that killings increase the amount of popular humiliation, frustration, and anger, more than do arrests (see, e.g., Walzer, 1977, 213). Assassinations might also do more damage than arrests to both existing authority structures and the subordinate rival's optimism about the pros-

Table 9.1. A Counterterrorism Policy Evaluation Matrix

	Assassinations	Arrests	Closures	Security fence
Fear of dominant rival reprisal				
Hatred/value-rationality of force				
Views on efficacy of violence				
Capabilities				
Political disintegration				
Economic distress				
Political Islam/cult. conservatism				
Diplomacy prospects				
Tally				

pects of peace. At the same time, we might expect assassinations to carry a greater deterrent impact than arrests. Also, the policy of arresting rather than killing militants can only enhance the dominant rival's leverage in future rounds of bargaining. It may well be difficult to estimate the relative effects of assassinations and arrests on other individual elements of the model. Let's take capabilities for example. Assassinations can only reduce the subordinate rival's reservoir of knowledge needed to carry out attacks more than do arrests. We might also expect that assassinations reduce more than do arrests the quality of the leadership by bringing to power individuals who are less experienced and savvy, and less instrumentally rational and more short-sighted, than old ones. Yet, the added increment of discontent associated with killings might enlarge the pool of individuals willing to personally facilitate and commit violent acts.[28]

Let's briefly broach one other comparison. Earlier, it was mentioned that the subordinate rival may deem that relatively moderate physical punishments it suffers do not outweigh the gains on the essential stakes it may derive from fighting. In cases of asymmetric protracted conflict, there is another possible type of deterrent, in addition to physical punishment, and we can seek to evaluate the relative performance across the model's criteria of the two different types. Specifically, the dominant rival may seek to make unilateral changes to the current disposition of the essential stakes of the conflict as a form of punishment for subordinate rival violence. To elaborate, the dominant rival can respond to subordinate rival violence not only with repressive military tactics—such as travel restrictions, curfews, arrests, assassinations, deportations, suppression of demonstrations, and so forth—but also by making unilateral grabs regarding the essential stakes of the conflict—such as further land expropriation and settlement and denying members of the subordinate nation access to disputed natural resources and religio-historical sites. We could see these latter forms of punishment as having an advantage over physically repressive counterterrorism/insurgency acts in that, all other things equal, they will directly reduce the subordinate nation's estimates of the efficacy of violence for achieving gains on the essential stakes. In other words, the dominant rival taking such actions can lead the subordinate rival to believe that the rebellion is taking it farther from its political goals.[29] Another reason that the dominant rival may seek to make unilateral moves on essential stakes is that doing so might minimize the damage to its reputation for resolve if it were to sit down and negotiate a settlement in the wake or midst of the cessation of violence.[30]

Of course, this strategy has its own set of intrinsic limits. The same type of moral constraints that restrains excessive repression may restrain the number and size of unilateral grabs on the essential stakes. Many members of the dominant rival may well oppose such moves, wanting instead to progress to giving up territory in a negotiated settlement in the relatively near future. Particularly in the case of a democratic dominant rival, furthermore, while dominant rival grabs can reduce subordinate rival feelings that violence is efficacious, domestic debate on strategy within the dominant nation, particularly dissent from aggressive acts, may enhance subordinate rival feelings that violence is efficacious (Mack, 1975, 183, 185, 186–187).

Conclusion

It remains for future research to consider how best to refine the model across different types or cases of terrorism/insurgency, and to estimate the empirical associations between particular actions and elements of the model. Assuming that policy evaluations do not provide conclusive preference rankings, the political scientist might find solace in the idea that the rational modeling of counterterrorism strategy contributes to the square evaluation of the consequences of one or more policy options on the full range of key national interests, and to the honest acceptance of the value-tradeoffs such evaluation inevitably reveals. On this core value of Realist political philosophy, Max Weber writes,

> The primary task of a useful teacher is to teach his students to recognize "inconvenient" facts—I mean facts that are inconvenient for their party opinions. And for every party opinion there are facts that are extremely inconvenient, for my own opinion no less than for others. I believe the teacher accomplishes more than a mere intellectual task if he compels his audience to accustom itself to the existence of such facts. I would be so immodest as even to apply the expression "moral achievement," . . . if we are competent in our pursuit . . . we can force the individual, or at least we can help him, to give himself an *account of the ultimate meaning of his own conduct*. . . . Again, I am tempted to say of a teacher who succeeds in this: he stands in the service of "moral" forces; he fulfils the duty of bringing about self-clarification and a sense of responsibility. (Weber, 147, 152)

In this spirit, one topic for future research is to model variation in the gaps and biases of the strategic thought of those within the dominant nation and beyond with influence on the nation's security policy. To elaborate, what respective effects do people's particular personal experiences, ideological orientations and party affiliations, formal authority status, level of cognitive complexity, and the like, have on their strategic evaluations? (see also Jervis, 1976). We could hope, if soberly, that such research would reach some of the people and organizations involved in policy making.

Notes

1. Certainly, the leader who leads his or her country into war for the sake of personal interests is instrumentally rational in doing so. However, this is non-Realistic at the national-level of analysis.

2. A similar putative cause is brands of nationalism that are intrinsically violence-prone (e.g., Van Evera, 2001, 31, 48–50). Scholars often postulate the breakdown of a previously effective state apparatus, which had ensured the security and co-functioning of the members of separate groups. For example, see Posen (1993); Snyder (1993), 86; Snyder and Jervis (1999, 17, 22–23); Walter (1999); Brown (2001, 5–6, 8–9, 13–14); and Lake and Rothchild (2001, 128, 133).

3. Works of this type include Posen (1993), Jack Snyder (1993), Van Evera (2001), Kaufmann (1996), Snyder and Jervis (1999), and Lake and Rothchild (2001).

4. Additionally, given the direct role of the masses, opposition factions, and other nongovernmental organizations, members of the subordinate rival may prefer what might be called a dual-track strategy, whereby the government adopts one strategy, say, conciliation, toward the rival, and other elements within the nation adopt a confrontational strategy toward it.

5. Limited war encompasses two threats. "One is the threat to inflict costs directly on the other side, in casualties, expenditures, loss of territory, loss of face, or anything else. The second is the threat to expose the other party, together with oneself, to a heightened risk of a larger war" (Schelling, 1966, 105). In asymmetric protracted conflict, a threat of larger war would generally involve the intervention of one or more third parties on the side of the subordinate rival.

6. Corresponding to the explanatory weaknesses in work that sees horrific violence between individual members of groups who reside in close proximity as the result of histories of intergroup brutality and hatred, this work implies conflict management and resolution strategies that are inappropriate for asymmetric protracted conflict, notably, physically separating the rival populations or, alternatively, rebuilding an effective state apparatus and equitable political system encompassing both groups. Separation leaves unresolved essential stakes of the conflict. The very boundaries of the separation and the political arrangements accompanying the separation represent the essential sources of conflict in the first place. Thus, separation will not reduce and will quite possibly exacerbate the willingness to resort to force. It should be noted additionally that, while separating peoples previously living in the same neighborhoods and towns can only reduce

the opportunity for mass-level aggression, the groups will likely be rearranged into regions that are contiguous and that are perhaps bound by borders that are long, meandering, and thus permeable.

When national sentiment is strong, each group will basically by definition demand its own state. Extreme distrust between the rivals will further reduce the acceptability of a bi-national state, democratic or otherwise, which would entail each rival relinquishing its ability to unilaterally guarantee the security of its members (Morgenthau, 1950, 259). A bi-national state is all the less feasible when the geodemographic integration of the rivals is far from complete (see Brown, 2001, 7; Van Evera, 2001, 37–41). If the subordinate population is relatively large, furthermore, the dominant nation's institutionalizing its domination undermines its state's national character and democraticness.

Meanwhile, attributing violence to egoistic elites generally implies that a change in leadership contributes to conflict management. In reality, however, externally imposed leadership changes will only fuel the discontent and thus war-proneness of the subjugated nation, particularly to the extent that it sees its resort to violence as a rational instrument of its national interests.

7. This premise excludes at least two other national-level concerns that may factor into a dominant rival policy maker's calculations, the quality of relations with third parties, and the possibility of a pretext for engaging the subordinate rival in a nearly all out war so as to destroy the subordinate rival's domestic authority infrastructure and/or territorial infrastructure. These omissions allow us to focus on the purer basic security calculation.

8. Pape, concerned primarily but not exclusively with conventional interstate war, suggests that the feeling of efficacy must be brought to nil before the target becomes unwilling to bear the costs of war. "If the victim can be persuaded that it is militarily impossible for him to achieve or maintain his objectives, then levels of costs which were bearable as long as there was a chance of success become intolerable" (Pape 1992, 424). He also writes, "risks of disastrous defeat are often not recognized . . . until these are made inescapably obvious by events. This makes the coercer's task of demonstrating the consequences of failure to concede all the more difficult . . . states . . . may not recognize the need to surrender until all ambiguity has been eliminated" (Pape, 1992, 434). Yet, later in the paper, he is less categorical: "If the target doubts its military capability to hold or take the territory at issue, it may be unwilling to pay the costs of continued resistance" (Pape 1992, 431). Mack (1975, 178) sees the subordinate rival as needing certainty of victory to want to bear the costs: "The certainty of eventual victory . . . is the key to . . . the willingness to absorb costs."

9. Dominant rival actions will likely not suffice to capture all weapons and weapons production material, which for that matter are likely to be easy to conceal and transport. Knowledge of weapons production and maintenance and operations logistics is largely impervious to physical repression and may be relatively easy to transfer from one individual to another.

10. Any de-escalatory effects of a rising feeling that violence is inefficacious can be muted by two forces. Subordinate nation proponents of violence will feel a need to save face in order to both maintain their reputation for resolve vis-à-vis

the dominant nation and protect them from having to admit failure domestically. Leaders and activists may thus find it difficult to stop violence in the absence of solid face-saving opportunities, even if they deem violence ineffective for achieving national goals. The second additional connection between inefficacy and continued violence is captured by what Robert Merton (1968, 193–194, 203–207, 238–241) calls "ritualism." "Ritualism" corresponds to accepting the institutionalized means while rejecting the established goals. Here, the member of the subordinate nation pursues violence as an end in itself, out of indignation, similarly to preserve self-esteem (Merton, 1968, 203), perhaps in fact out of habit, and/or out of a need to achieve security in relations with others within the nation (see Merton, 1968, 204, 239, 240). This last motive is closely related to "two-level game" thinking. By this view, resistance and intransigence on pre-June 1967 borders have the status of norms or duties. To deviate from them may bring disapproval, charges of inadequate resolve, and sanction (see Merton, 1968, 192, 193).

11. The separation of fear and hatred, and for that matter Machiavelli's "love" and "respect," may be more relevant in such conflicts as the U.S.-led wars in Iraq and Afghanistan than in asymmetric protracted conflict.

12. One might hold that Israelis who view the Palestinians as wanting to destroy Israel in the distant future will deem any increase in Palestinian negative affect resulting from Israeli repression to be marginal. Of course, this view encourages opposition to making substantial concessions on essential stakes such as territory, repatriation of Palestinian refugees, and so forth. Yet, a Palestinian may intend for the destruction of Israel at some point in the future in the wake of a dramatic shift in the balance of power yet oppose violence prior to such a shift. Indeed, a Palestinian may support a negotiated land-for-peace settlement in the short-term as a means to making a heady geopolitical challenge to the integrity of Israel in the future. Thus, the existence of Palestinians who support the future destruction of Israel does not in itself necessarily make any increases in will to attack Israel in the short-term marginal.

13. It is conceivable that certain dominant rival counterterrorism/insurgency actions will garner the subordinate rival added foreign sympathy, itself a basic dimension of power, political power rather than violence capability, and a contributor to subordinate rival feelings of efficacy. Yet, subordinate rival violence can just as well reduce its sympathy abroad.

14. Mack (1975) writes on domestic French opposition to the French-Algerian war. "It was not so much the inhumanity of the war per se that generated opposition in France; ... The major cause of opposition lay not in the enormous costs of the war to the *Algerians* (though this was a factor), but in the costs of the war to the French themselves" (Mack 1975, 180). Mack (1975, 180) does however write, "the barbarous methods used by [French General] Massu to achieve that victory, including the widespread use of torture, were instrumental in catalyzing opposition to the war in metropolitan France." Geographical distance and size of the subordinate population is a variable that can influence the costs of counterinsurgency. "Mao and Giap ... the principal contradiction which the imperialist army must confront on the ground derives from the fact that forces dispersed to control territory become spread so thinly that they are vulnerable to

attack.... For the external power to overcome this contradiction requires a massive increase in metropolitan forces; but this immediately increases the domestic costs of the war.... Any attempt to resolve one contradiction will magnify the other" (Mack, 1975, 187).

15. Pape expresses the same idea with respect to the Vietnam war: "given Hanoi's resolve, the threat of limited conventional bombing of industrial targets did not pose the risk of sufficiently brutal civilian hardship to overwhelm Hanoi's territorial interests" (1992, 440) adds an interesting empirical observation, "In fact, risk strategies [modest levels of civilian punishment] are hardly ever used except when assailants are subject to political constraints which prevent them from waging full-blown punishment campaigns."

16. I am indebted to Wendy Pearlman for emphasizing the importance of Palestinian fragmentation in Palestinian-Israeli relations, and in so doing inspiring me to devote the thought and attention to this general variable that have led to the hypotheses involving disintegration described in this section of the study.

17. Certainly, whether inter-elite/activist disintegration contributes to a radicalization of strategy depends on the distribution of popular strategic preferences.

18. Also, people may embrace Islam as a means of rationalizing feelings of inefficacy. Religion can help rationalize retreatism, meaning the rejection of both the society's established goals and established means without seeking to effect any change in the society's goals and norms (Merton, 1968, 193–194, 207–209, 241–244; see also Lewin, 1997 [1948], 91), à la "present difficulties are God's will; God knows what is best" (see Merton, 1968, 201–203; Deutsch, 1973, 147).

19. Wendy Pearlman has emphasized a closely related relationship in emphasizing the deleterious impact of Palestinian fragmentation on intra- and interfactional and PA-factional *coordination.*

20. Of course, believing that force is making the dominant nation more willing to make concessions on essential stakes can increase subordinate rival belief that force is working.

21. Whether a breakdown in the security apparatus of the subordinate nation contributes to peace and the value lost to the dominant rival by destroying it, largely depend on the willingness of the security apparatus to prevent violent attacks. As Rashid Khalidi (2002, 6), puts it, "after actively, often savagely, repressing such attacks from 1996 through 2000, the PA's security organs ceased to have the legitimacy and the political ability to do so [to not crack down on Palestinian violence], even before their capabilities were systematically dismantled by Israeli attacks on police stations, barracks, prisons and security headquarters beginning in February 2001" (Khalidi 2002, 6). Quite in contrast, Coser (1956, 129–133) suggests as a general rule that, if our co-existence in some form or another with the rival is inevitable, then it is best for us that the rival be organized.

22. Lewin (1997 [1948], 91) adds: "the very weight which the distant goal has for the individual who takes it seriously, the very fact that he is dissatisfied with the present situation, make it difficult for him to give sufficient consideration to the actual structure of the present situation, or to conceive realistically what step in the present world can be taken to achieve this end."

23. For many Palestinians the shift to a preference for liberating all of Palestine seems to have happened early in the intifada, perhaps quite automati-

cally with the start of the intifada, and thus before feelings of inefficacy set in among Palestinians.

24. We should be careful to distinguish this latter scenario from retreatism.

25. Assuming that people tend to readjust to gains more quickly than to losses, the dominant nation will come to view its extended restriction on the movement of its rival's members and goods as the status quo and this policy may in fact recede from the consciousness of the dominant nation. The subordinate nation will continue to view its restricted movement as an unacceptable deviation from the preceding status quo. On this backdrop, discrete acts of overt hostility conducted by the subordinate rival are likely to appear more escalatory to the dominant rival than to the subordinate rival. The subordinate rival may indeed worry that its refraining from acts of violence would do more harm to its reputation for resolve than good to its image as non-hawkish.

26. One might deem it responsible, all other things equal, to discount the value of positive outcomes we expect will result from our actions in the distant future relative to the value of negative outcomes we expect will result from our actions in the near future, on the premise that outcome estimates are less reliable the further in the distant future the outcome has to wait if it is to materialize.

27. Clearly, any dominant nation act of repression that does not meaningfully reduce subordinate rival capabilities and/or increase subordinate rival fear and/or reduce its resolve aggravates dominant rival security. This point might seem unremarkable, if not for the distinct possibility that the dominant nation may sometimes simply be intent on humiliating the subordinate rival. Israel restricting Yasser Arafat to his Ramallah headquarters, and destroying all of the buildings surrounding the one in which Arafat was located, all done in the name of "isolating" Arafat internationally, might be an example of such irrationality. Note that a much simpler model than the one in this study suffices to demonstrate this point.

28. A policy of killing militants may also reduce the will of relevant third parties to engage in cooperative relations with the dominant rival. It might well be the very factor that sways third parties otherwise sympathetic to the dominant nation's security crisis to an intransigent stand toward the dominant nation. The added international condemnation could only reduce the leverage of the dominant rival.

29. It is conceivable that the subordinate rival even comes to see the essential-stake status quo ante-rebellion as a gain.

30. Pape (1992) poses the interesting dichotomy between punishing the target's civilian population and "denial," convincing it that "it is militarily impossible for him to achieve or maintain his objectives," namely control over territory (1992, 424). He argues that the latter strategy is generally more effective than the former in getting the target to stop fighting. He emphasizes that the coercing state does not have the opportunity, primarily the physical ability, to inflict sufficient suffering on the rival civilian population and that the state or government of its rival is willing to bear heavy civilian costs. The reasoning behind his argument mostly presumes conventional inter-state fights (see Pape, 1992, 425, 438–440, 464, but also 428–429). At times, in discussing denial, Pape does not even argue that damage to military forces reduces ability to control territory, but rather that

damage to military forces conditions the balance of military capabilities (Pape, 1992, 442, also 473, fn. 100). At times, in discussing "denial," he focuses simply on the conventional military defeat of the rival (Pape, 1992, 426, 443, 464, 465). Pape recognizes that it can be difficult to defeat a guerrilla movement with conventional military force. Yet, his focus on denial as preventing the ability of the subordinate rival to militarily directly acquire or hold territory misses that guerrillas can be denied statehood, a certain city as capital, and indeed occupying power withdrawal from disputed territory. In other words, Pape's thinking gives little attention to the idea that the target of the compellence can suffer *costs* on essential stakes of the conflict as the war unfolds. Of course, additionally, in asymmetric protracted conflict, denial is at least as much a political party/state bureaucracy affair as it is a military one. Thus, Pape's claim that "Denial is more likely to succeed against conventional than guerrilla strategies. . . . Guerrillas should be largely immune to coercion" (Pape, 1992, 443) is not relevant to denying gains on essential stakes in cases of asymmetric protracted conflict.

References

Arreguín-Toft, I. (2001). How the weak win wars: A theory of asymmetric conflict. *International Security* 25 (1), 93–128.
Azar, E. E. (1985). Protracted international conflicts: Ten propositions. *International Interactions* 12 (1), 59–70.
Azar, E. E. (1990). *The management of protracted social conflict: Theory and cases*. Hampshire, England and Brookfield, VT: Dartmouth.
Barghouti, M. (2002). Interview, August 11, 2002. *Al-Majallah*. London.
Brown, M. E. (2001). The causes of internal conflict: An overview. In M. E. Brown, O. R. Cot Jr., S. M. Lynn-Jones & S. E. Miller (Eds.), *Nationalism and ethnic conflict* (Rev. ed.). Cambridge, MA: MIT Press.
Brynen, R. (1994). The Palestinians and confidence building measures in the Arab-Israeli conflict: The implications of statelessness. In G. Ben-Dor & D. B. Dewitt (Eds.), *Confidence building measures in the Middle East* (pp. 33–70). Boulder: Westview Press.
Coser, L. (1956). *The functions of social conflict*. New York and London: Free Press.
Deutsch, M. (1973). *The resolution of conflict: Constructive and destructive processes*. New Haven and London: Yale University Press.
Jad, I. (2002, April 29). A road littered with disappointment. *Bitter Lemons* 15.
Jarbawi, A. (2001, October). Critical reflections on one year of the intifada. *Between the Lines*. www.between-lines.org/archives/2001/oct/Dr_Ali_Jarbawi.html
Jervis, R. (1976). *Perception and misperception in international politics*. Princeton, NJ: Princeton University Press.
Kaplan, R. D. (1991, June). History's cauldron. *Atlantic Monthly*, 93–104.
Kaplan, R. D. (1993, April 18). A reader's guide to the Balkans. *New York Times Book Review* 1, 30–32.
Kaufmann, C. (1996). Possible and impossible solutions to ethnic civil wars. *International Security* 20 (4), 136–175.

Kecskmeti, P. (1958). *Strategic surrender: The politics of victory and defeat*. Santa Monica, CA: Rand.
Khalidi, R. (2002). Toward a clear Palestinian strategy. *Journal of Palestine Studies* 32 (4).
Lake, D. A., & Rothchild, D. (2001). Containing fear: The origins and management of ethnic conflict. In M. E. Brown, O. R. Cot Jr., S. M. Lynn-Jones & S. E. Miller (Eds.), *Nationalism and ethnic conflict* (Rev. ed.). Cambridge, MA: MIT Press.
Lewin, K. (1997 [1948]). *Resolving social conflicts*. New York: Harper Bros.
Lichbach, M. I. (1987). Deterrence or escalation? The puzzle of aggregate studies of repression and dissent. *Journal of Conflict Resolution* 31 (June), 266–297.
Lichbach, M. I. (1995). *The rebel's dilemma*. Ann Arbor: University of Michigan Press.
Machiavelli, N. (1985 [1513]). *The prince*. (H. C. Mansfield Jr., Trans.). Chicago and London: University of Chicago Press.
Machiavelli, N. (1997 [1513]). *The prince*. (A. M. Codevilla, Ed. and Trans.). New Haven, CT: Yale University Press.
Machiavelli, N. (1996 [1517]). *Discourses on Livy*. H. Mansfield Jr. & N. Tarcov, Trans.). Chicago: University of Chicago Press.
Mack, A. (1975). Why big powers lose small wars: The politics of asymmetric conflict. *World Politics* 27 (2), 175–188.
Maslow, A. (1943). A theory of human motivation. *Psychological Review* 50 (4), 370–396.
Merton, R. (1968). *Social theory and social structure*. New York: Free Press.
Morgenthau, H. J. (1950). *Politics among nations: The struggle for power and peace*. New York: Knopf.
Pape, R. (1992). Coercion and military strategy: Why denial works and punishment doesn't. *Journal of Strategic Studies* 15 (December).
Posen, B. R. (1993). The security dilemma and ethnic conflict. *Survival* 35 (2), 27–47.
Rosen, S. J. (1972). War, power, and willingness to suffer. In B. Russett (Ed.), *Peace, war, and numbers*. Beverly Hills: Sage.
Schelling, T. (1966). *Arms and influence*. New Haven, CT: Yale University Press.
Snyder, G. H. & Diesing, P. (1978). *Conflict among nations: bargaining, decision making and system structure in international crises*. Princeton, NJ: Princeton University Press.
Snyder, J. (1993). Nationalism and the crisis of the post-Soviet state. *Survival* 35 (1), 5–26.
Snyder, J., & Jervis, R. (1999). Civil war and the security dilemma. In B. F. Walter & J. Snyder (Eds.), *Civil wars, insecurity, and intervention*. New York: Columbia University Press.
Van Evera, S. (1994). Hypotheses on nationalism and war. *International Security* 18 (4), 5–39; reprinted in M. E. Brown, O. R. Cot Jr., S. M. Lynn-Jones & S. E. Miller (Eds.), *Nationalism and ethnic conflict* (Rev. ed.). Cambridge, MA: MIT Press.

Walter, B. F. (1999). Designing transitions from civil war. In B. F. Walter & J. Snyder (Eds.), *Civil wars, insecurity, and intervention.* New York: Columbia University Press.

Zartman, I. W. (1989). *Ripe for resolution: Conflict and intervention in Africa.* New York: Oxford University Press.

Chapter 10

Getting It Right

Understanding Effective Counterterrorism Strategies

William Josiger

Introduction

The terrorist attacks of September 11, 2001, will leave a deep scar on the United States for generations to come. Unfortunately, this devastation encourages scholars and policy makers to narrowly focus their attention on these events and ignore the long and even more devastating history of terrorism. Terrorism is not a new problem; terrorists have challenged legitimate governments and threatened civilian populations for centuries.

Over the past three decades, democratic governments accumulated sufficient experience responding to terrorism, and scholars can assess the effectiveness of their policies and the impact these policies had on the fabric of democracy (Wardlaw, 1994). This chapter addresses the question of whether we can draw some general conclusions about effective counterterrorism policies by examining these other governments' experiences, in particular those of Spain, the United Kingdom, and France.

In the 1970s and 1980s, terrorist groups across Western Europe intensified their attacks to the point that at least one author commented, "democracy itself might not survive" (Charters, 1994, 1). By the mid-1990s, however, governments had gained the upper hand. These reversals were not merely the result of the end of the Cold War's ideological struggle; rather, they reflected the effective enactment of counter-terrorism policies at the national, regional, and international levels. The governments of Spain, the UK, and France may not have declared war on terrorism as boldly as President Bush did in the wake of September 11, but they fought back successfully nonetheless. In fact, there may be some lessons from these cases that are applicable to the U.S. in its current global war against terrorism. Creating an effective counterterrorism strategy need not be akin to reinventing the wheel; by taking a "look ... at what has worked and what has not in the real world," I hope to highlight some successes, so they can be repeated, and failures, so they can be avoided (Alexander, 2002).

I organize this chapter into four parts. Part one provides a brief definition of terrorism along with five of its most commonly identified types: right-wing, left-wing, nationalist/separatist, religious, and single issue. Part two addresses three objections that critics might raise in opposition to this type of comparative study. Briefly, they are: you cannot compare democracies, types of terrorism, or counterterrorism policies. In part three, I compare each of the cases, focusing on the types of terrorism the government faced, the range of counterterrorist measures employed, and the effectiveness of these policies (Charters, 1994, 3). The fourth section concludes with some broad comparisons and general lessons.

Definition of Terrorism

There are several reasons why terrorism is difficult to define (Cronin, 2002). First, labeling an action as terrorism or a group as terrorist may reflect an ideological or political bias (Moxon-Browne, 1994). Second, definitions appear to vary over time; during the French Revolution terrorism had a positive connotation.[1] In fact, some terrorists and terrorist groups have since achieved legitimacy, for example, Nelson Mandela and the African National Congress in South Africa (Cronin, 1998, 121). Third, definitions vary across, and sometimes within, governments and from scholar to scholar (Schmid, 1993). These challenges aside, a proper definition of terrorism is important for both scholars and policy makers because it helps build a common terminology (Charters, 1994, 2). This, in turn, makes it easier to delineate terrorist acts from simple political violence and common criminal acts.

For the purposes of this chapter, I define terrorism as the calculated threat or use of violence designed to create an overwhelming fear in a larger target population, perpetuated by individuals, subnational groups, or state actors to attain political, social, or economic objectives (Alexander, 2002, 4). This definition contains four main points: first, there is the threat or use of violence; second, this threat or use of violence is a means to achieve some broadly defined goal; third, the target audience is larger than the immediate victims; and fourth, the intent is to create fear within this larger target audience.

This definition, while instructive, should be viewed more as a working aid or heuristic device for three reasons. First, scholars will disagree over whether a particular event or event falls within the bounds of any definition of terrorism, including the one presented here (Cronin, 2003, 281).[2] Second, the perspective of academics tend to differ from those of policy makers, and these differences will, most likely, impact what each group perceives what is and what is not terrorism.[3] Third, every government has the right to define terrorism as it deems fit; some may employ a narrow definition, others a broader one (Alexander, 2002, 3).[4]

Not all terrorism challenges governments and threatens civilian populations to the same degree, so it might be useful to create a typology to compare different types of terrorism.[5] One approach is to distinguish between domestic—confined within the borders of one country—and international—involving the citizens of more than one country—terrorism (Wilkinson, 2000, 19). In reality, while common, this distinction is not particularly useful; in fact, it is difficult to find examples of purely domestic terrorist groups.[6] In a globalizing world, the distinction between domestic and international is blurred; even so-called domestic terrorist groups tend to seek financial assistance, weapons, training, and safe havens in other countries, and some even carry out attacks against their home countries' interests abroad (Wilkinson, 2000, 19).

A more manageable typology categorizes groups together according to their primary motivations (see, for example, Chalk, 1996, 23; Wilkinson, 2000, especially chapter 2, 19–40). Different motivations tend to lead to different styles and structures, therefore, understanding the type of terrorism can provide insight into group dynamics and the likeliest form of violence (Cronin, 2003, 285). Scholars generally identify four main categories of terrorism: left-wing, right-wing, nationalist/separatist, and religious, while a fifth, single-issue terrorism, is less commonly referenced. As with any typology, there are some limits with these classifications; in particular, these categories are not always mutually exclusive (Cronin, 2003, 285). For example, nationalist groups tend to have left-wing ideologies and religious groups often combine political or nationalist and religious motivations (Cronin, 2002, 122). In these cases of overlap, scholars must carefully analyze the group and categorize it based on its primary motivation.

Left-Wing Terrorism

Typically, these organizations form as a result of dissatisfaction with the ruling political structure and pursue revolutionary or anti-authoritarian agendas (Cronin, 2003, 285). These groups are ideologically motivated, advocate utopian objectives, and view themselves at the forefront of a worldwide struggle, but generally have difficulties defining clear, long-term visions. Studies suggest members are generally well educated. Examples include the Italian Red Brigades, the RAF, Japanese Red Army, GRAPO (Spanish October 1st Antifascist Group), and Action Direct. Of the five categories, left-wing terrorists were the most caught up in the ideological struggle of the Cold War and the most likely to suffer setbacks after the collapse of the Soviet Union.

Right-Wing Terrorism

These groups generally claim to defend the status quo, form in reaction to left-wing terrorism, receive support from parts of the society that feel their privileged status at risk, and are not as cohesive as their left-wing counterparts.[7] In the United States, the most recognizable right-wing terrorist group is the Ku Klux Klan, while European examples include the French Federation d'action Nationale Européenne, the German Alternative, and the Italian Armed Revolutionary Nuclei.

Nationalist/Separatist Terrorism

These groups claim to represent the perceived victims—ethnically, territorially, or nationally defined—of some form of government imposed injustice. The groups' goals of national self-determination or increased regional autonomy tend to resonate with the local population and nearly all receive some form of active or passive support from regions beyond their own home areas, particularly from émigrés living abroad. This support base is most likely the key to the greater average longevity of these groups; however, it also poses restrictions on attack and targeting strategies (Wilkinson, 2000, 19). Finally, nationalist/separatist groups employ a wider range of political strategies than other terrorist groups. Examples include the PIRA, ETA, and the PFLP-GC.

Religious Terrorism

These groups adhere to religious dogma and see their missions in terms of a battle between good and evil, and their members are highly dedicated with many willing to sacrifice themselves. Religious terrorists are also motivated by political concerns, and it is often difficult to distinguish the two (Ranstop, 2003, 122). For example, several Middle Eastern groups combine political and nationalist motivations tied to the Palestinian-Israeli conflict with fundamentalist religious justifications. Islamic groups, however, do not hold a monopoly on religious terrorism; in fact, there are militant fundamentalist groups in almost every major religion. Sikhs, Hindus, Jews, and Christians have all resorted to terrorism (Wilkinson, 2000, 20).

Single-Issue Terrorism

Single-issue terrorists are not trying to make the system more egalitarian, as are left-wing terrorists, or carve out a homeland for themselves, as are national/separatist terrorist, or usher in a new age through violence, as are religious terrorists. Rather, they want to change a specific policy or practice within the targeted society (Wilkinson, 2000, 20). There is no typical single-issue terrorist; they come from all walks of life and social levels. Animal rights, the environment, and abortion are just three of the issues that motivate single-issue terrorists (Davidson Smith, 2003, 264). Examples include the Animal Rights Militia, the Earth Liberation Front, Earth First!, and various anti-abortion groups.

Some Objections

In this section, I address some objections that opponents might raise. Briefly, these objections are: we cannot compare different governments, different types of terrorism, nor governments' responses to terrorism. These objections, although incorrect, still require some attention. The first objection is the easiest to dismiss. We can, in fact, compare governments. Comparative analysis will always be problematic; as one scholar puts it, "any attempt to compare the political, legislative, legal, police, and other policies and practices of ... countries raises a number of methodological issues" (Charters, 1994, 2). That said, the entire discipline of comparative politics revolves around doing just this, and over the years, comparativists have overcome many methodological barriers. The fact that this study is concerned with one particular type of government, democracy, makes this comparison easier. Democratic governments have a number of features in common: multiparty political cultures, elected legislatures, responsible government, rule of law, institutionalized structures, procedures for law enforcement, and a heritage of fundamental democratic principles and civil rights, such as freedom of speech and the freedom of the press (Charters, 1994, 2). Comparative analysis is not just about similarity, it also involves noting differences to better understand how each government functions and responds to challenges in its own ways (Charters, 1994, 2). In other words, the "uniqueness" of each case can also provide insight.

The second objection poses a greater obstacle to this study. At its core, it questions our ability to compare different types of terrorism. By focusing too much attention on what makes each terrorist group or each terrorism subtype different, critics who raise this objection ignore what these groups and subtypes have in common. Although terrorist groups may have different motivations, at its heart, terrorism is still about using violence to create fear.[8]

The third, and final, objection is the most important, but like the others it does not hold up under careful examination. One of the challenges democracies face in responding to terrorism is creating the right balance between security and the protection of civil liberties and democratic practices. Clearly, the differences between governments ensure that results will vary, but the types of countermeasures democracies take against terrorism, even if somewhat different, are still similar enough to permit comparison (Charters, 1994, 3).

Regardless of the country, the aftermath of a terrorist attack still involves consequence management, clean-up, rebuilding, and investigation of a criminal or intelligence nature. Even some American policy makers and elected officials before September 11, 2001, acknowledged the possibility of learning from other countries' counterterrorism efforts. For example, several members of the Senate and the House of Representatives, recognizing that other countries had more experience dealing with terrorism within their borders, requested that the General Accounting Office "provide information on (1) how other governments are organized to combat terrorism and (2) how they allocate their resources to combat terrorism" (Government Accounting Office, 2000, 3).

In this chapter, I define a successful counterterrorism policy as one that balances security with the protection of democratic principles and civil liberties (Charters, 1994, 1–2). A central problem for all democratic government lies in understanding the nature and extent of a terrorist threat and in responding to that threat with rational, appropriate, and consistent countermeasures without undermining or altering democratic practices and traditions (Wardlaw, 1994, 5). Creating effective counterterrorism policies is a difficult process; the real key is to balance the threat and response in such a way as to avoid fundamental changes to democratic forms (Wardlaw, 1994, 7). In order to do this, the government must make every effort to avoid overreacting in the immediate aftermath of a terrorist attack.

Governments can enact counterterrorism policies on three interrelated levels: domestic, regional through organizations like the EU and EUROPOL, and international through the UN and INTERPOL. At the domestic level, there is a broad spectrum of possible responses. One way to organize these measures is to label them moving from severe—those designed to suppress or eliminate terrorism, typically labeled punitive or hard-line—to the more accommodative measures—designed to understand the terrorist demands, usually labeled therapeutic (Moxon-Browne, 1994, xv).[9] The hard-line approach requires the combination of harsh and effective temporary measures designed to isolate and eliminate terrorists and their logistical support structures (Wilkinson, 2000, 15). The key is to maximize the risk of punishment while minimizing the potential reward of terrorism (Wilkinson, 2000, 15).

Putative counterterrorism strategies fall into two categories: the criminal justice model, and the war model (Chalk, 1996, 97). The typical state response is the criminal justice model, which means that the primary responsibility for counterterrorism belongs to the police and the judiciary. The war model, on the other hand, places primary responsibility in the hands of the military forces.[10] Scholars identify several putative measures. Governments can deploy military forces to provide support to law enforcement officials—for example, British troops deployed in Northern Ireland and Spanish sailors and soldiers in the Basque region, or create special, highly trained, counterterrorism teams. However, both these measures have the potential to undermine the government's legitimacy if the public perceives they are too violent. Next, the government can grant special powers to law enforcement officials for a limited time to stop, question, detain, and arrest suspected terrorists. The government may tie these increased police powers to a series of judicial measures, for example, internment without trial, detention without charge, elimination of juries, suspension of the right to remain silent, or even restrictions on organizations and publications.

Continuing with the spectrum of responses, toward the accommodationist end governments can enact political, economic, and social measures or devolve political power, as the British, French, and Spanish tried. Legislation governing displays of ethnic culture or economic measures designed to stimulate employment, improve housing, education, or infrastructure, if properly implemented and under the right circumstances, could reduce the grievances that sometimes give rise to terrorism.

Cases

This section presents and analyzes several cases of terrorism, which demonstrate the thesis of this chapter in several national experiences.

The Spanish Experience

The Spanish experience with terrorism revolved mostly around the actions of the Basque separatist group ETA.[11] During the Spanish Revolution, the region fought against Franco, and after his victory, Franco suppressed the Basques' cultural identity (Das & Kratcoski, 2003, 274).[12] Young Basques dissatisfied with the efforts of the Basque Nationalist Party to gain some autonomy for the region formed ETA in 1959 (Hewitt, 1984, 18). The group did not originally advocate armed struggle, rather, it turned to terrorism in the face of Franco's continued cruelty.

ETA's first terrorist attacks came in the late 1960s and, in 1973, the group killed the Spanish Prime Minister and Franco's heir-apparent, Admiral Carrero Blanco.[13] Second only to the PIRA in terms of the scale of terrorism committed by a national/separatist group in Western Europe during the Cold War, between 1969 and 1989 ETA killed more than 600 people, fully 75 percent of all terrorist fatalities in Spain during that period (Chalk, 1996, 56, see also his tables A11 and A12). Its victims included government officials, members of the military and security forces, moderate Basques, tourists, and bystanders. In fact, a third of ETA's victims during the 1970s and 1980s were civilians—bystanders caught in attacks against government or security forces, or deliberately targeted during indiscriminate bombing campaigns.

Spain under Franco was not a democracy; therefore, I limit my analysis to counterterrorism policies enacted after his death. The 1978 constitution established a new Spanish democracy grounded in the rule of law, and, in August 1979, this new government adopted the statute of autonomy for the Basque region. Although the Spanish transition to democracy—and the associated removal of many of Franco's anti-Basque policies—represented one of the most important political achievements in Europe during the 1970s, ETA continued its terrorist campaign and actually intensified its attacks. Despite the move toward more moderate counterterrorism measures during 1977 and early 1978, the Spanish government enacted steadily more repressive and coercive policies through the end of the 1970s; interestingly, this trend held for both conservative and socialist governments (Clark, 1990, 37).[14] The most important Spanish counterterrorism measures included police and judicial actions, negotiation, a program of integration for the members of ETA who renounced violence, dispersion of prisoners, and international cooperation (Remiro Brotons & Esposito, 2002, 170). Although some specific policies, dispersion of prisoners, for example, harmed the cohesion of ETA, overall the Spanish case is not a success story (Remiro Brotons & Esposito, 2002, 170).

LEGISLATION IN THE SPANISH CASE

In the immediate aftermath of Franco's death, the fledgling Spanish democracy made considerable progress toward reversing many of Franco's repressive policies, partly in the mistaken belief that these changes would bring an end to ETA terrorism. Between November 1975 and March 1976, the Spanish government issued three amnesty decrees designed to clear Basque prisoners accused of politically related crimes against the state.[15] In October 1977, the legislature approved a general amnesty for political prisoners, and by early 1978, there were an estimated 5 to 10 Basques in prison for politically motivated crimes (Clark, 1990, 38).[16] In early 1978, parliament abrogated Franco's terrorism prevention law and disbanded the special courts, established under Franco, to try terrorists. By early 1978, ETA was still an illegal organization, but Spain had no permanent counterterrorism legislation. Accused terrorists were treated like common criminals, tried in the same courts, under the same rules, and detained with ordinary criminals.

In February 1978, the Spanish government found itself at a crucial turning point: ETA violence continued despite Franco's death, the transition to democracy, or the radical changes in the government's position toward the Basques. Public pressure mounted on the government to implement new counterterrorist policies and meet the continued ETA threat. On June 28, 1978, journalist Jose Maria Portell was killed outside his house in Bilbao, most likely by ETA members. In the aftermath of the attack, the government enacted three new counterterrorism laws, all without the approval of the full parliament. The first, Law 21/1978, gave police, with court approval, the ability to hold an individual without charges for more than 72 hours, intercept mail, and tap phone lines (Jimenez, 1993, 117). The law also restricted judges' ability to grant amnesties and pardons for certain types of terrorism-related crimes and release suspects on bond before trial. The second law, known as the Special Measures toward Crimes of Terrorism Committed by Armed Groups (Law 56/1978), took effect in December 1978 and authorized police to hold suspects incommunicado for up to 10 days. In January 1979, King Juan Carlos issued the third law in the form of a decree. It increased the penalties for terrorism-related crimes, transferred control of maximum security prisons to the national police force, further restricted the rights of convicted terrorists to seek provisional release from prison, and criminalized apologia of terrorism—printing or saying anything that could be construed as defending or supporting terrorism.

Together, these three laws gave authorities wide-ranging powers to arrest and try ETA members. However, critics viewed the laws with suspicion and labeled them unconstitutional because the government enacted them under emergency provisions without the approval of the full parliament. To alleviate these concerns, parliament passed Organic Law 11/1980, the Organic Law on Citizen Security, on October 29, 1980. It effectively replaced and codified the provisions of the preceding laws and remained the basic Spanish counterterrorism law for almost four years (Clark, 1990, 42).

In the early months of 1981, a series of violent ETA attacks and a failed coup attempt rocked the Spanish state to its core and, once again, the immediate government response involved beefing up counterterrorism legislation. In May 1981, the government broadened its definition of terrorism to include the embrace of any attack against the integrity of the Spanish nation or any effort to secure the independence of a part of its territory, even if undertaken through nonviolence (Clark, 1990, 47). This definition was so broad that it allowed the government to label almost any expression of separatism as an act of terrorism. The law also widened the range of available options to deal with media apologia of terrorism. Officials could now close or physically occupy the offices of print or broadcast media outlets accused of apologia.

Starting in October 1982 with the parliamentary victory of the Spanish Socialist Workers Party, counterterrorism policy grew more coercive. Partially in response to right-wing opponents who claimed the socialists were too soft on terrorism, the new government strengthened Spain's criminal and criminal procedure codes (Clark, 1990, 52). In December 1984, parliament passed Organic Law 8/1984, which reaffirmed most of the police powers found in earlier laws and, more importantly, went beyond existing legislation in several areas: it increased penalties for crimes related to terrorism and created a new category of crimes for attacks against members of the armed forces. The new law also authorized judges to punish individuals charged with apologia of terrorism with the same penalties imposed against actual terrorists, ban political parties and other groups led by convicted terrorists, close down print media organizations that supported terrorist aims, and detain, without trial, suspected terrorists for up to two and a half years. In 1987, several sections of Organic Law 8/1984 lapsed automatically, and in the face of continuous public pressure, the Socialist government announced its desire to repeal the entire law (Jimenez, 1993, 117). Around the same time, the government reduced the amount of time an individual could be held incommunicado from ten to five days and, henceforth, authorities would not charge apologists with a crime, provided they were not involved in any actual terrorist attacks (Remiro Brotons & Esposito, 2002, 171). In May 1988, parliament passed two laws reforming the criminal and criminal procedure codes and, for the first time in almost a decade, Spain did not have any special counterterrorism legislation.

POLICE

If the criminal justice system was the Spanish authorities' primary weapon in the fight against terrorism, then arrests and detentions formed the backbone of this approach. In 1978, when the new government limited military jurisdiction, the national police forces were not ready to assume their new counterterrorism roles (Remiro Brotons & Esposito, 2002, 171). At the time, before the Basque autonomous government existed, national law enforcement agencies, most notably the national police and the paramilitary Guardia Civil (GC), performed the police functions within the Basque region. In September 1978, the Minister of the Interior, Martin Villa, began what would be the first of several reorganizations of Spanish law enforcement in an attempt to address these deficiencies. Villa created a new counterterrorist police unit in Bilbao and Spain's first national counterterrorist police units the Special Operations Group (GEO) and the Rural Antiterrorist Groups (GAR).

A second round of reforms came after a series of terrorist attacks in March 1981. In response, the government sent police and GC reinforcements to the Basque region, deployed regular military units to patrol the French border and the Bay of Biscay, and established a unified command within the Ministry of Interior to coordinate all counterterrorism efforts. The most important change to the Spanish law enforcement structure came in October 1982 when the Basque autonomous police force, the Ertzainza, took over responsibility for police duties within the region. Although the creation of the Ertzaina addressed a key ETA goal, this new police force introduced considerable ambiguity into the evolving Spanish law enforcement structure (Remiro Brotons & Esposito, 2002, 171). In October 1983, the government created a new agency, the Police Intelligence Council, to study police issues, propose counterterrorism measures, and better coordinate with the Minister of Interior.

Negotiation in the Spanish Case

It is a dangerous and difficult process for a democratic government to negotiate with terrorist groups. First, the process lacks the transparency that is a foundation for democracy (Remiro Brotons & Esposito, 2002, 170). Second, negotiations give terrorists a platform to broadcast their ideology, or worse, could give them political credibility. Third, terrorist goals tend to be unclear and shift over time, which could drag negotiations out. Clark, however, maintains that negotiations have some benefits: for example, they can bring a temporary lull in the fighting, reduce the level of emotion and anger, help foster mutual trust and confidence among the different sides, and, in some cases, they may be the only way to stop the violence (Clark, 1990, 2). Between 1975 and 1988, there were 20 to 30 serious attempts to negotiate between the Spanish governments and ETA and its ETA-related groups (Clark, 1990, 3). Although there is no evidence to suggest that any of these negotiations ended successfully, and despite the Spanish governments' public insistence that it only dealt with ETA through the criminal justice system, the number of attempts indicates that negotiation, at the very least, played some role in the Spanish government's overall counterterrorism strategy.[17]

Reintegration in the Spanish Case

Successive Spanish governments tried to undermine ETA's strength by offering pardons, amnesties, and reintegration into society to terrorists if they cooperated and collaborated with the authorities. In September 1983, the government put into effect the so-called "Plan ZEN" (ZonaEspecial del Norte or Special Northern Zone). Although the plan was a political nonstarter, it did try to copy the Italian model of offering reintegration to convicted or exiled terrorists if they would agree to collaborate with the government (Clark, 1990, 57). Governments need to be extremely cautious when implementing reintegration policies because they can substantially lower the cost of participation in terrorist activity.

Dispersion of Prisoners in the Spanish Case

Starting in the spring of 1983, the government transferred ETA prisoners to a handful of maximum-security facilities, all under the control of a special unit of the GC (Clark, 1990, 55). Not surprisingly, consolidating prisoners in a few locations—by 1988, the majority were concentrated in three prisons—encouraged the creation of a parallel jailhouse ETA structure (Remiro Brotons & Esposito, 2002, 173). That year, hoping to undermine this cohesion, the government reversed course and dispersed the prisoners around the country. The dispersion policy did undermine ETA cohesion within the prisons, but, at the same time, it fostered a sense of resentment among families that now had to travel long distances to see incarcerated relatives (Remiro Brotons & Esposito, 2002, 173).

International Cooperation in the Spanish Case

An important part of Spain's response to terrorism took place at the international level. In particular, because the historic Basque homeland straddles the Spanish border with France, cooperation with the French was critical. For almost a decade after Franco's death, the French still thought of ETA as an internal Spanish problem (Clark, 1990, 36). The French sanctuary policy—the French government would give terrorists refuge so long as they did not attack French interests—spurred Spanish condemnation and, in one of the low points of the Spanish experience, prompted the creation of several right-wing clandestine groups that brought the fight to ETA terrorists in France. The most notable of these groups, the GAL (Grupos Antiterroristas de Liberacion), operated, with at least tacit Spanish government approval between 1983 and 1986 and reportedly killed 27 people, most of them Basques living in France (Remiro Brotons & Esposito, 2002, 177).

While Paris was at first reluctant to help Spanish authorities, as it became clear that the Spanish transition to democracy was, in fact, permanent, French claims that ETA terrorists were legitimate freedom fighters against a repressive regime were increasingly difficult to sustain. Starting in 1976, successive French governments put pressure on Basques living in France and in June 1978, French president Valery Giscard d'Estaing announced that his government would no longer consider Basques political refugees (Clark, 1990, 46). By 1983, France and Spain established a permanent system of informal consultations and held a ministerial seminar every six months to discuss issues related to terrorism (Remiro Brotons & Esposito, 2002, 180). In 1984, Spain's long-standing desire for extradition of ETA terrorists from France finally materialized, despite the ongoing campaign of violence by Spanish right-wing antiterrorist groups within France. It is interesting that one of the biggest breakthroughs in the Spanish fight against ETA came about in Paris. Within two years, the tougher French policies on deportations and extraditions had significantly weakened ETA's infrastructure in France and brought about a decline in terrorist activity on the Spanish side of the border. During the late 1980s and early 1990s, together, the police forces of the now cooperating states dealt ETA several stunning blows. In 1986, French authorities shut down an ETA finance center hidden in a furniture store and, in March 1992, arrested several ETA leaders.

Conclusions for the Spanish Case

How successful were the Spanish with dealing with the ETA? Although ETA attacks diminished considerably by the early 1990s, it can be argued that, from a general perspective, Spanish counterterrorism efforts were not successful (Remiro Brotons & Esposito, 2002, 184). In its bid to fight ETA, the Spanish government enacted policies that infringed on the country's nascent democratic foundation. Its broad definition of terrorism allowed the government to try any citizen who expressed support of separatism and provisions of Organic law 8/1984 had a chilling effect on the Spanish public. The violence attributed to the right-wing reactionary groups and the evidence connecting these groups to the Spanish government, in particular the GAL, clearly undermined the rule of law in Spain.

The Spanish experience with terrorism also highlights several important lessons. The first is that a democratic transition may not be sufficient to change the demands of a terrorist group: the Spanish transition to democracy was accompanied by an increase in terrorist violence by ETA. Second, the government and police forces must always respect the rule of law, and governments cannot tolerate violent reactionary groups. Third, government restrictions on the media are at odds with the foundations of democracy and the free exchange of ideas. Fourth, international cooperation is critical; in the Spanish case, one of the most effective policies against ETA was enacted in Paris.

The United Kingdom Experience

The United Kingdom (UK) faced several different terrorist challenges over the past 30 years. The major challenge came from the Provisional Irish Republican Army (PIRA), formed in Ulster, Northern Ireland, for the purpose of unifying Ireland. The group's activities included bombings, assassinations, kidnapping, extortion, and robberies. Catholic splinter groups and Protestant opponents of a political solution to the Northern Ireland situation also resorted to terrorism during this time. Between 1969 and 2000, the different groups involved in Irish terrorism killed nearly 3,300 people (Taylor, 2002, 201). Nor was Northern Ireland the only issue that motivated terrorist attacks within the UK; the British experience with terrorism was also connected Middle Eastern nationalist and religious groups, state-sponsored attacks, and a wave of anti-colonial terrorism.[18]

Middle Eastern religious and nationalist terrorist groups hijacked and destroyed aircrafts, kidnapped and killed British nationals abroad, and conducted bombings and assassinations within the UK. Most of the attacks by Middle Eastern groups were not directed against the UK or UK citizens, rather the targets were often foreign nationals located in the UK.[19] Foreign governments attacked opposition and dissident groups within the UK and certain ethnic groups, the Sikhs, for example, used terrorist tactics to bring attention to their problems (Bonner, 1993, 172). The UK also experienced attacks abroad, including terrorist attacks against tourists traveling outside the country, military forces deployed with NATO in Western Europe, and overseas offices of British companies (Taylor, 2002, 18; Warner, 1994, 15).

Counterterrorism policy in the UK had several key features: a firm commitment to the rule of law, an absolute refusal to surrender to terrorist demands, a desire to promote international law and cooperation, and a belief that terrorists were common criminals (Warner, 1994, 18). As in Spain, the primary British counterterrorism tool was law enforcement officials, sometimes with special units, employing the ordinary criminal law (Bonner, 1993, 172).[20] Other measures included the drafting of emergency legal powers, extra-judicial executive processes, the strengthening of domestic intelligence organizations, target hardening to reduce the damage from bomb attacks, the deployment of the military in support of police forces, and the arming of police officers (see Warner, 1994, 19–26; Taylor, 2002, 198; Bonner, 1993, 171). British counterterrorism officials also acknowledged that fighting terrorism was about more than increased security and focused on some political, economic, social, and psychological measures (Bonner, 1993, 190).

Legislation in the UK Case

In the 1970s and 1980s, Parliament enacted a series of laws to reduce terrorism in Northern Ireland and Great Britain. These measures were not always successful at stemming the tide of terrorism; in fact, some scholars argue that these laws were counterproductive (O'Connor & Rumann, 2003, 1662). Prior to July 2000, there were three principal legislative measures governing terrorism in UK: the Northern Ireland (Emergency Provisions) Acts (NIEPA) of 1973, 1978, 1987, 1991, and 1996; the Prevention of Terrorism (Temporary Provisions) Acts (PTA) of 1974, 1976, 1984, and 1989; and the Prevention of Terrorism (Supplemental Temporary Provisions) (Northern Ireland) Orders 1976 and 1984 (O'Connor & Rumann, 2003, 1665–1666). Terrorism, according to these and other British laws, was a criminal undertaking and not a political act; in fact, the government specifically rejected calls to create an offense of terrorism (Taylor, 2002, 188). Rather, the British held that terrorists commit serious, though nonetheless ordinary, crimes such as murder, kidnapping, and causing explosions. The PTA, which was subject to annual parliamentary review, contained the key counterterrorism powers applicable throughout the UK: extended powers of arrest and detention; provision for the exclusion of suspected terrorists from Great Britain; the proscription of certain organizations; and the creation of new offenses related to supporting terrorism. Parliament originally formulated the PTA's extended powers of arrest and detention to apply only to Irish terrorism but, after 1984, police could use these powers against Middle Eastern groups as well (Warner, 1994, 21).

The Northern Ireland (Emergency Provisions) Act of 1991 contained additional counterterrorism measures applicable to Northern Ireland: it reiterated that terrorists were ordinary criminals; gave police and security forces the power to stop, question, and search any person after a terrorist attack and to search individuals for weapons in public places; required that the Secretary of State license all banks and investment firms; required banks to report suspicious transactions; criminalized the possession or handling of terrorist money, and substantially lowered the threshold of criminal liability for these offenses (Bonner, 1993, 179–181). Within Northern Ireland, terrorist trials took place without a jury in so-called Diplock Courts.

British law provided for extra-judicial measures when the criminal justice approach would not work. The UK reserved the right to refuse entry to or deport foreigners suspected of terrorist ties on national security grounds under immigration laws. Moreover, immigration officials could prevent Irish citizens from entering the UK and British citizens from reentering Great Britain if they were a suspected IRA terrorist. Finally, authorities could intern terrorist suspects without trial, a process only used in Northern Ireland from 1971 to 1975 (Bonner, 1993, 184–185).

Police in the UK Case

The primary government organizations designated to respond to terrorism and terrorist acts within the UK were the country's 50 or so police forces. While centrally planned, the UK system allowed for genuine delegation of responsibility. The Home Secretary was responsible for all security and counterterrorism issues (Taylor, 2002, 190).[21] Within the Home Office, the Terrorism Protection Unit (TPU) had primary responsibility for coordinating responses. Great Britain did not have a centralized nationwide police agency; rather, responsibility for police matters fell to the independent provincial forces. This decentralized arrangement necessitated a high degree of coordination and cooperation between the different forces and also raised the problem of interforce rivalry (Bonner, 1993, 196). The daily operational deployment of counterterrorism measures fell to the chief constable of the relevant local police force, who also had primary responsibility for responding to terrorist attacks and the power to pull in resources from other jurisdiction or agencies, including the domestic Security Service (MI5) (Taylor, 2002, 190).[22] Formalized procedures existed to provide the experience and knowledge of MI5 and, in select cases, MI6, to the relevant police authorities during a crisis (Taylor, 2002, 196).

In contrast to the decentralized police system within Great Britain, in Northern Ireland there was only one police force, the Royal Ulster Constabulary (RUC). Although the British Army deployed in support of the RUC in 1969, since 1976, the policy was one of police primacy (Bonner, 1993, 197). Within Northern Ireland, the RUC had wide-ranging powers to arrest, detain, search, seize assets, and cordon off areas. The key to responding to terrorist incidents throughout the UK was a single set of standard operating procedures. Police authorities, emergency services, government ministries, and the security services all used the same set of procedures, which minimized errors and confusion and enabled rapid, coordinated responses to terrorist attacks (Taylor, 2002, 192). To ensure that authorities followed these procedures, the TPU coordinated a series of tabletop and live exercise each year (Taylor, 2002, 192).

Supergrass in the UK Case

Similar to the efforts in Spain and Italy, the British judges reduced sentences for terrorists who collaborated with the authorities. The Supergrass strategy provided for converted terrorists to testify in court against their co-conspirators or accomplices.

Economic, Social, and Psychological Measures

The British government recognized that increased security would not, on its own, solve the problem of Irish terrorism, so it enacted various policies to reduce some of the underlying grievances. Specifically, the government reformed voting procedures, increased housing allocations, and passed fair employment legislation (Bonner, 1993, 190). Unfortunately, most did not achieve their desired effect.

International Cooperation in the UK Case

The UK strategy to fight terrorism placed importance on international legislation and various international mechanisms. The UK was a regular participant in INTERPOL and the TREVI group and employed economic sanctions against states that supported terrorism (Bonner, 1993, 198).[23] In 1978, the UK signed the Bonn Summit Declaration, which resolved that in cases where a country refused to extradite or prosecute an aircraft hijacker, other governments would take immediate action to cease all commercial air traffic with that country (Bonner, 1993, 187). Finally, the UK signed multilateral treaties on extradition of terrorist suspects and a series of bilateral treaties with the U.S. that barred the application of the political offense exception in certain violent cases.

Conclusions for the UK case

The British case provides insight into the effectiveness of counterterrorism policies against different types of terrorism because, for the most part, the government used the same measures with varying results. In particular, when there is no domestic support for terrorists—for example, with the Middle Eastern nationalist and religious groups—law enforcement measures based on firm policies can be successful. However, when the terrorists do maintain a domestic constituency, as the PIRA did, firm counterterrorism measures without accompanying political, economic, or social measures will only contain the terrorist threat (Alexander, 2002, 386). The British experience also demonstrates the benefits of acting within the rule of law, dealing with terrorists in a criminal justice system, gathering intelligence, not making concessions to terrorist demands, and international cooperation (Bonner, 1993, 201; Alexander, 2002, 386).

The British experience also highlights some of the potential problems associated with a decentralized police force. First, because each provincial police force had a Special Branch responsible for terrorism, there was substantial duplication. Second, although local chief constables could call in support from other sources, not every police force had the necessary experience to properly handle an investigation, and those forces that did, such as the London Metropolitan Police, might have been viewed as rivals. Finally, it was likely that an investigation into a terrorist attack would expand beyond the jurisdiction in which the attack occurred. In these situations, despite the existence of policies and procedures, it is possible that inter-force rivalry may have caused problems. Similar to the Spanish experience, the British sometimes enacted policies that did more harm than good. The best example of this was the provisions of the PTA; even British Law Lords criticized the harsh character of the PTA and its violation of fundamental democratic liberties (Warner, 1994, 19–20). The proscription of certain organizations, for example, which included prohibition on members or supporters being heard directly on the broadcast media, was criticized as an unjustifiable restriction on the public's right to know its enemy in an otherwise free society (Bonner, 1993, 180). Some of the extra-judicial proceedings, while effective, were nonetheless contrary to democratic principles. Even the Supergrass policy, which tried to encourage terrorists to testify against their co-conspirators, eroded public confidence. In Great Britain, a jury could convict an accused terrorist based solely on the uncorroborated testimony of a Supergrass, that is, a converted accomplice, provided the judge warned the jury about the dangers of deciding guilt or innocence on a single piece of testimony. In Northern Ireland, the Diplock Courts did not have juries, so the required warning amounted to nothing more than a judge reminding himself to be careful (Bonner, 1993, 184).

The Experience of France

Over the past 20 years, French counterterrorism policy evolved substantially from the much maligned sanctuary policy of the early 1980s, and French capabilities developed to match the government's new stance against terrorism. In 1999, the French warned Canadian authorities that an Algerian was planning terrorist attacks in North America, a vast improvement from the early 1980s, when the government could not correctly identify terrorist threats within its own borders (Shapiro & Suzan, 2003, 67–68). France faced four different types of terrorism: nationalist/separatist from the Basques, Corsicans, and Palestinians; left-wing from Action Directe (AD); right-wing from groups such as the Federation d'action Nationale Européenne; and religious from Middle Eastern groups (Guillaume, 1993, 131). Active from 1979 to 1987, AD carried out attacks against French businesses and governments as well as targeted assassinations. In 1980, French authorities almost wiped the group out by arresting its leaders. However, the next year, the Mitterand government released most of these terrorists under a newly enacted amnesty law and AD quickly returned to its terrorist campaign (Harrison, 1994, 105). Starting in 1980, Middle Eastern religious and nationalist groups shifted the focus of their efforts off of government officials to the general French population, carrying out attacks against synagogues, trains, restaurants, and railway stations (Guillaume, 1993, 131). Right-wing and regional separatist terrorism were the least threatening, typically involving attacks against property (Shapiro & Suzan, 2003, 69).

France had a seemingly ambivalent, even contradictory, approach to the problem of terrorism. In the late 1970s and early 1980s, on one hand, officials vigorously suppressed groups suspected of involvement in terrorism while, on the other, some policies appeared to favor a hands-off approach (Harrison, 1994, 103). Several contradictory influences guided French counter-terrorism policy: first, officials wanted to preserve the French tradition of political asylum for foreign activists; second, the French public felt that revolutionaries could use violence to achieve their goals; third, officials wanted to minimize the political risks associated with policies toward the Middle East by remaining as neutral as possible on the issue of the Palestinian homeland; and finally, officials wanted to fulfill international counterterrorism responsibilities but do the bare minimum to avoid scraps with allies (Harrison, 1994, 111).

Broadly speaking, French countermeasures to fight terrorism included legislative changes to the criminal and criminal procedure codes, the reorganization of police structures and operations, and, at the international level, increased cooperation in the areas of legal conventions, diplomatic initiatives, and policing (Guillaume, 1993, 131). Interestingly, as in the Spanish case, French socialist and conservative governments enacted similar policies, and both faced challenges from within the political arena on their handling of counterterrorism (Harrison, 1994, 111).

The French Sanctuary Doctrine

The sanctuary doctrine held up in France until the early 1980s. At its most basic level, the sanctuary doctrine required that French policy and soil would be as neutral as possible with respect to the issues that motivated terrorism, for example, by remaining quiet on the Basque issue and Palestinian-Israeli conflict. The policy was a fairly successful tactic for preventing terrorist violence in France, but it had some serious flaws which grew more pressing over time. In particular, the sanctuary doctrine created political problems with other governments, particularly those that were fighting against terrorist groups that France sheltered, for example, Spain and Israel; required that French authorities maintain secret contact with terrorist groups; only worked when the terrorists did not directly challenge French interests or seek to change French policy; and reflected a lack of confidence in the ability of the French police to prevent or respond to terrorist attacks (Shapiro & Suzan, 2003, 70).

Legislation in the French Case

When he came to power in 1981, Mitterand and his government followed a soft-line policy toward terrorism (Wilkinson, 2000, 99). The government granted amnesty to hundreds of terrorists in jail, including several leaders of AD who quickly returned to violence; disbanded the State Security Court, despite its almost 20 years of experience dealing with terrorism; abolished the death penalty; affirmed the French sanctuary policy; and refused to extradite terrorist suspects (Wilkinson, 2000, 99; Harrison, 1994, 113; Moxon-Browne, 1986, 133). These measures were popular at the time but lost their appeal in 1982 when AD and other terrorist groups undertook a campaign of violence in Paris (Harrison, 1994, 114). Internationally, these policies did not go over well with neighboring governments, in particular the Spanish, who were incensed by the French refusal to extradite terrorists (Moxon-Browne, 1986, 134). Toward the end of April 1982, in reaction to the resurgence of attacks from AD and Palestinian groups, Mitterand announced a new hard-line policy toward terrorism. He created the new position of Secretary of State for Pubic Security, set up a council on terrorism within the government to coordinate and oversee counterterrorism policy, banned the sale of certain weapons, enacted stricter border controls, undertook surveillance on some diplomats, banned AD, reinforced police forces throughout the country, created a computerized data bank on terrorists, and increased cooperation with other European governments (Harrison, 1994, 114–115;

Moxon-Browne, 1986, 134; Wilkinson, 2000, 99). In November 1982, the cabinet also restricted the right of asylum (Harrison, 1994, 114).

In September 1986, the new Chirac government passed two important laws addressing terrorism. Specifically, these laws extended the detention of adult terrorist suspects from two to four days; permitted amnesties for individuals who helped prevent a terrorist attack, even if they were involved in planning the attack; created a compensation fund for victims of terrorist attacks; and imposed lengthy mandatory jail sentences on certain crimes relating to terrorism (Guillaume, 1993, 132; Wilkinson, 2000, 99). The new law also centralized terrorist trials within a new court, the "Parquet General," in Paris, with a jury of seven professional magistrates and a core group of prosecutors dedicated solely to terrorist cases (Shapiro & Suzan, 2003, 75–77; Guillaume, 1993, 132). The second law, often referred to as the loi Pasqua, after Chirac's Minister of Interior, required renewal after six months and, most notably, defined terrorism in broad terms as those acts that "aim to gravely trouble public order by intimidation or terror." (Harrison, 1994, 115). The government also passed an Amnesty Law in 1988, although learning from past mistakes after the debacle surrounding the 1981 amnesty, this one was not so broad.

Police in the French Case

As with the British and Spanish cases, the French viewed terrorism from the lens of the criminal justice model. Officials increased the French capacity to suppress terrorism on French soil by strengthening the police and judicial apparatus. Police went after the terrorists' logistical networks, which they viewed as the weak links. The French government faced two obstacles: a lack of coordination and centralization of counterterrorism policies internally, and a politicization of the struggle against terrorism (Shapiro & Suzan, 2003, 75). At least seven different police services in four different cabinet ministries had a variety of overlapping responsibilities in matters relating to terrorism. These agencies rarely met and distrusted each other (Shapiro & Suzan, 2003, 75). In a particularly telling incident, one of these agencies collaborated with the New Zealand police to prove the complicity of a second agency in a terrorist attack in Auckland harbor (Shapiro & Suzan, 2003, 75).

The fact that there were three French security and intelligence services did not make matters any easier (Harrison, 1994, 119). The first two were the DGSE under the Ministry of Defense, which held responsibility for foreign intelligence but in practice operated domestically as well, and the DST, part of the Ministry of Interior, which was nominally in charge of counterterrorist intelligence on French soil, but did not always consult the police or other agencies and tended to get involved in politics and diplomacy (Harrison, 1994, 120). The third agency was the RG, a directorate within the national police, which lorded over the country's terrorism computer database that it was supposed to share with the other security, police, and intelligence agencies, but typically did not (Harrison, 1994, 120).

The legislative measures enacted during the 1980s were accompanied by improvements in the organization and methods of the various police forces. For example, in 1983, the Ministry of Interior created a special database named VAT (violence, assassination, terrorism) to keep track of terrorist related incidents, organizations, and individuals. In 1984, the government created a coordinating body, also within the Ministry of Interior, to increase the effectiveness of the various services operating in the field of counter-terrorism (Guillaume, 1993, 133). In 1986, Mitterand created an ad hoc counterterrorism cell within the presidential palace that the established police and security forces immediately resented (Shapiro & Suzan, 2003, 76).

International Cooperation in the French Case

Starting in the early 1980s, the French embraced international measure to fight terrorism. In April 1986, after suffering through a wave of violent terrorist attacks, the French government finally took its international responsibilities seriously. In July, it expelled the first of 70 Basques and, with one raid, crushed ETA financial and money laundering operations. This was an important departure from French policy under the sanctuary doctrine, and it not only helped the French fight terrorism, it was pivotal in the Spanish fight against ETA. Since then, French international efforts have focused on three areas: judicial, diplomatic, and police cooperation. The French participate in international conventions aimed at extending the jurisdiction of national courts with regard to certain crimes and to facilitate the extradition of criminals (Guillaume, 1993, 133). In addition to cooperation with the Spanish authorities, France maintains formal and informal ties with other neighbor states and participates in TREVI.

Conclusions for the French Case

The French counterterrorism experience weighs on the negative side. Whereas UK and Spain overreacted to their respective terrorist threats, France underreacted. During the early 1980s, France did not balance security and democracy. The French government purchased freedom, through the sanctuary doctrine, at the expense of security, and the cost in human lives was high (Harrison, 1994, 129). Although France dealt successfully with AD and, starting in the early 1980s, played a major role in the Spanish efforts against ETA, overall, France was not so successful in its efforts to combat the spillover of Algerian terrorism and other terrorist incidents related to the Middle East (Wilkinson, 2000, 100). France's sanctuary policy made the country a terrorist safe haven. While the performance of the security and intelligence services was less than impressive, it is not clear that these different services overcame their coordination problems (Harrison, 1994, 128).

The French case demonstrates, first, the power of a centralized and specialized judicial process which enabled a core group of prosecutors to build solid cases against terrorists, connect these cases together in a way that might not have been possible if terrorists were tried in various local jurisdictions, and pool resources to really push the cases through the system in a timely manner. Second, it illustrates the importance of international cooperation—once again, French support was absolutely critical to Spain in its fight against ETA. Third, it shows the need for coordination, cooperation and trust between the intelligence, security, and police forces.

Conclusion

This chapter stems from the idea that democratic governments have accumulated enough experience dealing with terrorism to allow scholars to comparatively assess the effectiveness of different policies. By recognizing that we can compare democratic governments, different types of terrorism, and counterterrorism policies, I hoped to draw some general conclusions. The three cases detailed above demonstrate that democracies can succeed in reducing terrorism to manageable proportions without betraying the values that set them apart from other political systems (Wardlaw, 1994, 7). The range of responses studied in the cases include: police reorganization; modification of criminal and criminal procedural codes; amnesties, pardons, and attempts at reintegration of converted terrorists; various political, economic and social measures designed to address underlying grievances; and international cooperation. Some were effective, others were not.

Several broad themes are evident. First, all three countries treated terrorists, with little exception, as ordinary criminals. This is not to say that the governments did not take terrorism seriously; rather, they hoped to undermine the terrorists' political motivations essentially by ignoring them. By charging terrorists with ordinary, though nonetheless serious crimes, the governments sought to avoid claims that they were arresting terrorists for their ideas (i.e., left-wing or nationalist). When treating terrorists like criminals was not sufficient to protect the security of the population, then these governments began to selectively criminalize some activities related to terrorism, providing financial support to terrorists or publicly supporting terrorist aims.

The British and Spanish cases also demonstrate an important point about overreacting to terrorism, especially in the aftermath of successful terrorist attacks. In both of these cases, governments enacted policies in the aftermath of successful attacks that were later heavily criticized. This brings up an even more important and fundamental point: in a democracy, the response to terrorism must always respect the rule of law. The fallout from the at least tacit approval of the GAL's assassination campaign against ETA terrorists by Spanish authorities negatively impacted Spaniards' views of their governments for nearly 15 years. Similarly, the Spanish Organic Law that treated apologists as if they were terrorists and the British law that restricted the broadcast media from airing terrorist supporters were both inconsistent with these countries' democratic traditions and only served to undermine the governments' efforts.

As I pointed out earlier, defining terrorism is not an easy task, but all too often government definitions of terrorism fail to truly appreciate the nature of the terrorist threat. In the British case, up until 1984, the government viewed terrorism mainly through the lens of the Northern Ireland question; Middle Eastern nationalist and religious terrorists were not subject to the same police powers that Irish terrorists were. In the Spanish case, the government defined terrorism too broadly, such that almost any expression of separatism could be labeled as terrorism.

If these cases demonstrate that governments can deal with terrorism within the existing structure of their criminal justice systems, then it also points to the importance of police forces to enforce these laws. All three countries had trouble fostering coordination and cooperation between and among the different police, intelligence, and security agencies involved in terrorism. Lack of cooperation does not necessarily mean that the members of one agency are callous or insincere about their jobs; rather, failure to cooperate with other agencies could be the result of a lack of standardization or a misunderstanding about an agency's central mission or area of responsibility. In order to be effective, police forces must be given sufficient resources, but also sufficient guidance and guidelines. The many reorganizations undertaken in each of the three cases demonstrates that getting these latter two points right is not an easy task.

Both the Spanish and French experiences point to the importance of international cooperation. French support to Spanish efforts against

ETA was absolutely critical. In fact, the use of international mechanisms to combat terrorism was important in all the cases. For example, all three countries participated in a number of international conventions on the suppression of terrorism and the UK negotiated a series of bilateral treaties with the U.S. designed to prevent the use of the political offense exception in most extradition proceedings.

Notes

1. At that time it referred to the means the revolutionary state used to consolidate its power and impose order. See Cronin, 2002, 121, and Hoffman, 1998, 15.

2. There are, however, certain fundamental aspects that most scholars agree belong in any definition of terrorism.

3. The official UK definition of terrorism was, for a time, closely tied to the issue of Northern Ireland.

4. Rather than posing an insurmountable problem these different national conceptions can serve as a further point for comparison.

5. Given the variety of structure, belief, and membership any attempt to generalize across groups and sort them into categories will not prove entirely successful but the effort will provide a more orderly way to study the impact of counterterrorism policies. See for example Chalk, 1996, 24.

6. The PIRA, commonly referred to as a domestic terrorist group received funding from American citizens, weapons, and training from Libya, and carried out attacks against British interests throughout Western Europe.

7. The impact that this lack of organization has on the groups' capability to carry out violence is not clear. Some argue that right-wing groups tend toward more limited violence while others claim these groups are rasher when it comes to the use of violence. Compare Cronin, 2003, 285, to Malik, 2000, xii.

8. An extension of this objection is that the U.S. cannot learn anything from the Spanish, British, and French experiences because the U.S. faces a different type of threat then these states did. This is simply not true, both the UK and France dealt with religiously motivated terrorism during the period covered in this chapter.

9. The term hard-line is most often associated with Wilkinson (see Wilkinson, 2000, 95, or Wilkinson, 1986).

10. In general, declaring war on terrorists could be a bad idea because it implicitly acknowledges the terrorists' political role for further discussion see Chalk (1996, 97).

11. A second group, the left-wing GRAPO, also operated in Spain starting in 1975. During its reign of terror the group killed close to 80 people. For more information on GRAPO see Jimenez 1993, 113–114.

12. Franco even went so far as to outlaw the Basque language, Euskera.

13. For a good history of this assassination see Janke, 1986, 137–140.
14. Indeed, the leftist government was a much stauncher opponent of ETA than its rightist predecessors.
15. Along with Clark, I am hesitant to call the Basques in prison around the time of Franco's death terrorists. See Clark, 1990, 38.
16. This was down from a high of around 750 in 1975.
17. For details, see Remiro Brotons and Esposito 2002, 172, and Clark 1990, 447–466.
18. See Taylor, 2002, 199–211, for an excellent discussion of the different forms of terrorism the UK faced.
19. Taylor (2002) and Warner (1994, 13) provide two examples to illustrate this point; the PLO and the splinter Abu Nidal Organization fought an internecine struggle within the UK and Palestinian groups tried to assassinate the Israeli ambassador to the UK and destroy Israeli aircraft inside the UK.
20. British law makes an important distinction between terrorism related to Northern Ireland and terrorism not concerned with Northern Ireland. In cases of the former the police have access to special powers of arrest and extended detention without charge that are not always applicable in case of terrorism not related to Northern Ireland.
21. Although Scotland and North Ireland had independent police forces they were subordinate to the Home Secretary on counterterrorism issues.
22. MI5 was given the lead in counterterrorism intelligence in the early 1990s.
23. Part of the EC, the TREVI group was a forum where police chiefs, ministers, and other senior officials met regularly to discuss intelligence and police matters; the group also collected data on terrorist related activities, such as arms smuggling and financing. See also Charters 1994, 30, 32.

References

Alexander, Y. (Ed.). (2002). *Combating terrorism: Strategies of ten countries*. Ann Arbor: University of Michigan Press.

Bonner, D. (1993). United Kingdom: The United Kingdom response to terrorism. In A. P. Schmid & R. D. Crelinsten (Eds.), *Western responses to terrorism*. London: Frank Cass.

Chalk, P. (1996). *West European terrorism and counter-terrorism: The evolving dynamic*. New York: St. Martin's Press.

Charters, D. A. (Ed.). (1994). *The deadly sin of terrorism*. Westport, CT: Greenwood Press.

Clark, R. P. (1990). *Negotiating with ETA: Obstacles to peace in the Basque Country*. Las Vegas: University of Nevada Press.

Cronin, A. K. (2002). Rethinking American sovereignty: American strategy in the age of terrorism. *Survival* 44 (2).

Cronin, A. K. (2003). Transnational terrorism and security. In M. E. Brown (Ed.), *Grave new world: Security challenges for the 21st century*. Washington, DC: Georgetown University Press.

Das, D. K., & Kratcoski, P. C. (Eds.). (2003). *Meeting the challenges of global terrorism: Prevention, control, and recovery.* Lanham, MD: Lexington Books.

Government Accounting Office. (2000). *Combating terrorism: How five foreign countries are organized to combat terrorism.* GAO/NSIAD-00-85 (April).

Guillaume, G. (1993). France and the fight against terrorism. In A. P. Schmid & R. D. Crelinsten (Eds.). *Western responses to terrorism.* London: Frank Cass.

Gutteridge, W. (1986). *Contemporary terrorism.* New York: Facts on File Publications.

Harrison, M. M. (1994). France and international terrorism: Problem and response. In D. A. Charters (Ed.). *The deadly sin of terrorism.* Westport, CT: Greenwood Press.

Hewitt, C. (1984). *The effectiveness of anti-terrorist policies.* Lanham, MD: University Press of America.

Hoffman, B. (1998). *Terrorism today.* New York: Columbia University Press.

Janke, P. (1986). Spanish separatism: ETA's threat to Basque democracy. In W. Gutteridge (Ed.), *Contemporary terrorism* (pp. 137–140). New York: Facts on File Publications.

Jiminez, F. (1993). Spain: The terrorist challenge and government's response. In A. P. Schmid & R. D. Crelinsten (Eds.), *Western responses to terrorism.* London: Frank Cass.

Malik, O. (2000). *Enough of the definition of terrorism.* London: Royal Institute of International Affairs.

Moxon-Browne, E. (Ed.). (1994). *European terrorism.* New York: G.K. Hall.

O'Connor, M. P., & Rumann, C. M. (2003, April). Into the fire: How to avoid getting burned by the same mistakes made fighting terrorism in Northern Ireland. *Cardoza Law Review* 24.

Ranstop, M. (2003). Terrorism in the name of religion. In R. D. Howard & R. L. Sawyer (Eds.), *Terrorism and counter-terrorism: Understanding the new security environment.* Guilford, CT: McGraw-Hill/Dushkin.

Remiro Brotons, A., & Esposito, C. (2002). Spain. In Y. Alexander (Ed.), *Combating terrorism: Strategies of ten countries.* Ann Arbor, MI: University of Michigan Press.

Schmid, A. P. (1993). The response problem as a definition problem. In A. P. Schmid & R. D. Crelinsten (Eds.), *Western responses to terrorism.* London: Frank Cass.

Shapiro, J., & Suzan, B. (2003). The French experience of counter-terrorism. *Survival* 45 (1).

Smith, G. D. (2003). Single issue terrorism. In R. D. Howard & R. L. Sawyer (Eds.), *Terrorism and counter-terrorism: Understanding the new security environment.* Guilford, CT: McGraw-Hill/Dushkin.

Taylor, T. (2002). United Kingdom. In Y. Alexander (Ed.), *Combating terrorism: Strategies of ten countries.* Ann Arbor, MI: University of Michigan Press.

Warner, B. W. (1994). Great Britain and the response to international terrorism. In D. A. Charters (Ed.), *The deadly sin of terrorism.* Westport, CT: Greenwood Press.

Wardlaw, G. (1994). The democratic framework. In D. A. Charters (Ed.), *The deadly sin of terrorism*. Westport, CT: Greenwood Press.
Wilkinson, P. (2000). *Terrorism versus democracy: The liberal state response*. London: Frank Cass.
Wilkinson, P. (1986). Terrorism versus democracy: The problems of response. In W. Gutteridge (Ed.), *Contemporary Terrorism* (pp. 3–28). New York: Facts on File Publications.

Chapter 11

Negotiating with Terrorists and the Tactical Question

I. William Zartman and Tanya Alfredson

Introduction

Governments involved in internal conflicts are constantly faced with the question of whether and when to negotiate with the rebels whom they termed terrorists.[1] Often the rebels seek negotiations, if only to set the terms of takeover,[2] but negotiations legitimize their movement and acknowledge its status as spokesman for a part of the government's population, as well as rewarding it for its violence against civilians and government forces. But governments frequently, if not inevitably, evolve in their views of the rebels as a negotiating partner. A quick count indicates that 21 of the 26 cases of negotiation in civil wars between 1900 and 1989 (including negotiated surrender and unstable negotiations) were instances where governments negotiated with former terrorists (Stedman, 1991, 6–7). The interesting subject of inquiry, then, is the reasoning behind a government's decision to negotiate with its terrorists and the impact of that decision (i.e., the effectiveness of that reasoning) on them.

Terrorism is defined by United Nations Security Council Resolution (UNSCR) 1373 as violent or criminal acts designed to create a state of terror in the general public and by the United States government as premeditated, politically motivated violence perpetrated against noncombatant targets by subnational groups or clandestine agents, usually intended to influence an audience. They may be divided into analytical categories (Zartman, 2003). Absolute terrorists are those for whom the act is an end in itself, conducted for a reason but completed when accomplished; suicide bombers are an example. They may be subdivided into total absolutes, the suicider, and conditional absolutes, the operative removed from the target who sends out the improvised explosive devices (IEDs), rockets, or suiciders as a means to the total elimination of the enemy.

This analysis considers total absolutes to be beyond negotiation, by definition. At the extreme, it may be possible to talk a would-be suicider with a weak sense of purpose out of his mission, much as some women have been able to talk would-be rapists out of their act, but that is the subject of a psychological exercise and beyond this analysis. In passing, however, it is important to recognize that both actions are often based on a feeling of total frustration and social powerlessness, giving rise to a need to make a potent act, to once and for all assert oneself against the crush of society and more broadly against the external world, which is perceived to rob the actor of any other possibility of decision. Changing such a perception, necessary as the basis for negotiation, is extremely difficult and time-consuming.

On the other hand, contingent terrorists are those for whom the act is a means to an immediate goal, usually to be obtained by negotiation; hostage takers are an example. The categories are hermeneutic and not hermetic. Any group or movement is likely to contain many types of individual terrorists and not all group members may be terrorists. Since the analysis concerns the opportunity and effect of negotiation, it addresses rebel groups violent rebels are termed terrorists by their governments, without contesting the detailed validity of the charge. The question remains: Why or when does a government that previously saw its rebels as illegitimate perpetrators of violence now decide to negotiate with some or all of them, and with what effect?

Questions

The question of negotiating with terrorists is a dual decision that begins as a simple 4x4 matrix or tree: party A's decision to negotiate or not facing party B's decision to negotiate or not.

But that is too simple to be real or interesting. The question also has to do with the internal dynamics of the *other* side. At the beginning

Table 11.1. A Negotiation Matrix

		A Don't Negotiate	A [Some Negotiate]	A Negotiate
B	Don't Negotiate	t/s ◊ ⇔	[q/q]	p/p
	Negotiate	r/r	[q/q]	s/t

of the violent conflict, the government will probably have considered the rebels to be not worthy of negotiation because of their violent tactics and not willing to negotiate because of their millennial goals, classifying them as spoilers and calling them terrorists. There are plenty of evolutions possible from this initial situation, but in most cases the government will finally reverse itself and decide to negotiate. In some cases or under some conditions the government moves from "Don't Negotiate" as the rebel group splits into a spectrum of factions and the government negotiates with some of them. The question addressed here, restated, is: Why and when does the government decide to negotiate with one or more rebel factions, and what are the implications of that decision for the rebels? At this point the decision panels become more complex and more interesting.

Both sides are confronted with the Tactical Question (TQ), a major concept in social action on which little has been written (Zartman, 2008). TQ is one of the major (and unexplored) distinctions in social movements and political interaction. Political groups and social movements are continually faced with the question of whether to seek to prevail by cooperative or combative measures, the issue so well illustrated some time ago by Aesop in his story of the contest between the sun and the wind seeking to make a man remove his coat. Sociopolitical movements coalesce and fracture over the Tactical Question. It defines the Rubicon as social movements move from the petition to the consolidation phase (Zartman, 1995), and it becomes the dividing issue when such movements get bogged down in prolonged contestation. Thus, rebel movements can be assumed to always contain a spectrum of TQ positions, even if the extremes may not be filled at any given moment. In terms of the present inquiry, this means an array of positions on whether to use violence (terrorism) and whether to negotiate, correspondingly.

There are many possible dynamics in the rebels' decision. The main organization may be split internally on the question, for purely tactical reasons, for reasons of fatigue and despair, or for personal reasons, with one faction seeking to achieve benefits for themselves from political engagement with the government. The rebel movement may have moderated, the seekers of political solutions having won out over the violence advocates. Or it may be faced with competition from the outside from new organizations espousing either the negotiating option or the violent option, arising from TSQ dissatisfaction with the main organization's progress to date.

On the government side, the spectrum in parties is assumed to be less relevant but the same spectrum exists on decision options. Are rebels illegitimate terrorists (and so Don't Negotiate), are they legitimate partners with whom to seek a new political outcome (Negotiate), or are there factions within the rebels' side who are legitimate or tactical partners (Some Negotiations)? Whereas the rebels' decision is likely to be taken in the light of the factions' views of the proper way of achieving their own goals, government's decision involves not only that same issue but also consideration of the effect of that decision in turn on the rebel movement. Thus, the government has its own Tactical Question (TQ) in the choice between negotiating with the moderates and negotiating with the terrorist extremists, and in any case, it must decide how to treat the terrorists/extremist even if it decides to negotiate only with moderates. In other words, as has not been fully explored as yet, the decision to negotiate with terrorists is not merely a decision of whether to negotiate but also a decision of with whom to negotiate.

The decision can be based on various secondary or tactical calculations that lie behind the decision to negotiate. An offer to negotiate can contribute to strengthening the rebels' political faction and moderating the movement's position. It can also contribute to splitting the organization, enticing one faction to negotiate and making the other a spoiler. It can also respond to a new organization, either by offering a political settlement to a new group of moderates or by making common cause with the rebel organization against a more radical competitor. But it can also seek to prevent the radicals from playing an effective spoiler's role by including them in a comprehensive settlement.

Although the Tactical Question (TQ) is basic to the decision to negotiate, ethical questions are involved as well. Why should terrorists be rewarded for their terror by being included in the distribution of benefits from a settlement? Why should new spoiler groups be encouraged to break away from the main movement, with benefits to buy them into the agreement? Why should extremists and terrorists hold up an otherwise conclusive agreement for a new political system, simply to cater to their spoiler demands? But, on the other hand, why should not those who are part of the problem be necessarily part of the solution? Not simply moral dilemmas, these are aspects that make the Tactical Questions (TQ) a big cloud that casts its shadow over the negotiation decisions.

Negotiations

To return to the typology, if total absolutes are beyond negotiation, as posited, contingent terrorists are seeking to negotiate.[3] They want to get full price for their hostages or their targets. Hostages are negotiating capital or bargaining chips, that is, items of no intrinsic value to the bargainer but created for the purpose of bargaining away (Faure, 2003); targets for rockets and IEDs are much the same although the casualties caused are a side effect that keeps the terror alive. Contingent terrorists try to overcome their essentially weak position by appropriating a part of the other side and trying to get the best deal out of the other side's efforts to get that part back, to make itself whole again. Absolute terrorists do not want society to be whole again; they want it wounded and bleeding. To be able to do so, terrorists must believe in the rightness of their cause to counterbalance their asymmetrical power position, whether that sense of justice that comes from revelation, from revolution, or from revulsion, through their belief that the world owes them this right as a result of its own basic discrimination or corruption (nationalists and criminals, respectively).

In between the two groups are the conditional absolute terrorists, who do have something to negotiate about—territory, independence, conditions—even if their violent tactics are absolute. Conditional absolutes are not contingent; they do not seek negotiation as part of their act and their tactics are not divisible into two parts, grasping hostage capital and spending it. But their demands are potentially negotiable, leaving that potentiality to be developed by the negotiating partner. The distinction suggests appropriate negotiating—or prenegotiating—tactics. It is important to divide the terrorists, pulling the contingents and conditional absolutes away from the total absolutes through the prospect of something real and attainable.

The problem in the case of contingent terrorists is not that they are not interested in negotiating but that the world does not accept their deal. But that is merely an extreme case of a typical negotiating situation. To that situation there are two appropriate negotiating strategies—lower their terms or change their terms. Lowering terms involves showing terrorists that their original goals are unattainable, changing their expectations, lowering their security point (BATNA), increasing the attractiveness of lesser alternatives and emphasizing their attainability. Treatment as equals, developing the legitimacy of a solution, building the terrorists' independent decision-making capabilities, and expanding options are all ways of moving the hostage takers off position bargaining and opening the possibility of a fruitful search for mutually satisfactory solutions, only available when they can think in terms of lowered expectations and so of lowered demands.

The key to successful negotiations is to change the terrorists' terms of trade from their demands to their fate. When they see that there is no chance of their demands being met but that their future personal situation is open to discussion, innumerable details become available for negotiation. Closing and opening must be carried out in tandem, indicating that while one avenue or problem is closed for discussion, the other is open and personally more compelling.

Terrorists tend to focus on their original terms of trade—release of hostages or cessation of bombardment in exchange for fulfillment of demands—and are little open to looking for reductions and alternatives. As in any negotiations, when they become convinced that a search for a solution is legitimate and acceptable to both sides, they become joint searcher for a solution to a problem rather than adversaries. To entice them into this common pursuit, they need to be convinced that the other side is willing to consider their interests.

Spector (2003) says, "If state leaders have the political will to promote negotiation as a response to terrorism, they will need to attend to terrorists' interests, not only their actions, strategies and tactics.... To overcome the no-negotiation impediment, state leaders will need to respond in a special way, seek to understand terrorist interests, translate those interests into politically acceptable terms, and respond to them appropriately."

There is room for a wide range of tactics. Take-it-or-leave-it offers and firmness on the agenda are required at some times, whereas at other times invitations to further refinement and creative thinking are appropriate. When the hostage taker is in a known location—in fact a hostage—along with his hostages, time is on the side of the negotiator, a point that the terrorist may seek to reverse by either killing or releasing some of his hostages; when the hostage taker or bomber is on the loose, time is on his side. Once relations with terrorists get into the bargaining mode, however, they are open to the same shifts and requirements of tactics as any other negotiation. The position of the authorities as holders of the upper hand—one-up negotiators, in Donohue's (2003) terms—rather than full equals leads to unproductive tactics, position politics, and hostile bargaining on the part of the terrorist that is unproductive of integrative outcomes. There is a "need to achieve a gradual process of creating conditions which will enable the terrorists to securely conclude the crisis, . . . undermining the terrorists' psychological safe-zone, constructing legitimacy for the negotiated agreement," in Crystal's words (2003).

All this is not to suggest either that the demands of terrorists are to be considered legitimate in principle and only require some tailoring around the edges, or that negotiation is an easy process, or that concessions do not encourage contingent as well as absolute terrorists. The answer to the question of whether negotiations can be conducted with terrorists is that contingent terrorists in fact are looking for negotiations and that even conditional absolute have something negotiable in mind; but the answer to the next question of how much of their demands can be considered acceptable depends on the demand's content and on the importance of freeing the hostages or stopping the bombing. Since negotiation is giving something to get something, what can the government be expected to give to get the terrorists to give up their violence *and* moderate their demands at the same time? (Hezbollah and Hamas were brought into the Lebanese and Palestinian democratic system in exchange for neither.) What the terrorists are expected to give is clear: What will the government pay for it? The government has to convince the terrorist parties that it is willing to make substantial compromises and compensations. Terrorism is a brutal business and its particular type of violence is powerful money to buy government concessions.

This latter consideration again relates in turn to the danger of encouragement. Here it is not the matter of negotiation per se that encourages contingent terrorism but rather the degree of their demands that they are able to achieve by negotiation. If negotiating leads the terrorist to a purely symbolic result—a radio broadcast or a newspaper ad presenting his position—he is more likely to decide that the result is not worth the effort rather than to feel encouraged to do it again. Or if negotiating leads the terrorist to a bargain for his escape and totally neglect his original demands, he is not likely to feel encouraged to make another try. Thus, in the case of contingent terror, any encouragement would come from the results but not from the act of negotiating itself.

Similarly, the negotiator needs to offer the conditional absolute terrorist concessions to his demands as the payment for his abandonment of his violent terrorism and not as concessions to the pressure of the terrorism itself. If the negotiator should make concessions to the terrorist as part of the negotiation process, so must the terrorist do, and the absolute terrorist organizer does have something to offer as payment—his choice of terrorist tactics. Thus the answer of the negotiator to his public's fears of appeasing and legitimizing terrorism lies in the deal he is able to extract from the terrorist and in his need to focus on the fate of the victims.

The government decision to negotiate with "ex"-terrorists is based on its own Tactical Question estimates of the chances of reaching an acceptable agreement but is also inevitably tied up with the tactical attempt to try to encourage TQ splits in the rebel movement and to try to isolate the "real" terrorists/extremists. At the same time, the rebels' decision and their hawk/dove split is a reflection of its own Tactical Question, which in turn hangs on various estimates of three elements: (1) the chances of reaching (2) an acceptable proportion of the goal in (3) an acceptable amount of time. These are too many variables to put into a matrix or correlate through a questionnaire, so a preliminary investigation into the questions of when and why will have to be made through a few case studies.

Cases

This section shows case studies in support of the ideas presented in this chapter. We discuss the experience in Rwanda, Sierra Leone, Macedonia, Kosovo, and Palestine.

Rwanda 1993

At the time of their signing in August of 1993, the Arusha Accords had won waves of approval from international observers who saw in the Arusha process a model for conflict mediation. Seven months later, all hopes imploded when extremist Hutu leadership launched a genocidal attack on the Tutsi population and targeted butcherings of moderate Hutu leaders and their families. Leadership from two extremist Hutu parties—the Mouvement Révolutionnaire National pour le Développement (MRND), President Habyarimana's party, whose position in the planned Broad-Based Transition Government (BBTG) was to be drastically diminished, and the Coalition pour la Défense de la République (CDR), which the Arusha agreement excluded outright—were implicated in the genocide. In the brutal aftermath of the genocide, observers have asked whether the decision at Arusha to exclude the terrorist leadership of the CDR from the BBTG was a fateful misjudgment.

The situation was complex. There were two competing tensions from the TQ at the heart of the Arusha process—a violent struggle since 1990 between rebel Tutsi leaders of the Rwandese Patriotic Front (RPF) and the Habyarimana Government of Rwanda over the rights of Tutsi refugees in Uganda to return to Rwanda, and a political contest between the government and a growing pool of agitators who clamored for political inclusion and the creation of a multiparty system. The *akazu* (radical inner clique), comprising the CDR and the radical element of the MRND, were as much a product of the ideological divisions concerning domestic multiparty power sharing as of racist schisms over the Tutsi/RPF question. Launched in March of 1992, the CDR was the *akazu*/MRND response to the proliferation of opposition parties under incipient multipartyism. With respect to the RPF and the Rwandese Tutsi, CDR leadership had brandished a radically intolerant, racist ideology quite openly, from the war's inception. At its helm were radical racist leaders, including Mme Agathe Habyarimana and Théoneste Bagasora who was able to cling to his position in the military, became a delegate to the talks at Arusha, and ultimately proved to be one of the chief architects of the genocide.

Multipartyism began to take form after President Habyarimana signed a power-sharing agreement with the "United Opposition" (composed of the Mouvement Démocratique Républicain [MDR], the Parti Socialiste Démocratique [PSD], Parti Libéral [PL], and the [PDC]) on March 14, 1992. When the coalition government was convened on April 5 with a mandate to begin formal peace talks with the RPF at Arusha, the CDR objected to the mandate and was not included in the new coalition government (Jones, 2001, 63). When a cease-fire agreement was signed between the government and the RPF on July 5, the MRND ministers boycotted cabinet meetings, accused Habyarimana of "selling out" to the opposition in order to keep his own place in government, and organized demonstrations in support of its position (Prunier, 1995, 128–129, 161).

A commitment signed on July 18 by the RFP and the government to join in a multiparty transition government (BBTG) triggered immediate street protests organized by the CDR and the MRND, which had already rejected the February 19, 1991, Dar as-Salaam agreement between the government and the RPF. Demonstrators clamored for a new "broad-based" cabinet that would consult CDR membership and respect their positions. Killings by MRND extremists occurred in Kibuye within days and MRND leaders charged that the new government under Prime Minister Dismas Nsengiyareme (MDR) was failing in its obligation to represent all parties. Although CDR representatives were included in the formal government delegation to the Arusha talks, which officially began in August of 1992, neither the CDR nor the hard-line members of the MRND had formally accepted the process.

At first, in early November and throughout the month, President Habyarimana came out in support of the CDR in its bid for inclusion in the BBTG. From the outset, the U.S. and others had advocated inclusion of the CDR in the peace process based on the theory that it was safer to work with the enemy than to isolate him. Several have argued that Habyarimana's choice should be understood within the context of conflicting pressures from the demands of World Bank/IMF structural adjustment programs, introduced by 1990, which required Habyarimana to cut social services and give in to the demands of donors to advance multipartyism (Stettenheim, 1999; Anderson, 2000). Whether Habyarimana's position was motivated by allegiance to the CDR, by fear of further marginalizing by the CDR, or by a desire to simply stall the process is not clear.

During the power-sharing talks held during the fifth meeting at Arusha (November 22 to December 22), the RPF flatly refused to allow the CDR to take a place in a coalition government. Ultimately the RFP prevailed, and Habyarimana gave way on this point in December. By the end of the month, it was clear to the CDR that they had no option other than detachment from the political process. The final protocol signed on December 22 left the MRND with 5 out of 21 ministries in the BBTG and 11 out of 59 seats in the Transitional National Assembly (TNA), and formalized the decision to isolate the CDR by denying it participation in either the government or parliament. A condolence seat in parliament awarded on January 9, 1993, was rejected by the CDR (Joint Communique, 1993). Within days, the CDR and the MRND led demonstrations over the CDR's exclusion. Violence followed, with a massacre of more than 300 Tutsi in the Ruhengiri and Gisenyi provinces in late January (Jones, 2001, 81–82). The CDR, initially supporting Habyarimana, emerged as a formal opposition party in 1993. By then its opposition had already turned into terrorist tactics.

The January 1993 power-sharing agreement, in combination with the military unification plan signed at the final meeting in Arusha in August giving the RPF forces 50 percent of the rank and file and 40 percent of the officers in the revised armed forces, has been criticized for leaving the CDR and hard-line MRND with an unworkable solution that pushed them forward to genocide. But for the majority of actors involved, the decision to sideline CDR members appears to have been taken prior to the onset of the Arusha talks. Unless the party could stomach a radical shift in its demands, its exclusion had already largely been determined by its own TQ choice. Seeing negotiations for both internal multipartyism and inclusion of the Tutsi RPF-proceeding apace, the *akazu* mentality saw genocidal violence as the only option. Though the CDR continued to lobby for its inclusion in a future government, some observers note that its efforts at altering the diplomatic course from this point forward suddenly seemed diminished, perhaps an indication its decision to shift to terrorist violence. Even if the CDR had been willing to participate it is quite likely that its aims would always be irreconcilable with multiparty participation, both to its leadership and to its membership.

Unlike the CDR and the RPF, the opposition parties had a decision-making process that is better characterized as that of a gambler rather than an ideologue. Many opposition members proved to be less committed to strong positions on the RPF question than to winning at the domestic numbers game, casting in bets with those parties who seemed most likely to secure their own place at the winners table of the internal power struggle. Though it had gained access to the multiparty system, the United Opposition ultimately subverted multipartyism in principle. On numerous occasions throughout the negotiations, the coalition delegates to the talks conducted themselves in open disregard to the position of the Habyarimana government. Foreign Minister Ngulinzira initialed the agreement at the September 7–8, 1992, meeting at Arusha on power sharing, unification, and political cooperation without the support of Habyarimana (Jones, 2001, 80). When talks broke down following the

CDR massacres in January 1993 and the devastating siege by the RFP in late February 1993, coalition partners met with the RFP in Bujumbua to restart negotiations without the support of either Habyarimana or indeed their own ranks.

Although it is true that even without such efforts by the old opposition the peace process may have been permanently stalled, their failure to attend to their own constituency made the coalition parties vulnerable to internal divisions and made them ultimately lose control of the peace as well. Breakaway factions of the old opposition parties met with the "Common Front" of the MRND, CDR, seven minor opposition groups, and the four new "Power Parties" (Power-MDR, Power-PL, Power-PSD, and Power-PNC), meeting under Habyarimana and called with blessings from France. The meeting concluded with a resolution condemning the delegates at Bujumbura, the RFP, and the division between the Prime Minister and the President.[4] Lindsey Hilsum (1994) has argued that Habyarimana was pursuing a two-track strategy throughout the peace process by working with the peace process through his affiliation with the MRND (a signatory to the Arusha Accords) while also working outside of the political system through the CDR. But if Habyarimana sought to keep all of his options open, both he and the Opposition ultimately lost control of both processes.

Several observers have faulted the RPF for challenging the resilience of a negotiated peace through its excessive inflexibility and through its insistence on demands that turned Arusha into a "victor's deal." (Steinham, 1999; Jones, 2001). On the inclusion of the CDR in the new BBTG, the RPF was intransigent. That intransigence is explained in part by historical and current mistrust of Hutu radicalism, expressed in reports by RPF radio on October 25, 1992, of "persistent rumors" of a Hutu plan to massacre civilians indiscriminately (Prunier, 1995, 168). However, numerous accounts also emphasize that the RPF simply proved itself more capable in pressing its demands. Its leaders approached the talks with a clear and detailed position, surpassing the opposing party both in terms of negotiation skill and moral high ground in the eyes of the international facilitators. Above all they were unified, whereas the government delegation was in a constant state of acrimony and internal division. Moreover, by late December 1992 to January 1993 when the power-sharing agreement was finally crafted, and even more so after its enormously successful February 8 offensive, the RPF had shown it had the muscle to impose its demands (Stettenheim, 1999).

The question of whether the CDR was includable or excludable may never be answerable. When the decision is taken to isolate terrorists, the parties taking the decision must have an idea that such an action is possible, but when the decision is taken to include them, the other parties must be able to carry the terrorists with them and to carry through with their agreement even if the terrorist defects and not feel forced to defect along with it. Jones (2001) has argued that there was never any indication that the *akazu* was ever willing to consider a negotiated settlement with the RPF; it would have defected in as well as out of the Arusha Agreements. Whether it would have played along in signing the agreement and then (a faction of it, at least) defect, or simply defect from the beginning, making an agreement impossible, is hard to postdict. What is certain is that those who bought into the agreement did nothing or were not able to contain the CDR (ex-FAR and *interahamwe*) terror after the agreement was signed.

Sierra Leone 1996–1999

The Revolutionary United Front (RUF) invaded Sierra Leone in 1991 with only a small force of several hundred men (Abebajo, 2002).[5] Because of their small force, the rebels were initially not taken seriously and characterized as vassals of Liberian warlord Charles Taylor or bandits. Already a few months after their appearance in Sierra Leone, Joseph Momoh announced an opening of the political system and invited the RUF to join. However, this was not accompanied by an invitation to direct talks and Momoh continued to believe that the rebels were not a serious threat, especially after they were stopped by the Sierra Leonean army, troops from Guinea, and Liberians opposed to Taylor.

Nonpayment of the soldiers for several months in 1992 triggered a coup of army officers generally disillusioned by the corrupt, ineffective government and led by the young officer Valentine Strasser. Initially it seemed that Strasser's National Provisional Ruling Council (NPRC), which shared some of the RUF's original goals to end corruption and political misrule, would follow a different approach to the Tactical Question and try to pursue a dialogue with the terrorists. However, the new leaders quickly repeated the mistake of the predecessor regime and disqualified the rebels as "bandits sent by Charles Taylor" who can be brought under control. Strasser's successor Julius Maada Bio later recalled that the young soldiers who took over power became convinced that, with the new resources and possibilities at their disposal, they should defeat the rebels militarily, rather than negotiate (Gberie, 2000). However, as the rebels succeeded in expanding their territory and bringing important diamond areas under their control, Strasser declared a unilateral cease-fire in December 1993. The rebels' advance toward Freetown was accompanied by an even worsening economic situation. With the fall of the Sierromco aluminium and Sierra

Rutile mines to the rebels, the NPRC lost its principal foreign-exchange earner (Hirsch, 2001, 37). Although the NPRC was supported by Nigerian and Guinean troops, it was on the defensive, and subsequently had to seek external and internal support to improve its position.

After the failure of a "private security force" of Nepalese Ghurkas, the NPRC hired the mercenaries of Executive Outcomes (EO) from South Africa. Although it was only a small force of about 10 officers and 200 soldiers, it made a strong impact on the civil war. When EO entered the war on the government side in 1995, the rebels were only 20 miles from Freetown. The military situation quickly changed in favor of the government, which succeed in recapturing large portions of the country. The government position was further strengthened when EO established an informal cooperation with the southern-based rural militias, the Kamojahs.

However, the troops of EO were expensive, and the NPRC soon faced severe problems to pay them. Economic activities had ground to a halt in the country, which was basically dependent on the IMF. Consequently, by December 1995, EO threatened to leave the country again, which would make the rebels victory only a matter of time. As a reaction to this situation, Julius Maada Bio took over power in a palace coup and sent Strasser into exile (Abebajo, 2002, 37–40; Bangura, 1997, 227–240). On the day he was sworn in, Bio shifted his TQ position and made a public appeal to start negotiating with the RUF without preconditions. He reportedly had personal stakes in the talks, as his elder sister and her husband had been abducted by the RUF in 1991, and apparently become leading RUF officials (Gberie, 2000). Talks continued after a democratically elected government under Lansana Kabbah of the Sierra Leonean People's Party (SLPP) took over power in March 1996.

The new civil government faced the same urgency to reach an agreement as its military predecessor. The conditions in the Sierra Leonean Army were so bad that many soldiers saw a better future in joining the rebels in looting the country, and the distinction between these two groups became increasingly blurred, as expressed in the name "sobels" (soldier-rebels). When the military situation changed in favor of the government, the government forces and their militia allies failed to destroy the RUF headquarters in Kailahun and to recapture the remaining areas under RUF control. The government therefore only could negotiate an agreement to end the war. On the other side, the lack of popular support and the severe military pressure on the rebels was hurting the rebels. The parties had arrived at a momentary stalemate, which led to the Abidjan Agreement in November 1996, mediated by the Ivorian government,[6] UN, OAU, and Commonwealth representatives, and the London-NGO International Alert.

Spoilers of the peace agreement came from both sides, showing that the distinction between soldiers and rebels was not clear. The withdrawal of Executive Outcomes before the establishment of a Neutral Monitoring Group intended to monitor the breaches of the cease-fire, which was agreed on in the peace agreement, seriously weakened the government position. Rebel leader Foday Sankoh was arrested in Lagos in March 1997, where he attempted to buy weapons to continue his fight. However, the group that forced the democratic government of President Kabbah to flee from Freetown came from its own troops. Junior officers from the already discredited army faced further marginalization by Kabbah's decision to continue relying on other forces than the army, namely the Nigerian-led ECOMOG troops and the Kamojahs (Bangura, 1997, 222). The revolting officers created a new level of collusion with the rebels when they formed the Armed Forces Ruling Council (AFRC) and invited the RUF to join their junta. The exiled Kabbah government had to negotiate its return to Freetown with the joint AFRC-RUF junta, even though the junta lacked any international recognition, reaching an agreement in Conakry in October 1997 (ECOWAS, 1997).[7] However, the junta could ultimately only be removed by force and in February 1998, ECOMOG forced them out of Freetown and restored the democratic government.

ECOMOG troops, led by Nigeria, became the de-facto army of the government of Sierra Leone. After the death of Nigerian dictator Sani Abacha in June 1998, the candidates for the upcoming democratic elections signaled the withdrawal of troops from ECOMOG. More than 800 regional peacekeepers had died in the civil war by the end of May 1999, and its involvement in the peacekeeping operations cost Nigeria about US$1 million per day. Also, in other neighboring West African countries public opinion had shifted against a peacekeeping involvement in Sierra Leone, further weakening the government's position (Rashid, 2000). In mid-1999 it once again entered negotiations with the RUF; as three years earlier, the government was pressured to reach an agreement by the withdrawal of key military forces from its side. Additionally, especially after the devastating attack of AFRC-RUF forces on Freetown in January 1999, the conflict achieved increased international attention and pressure to reach an agreement. Rashid (2000) aptly summarizes the TQ positions the two sides face before entering negotiations:

> [For Kabbah], refusal to negotiate would mean accepting de facto partition of the country, the potential loss of regional and international sympathy and support, and continued instability and violence—especially since all parties were beginning to conclude that the war was unwinnable. (. . .) For the AFRC-

RUF, refusal to pursue negotiations meant holding territory illegally, risking unrest within the army faction and offending its regional supporters. The alliance could either transform its control over these areas to freedom for its leaders, amnesty for its war crimes and legitimate political power through negotiations, or continue to fight an unwinnable war and be treated as pariahs.

The two warring parties signed the peace agreement of Lomé in July 1999, which was similar to the Abidjan Accord, but included the deployment of a UN peacekeeping mission (UNAMSIL) that took over from ECOMOG (Peace Agreement, 1999). Like the previous agreement it did not bring sustainable peace at first. Again, Sankoh and the RUF wanted to continue their fight after the foreign troops left, that is, after the final departure of ECOMOG on May 1, 2000, and violently resisted the replacement through UN troops. However, this time the international community responded assertively to save the peace. Great Britain intervened militarily to stabilize the situation in May 2000. Shortly thereafter, the UN issued an embargo on so-called "conflict-diamonds," therefore cutting off the rebels' means, and UNAMSIL was strengthened through an increase in troops.

Several factors combine to explain why the government of Sierra Leone changed its position on the TQ and entered into negotiations with the terrorist movement (RUF) in 1996 and, on failure of the ensuing Abidjan agreement, continued until 1999. First, and most importantly, the development of a costly stalemate made the situation ripe for negotiations. Neither side was able to achieve a military victory. The government and its army were unable to defeat the rebels militarily. The state collapse in Sierra Leone, resulting from extended exploitation of the country by the ruling elite of the All Peoples Congress (APC) (1968–1992), also left its marks on the army, which consisted of badly or not at all paid and poorly equipped soldiers and officers. The poor condition of the army led to a dependency on foreign troops in the fight against the RUF, which came from "private security forces" (i.e., mercenaries) and later from regional and international peacekeeping forces of the Economic Community of West African States (ECOWAS) and the UN. Even more, the frustration and disillusion within the army led many officers and soldiers to change sides and to collude with the rebels. Although the deployment of mercenaries, together with the support of local tribal militias (kamojahs) in the first half of the 1990s changed the military situation in favor of the government, it failed to achieve a military victory over the RUF and put the government under severe financial pressure. This could be solved by bringing the hostilities to an end and ceasing the employment of expensive foreign mercenaries. It was this inability to achieve a military victory and dependency on foreign troops that brought the government to the negotiating table. In 1995/1996 the RUF, too, had experienced heavy losses and was on the defensive. Additionally, its terrorist tactics alienated popular support. In the fall of 1996, both warring parties perceived a peace agreement as the expedient solution.

Second, the element of leadership and valid spokespeople on all sides contributed to the presence of ripeness. On the rebel side, Foday Sankoh leadership of the rebels was relatively uncontested. His historically strong, even charismatic position within the RUF was proven after he was held in Nigeria for more than a year, beginning in March 1997. Attempts to remove him from the RUF's leadership were prevented by his loyal deputies, mainly by Sam Bockarie, and he was again the key person on the RUF's side to renew negotiations in Lomé in 1999. Both the government and the mediator saw this situation and sought to capitalize on it. The strong interest of the Ivorian leadership to resolve the conflict resulted in an active mediation effort, which was supported by other regional and international actors.

Macedonia

The second Macedonian crisis came a decade after the first that accompanied the country's secession from Yugoslavia in 1991, and was largely an overflow of the Kosovo crisis of 1998 to 1999 next door.[8] The formula for the independence agreement, involving entrance into the EU (European Union) in exchange for reliance on the democratic process for satisfaction of ethnic grievances, had begun to wear thin toward the end of the decade. Ethnic Albanians began to pose the Tactical Question, lose faith in the democratic process, and look to stronger measures to make their cause heard. In the 1998 elections, the government led by the Social Democratic Alliance (SDSM) was replaced by a coalition of a right-wing nationalist party, the Internal Macedonian Revolutionary Organization-Democratic Party of Macedonian Unity (VMRO-DPMNE), the moderate Democratic Party of Albanians (DPA), and the small Liberal Party (LP). Another Albanian party, the Party for Democratic Prosperity (PDP), formerly part of the socialist coalition, lost ground over the decade, and then in 2001 lost members to the newly formed National Democratic Party (NDP), with ties to the Kosovar militants in Serbia. The same year as the elections (but with no relation), the UN Preventive Deployment Force (UNPREDEP) that had been in place since independence was terminated by a Chinese veto.

Although it allegedly had been forming over the previous year, the National Liberation Army (NLA)[9] came to the surface on January 23, 2001, when it claimed responsibility (in Communiqué, 4) for an attack on a village near the Kosovo border. The NATO Secretary-General labeled the group "a bunch of thugs," the EU representative declared that "it would be a mistake to negotiate with terrorists in this particular case," and the government sent its army (ARM) and border police against it.[10]

The goals of the NLA were not clear, and its command as well as its troops were not unified (much as in the case of the KLA in Kosovo three years earlier). Although the previous situation had been designed to deal with the rights and aspirations of Macedonian Albanians within a democratic process, militants' goals tended toward federalization. However, government unity was also shaky, and parties were positioning themselves for a possible election campaign. Under enormous pressure from the EU, NATO and OSCE since late March, all the above-mentioned parties joined in a government of national unity on May 13 and declared a cease-fire in order to bring in the PDP, where still-recalcitrant PDP members broke away to form the NDP. However, the "parties are not natural bedfellows," officials from the two ethnic categories did not speak to each other, and the government did not function (IGC, 2001, 8, 14).

The first negotiations were within rather than between the "sides." Robert Frowick, Special Envoy of the Chairman-in-Office of the Organization for Security and Cooperation in Europe (OSCE), launched a three-phase process that began with the cease-fire and was to be followed by substantive confidence-building measures and then institution of control mechanisms to integrate some NLA leaders into public life. But first, the ethnic Albanians needed to unify and clarify their goals, for which DPA and PDP leaders met secretly with NLA leaders in Prizren on May 22. The Prizren Document accomplished its purpose and allowed the party leaders to speak in the name of the ethnic Albanians including the NLA. However, a press leak destroyed the process and brought out denunciations from the VMRO-DPMNE president and prime minister (covering their own plans to break the cease-fire) and adamant opposition from the EU; NATO pressed for negotiations, while the U.S. remained coy on its support for Frowick and negotiations involving the NLA.

Negotiations can be said to have begun on June 13 with the president's meeting with international mediators and his announcement of a vague five-point plan. They were conducted by the VMRO-DPMNE president and prime minister and SDSM former prime minister, for the ethnic Macedonians, and by the DPA and PDP leaders for the ethnic Albania side, leading to the Ohrid Agreement of August 8, signed on August 13; the process followed much the same path as laid out by Frowick.

Thereupon, NATO and NLA representative began direct negotiations on NLA disarmament, reached on August 14; however, as early as late June NATO representatives and NATO forces in Kosovo (KFOR) arranged a separation of NLA and ARM forces at Aricinovo near Skopje, and on July 24–26 renegotiated a cease-fire from three weeks earlier with NLA leaders (IGC, 2001b, 4, 5, 7).

Curiously, the question "Why did the government and international mediators negotiate with the 'terrorist' NLA?" has to be paired with the prior, reverse question, "Why did they not?" in order to produce the more precise question, "When did they negotiate with the NLA, and why?" In fact, after May, negotiations took place with the NLA both directly and indirectly. Negotiations took place directly, simply, when they had to, that is, when a directly military situation required immediate contact outside the political framework, as in Aricinovo or as on post-agreement disarmament. They did not take place "when they did not have to," that is, once the Prizren agreement brought the ethnic Albanian parties and rebels onto one track on their goals and representation; the question of direct negotiations with the "terrorists" was circumvented.

The further question of "Why negotiate at all in the Macedonian violent conflict?" is answered by the notion of ripeness. The mutually hurting stalemate (MHS) began to develop throughout the NLA actions and ARM reactions, more slowly on the government side than on the ethnic Albanian side after Prizren (Ruso, 2003, 29–30). Although it continued to be tested throughout the negotiations, the MHS can be said to have been perceived by both in June, when the NLA occupied Aracinovo, on the edge of Skopje, on June 6, and the ARM attempted to dislodge it on June 22 and failed, leaving NATO to negotiate a mutual disengagement. The Prizren agreement established the parameters of a Way Out (WO), the other element of ripeness, by indicating its concerns and eliminating a territorial demand, with the more specific notions of a mutually acceptable formula to be worked out in the negotiations. Thereafter, the international mediators focused their attention on the government, parts of which returned to violence, since the NLA and ethnic Albanian parties generally retained their perception of ripeness.

Just before the Ohrid agreement was signed, the NLA began to split (a common TQ reaction as agreement approaches) and on the week of the agreement the worst outbreak of violence occurred, claimed by a new Albanian National Army (ANA/AKSH) (ICG, 2001c). The extremist move, however, was not enough to upset the agreement. There does not appear to have been any tactical consideration on the part of the mediators (let alone the government) to isolate extremists through negotiation with the mainstream terrorists. To the contrary, the mediators (and government) worked to get the entire ethnic Albanian side, as well as the entire ethnic Macedonian side, into the agreement. Nor was there any effort to test the authority of Arben Xhaferi and Imer Imeri, the DPA and PDP leaders, or Ali Ahmeti, political leader of the NLA. Their efforts were to reach a substantive formula that would keep both sides in the agreement.

Kosovo

The tactical choices of four key players concerning the use of violence and the policy of exclusion of other groups roughly defined five phases in the conflict between Kosovo Albanians (Kosovar) and government of Yugoslavia between 1989 and 1999. Though the Yugoslav government (FRY) under Slobodan Milosevic, the Kosovar Democratic League (LDK) under Ibrahim Rugova, the Kosovar Liberation Army (KLA) rebel leaders, and the NATO/Contact Group nations each refused to deal with what was viewed as a terrorist opponent at various points in the conflict, in each case this strategy served different goals, ideologies and tactical considerations. As the conflict evolved, relations shifted from (1) Western favor for the LDK but Milosovic's refusal to negotiate with both LDK and KLA as terrorists, then (2) Western support in early 1998 for a dialogue between the Milosevic government and the LDK that excluded the KLA and concentrated on confidence-building measures between the two parties, to (3) Western and Kosovar attempts to create a unified KLA/LDK team, to (4) an effort to forge a set of bilateral agreements between the Milosovic government and western intermediaries in October of 1998, to finally (5) Western confrontation of Milosevic with an ultimatum to either submit to a compromise arrangement that included both the LDK and the KLA or else face a NATO aerial campaign (which he did in the end, in reverse order).

Not until 1999 was the KLA brought into direct talks with the FRY. Moreover, although U.S. sources were in contact with the (sometimes elusive) KLA leadership from the summer of 1998, at no time prior to the Rambouillet process were such talks designed to end in any formal contractual arrangement with the KLA (Touval, 2002; Zartman, 2005). The refusal by the KLA to enter into discussions with Milosevic throughout the fall of 1998 mimicked the reality of the group's exclusion from the process, and reflected the KLA's lack of trust both in Milosevic willingness to enter into earnest compromise and in the commitment of the international mediators to fill the security vacuum that would result from a proposed KLA disarmament (Walters, 2001).

1989-1997

The separatist LDK party formed around a principle of passive resistance after the autonomous status of Kosovo was revoked in 1989. In 1992 Kosovo Albanians voted (in an illegal election sponsored by the LDK) to declare Kosova a newly independent Republic with Rugova as its head. For the remainder of the decade Rugova worked to elaborate a parallel system of government in the hope that the unofficial Kosovo government would someday be rewarded with de facto authority—in fact, a hopeful formula for agreement. By 1997 ongoing human rights abuses and an unemployment rate of 70 percent among Kosovo's ethnic Albanians continued to provide evidence of Milosevic's imperviousness to passive resistance and rejection of the formula. When the 1995 Dayton peace accords brought redress to Muslims fighting Serbs in Bosnia but failed to reward the peaceful struggles of Kosovo Albanians, the KLA emerged, premised on the conviction that independence for Kosovo could not be won without violence.

At the outset of the conflict the FRY refused to deal with any element of the Kosovar separatist movement. Kosovo had powerful historical significance for many Serbs who believed the land was the cradle of the Serbian nation; Milosevic had used Serbian nationalist sentiment over the issue in order to secure his own rise to power. As such, throughout most of the 1990s both the pacifist LDK (whose activities were largely tolerated by the government of Yugoslavia) and the guerrilla KLA movement (whose presence between its formation in 1993 and 1998 was scarcely visible) were classified as terrorist by the FRY. Yugoslav military superiority was buttressed by the public assertion that the question of Kosovo was strictly a matter of internal concern. The aim of exclusion was not to foster a situation conducive to productive compromise, but to escape the responsibility to compromise.

JANUARY 1998–MAY 1998

The first half of 1998 marked the first TQ positional shift. Under external pressure, Milosevic abandoned the classification of the LDK as a terrorist group and professed his willingness to explore talks with Rugova, but stood by his refusal to accept the KLA into the process. In January 1998, the international Contact Group had begun to increase diplomatic pressure for a solution "between the status quo and independence" to the Kosovo problem. In a strategy designed to induce a TQ division in the Kosovo resistance movement, the FRY combined its official overtures toward the LDK with a series of violent operations against the KLA. In February–March the Serbian army launched a series of offensives against KLA strongholds in Qirez and Likosane and the Drenica Valley that claimed the lives of nearly 90 ethnic Albanian civilians. Such brutality evoked outrage among international observers, and the Contact Group immediately stepped up their demands for progress. Milosevic responded by sending a delegation to meet with Rugova in Kosovo on March 12 but also insisted that Rugova denounce the KLA, abandon the LDK demand for foreign mediation, and drop his insistence on acceptance of independence as a precondition for negotiations. These conditions challenged Rugova to countermand the positions of his own party only weeks before scheduled elections when more radical political leaders such as Adem Demaci (then LPK) and Bujar Bukoshi were waiting in the wings (Hedges, 1999, 29).[11] More importantly, these conditions, only days after the attacks in Drenica, challenged Rugova to risk assassination by the KLA *(Economist,* 1998, 53–54).

Despite such setbacks and thanks in large part to an intensive effort by U.S. Balkans envoy Richard Holbrooke, Milosevic and Rugova met two months later on May 15 and concluded an agreement to begin talks to discuss formal negotiations.[12] But within 10 days, the Serbs launched a major counter offensive against the KLA in Decani, resolving the TQ for the Kosovar. Rugova called an immediate halt to the fledgling talks and KLA activity blossomed into full-scale guerilla war with many local LDK leaders taking up arms to command village units of the KLA resistance (Holbrooke, 1999; Judah, 2000, 157).

JUNE 1998–AUGUST 1998

Milosevic continued to exclude the KLA as a divide-and-defeat (rather than a divide-and-deal) strategy, and the army made massive incursions into the Drenica region that set tens of thousands of Kosovar in flight. Such events convinced the U.S. to reclassify the KLA from a "terrorist group" to a potential compromise partner, and to launch an active campaign to bring the LDK and KLA into a new unified Kosovo delegation. As one negotiator noted, "it was obvious to everyone that it was not confidence building measures that we needed but deep political changes on the ground and for that, we needed the KLA." By the fall of 1998 members of the Contact Group, who had once sided with the Yugoslav government in denouncing the KLA as a terrorist organization, had come to view Milosevic as bearing direct responsibility for the KLA's rise from obscurity.

AUGUST 1998–OCTOBER 1998 AGREEMENT

The framework shifted again in mid-August when quite unexpectedly the LDK abandoned the effort to build a coalition government and announced a reformulation of the Kosovar negotiating team to the exclusion of the KLA, while the U.S. turned to crafting an agreement restraining Milosovic, without Kosovar involvement. The resulting Milosevic-Holbrooke agreement, signed on October 13, affirmed Milsovic's commitment to comply with the demands set forth under UNSCR 1199 to commence an immediate cease-fire, withdraw forces from Kosovo, facilitate a return of Albanian refugees, and to accept verification procedures. Though the agreement called on all parties to cease hostilities, neither the Rugova government nor the KLA were parties to the arrangement and as such, neither were bound legally to observe it.

The cause of the breakdown in the effort to create a unified Kosovo delegation in August, and the reasons for the decision by the Holbrooke team shortly thereafter to pursue a unilateral agreement with Milosevic are less than clear. Opposition leader Mehmet Hajrizi has claimed that the Kosovar had been on the brink of agreeing on a coalition government to include the KLA when the Rugova government suddenly rescinded its cooperation and formed a smaller negotiating group (BBC, August 18, 1998). If the goals of the two factions were the same, differences remained on the TQ. On August 15, LDK negotiator Fehmi Agani claimed that although his delegation "never set the independence of Kosovo as an imperative or rather as a condition for negotiations, ... that does not mean that we should give up our right to try and prove why an independent Kosovo is possible ... we include independence for Kosovo as one of the possible solutions and will work towards it" (BBC, 1998). The KLA may have been unwilling to compromise in its demand that talks be held on the condition of independence, but KLA concerns also appear to have rested on questions of process. After Agani proposed that the Serbs and Kosovar meet with U.S. envoy Christopher Hill to set an agenda and establish a timetable for new talks, Demaci, as KLA political representative, announced that the KLA would not accept an offer to negotiate with the Serb regime until the Serbian regime "shows it is serious about negotiating," by stopping all military offensives and withdrawing its police and military units from the province" (BBC, 1998; *Deutsche Presse Agentur*, 1998). Others have expressed the view that the deal fell apart simply because Rugova was opposed to sharing power with anyone, including moderate opposition leaders in addition to the KLA. After the Serbian onslaught had driven the number of refugees and internally displaced persons into the hundreds of thousands, however, the Rugova government may have felt it would be better able to appeal to Milosevic to curtail Serb offensives if the KLA was sidelined, given its own position of weakness. Whatever the reasoning, two days after the Kosovo government abandoned the effort to form a Kosovo coalition, Demaci indicated that any talks held by Rugova without the KLA were "meaningless' " (*Deutsch Presse-Agenturn*, 1998).

Instead, as a consequence of its exclusion, the KLA continued to affirm its commitment to violence and issued a statement on October 17 that the organization would punish anyone who signed an agreement that obstructed the goal of independence (CNN, 1998).[13] Yet by placing the protection of Kosovo citizens, the KLA, and even of the international verification force in the hands of the Serb police force the Holbrooke-Milosevic agreement did just that (DOD, 1998). Within little more than a week the KLA, not a signatory of the agreement, moved into the territories vacated by withdrawing Serbian forces and clashes ensued. Milosevic felt betrayed by the western allies; in consequence in turn, he began plans for a massive counteroffensive, Operation Horseshoe (Daalder & O'Hanlon, 2000, 58). From that point forward, a number of officials have commented that the wind appeared to have gone out of the sails of the peace process.

Given the warnings, why would the international community turn next to try to strike a deal with Milosevic to the exclusion of both the KLA and the LDK? In the months following the breakdown of the October agreement a Western diplomat commented on the inability of the west to prevent KLA encroachments following the October agreement by saying "we don't have leverage on the KLA" (O'Connor, 1998). Internal sources suggest that the primary reason for the exclusion of the KLA stemmed more from the belief that the KLA was too small to matter combined with the limited commitment among the Contact partners than from any ideological aversion to negotiating with terrorists per se. The United States had not been opposed to dealing with the KLA in principle; it had been doing so formally since the summer months (and informally since the spring) (Zartman, 2005). Moreover by September Ambassador Christopher Hill had established a reliable conduit to and from the KLA authority. Through these contacts State Department officials felt they had received assurances of tacit support for the plan by the KLA (though it was understood that the KLA would not take this position publicly) so that efforts to urge compliance by the rebel group continued in direct talks between Ambassador Hill and the KLA (DOD, 1998). One senior official has explained that by August 1998, the view at the State Department was that the popularity of the KLA had reached its nadir and as such that the KLA would not have the capacity to mount a meaningful offensive once Serbian withdrawal was achieved (Zartman, 2005). But this appears to be contradicted by the steady growth in the size of the KLA throughout this period as well as by the fact that there was at least an informal effort in place to obtain KLA a buy-in.

The best explanation for Western decision making comes from the underlying motives and goals of international parties. Daadler and O'Hanlon (2000, 57–58) have argued that the goal of the Holbrooke-Milosevic agreement was to resolve the immediate humanitarian crisis as 300,000 Kosovar Albanian refugees were threatened by exposure to the approaching winter. Though the West may have underestimated real support for the KLA in Kosovo, Western leaders chose to deal with Milosevic to the exclusion of the Albanian parties (and against expressed concerns by the KLA) because the deal was never about crafting a long-term political compromise to resolve the underlying causes of the conflict. Security Council Resolution 1199 (the framework for the Milosevic-Holbrooke agreement) called on both parties to cease hostilities. Pushed into compliance by the threat of NATO airstrikes, Milosevic viewed the potential for KLA forces to exploit the Serbian withdrawal as his primary concern as the withdrawal agreement was being fashioned. But rather than bring the KLA in to deal directly with Milosevic, Western diplomats reassured Milosevic that Serbian compliance would "put the onus on the KLA" to act appropriately, and even suggested that NATO and KVM forces could be used to ensure that they did.

JANUARY 1999

An attack by Serbian forces on Racak on January 15, 1999, that left 45 ethnic Albanians dead despite the presence of international OSCE observers, "shattered the credibility of the [October] cease-fire agreement and showed how fragile and inadequate the international intervention in Kosovo really was," in the words of Veton Surroi (who would later sit on the Kosovo delegation at Rambouillet). Racak dramatized the fact that OSCE verifiers could observe a crime but could not protect anyone. Racak galvanized the international community around the goal of resolving the conflict and overcame the last reluctance to negotiate—and force Milosevic to negotiate—with both Kosovar factions. This meant finally bringing into practice what the U.S. had already realized in the summer of 1998, that a durable solution could only be achieved through the inclusion of all of the relevant parties.

The failure of the October agreement also pressed home the need to obtain a KLA buy-in in order to neutralize concerns that KLA forces would exploit a NATO threat to attack Serbia by provoking Serbian authorities. That buy-in was enforced by making the threat of air strikes against Serbia conditional on moderation by the KLA and an acceptance of "non-negotiable principles" outlined in a draft accord by the Kosovo Albanian delegation. Some sources conjecture that the talks at Rambouillet were devised under the western misapprehension that if Milosevic could be threatened into obedience, the Kosovar would willingly follow (Daalder & O'Hanlon, 2000, 65). In fact, Rambouillet offered several things to the Kosovar absent from the October agreement, not the least of which was the fact of inclusion. Not only were the Kosovar to be part of the deal-making process, the Kosovar Albanian delegation at Rambouillet was itself to be inclusive, comprising representatives of the KLA in addition to the Rugova government.

Though Demaci would step down as political representative for the KLA in early March over his insistence that the accords at Rambouillet cement a commitment to call a popular referendum on independence in three years instead of a pledge "to determine a mechanism for a final settlement . . . on the basis of the will of the people and the opinions of relevant authorities," ultimately the provisions laid down at Rambouillet addressed Kosovo Albanian security concerns. The combination of incentives and warnings used to induce all parties to Rambouillet finally amounted to the first coherent strategy toward peace since the start of the conflict. For the first-time motives, goals and means of the internationals had come into alignment, overcoming the refusal to negotiate with groups that, in the process, had become more, not less, "terrorist."

Palestine

The Oslo process represents a watershed in the Middle East peace process as the first time the Israeli government entered into direct discussions with the Palestine Liberation Organization (PLO), formerly qualified as a terrorist organization. Though the choice was indeed historic, the decision made by the Rabin government to deal with the PLO was predicated on several more fundamental conceptual shifts that brought the Tactical Question into a context more amenable to inclusion. However, the PLO with its core group al-Fatah was not the only Palestinian organization branded terrorist. Other, more extreme wings of the Palestinian nationalist movement outside the PLO such as Abu Nidal's group, George Habash's People's Front for the Liberation of Palestine (PFPL), and Hamas were and have remained on the list of terrorists.

When the UNSC resolution 242 formalized the formula for the Middle East Peace Process as a tradeoff of territory for security, in 1967, the PLO ascribed to the "3 Nos" of Khartoum—no recognition, no negotiations, no peace. The PLO began to seek a way to enter into a dialogue with Israel 10 years later, when Abu Mazen (Mahmoud Abbas) led a successful movement within the PLO to seek constructive engagement with "democratic forces" in Israel (Corbin, 1994, 25). Before the end of the Cold War and after the first intifada, the PLO formally signaled its acceptance of the state of Israel in two documents presented at the November 1988 meeting of the Palestinian National Council (PNC) in Algiers. The first was a political communiqué in which the PNC declared its commitment to reaching a comprehensive settlement with Israel "within the framework of the UN Charter and relevant Security Council Resolutions," granting implicit recognition of the State of Israel by accepting UNSC Resolution 242. The second document was the "Palestinian Proclamation of Independence," which claimed independence "under the provisions of international law including General Assembly Resolution 181(II) of 1947," which called for the partition of the British Mandate into two States, Israel and Palestine. These documents were followed in December by an explicit statement by PLO Chairman Yasir Arafat recognizing the State of Israel and condemning all forms of terrorism at the General Assembly meeting of the UN in Geneva (because the U.S. would not let Arafat, as a "terrorist," into New York).

Immediately following his address, the U.S. announced the opening of a dialogue with the PLO. But the PLO was still not admitted into the Madrid Conference three years later. Israel's involvement in the Madrid talks beginning in 1991 was conditioned on the exclusion of the PLO and Palestinians from East Jerusalem and the Diaspora from the process. The rationale was that "[Prime Minister Yitzak] Shamir believed that permitting a resident of East Jerusalem to participate would amount to an Israeli concession on the status of Israel's capital" (Markovsky, 1996, 14). By extension the decision to exclude the PLO and the Diaspora was a tactical choice designed to usurp the legitimacy of these group's demands. Prime Minister Yitzhak Rabin's rejection of a request by Abu Mazen to open a channel of communication with the PLO through Egypt as late as October of 1992 indicates that the PLO's stated readiness to deal did not serve as a defining factor in the Israeli decision-making process on whether to engage with the PLO (Corbin, 1994, 26).[14]

Israel's refusal to deal with and recognize the PLO prior to the opening of the Oslo channel was rooted in several factors, including deep-seated mistrust of Palestinian aims, preoccupation with national security concerns, opposition to giving in to acts of terror, and lack of confidence in the ability or will of the PLO leadership to deliver peace. The refusal to deal with the PLO reflected a dominant ideological commitment to realizing the dream of a Greater Israel, particularly on the part of the Likud party, and a lack of urgency in the Israeli mindset concerning the need to resolve the crisis.

In the late 1980s and the early 1990s a combination of internal and external events brought a new sense of urgency and planted the seeds for a perceptual TQ shift in the way some segments of the Israeli public began to assess the conflict. The decision to engage the PLO in constructive dialogue was a tactical choice made by the Rabin government consistent with a set of reframed goals suited to this new context. Jane Corbin (1994, 15) has argued that the most important force behind the Oslo process was "the rise to prominence and political influence" of figures on both sides of the conflict who believed in the necessity of coexistence. These figures include Norwegian facilitator Terje Larsen, Israel's Deputy Foreign Minister Yossi Beilin, Foreign Minister Shimon Peres, and PLO Finance Minister Abu Ala (Ahmed Qorei). Such efforts would scarcely have gained visibility if those at the apex of the concentrated decision-making structures of the Israeli government under Rabin and of the PLO under Arafat had not created or been compelled to create a space for them to explore their vision.

Before the first intifada the Likud government maintained that Israel could address its external conflicts with its Arab neighbors independently of Israel's domestic concerns. Likud viewed Palestinian nationalism in the West Bank as an instrument of the PLO that had no organic basis. The spontaneity and depth of Palestinian participation in the 1987 intifada revealed such views to be grossly at odds with reality (Markovsky, 1996, 8). In later years Uri Savir, one of the chief negotiators for Israel at Oslo, would argue that the 1987 uprising and the heavy-handed Israeli response to the uprising presented a pivotal moment in the Israeli consciousness, triggering a rising tide of domestic ideological opposition to the Israeli occupation (Corbin, 1994, 79; Savir, 1998).

Externally, the evaporation of Soviet influence and the rise of religious fundamentalism in the Middle East created a new dimension of interest in the region. Savir has suggested that Israel's decision to pursue an agreement with the PLO was a reaction to the PLO's new willingness to negotiate with Israel as a result of systemic changes arising at the end of the Cold War (Savir, 1998, 4–5). In Iran poverty provided a growing base of young men for whom the call to violence rung with appeal. Secretary of State James Baker, in an address to the American-Israel Public Affairs Committee in May 1989, counseled Israel to abandon its dreams of a Greater Israel and to accept its need to relinquish control over portions of the Occupied Territories (Markovsky, 1996, 10; Baker, 1999). The message was soon followed by an announcement that Israel would need to halt its expansion of Jewish settlements in the occupied territories as a condition for continuance of U.S. government financial aid and loan guarantees. The new domestic economic conditions created by American policy helped to galvanize a perceptual shift among segments of the Israeli population and for the first time set the Palestinian problem on a timetable defined by pressing domestic economic concerns. In the words of Markovsky (1996, 84), "Israel was moving away from some of its pioneering ideological moorings and becoming a more middle-class society."

Rabin's first major departure from preceding Israeli policy was not his choice to deal with the PLO but his reframing of the Palestinian problem to incorporate domestic economic realties and regional security concerns. In his May 1992 election campaign the Labour Party leader directed his appeal to Israel's Jewish working class who were feeling the impact of cutbacks in U.S. loans and economic assistance. Rabin triumphed over Shamir's incumbent Likud government on a promise to bring peace within a year.

The new Prime Minister further distanced himself from his predecessors early in his term in differentiating between strategic and political settlements in the occupied territories, in adopting certain conciliatory terminology and in his public expression of willingness to negotiate autonomy (territory for security, renamed "peace through security") (Corbin, 1994, 54).

With the vision of the end game reframed, the Tactical Question became how to achieve the best possible outcome for Israel inside a newly accepted set of realities. In the past, Israel's strategy had excluded the PLO for the purpose of delegitimization, consistent with the existence of an opponent who stood on a platform that denied the right of the nation to exist. Another explanation for the Israeli tactical choice to deal with the PLO lies in the Israeli assessment of Arafat's capacity to provide security. Joel Singer has stressed Abu Alaa's role during the Oslo process in vouching for Arafat's ability and will to end terrorism against Israel; "Rabin became fond of saying that the PLO would be able to handle Hamas because it would not be hampered by civil liberties constraints." (Markovsky, 1996, 53). The Israeli team's faith in Arafat's capabilities were pivotal to the decision to deal with the PLO, although apart from the fact that the remark in itself appears to contradict the spirit of lasting peace, Rabin did have information that indicated Arafat's power in this area was not boundless. PLO spokesmen stated in March that Arafat's agreement to a cease-fire would not apply to the intifada or attacks by rejectionist groups like Hamas over whom the PLO had no control. Indeed, circumstances suggest that the moment chosen by Israel to make a deal was one in which the PLO chairman's capability to deliver his population was at its weakest.

The TQ shift came at a time when Israel's bargaining position against Arafat was presented with a new level of opportunity. The PLO chairman's standing was shaken when much of the Arab world reacted with condemnation to his pledge of support for Saddam Hussein's annexation of Kuwait. The well of contributions from Saudi Arabia and Kuwait that had accounted for half of the organization's financial resources suddenly ran dry, forcing the organization to restrict many of the activities that had been essential to its popular base.

The Oslo talks gained official Israeli attention after exploratory efforts demonstrated that the PLO would be more pliable than the official Palestinian delegation in Washington (Corbin, 1994, 76).[15] In pursuing a deal with the PLO at the moment when Arafat's vulnerabilities were at their height the Rabin government seemed poised to capitalize on a historic opportunity to wrangle concessions from the PLO chairman, perhaps at the price of a reduction in security guarantees. As Arafat's power and influence waned, both Israel and the PLO anxiously noted the strength of Hamas wax.

As elements in the left of Rabin's government came to realize, an alternative dimension of the problem was that Arafat's declining influence began to make him reevaluate his own TQ and to reclaim his lost stature by adopting a harder line more consistent with that of Hamas. The PLO had felt it had to cast its support behind Hamas by blocking Washington negotiations in protest of Rabin's expulsion of 415 Hamas militants in December 1992. With Arafat under fire for the Jerusalem concession and for severing welfare payments to 50,000 Palestinian families due to the PLO's financial difficulties, Rabin realized that he might not have the PLO around to deal with much longer and a new leadership might be worse (Corbin, 1994, 148).

It is clear that over the course of Rabin's first term in office, pressures mounted to deliver on his campaign pledge to bring peace. With the Madrid/Washington talks going nowhere the Israeli government explored other options for making a deal (Corbin, 1994, 17, 54, 156; Savir, 1998, 5; 1996, 164). At first, Rabin tried for a backchannel agreement with Syria. But Syrian demands ultimately proved to be unworkable, and Rabin's conclusion that a withdrawal from the Golan Heights would be both strategically and politically riskier than the deal he believed he could cut with the PLO was a deciding factor in his decision to pursue the Oslo Accords (Makovsky, 1996, 115).

Finally, the fact that Israel's dealings with the PLO as part of the Oslo Process were sandwiched between the two Israel's two offensive maneuvers against extremist Hamas (the mass deportations in December 1992) and Operation Accountability against Hezbollah guerillas in Lebanon in July, indicates that the Rabin government intended not only to establish its footing with the PLO in the face of a rising extremist threat, but also to drive a wedge between the PLO and the extremist factions. On the other hand, Israel may have had hopes of using talks with the PLO as a means to secure a peace dividend with its Arab neighbors. During a meeting with Secretary of State Warren Christopher, shortly before the conclusion of the Oslo Accords, Foreign Minister Peres emphasized that a U.S. commitment to push regional States to reconcile with Israel would be vital to the success of the Oslo process (Makovsky, 1996, 75).

The opportunity to deal with the PLO presented Israel with a number of potential opportunities. If a deal could be made, the payoff would be a reduction in PLO sponsored terrorism and a boost to Israel's standing in Arab world. Israel's risk in entering into a partnership with the PLO was that it would not work, but that risk was somewhat mitigated by the provisions of the Accords, which passed responsibility for controlling radical elements to the PLO. From whatever angle, such benefits could be within reach only through negotiations with the PLO to make it a former terrorist and to isolate those who continued to practice terrorism.

Conclusion

The lessons that can be drawn from this brief chapter are highly tentative; they are merely hypotheses supported enough by a few cases not to be thrown out but scarcely firm conclusions. Such support, however, warrants further investigation, because of the importance of the question. Why and when do governments, mediators, and others who brand their opponents as terrorists revise their answers to the Tactical Question and end up negotiating with them?

The first answer is, because and when they have to, that is, when they have to establish an agreement and need the involvement of the terrorists to do so. When NATO had to negotiate with the Macedonian KLA to reestablish a cease-fire or organize disarmament, it rose to the occasion. When the Kosovar KLA proved itself necessary to the final settlement, whether as a partner or as a bait for Milosovic's participation, the U.S. began the difficult job of locating a valid spokesman and talked to them. On the other hand, when a sufficient agreement could be achieved with the moderates but without the terrorists, mediators and opponents tried to do so. Both KLAs had to prove their indispensability to an agreement to be included; the mediators and the government of Rwanda thought the CDR dispensable and excluded it, whatever other calculations were present in the mind(s) of the government. When Rabin negotiated with the PLO, it was because he saw it as the only way to deliver on his electoral promise to bring peace within the year, Syria having proven obdurate and the Washington/Madrid talks without the PLO sterile.

This decision in turn depends on the belief that the opponent can deliver on a commitment and make the agreement effective. Thus, two estimations are involved: the possibility of an agreement and the possibility of implementation, and both must be positive (or at least hopeful, depending on the need of the deciding party for an agreement). Of course, in some cases, the first question suffices, if the agreement succeeds in putting the monkey of responsibility squarely on the back of the other. Israeli calculations on the Oslo negotiations with the formerly terrorist PLO illustrate both situations. A negative estimation kept the mediators from pushing for negotiations with the KLA through 1998 and then a positive estimation led them to reverse their TQ answer thereafter. The RPF's estimation of the *azaku* around Arusha was negative all the way through, despite pressure from the mediators. The weak government's estimation in the first case was positive, but the RUF never had any intention of holding the agreement, which repeatedly collapsed

A second answer, a sharper form of the first, is, when there is a mutually hurting stalemate. In the first answer, governments and mediators negotiated when they had to because it was useful; in the second answer, they negotiated with both sides were stymied and suffering if they did not negotiate. As in any ripe situation, both parties have to be unable to escalate their way out of a painful situation, perceive the possibility of a way out, and have valid spokespeople for their negotiations (Zartman, 2000). In Kosovo and Macedonia, the parties finally realized they were cornered, although it took a while in Kosovo; in Rwanda, they did not, with horrible results. In the Middle East, Israel and the PLO were painfully stalemated, not in Palestine but in Washington, and needed a way to meet their own campaign pledges and to face the common external enemy, Hamas, the "real" terrorist (Pruitt, 1997). Sierra Leone is the clearest example of a mutually hurting stalemate that brought government and terrorists together, but in a flawed agreement.

A third answer is, when a moderating unity of goals is achieved among the various rebel groups, moderate and radical. Unity frequently tends to pull the terrorists away from their extreme stands, although governments tend to fear that it will radicalize the moderates (a logical possibility) and legitimize the goals of the terrorists. However, the slim record presented here shows that unity made negotiation possible, as in Macedonia and Kosovo, and that the absence of unity merely set up the extremists to conduct their terror, as in Rwanda. The key to the Macedonian Albanians' negotiations with the government was their unity, so that moderates could speak for all, after Prizren. The mediators again worked for unity among the Kosovar, even if they switched the focus of their strategies to Milosovic on occasion; getting the latter on board at Rambouillet depended on Kosovar unity as a negotiating partner. The jury is still out in Palestine; Oslo was a tactic to steal victory from Hamas and was unsustainable, but the tactic of the PLO under Abbas was then to seek unity with Hamas in order to curb terrorism and gain legitimacy for broader goals.

The major impediment to the mediators' strategy of unite-and-resolve was the mediators' own unclarity of an acceptable outcome (including its sense of the popular legitimacy locally, regionally or globally of the rebels' demands as opposed to the resistance capabilities on the government side). Whereas Macedonia was a case of a single salient solution, Kosovo was a case of a two-solution problem; objectively, there is no stable intermediate solution as in Macedonia (Zartman, 2005, 2006). Rwanda is a curious intermediate case: There was a single salient solution—a multiparty government, as provided at Arusha—but it was not stable, given the terrorists' unshakable option for another salient solution, ethnic cleansing, and political takeover. For the mediator or opponent to press for the necessary factional coalescence, there must be a single salient acceptable solution for both sides to agree to.

A fourth answer, the reverse of the third, might be when negotiations are a way of creating a split and isolating manageable extremist spoilers. However, the cases provide no such examples. Complex strategic calculations, such as divide-and-defeat or exclude-and-split, do not fare well. Sophisticated tactics such as testing a leader's control by exclusion do not hold up in most cases. Even Israel's test of Arafat's ability to control terrorism seems to be straightforward, and indeed Rabin sought to pull Arafat into a peace agreement as an ally against Hamas, a strategy that his successor, Benyamin Netanyahu, could not conceive of (Kydd & Walter, 2002; and Bueno de Mesquita, 2004, to the contrary.) Indeed, exclusion becomes a self-proving hypothesis: The mediators made no tactical move to split the Macedonian Albanians, to the contrary. Refusal to negotiate with a faction because they are termed terrorists makes them real terrorists (whether they were or not beforehand) because they are excluded. The Kosovar KLA is a case in point. The mediator never sought to follow a tactic of split and isolate, although Milosovic did, with unrewarding results. In the process, the moderates are left unable to deliver on a deal because the excluded faction is able to upset the deal. The Rwandan CDR is a case in point. Not all excluded factions are strong enough to be effective as spoilers, but they will be cast as spoilers if excluded. This preliminary study based on four cases, however, can in no way answer the conundrum, "Were the terrorists radical enough to warrant exclusion, as posited in Rwanda, or were they radicalized—turned into terrorists—because of exclusion, as suggested in Kosovo?"

The fifth conclusion, also related to the previous ones, is, when the mediators lead the way. The mediators' presence and activity was absolutely crucial. The various mediators were always more ready to open negotiators—cautiously—with the accused terrorists and urged the governments to do so, often preparing the way with their own mediation, conditions, and actions. But the mediators were not simply soft on terrorists: They worked on the extremists to fulfill the conditions helpful to their being accepted as negotiation partners. When they did not, the government held firm on a policy of exclusion. It was the mediators who produced unity in Macedonia and Kosovo, by helping to provide security to assuage the rebel groups' fears that their government opponents would not abide by a negotiated commitment; the U.S. tried for Rwandan (Hutu) unity but was unable to achieve it. Mediators pressed for negotiations with the terrorist RUF in Sierra Leone; while the result put the chicken coop in the hands of the foxes, it pull them into the open, where Sankoh could be arrested again and the rebels crushed by the British.

The final answer is the most tentative: When the terrorists revise their goals or their nature. It is tentative because it is not clear how much revision is necessary or whether inclusion or the possibility of inclusion triggers revision or revision triggers the decision to include. Macedonian Albanians at Prizren made plain their willingness to accept a democratic solution, dropping a geographic solution as a threatened goal; but Kosovar Albanians were quite imprecise about their softening of the demand for an immediate promise of independence. The *akazu* retained their opposition to ethnic or party power sharing, justifying the exclusion to which they were subjected. In the still-open case of Palestine, the PLO clearly changed its goals, less clearly changed its methods, but became fully committed to the negotiations and their results; Hamas (and Hizbollah, too, in Lebanon) has accepted the constraints of democratic elections but has not renounced its zero-sum goals. But the conditions of negotiation—compromise, persuasion, positive-sum outcomes—and of democracy themselves—legitimacy of all parties, need to appeal widely, acceptance of popular judgment—impose limitations on terrorists that can mark the beginning of the socialization process toward inclusion.

The answer seems to be that moderation is a process, not a status; a party seeking a solution must be able to see indication of a change in goals or nature in the terrorists that it feels can be encouraged by engaging the terrorists in negotiations. There must be some empirical indication of change to lead to negotiation and some analytical indication that negotiation will intensify the change. Initially, the erstwhile terrorist is unlikely to change its ends, only its means, but engagement in negotiation and the new situation it produces can gradually produce deeper changes.[16] But it is still a chicken-and-egg process, until more research is done, and even then may ultimately be a matter of political or diplomatic "feel."

Notes

1. This chapter is based on the "Negotiating with Terrorism" Project of the Processes of International Negotiation (PIN) Program, Institute of Applied Systems Analysis (IIASA) in Laxenburg (Austria).

2. Both Osama bin Laden and Mahmood Ahmedinajad have offered to negotiate, although primarily for terms of Western surrender and withdrawal.

3. The following discussion is based on Zartman (2003).

4. Another example: Stettenheim (1999, 231) says the June 24, 1993, agreement signed (on division of military) by Ngulinzira was rejected by Habyarimana and Ngulinzira was recalled but Ngulinzira refused and the negotiations continued. Jones (2001, 81) said Ngulinzira took the agreement back to Habyarimana who rejected it and sent Ngulinzira back to Arusha were a final deal was worked out (even more in favor of the RPF).

5. Case study by Christoph Koettl.

6. The government of Cote d'Ivoire played an especially active role in brokering a peace agreement. President Konan Bedié and Foreign Minister Amara Essy made it a top priority. Bangura recalls that the negotiation process coincided with the election of a new UN Secretary General, and that Essy was one of the four African candidates for the job. He might have felt that the brokering of a peace agreement would increase his chances to get the position. See Bangura, 1997, 222.

7. The juntas leaders were well aware that the NPRC's young leaders had lived on the countrys' wealth, bought properties abroad, and obtained UN-founded scholarships in England and the US in exchange for giving up power. See Hirsch 2001, 56.

8. I am grateful for the research assistance of Ben Rempell, "Shooting the Passengers: Changes in Power and Formula in the Macedonian Ohrid Negotiations," (SAIS, May 14, 2004) and Christopher Hattayer, "The Ohrid Framework Negotiations," (SAIS, July 2, 2004) in preparing this case.

9. Or in Albanian UCK, the same initials as the Kosovo Liberation Army in Kosovo.

10. Quotes from Radio Free Europe/Radio Liberty 2001; Garton Ash, November 29, 2001; and Hislope, 2003, 133. Even the International Crisis Group (April 5, 2001, 16) wrote, "The PDP should stop trying to get a seat at the table for the NLA."

11. These sentiments were echoed by three KLA fundraisers: Bardhyl Mahmuti, Jashar Shalihu, and Bilall Sherifi, in an interview given Landay April 15, 1998, 1.

12. At Milosevic's insistence, Rugova dropped his demand that foreign intermediaries be present as a condition for the talks. Though this concession left Rugova somewhat diminished in the eyes of both the LDK and the KLA, in practical terms the deal was somewhat of a compromise position for both leaders who agreed that while he would not be allowed in the discussion room, U.S. envoy Hill would be standing by throughout the meeting in the room next door. The KLA had joined the LDK in its request for foreign mediation to the conflict and therefore cannot be said to have maintained an ideological resistance to compromise even at this stage.

13. The KLA also offered to provide the unarmed verification teams protection from the Serbs.

14. Abu Mazen (M. Abbas) also reports that the PLO established contact with Ariel Sharon and was in the process of opening up a secret channel when Sharon severed the link after rumors of a connection began to circulate in the press (Abu Mazen). Similarly Jane Corbin (19) recounts prior efforts by Norway to put Arafat and Israel in direct contact in April 1983 through a meeting between Palestinian moderate Dr. Issam Sartawi and members of the Israeli Labor party, that ended when Sartawi was assassinated by the extremists (Abu Nidal's group). In 1987 Norway embarked on a bridge-building program that included funding Palestinian medical and humanitarian projects and a study by Larsen.

15. Also Abu Ala complied (on instruction from Tunis) with Savir's request to unlink the question of Jerusalem from the West Bank and Gaza (Corbin, 1994, 83).

16. Recalling the change in means of the National Party under F. W. de Klerk, which eventually led to a change in ends under the new political system (Zartman, 1995).

References

Abebajo, A. (2002). *Building peace in West Africa: Liberia, Sierra Leone, and Guinea-Bissau.* International Peace Academy Occasional Paper Series. Boulder, CO: Lynne Rienner.

Andersen, R. (2000). How multilateral development assistance triggered the conflict in Rwanda. *Third World Quarterly* 21 (3), 441–456.

Bangura, Y. (1997). Reflections on the Abidjan Peace Accord. *Africa Development* 22 (3–4), 217–241.

BBC Summary of World Broadcasts. (1998a, August 17). Ethnic Albanian official says atmosphere still not conducive to talks. [Source: Radio Montenegro, Podgorica, in Serbo-Croat 1330 gmt 15 August 1998].

BBC Summary of World Broadcasts. (1998b, August 18). Politician laments failure to unite Kosovo Albanians. [Source: 'Bajku,' Pristina, in Albanian 14 August 1998].

Bueno de Mesquita, E. (2005). Conciliation, counterterrorism, and patterns of terrorist violence. *International Organization* 59 (1), 145–176.

Corbin, J. (1994). *Gaza first: The secret Norway channel to peace between Israel and the PLO.* London: Bloomsbury and New York: Atlantic Monthly Press.

CNN. (1998). Kosovo liberation army wants a voice in peace talks. October 17, 7:00 PM EST.
Cristal, M. (2003). Negotiating under the cross. *International Negotiations* 8 (8), 549–576.
Daalder, I. H., & O'Hanlon, M. E. (2000) *Winning ugly: NATO's war to save Kosovo*. Washington, DC: Brookings Institution Press.
Deutshe Presse-Agentur. (1998, August 17). No peace talks until Belgrade stops offensive, say Kosovo leaders. BC Cycle 15:58 Central European Time.
DoD News Briefing. (1998). Capt. Mike Doubleday, DASD (PA), Office of the Assistant Secretary of Defense. October 29, 1:30 PM EST. http://www.defenselink.mil/transcripts/transcript.aspx?transcriptid=1759
ECOWAS. (1997). *Six-month peace plan for Sierra Leone. 23 October 1997–22 April 1998*. http://www.c-r.org/accord/s-leone/accord9/Conakry.shtml, accessed June 7, 2006.
The Economist. (U.S.). (1998, March 14). The Kosovo cauldron, 53–54.
Gberie, L. (2000). First stages on the road to peace: the Abidjan process (1995–96). In D. Lord (Ed.), *Paying the price: The Sierra Leone peace process, Accord 9*, available at http://www.c-r.org/accord/s-leone/accord9/index.shtml, accessed June 7, 2006.
Hedges, C. (1999). Kosovo's next masters? *Foreign Affair* 78 (3), 24–42.
Hilsum, L. (1994). Settling scores. *Africa Report* 39 (2), 14–17.
Hirsch, J. L. (2001). *Sierra Leone: Diamonds and the struggle for democracy*. International Peace Academy Occasional Paper Series. Boulder, CO: Lynne Rienner.
Holbrooke, R. (1999). War in Europe. Interview with *Frontline*. http://www.pbs.org/wgbh/pages/frontline/shows/kosovo/interviews
ICG. (2001a, June 20). Macedonia: The last chance for peace. *Balkans Report 113*.
ICG. (2001b, July 27). Macedonia: Still sliding. *Balkans Briefing Paper*.
ICG. (2001c, August 15). Macedonia: War on hold. *Briefing Paper*.
Joint Communiqué. (1993). *Issued at the end of the third round of the political negotiations on power-sharing between the government of the Republic of Rwanda and the Rwandese Patriotic Front, held in Arusha, From 24 November, 1992 to 9 January 1993*. Arusha, Tanzania: January 9.
Jones, B. (2001). *Peacemaking in Rwanda: The dynamics of failure*. Boulder and London: Lynne Rienner.
Judah, T. (2000). *Kosovo: War and revenge*. New Haven, CT: Yale University Press.
Kydd, A., & Walter, B. (2006). The Strategies of terrorism. *International Security* 31 (1), 49–79.
Landay, J. (1998, April 15). Inside a rebellion: Banking on war. *Christian Science Monitor* 1.
Makovsky, D. (1996). *Making peace with the PLO: The Rabin government's road to the Oslo accord*. Boulder: Westview Press.
O'Connor, M. (1998, December 4). Kosovo rebels gain ground under NATO threat. *New York Times*. A3.

Peace Agreement. (1996, November 30). *Between the government of the Republic of Sierra Leone and the Revolutionary United Front of Sierra Leone (RUF)*. http://www.c-r.org/accord/s-leone/accord9/Abidjan.shtml, accessed June 7, 2006.
Peace Agreement. (1999, July 7). *Between the government of Sierra Leone and the Revolutionary United Front of Sierra Leone*. http://www.c-r.org/accord/s-leone/accord9/Lome.shtml, accessed June 7, 2006.
Pruitt, Dean G. (Ed.). (1997). The Oslo negotiations. Special issue of *International Negotiation* 2 (2).
Prunier, G. (1995). *The Rwanda crisis: History of a genocide*. New York: Columbia University Press.
Rashid, I. (2000). The Lomé peace negotiations. In D. Lord (Ed.), *Paying the price: The Sierra Leone peace process, Accord 9*. Available at http://www.c-r.org/accord/s-leone/accord9/index.shtml [June 7, 2006]
Rusi, I. (2003). From army to party: The politics of the NLA. In *Ohrid and Beyond*. London: Institute for War and Peace Reporting.
Savir, U. (1998). *The process*. New York: Random House.
Spector, B. I. (2003). Negotiating with villains revisited. *International Negotiation* 8 (3), 613–621.
Stedman, S. J. (1991). *Peacemaking in civil wars: International mediation in Zimbabwe, 1974–1980*. Boulder and London: Lynne Rienner.
Stedman, S. J. (2000). Spoiler problems in peace processes. In P. Stern & D. Druckman (Eds.), *International Conflict Resolution after the Cold War*. Washington, DC: National Academy Press.
Stettenheim, J. (1999). The Arusha Accords and the failure of international intervention in Rwanda. In M. C. Greenberg, J. H. Barton & M. E. McGuinness (Eds.), *Words over war: Mediation and arbitration to prevent deadly conflict*. Lanham, Boulder, and New York: Rowman & Littlefield.
Walter, B. (2001). *Committing to peace: The successful settlement of civil wars*. Princeton, NJ: Princeton University Press.
Zartman, I. W. (2000). Ripeness: The hurting stalemate and beyond. In P. Stern & D. Druckman (Eds.), *International Conflict Resolution after the Cold War*. Washington, DC: National Academy Press.
Zartman, I. W. (2005a). *Cowardly lions: Missed opportunities to prevent deadly conflict and state collapse*. Boulder, CO: Lynne Rienner.
Zartman, I. W. (2005b). Analyzing intractability. In C. Crocker, F. O. Hampson, & P. Aall (Eds.), *Grasping the nettle*. Washington, DC: USIP.
Zartman, I. W. (2006). Process explanations. In G. O. Faure & F. Cede (Eds.), *Explaining negotiation failures*. Laxenburg: IIASA.
Zartman, I. W. (Ed.). (1995). *Elusive peace: Negotiating to end civil wars*. Washington, DC: Brookings Institution Press.
Zartman, I. W. (Ed.). (2003). *Negotiating with terrorists*. Leiden: Nijhoff.
Zartman, I. W. (Ed.). (2008). *Imbalance of power: Systems of world order after the Cold War*. Boulder, CO: Lynne Rienner.

Part Four

Responses

Chapter 12

Who Supports Terrorism?
Evidence from Fourteen Muslim Countries

C. Christine Fair and Bryan C. Shepherd

Introduction

Since the spectacular terrorist attacks on the United States on September 11, 2001 (9/11), quantitative analyses of terrorism and the subset suicide terrorism have proliferated. Much of these studies have focused on the supply of terrorist manpower and the attributes of terrorists. These findings have generally found that terrorists are generally male, better educated, and less likely to be from economically deprived backgrounds, relative to the populations from which they are drawn. The findings of various studies have been mixed with respect to marital status and propensity to be a terrorist (see Pape, 2003, 1; Cronin, 2003, 5; Berman & Laitin, 2004; Iannaccone, 1992, 1998, 2004; Harrison, 2004; Gold, 2004; Konrad, 2004; Krueger & Maleckova, 2002a, 2002b; Berrebi, 2003; Collier, 2000; Collier & Hoeffler, 2000; Bueno de Mesquita, forthcoming).

Although these supply-side studies continue to propagate, there have been no comparable quantitative efforts to examine the explanatory powers of demographic variables on *demand* or support for terrorism generally or suicide terrorism in particular.[1] As a consequence, there have been few systemic efforts to exposit determinants of the support that terrorism and terrorists garner among the population on whose behalf terrorist organizations claim to act and from which terrorist cadre and commanders are drawn.[2] Yet, understanding the determinants of the demand for terrorism is a fundamental piece of the analytical puzzle.

This research note seeks to address in modest measure these empirical lacunae by exploring aspects of the demand (or support) for terrorism using data that have been recently made available by the Pew Research Center. These data have not been extensively used for these purposes. These data are comprised of respondent level data for 7,849 adult persons across 14 countries with predominantly Muslim populations or large Muslim minorities within Africa, Southwest, South and Southeast Asia. We analyze these data to draw out who supports terrorism and what their characteristics are.

Consonant with the public and scholarly concern about suicide terrorism, in 2002 the Pew Research Center fielded a survey in countries with predominantly Muslim populations or with large Muslim minorities. Pew's survey instrument collected several kinds of data about the respondent and included a question that Pew hoped would query support for suicide terrorism. Unfortunately, while the question used by Pew gives primary emphasis to suicide terrorism, the phrasing of the question pertains to *all* varieties of terrorism. Pew has used these data to explicitly address countrywide aggregate support for *suicide* terrorism in these countries despite the problematic phrasing of this key question (see the Pew Research Center, 2002).

Our analysis (using summary statistics and regression analysis) finds that in many cases, females are more likely to support terrorism than males. We also found that younger persons are more likely to support terrorism than older people, but support for the tactic among older persons is still high in many countries. We find that those who are very poor are less likely to support terrorism, but those who are not poor are more likely to support it. Persons who believe that religious leaders should play a larger role in politics are more likely to support terrorism than those who don't hold this view.[3] Finally, we found that persons who believed that Islam was under threat were more likely to support terrorism than those who did not have such threat perceptions. Most importantly, we find that while these generalizations hold, the affect of these various variables vary throughout the fourteen countries in question. This makes the case that any intervention must be highly tailored to the target population in question, which in turn is highly specified using demographic and even psychographic data.[4]

The remainder of this research note will be organized in the following manner. The second section will describe the data and methodology employed here. The third section presents key findings from the descriptive analysis of these data. The fourth section details finding from the econometric modeling of support for terrorism. The fifth and final section concludes with a discussion of the results and their particular for counterterrorism efforts.

Attitudes Data

We employ the data from the Global Attitudes Survey 2002, conducted by the Pew Research Center. This dataset represents a general survey of respondents in 44 countries across the globe, but it specifically includes 14 countries that are either predominantly Muslim or have large Muslim minorities (henceforth we will use the inelegant short-hand "Muslim countries" to reference these states). Most of the samples were nationally representative. However, there were several countries where the samples were predominantly urban. For purposes of this analysis of Muslim countries, it should be noted that this caveat applies to samples for Egypt, Indonesia, the Ivory Coast, Mali, Pakistan, and Senegal.[5]

Fieldwork in all 44 countries, including those included in this analysis, was conducted between July and October 2002. Thus these national surveys were fielded well in advance of the U.S.-led operations against Iraq, which commenced in March of 2003. However, by the end of the summer of 2002 vigorous discussion had already taken prominent place in the media and within various multilateral forums, which intensified in the early months of 2003.

Within these countries with large Muslim populations, Muslim respondents were asked several questions related to their religious beliefs and their place in a modernizing and increasingly connected world. In addition, Muslims respondents in these Muslim countries were asked the following questions:

> Some people think that suicide bombing and other forms of violence against civilian targets are justified in order to defend Islam from its enemies. Other people believe that, no matter what the reason, this kind of violence is never justified. Do you personally feel that this kind of violence is often justified to defend Islam, sometimes justified, rarely justified or never justified?

Responses to this question comprise the outcome variable in this analyses. Responses ranged from one through four (1 = "Often Justified," 2 = "Sometimes Justified," 3 = "Rarely Justified," and 4 = "Never Justified"). Note that this question was not asked in Egypt (see Princeton Survey Research Associates International, 2002). For purposes of the descriptive statistics, we recoded this variable such that higher values indicate higher levels of support for the tactic. Thus, upon recoding, this variable took the values: 4 = "Often Justified," 3 = "Sometimes Justified," 2 = "Rarely Justified," and 1 = "Never Justified." For purposes of the regression analysis only, we recoded this measure as dichotomous variable (0- = Never Justified and 1 = Ever Justified) and analyzed it using both descriptive statistics as well as logistic regression.

We are cognizant that this question is inherently framed within the context of Islam. Ideally, we would prefer a question devoid of religious verbiage; however, because the assumption of this religious connection to suicide bombing and other forms of violence is so ubiquitous in the countries included, the allusion to it in this question is likely to be irrelevant. (Obviously, if we were looking at countries such as Sri Lanka or India where non-Islamist groups have employed the tactic, this phraseology of the question would be utterly inappropriate.)

As noted above, the question also conflates suicide terrorism (a subset of terrorism) with terrorism (the superset). Pew, despite this limitation, has used these data to make claims about the support for *suicide terrorism*, which may not be warranted. It is possible that people may feel very differently about suicide terrorism than they do about terrorism in general. It is also possible that given the primary emphasis on suicide terrorism, respondents may cue off this emphasis depending on how the question was administered during the fielding of the survey. Obviously, it is preferable that this question be disaggregated into specific queries about support for terrorism generally and suicide terrorism in particular.

We recommend that these issues (reference to Islam and the conflation of suicide terrorism with terrorism generally) be considered in future surveys.

Empirical Methods

This analysis utilizes both descriptive statistical measures to provide broad overviews of how support for terrorism varies within the respondent samples of the 14 Muslim countries by specific groups, such as age groups, gender, and marital status. (Because of the above-noted problem with the distribution of urban respondents, we were unable to provide cross tabulations of urban and nonurban respondents.) All summary statistics were derived using appropriate weights provided by Pew. Building on these summary statistics, we next utilize logistical regression to explain with greater complexity the variation in support for terrorism across the respondents in our sample.

We estimate regression models evaluating support for terrorism, using the dichotomous variable (0 = Never Justified, 1 = Ever Justified) as our dependent variable. Below we provide a discussion of the independent variables employed in our models and the theoretical and empirical bases for their inclusion.

Demographic Variables

Important demographic variables such as "sex" (female = 1), "age" (continuous 18–94) and "marital status" (married = 1, all other = 0) were included in our models because their characterization will be important to any public diplomacy campaign or targeted intervention. These variables are also important because the conventional wisdom is that young, unmarried males are the most likely candidate for participating in or supporting a terrorist campaign (Kleinberg, 2003; Ganor, 2000; Rubin, 2002; Hoffman, 2001; Paz, 2001; Camarota, 2002). This is true despite the growing literature on female terrorists (see Cunningham, 2003).

Proxies for Socioeconomic Status

Economic comparisons based on monetary units is difficult given the wide variety of currencies and their exchange rates and the complex and highly debated modeling techniques to control for purchasing power parity.[6] Instead, we used two proxy questions to instrument the effects of socioeconomic variables on support for terrorism. These questions asked, "Have there been times in the past year when you did not have enough money to buy food your family needed?" and "Have there been times in the past year when you did not have enough money to buy clothes your family needed?" Both questions had "yes" and "no" (recoded to 1 and 0, respectively) as available responses.

These proxies for economic resources are important to our understanding of the linkages between poverty and support for terrorism. According to depravation theory, we would expect one of two relationships between these economic variables. Individuals with neither food nor money to buy clothes would support violent behaviors as a result of frustration manifested in aggression or support for aggression. But relative deprivation theory also suggests that there may be a threshold point at which the relationships between poverty and support for terrorism change (Young, 1999).

On a similar conceptual note, the use of these variables permits us to explore aspects of Maslow's hierarchy of needs (Maslow, 1970). According to this theory, when basic needs are unmet, their satiation is the primary focus of motivation. Extremely economically deprived persons do not have the "luxury" of expending efforts toward issues unrelated to day-to-day survival. Once basic needs are met, the needs of the next level can be addressed. These issues will be explored through the use of these socioeconomic proxies in our model.

We also explored the impact of ownership of a cell phone and a computer to instrument for variation in support for terrorism. These variables are difficult to interpret because they can reflect at least two different aspects about those who possess them. On the one hand, owners of these technologies are likely to have higher socioeconomic status than those who do not have these items. In this sense these variables may behave like socioeconomic proxies and would comport with the above-noted predictions.

On the other hand, these variables also suggest a degree of connectivity and ability to access information in ways that nonowners would not have. Ownership of these items may also correlate to other means of accessing information or even suggest different ways of understanding information than non-owners. Clearly, this is not identical to socioeconomic status.

If seen as measures of connectivity and accessibility to information, there is no explicit prediction as to how ownership of a cell phone and a computer would explain variation in support for terrorism. If these variables are seen as indexing greater access to information, their affect could be in either direction. If the information they receive is accurate and contributes to their threat perception, then greater access to information would produce an increase in the propensity to support terrorism. Access to information may dispel myths and misinformation, but the ownership of these technologies is likely to be less important than the content of the information they convey. But this, too, may suggest opportunities for public diplomacy interventions.

Religio-Political Sentiments

We also included an explanatory variable that characterized respondents' religio-political sentiments. Specifically, respondents were asked to give their level of agreement or disagreement with the following statement: "Religious leaders should play a larger role in politics." Four response categories ranging from "1 = completely disagree" to "4 = completely agree" were available. There is no theoretical prediction as to how this variable may behave. If individuals believe that terrorists and their organizations are not religious leaders and if individuals believe that religious leaders should be more involved in politics (a maximum value of 1), this may augur decreased support for terrorism. Alternatively, if respondents view terrorist outfits as forms of religious leaders and they believe that religious leaders should have greater role in politics, then lower numbers for this variable would suggest higher support for terrorism. Similarly if religious leaders support terrorist activities, then support for these leaders should suggest greater support for terrorism. While a priori ambiguous, this variable is important because it helps characterize the legitimacy and authority that religious leaders play within politics and therefore may identify potential partners in a public diplomacy campaign.

Threat Perception Variables

We also included two variables that represent two different kinds of threat perceptions as predictors for support of terrorism. First, we included a variable that indicated agreement with the statement "The influence of other religions is the greatest threat to Islam today." Individuals who agreed with this were given a value of '1;' all others received a value of '0.'

The second threat variable instruments the influence of nationalist threats that are not explicitly imbued with religious sentiment upon support for terrorism. We used the individual's agreement or disagreement with the statement that "There are parts of neighboring countries that really belong to (respondent's country)." The four response categories ranged from "completely disagree" (a value of 1) to "completely agree" (a value of 4). This variable is important because it often argued that pivotal conflicts (e.g., Palestine, Chechnya, Kashmir) animate the sentiments of those who support terrorism and even motivate those who perpetrate the tactic. Presumably, explicating the role of these threat perceptions on support for terrorism may identify potential opportunities for public diplomacy interventions. (We summarize the empirical hypotheses in Table 12.1, next page.)

Additional Controls and Technical Details

In addition, we included dummy variables for each country to control for state-specific effects that are not explicitly controlled for in the model. Each regression model is benchmarked to Mali, which is the excluded case. (We chose Mali as the benchmark case because support for terrorism in that country is nearly identical to the overall sample mean.) Thus all country coefficients and the corresponding analysis are relative to Mali. Because the affect of some variables on support for terrorism may depend characteristics of the particular country, we permitted various interactions (e.g., between gender and the state in question) with these country-level dummy variables. However, most of these interactions proved to be statistically insignificant, as is apparent in the appropriate tables. The first model we estimate contains no interaction variables while the second through the fifth examine various interactions effects.

Table 12.1. Table of Empirical Hypotheses

Variable	Hypothesis
Female	There is no explicit prediction as to how gender would influence support for terrorism.
Age	There is no explicit prediction as to how age would influence support for terrorism.
Married	Conventional wisdom holds that married persons would be less likely to support suicide terrorism although there is no explicit prediction as to how marital status would influence support for terrorism.
No money for food	The literature on terrorism suggests that extremely poor persons may be less interested in social events such as terrorism given their immediate preoccupation with survival.
No money for clothes	There is no explicit prediction as this variable. One could argue that if one has enough money for food but not enough for clothing, he or she may be more concerned with social events such as terrorism. If this is the case, affirmative answers would predict an increase in support for terrorism. However, if this variable indexes extreme poverty, it could decrease support for terrorism.
Religious leaders should play larger role in politics	There is no explicit prediction for this variable as it would depend on the view of the respondent held of terrorist organizations.
Influence of other religions is a threat	Agreement with this statement would increase the likelihood of supporting terrorism.
There are parts of neighboring countries that belong to us	In countries with outstanding territorial disputes, agreement with this variable should increase likelihood of supporting terrorism.
Ownership of cell phone	There is no explicit predicted affect on support for terrorism.
Ownership of computer	There is no explicit predicted affect on support for terrorism.

Because our outcome variable is dichotomous, we have used the logistic regression method to estimate our five models. Because of the nonlinear basis of logistic regression, we cannot directly use the regression results to predict the direct effect of various variables in the model.

Instead, we must calculate the marginal effects of each of the variables. In the case of a dichotomous variable (value of 1 or 0), the marginal effect indicates the change in probability when that dummy variable value is changed (e.g., from zero to one), while holding all other variables at their sample means. In one case (role of religious leaders), the variable is a polychotomous variable (values 1, 2, 3, 4). To estimate the marginal affect of this variable, we calculated the change in predicted probability of support when that value is changed from 1 to 4, holding all other variables at their sample means. In estimating the effect of age, which is a continuous variable, we predicted the probability of supporting terrorism for various values of age holding all variables at the sample means and graphed these predicted values as a function of age.

In all analyses a generalized weight was applied, which was supplied by Pew Research Center. Sample sizes (which are affected by the application of the weights) are held constant within the regressions but vary in other areas, such as the presentation of the descriptive statistics. The number of valid respondents is presented in the relevant tables. We used SPSS version 11.0 for Windows for this analysis.

Descriptive Statistics

Across the 14 countries studied, the support for terrorism had a sample mean of 2.05. (Recall that a value of 2 indicates that terrorism is "rarely justified.") The country with the highest support for terrorism was Lebanon with a mean of 3.15 out of a maximum value of 4. The country with the lowest support was Uzbekistan with a mean of 1.22. The overall summary statistics for terrorism support among respondents of these 14 countries, as well the sample size and nation-wise composition of the sample is given below in Table 12.2 (next page).

We next disaggregate support for terrorism within the 14 countries by age (those younger than 40 and those 40 years and older), gender, and marital status. To do so, we performed pair-wise t-tests on the sample mean on the outcome variable (support terrorism). These results are presented in Tables 12.3, 12.4 and 12.5. (We used the Levene's Test for Equality of Variances to determine whether we should assume equal or unequal variances.) On the main we found that there were relatively few statistically different group means (at the 0.1 significance level or lower). This was surprising given the large sample sizes in some of these

Table 12.2. Descriptive Statistics for Support for Terrorism (Higher Mean Indicates Greater Support for Terrorism)

Country	Mean	N	Std. Deviation	Min.	Max.	% of Total N
Lebanon	3.15	554	1.05	1	4	7.06
Ivory Coast	2.55	98	1.13	1	4	1.25
Bangladesh	2.47	476	1.13	1	4	6.07
Nigeria	2.44	318	1.13	1	4	4.05
Jordan	2.34	873	1.06	1	4	11.12
Pakistan	2.20	1522	1.29	1	4	19.39
Mali	2.06	602	1.02	1	4	7.66
Senegal	1.91	644	1.09	1	4	8.21
Ghana	1.91	85	1.01	1	4	1.08
Uganda	1.83	110	1.04	1	4	1.40
Indonesia	1.77	925	0.97	1	4	11.79
Tanzania	1.61	230	0.92	1	4	2.93
Turkey	1.44	847	0.85	1	4	10.79
Uzbekistan	1.22	566	0.60	1	4	7.21
Sample Mean	2.05	7849	1.16	1	4	100.00

Source: Author tabulations using data obtained from the Pew Global Attitudes Survey 2002.

countries. However, it must be kept in mind, that these comparisons are not fully controlled. For instance, while we control for marital status in one comparison, individuals vary in all other respects (age, gender, SES, etc.). In a more fully controlled analyses where similar individuals are compared (e.g., regression analyses), the impact of any one characteristic (e.g., age, gender, marital status, SES) may become prominent both in terms of magnitude and statistical significance.

Our descriptive analysis has produced the following general observations:

- *Variation within age groups.* Statistically significant between-group variation was found in only in five countries. In Pakistan, Senegal, Turkey, Lebanon, and Jordan, respondents under 40 years of age were more likely to support the tactic than those who were 40 years or older (see Table 12.3 for details).

- *Variation by marital status.* Statistically significant between-group variation was found in three countries. In Ghana married persons were more likely to support terrorism than unmarried persons. In Pakistan and Tanzania, unmarried persons were more likely to support terrorism (see Table 12.4).

Table 12.3. Support for Terrorism Among Those 40 Years and Above and Those Below the Age of 40

Country Name	>= 40 Mean (N) (Std. Error)	< 40 Mean (N) (Std. Error)	T statistic
Bangladesh	0.67 (160) 0.037	0.71 (293) 0.027	−0.808
Ivory Coast	0.80 (11) 0.128	0.73 (87) 0.048	0.458
Ghana	0.64 (28) 0.092	0.45 (56) 0.067	1.707
Indonesia	0.46 (283) 0.030	0.43 (642) 0.020	0.897
Mali	0.62 (186) 0.036	0.60 (406) 0.024	0.560
Nigeria≠	0.75 (115) 0.41	0.69 (203) 0.032	1.024
Pakistan≠	0.45 (419) 0.024	0.52 (1048) 0.015	2.378**
Senegal≠	0.40 (208) 0.034	0.53 (436) 0.024	−2.995****
Tanzania	0.39 (112) 0.046	0.33 (115) 0.044	0.977
Turkey≠	0.21 (295) 0.024	0.26 (550) 0.019	−1.655*
Uganda	0.46 (28) 0.096	0.39 (76) 0.056	0.634
Uzbekistan	0.12 (204) 0.023	0.15 (362) 0.019	−1.109
Lebanon≠	0.83 (178) 0.029	0.90 (367) 0.016	−2.163**
Jordan≠	0.63 (344) 0.026	0.76 (529) 0.019	−4.010****

Notes: ≠ Indicates that equal variances were not assumed. **** Indicates significant at the 0.001 level, *** at the 0.01 level, ** at the 0.05 level, and * at the 0.1 level. Derived from author tabulations of data from Pew Global Attitudes Survey 2002.

Table 12.4. Support for Terrorism Among Married and Unmarried Respondents

Country Name	Unmarried Mean (N) (Std. Error)	Married Mean (N) (Std. Error)	T statistic
Bangladesh	0.77 (107) 0.041	0.69 (369) 0.024	1.550
Ivory Coast≠	0.78 (61) 0.054	0.67 (36) 0.079	1.121
Ghana	0.33 (21) 0.105	0.57 (63) 0.063	1.909*
Indonesia	0.46 (193) 0.036	0.43 (732) 0.018	0.566
Mali≠	0.58 (237) 0.032	0.62 (365) 0.025	1.051
Nigeria	0.68 (96) 0.048	0.73 (222) 0.030	−0.952
Pakistan≠	0.54 (410) 0.025	0.49 (1106) 0.015	1.844*
Senegal	0.51 (304) 0.029	0.47 (341) 0.027	0.969
Tanzania	0.47 (62) 0.064	0.32 (168) 0.036	2.060**
Turkey	0.26 (260) 0.027	0.23 (585) 0.017	0.829
Uganda	0.32 (22) 0.102	0.47 (88) 0.053	−1.247
Uzbekistan	0.14 (164) 0.027	0.14 (402) 0.018	−0.171
Lebanon≠	0.86 (282) 0.021	0.88 (269) 0.020	−0.933
Jordan	0.72 (229) 0.030	0.70 (637) 0.018	0.572

Notes: ≠ Indicates that equal variances were not assumed. **** Indicates significant at the 0.001 level, *** at the 0.01 level, ** at the 0.05 level, and * at the 0.1 level. Derived from author tabulations of data from Pew Global Attitudes Survey 2002.

- *Variation by gender.* Statistically significant variation between groups was found in only four countries. In Bangladesh, Pakistan, and Jordan females were more likely than males to support terrorism whereas females in Nigeria were less likely to do so (see Table 12.5).

We next explore the impacts of these variables more rigorously in the below-given discussion of our regression analyses.

Regression Analyses

The first logistic regression model that we examine includes support for terrorism as the dependent variable. Independent variables include the demographic, socioeconomic, political, religious, and threat perception variables as well as the dummy indicators for each country. (We present the regression results along with sample means in Table 12.10, page 304.) As described earlier, we calculated the marginal affects for those variables that were significant in the regression at least at the 0.1 level of significance (see Table 12.6). We are using this higher cutoff threshold because in many of these models, cell sizes are small.

Table 12.5. Support for Terrorism Among Males and Females

Country Name	Male Mean (N) (Std. Error)	Female Mean (N) (Std. Error)	T statistic
Bangladesh≠	0.65 (229) 0.031	0.76 (247) 0.027	2.649***
Ivory Coast	0.78 (47) 0.062	0.70 (51) 0.065	0.822
Ghana	0.56 (54) 0.068	0.42 (31) 0.090	1.205
Indonesia	0.44 (446) 0.024	0.44 (479) 0.023	0.153
Mali≠	0.58 (316) 0.028	0.64 (285) 0.029	1.456
Nigeria≠	0.76 (174) 0.032	0.65 (144) 0.040	2.178**
Pakistan	0.43 (922) 0.016	0.62 (600) 0.020	7.300****
Senegal	0.51 (337) 0.027	0.47 (307) 0.029	1.115
Tanzania	0.35 (121) 0.043	0.38 (109) 0.047	−0.456
Turkey	0.23 (429) 0.020	0.25 (418) 0.021	−0.539
Uganda	0.47 (62) 0.064	0.40 (48) 0.071	0.749
Uzbekistan	0.15 (290) 0.021	0.14 (276) 0.021	0.204
Lebanon	0.87 (300) 0.020	0.88 (254) 0.021	−0.395
Jordan≠	0.65 (462) 0.022	0.78 (411) 0.020	−4.362****

Notes: ≠ Indicates that equal variances were not assumed. **** Indicates significant at the 0.001 level, *** at the 0.01 level, ** at the 0.05 level, and * at the 0.1 level. Derived from author tabulations of data from Pew Global Attitudes Survey 2002.

Among the demographic variables explored in this model (age, gender, marital status), only age and gender were significant. The marginal effect of being female (relative to being male) was 7.65 percent (see Table 12.6). Using data from this model, we also predicted the probability of supporting terrorism as a function of age. (This graph is given in Figure 12.1, next page.) These data suggest that older respondents were less likely to support the tactic than those who are younger. What is notable that even at the highest age in our sample's range (62), predicted support is still above 45 percent.

Our analyses of variables on SES yielded interesting and complex results. Individuals who reported having insufficient funds for food during the course of the past year were *less* likely to support suicide terrorism than those without such problems (marginal effect of −6.6 percent). However, those who reported having inadequate money for clothing were more likely to support terrorism with a marginal effect of 4.28 percent. Individuals who owned their own cellular phone and their own computers were also more likely to support terrorism than those without such technologies with marginal effects of 4.25 and 8.75 percent respectively. Thus, whether one views these variables as denoting SES or informational access, both ownership of a cell phone and a computer indicate increased support for suicide terrorism, all else equal. (See data in Table 12.6.)

Table 12.6. Marginal Effects of Various Variables on Support for Suicide Terrorism

Country	Marginal Effect of Variable
Female	7.65% ****
Age	See Figure 12.1****
No money for food	−6.6%***
No money for clothes	4.28%**
Respondent owns a computer	8.75%***
Respondent owns cell phone	4.25%**
Religious leaders should play a larger role in politics (1-completely disagree, 4-completely agree)	20.91% Difference between complete agreement (1) and complete disagreement (4)****
Influence of other religions is a threat to Islam	6.77%**

Note: **** Indicates significant at the 0.001 level, *** at the 0.01 level, ** at the 0.05 level, and * at the 0.1 level. Derived from author tabulations of data from Pew Global Attitudes Survey 2002. Marginal affect calculated using estimates from Model 1, evaluated at the sample means.

Figure 12.1. Predicted Probability of Supporting Terrorism By Age, All Else Constant

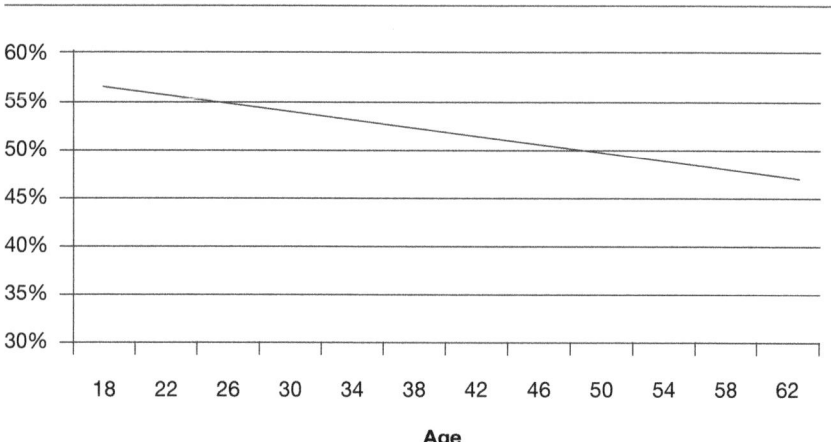

Note: Predicted probabilities calculated using estimates from Model 1, evaluating all variables at the sample means.

Respondent who felt that religious leaders should play a larger role in government were significantly *more* likely to support terrorism. The marginal effect of moving between complete disagreement (1) and complete disagreement (4) was 20.91 percent.[7]

Among the threat variables, in the uninteracted model (Model 1), territorial disputes were not significant. (Note that in ongoing work, we are examining country specific models. In some of these within-country models, this variable *is* significant even though it is not significant in this model of across-country effects.) The variable indicating respondent perceptions that Islam is under threat was significant (at 0.05 level) with a marginal effect of 6.77 percent.

To allow the affect of key variables to vary within the specific states, we ran several models, where we computed interactions of select variables with the country-level indicator. This is done during the statistical programming process by forming new variables comprised of products, for example: female x Bangladesh. Specifically, we computed interactions of country indicators with gender, threat perception, and the variable indicating the respondent owns computer. We selected these variables based on an examination of the t-test analyses, significance, and magnitude of the variables in the uninteracted model, and on our analysis of state-level models. The regression coefficients and the list of variables for these models are given in Table 12.10, page 304. Calculated marginal effects are given in Tables 12.7–12.9.

- In Model 2, we augmented the variables contained in Model 1 and added six interaction variables between gender and the state-level dummies. In general these interactions were not significant. Only four interactions were significant at the 0.1 significance level. Analysts who prefer a significance-level cutoff of 0.05 would not consider these interactions to be significant.

- In Model 3, we added to Model 1 six interaction variables between the threat (to Islam) perception variable and the country indicators, many of which were significant even at the rigorous 0.01 significance level.

- In Model 4, we augmented Model 1 with the interactions between the country indicators and computer ownership. (Note that in three countries, no respondent owned a computer.) Four interactions were significant at the 0.1 significance level.

- In Model 5, we included the variables in Model 1 and added all 16 interaction variables (e.g., dummy variables with threat, gender, and computer ownership). Many of these interaction variables were significant.

To examine the country-specific marginal effects of gender, threat, and computer ownership within the 14 countries, we predicted the probability of supporting terrorism using the appropriate models. In the case of gender and its interaction with country-level dummies, we built models to calculate the relative predicted probability of supporting terrorism for females and males in each state using results from Model 2. We were of mixed minds in performing this analysis and presenting results for all countries, as only four of the interactions were significant. Ultimately, we chose to present the estimated state-specific marginal effect for in Table 12.7 (next page), with the appropriate significance indicators. What is notable is that while the overall affect of gender predicted using Model 1 was positive, in three of the four statistically significant interactions, women were less likely to support terrorism than males. In Uganda, Senegal, and Turkey, females were less likely to support it with marginal effects of –17.47, –7.89, –4.98 percent respectively. In Indonesia, females

Table 12.7. Marginal Effects of Being Female on Support for Terrorism

Country	Marginal Effect of Gender
Uganda	−17.47%*
Ghana	−15.03%
Senegal	−7.89%**
Turkey	−4.98%*
Ivory Coast	−4.07%
Uzbekistan	−1.50%
Nigeria	−0.57%
Lebanon	−0.27%
Indonesia	1.07%*
Tanzania	8.14%
Jordan	8.79%
Pakistan	13.50%
Bangladesh	14.01%

Note: Country-wise marginal effects calculated using estimates from Model 2, evaluated at the sample means. All results are relative to the benchmark case of Mali. **** Indicates significant at the 0.001 level, *** at the 0.01 level, ** at the 0.05 level, * at the 0.1 level.

were slightly more likely to support terrorism with a marginal effect of 1.07 percent. These findings underscore the importance of understanding with great clarity the particular impact of particular demographic variables within specific target audiences.

We similarly calculated the marginal effect of threat perception on the predicted probability of supporting terrorism in countries examined using regression results from Model 3. These data are provided in Table 12.8. As these data illustrate, the impact of threat perception varies significantly within the states, but in all cases it is associated with increasing tendency to support terrorism. In Pakistan, Jordan, Nigeria, Indonesia, and Lebanon the marginal effect of having this threat perception was over 70 percent. As noted earlier, many of the interaction variables were statistically significant.

Finally, we calculated the marginal effect of computer ownership on predicted probability of supporting terrorism, using regression results from Model 4. These values are given in Table 12.9. (Note that several of the African countries had no respondents with computers and thus were not included.) In Model 1, the uninteracted model, computer ownership tended to suggest increased likelihood of supporting terrorism. However, when we allow the effect to vary within states through the use of the interaction variables, a much more nuanced picture emerges. In the four

Table 12.8. Marginal Effects of Threat Perception on Support for Terrorism

Country	Marginal Effect of Threat Perception
Ghana	2.03%
Bangladesh	4.21%**
Ivory Coast	25.57%
Uzbekistan	28.38%***
Turkey	33.97%***
Senegal	43.81%
Tanzania	55.38%**
Uganda	60.25%
Pakistan	70.62%****
Jordan	75.07%**
Nigeria	78.72%**
Indonesia	82.58%****
Lebanon	89.89%**

Note: Marginal effects calculated using estimates from Model 3, evaluated at the sample means. All results are relative to the benchmark case of Mali. **** Indicates significant at the 0.001 level, *** at the 0.01 level, ** at the 0.05 level, * at the 0.1 level.

Table 12.9. Marginal Effects of Computer Ownership on Support for Terrorism

Country	Marginal Effect of Threat Perception
Bangladesh	−29.57%*
Nigeria	−10.99%*
Pakistan	−9.11%*
Turkey	−7.95%*
Lebanon	−0.37%
Uzbekistan	−0.36%
Senegal	8.39%
Indonesia	22.79%
Ivory Coast	28.66%

Note: Marginal effects calculated using estimates from Model 4, evaluated at the sample means. All results are relative to the benchmark case of Mali. Countries where no respondents owned computers not included. **** Indicates significant at the 0.001 level, *** at the 0.01 level, ** at the 0.05 level, * at the 0.1 level.

Table 12.10. Logistic Regression Results for Support for Terrorism (Models 1–5) and Weighted Sample Means

Variable	Model 1	Model 2	Model 3	Model 4	Model 5	Sample Mean (Weighted)
	(B)	(B)	(B)	(B)	(B)	
Female	0.308****	0.444**	0.314***	0.307****	0.458**	0.44
Age	-0.009****	-0.009****	-0.009***	-0.009****	-0.008***	35.127
Married	-0.018	-0.01	-0.023	-0.018	-0.014	0.68
No money for food	-0.247***	-0.251***	-0.257***	-0.253***	-0.27***	0.4
No money for clothes	0.172**	0.172**	0.182**	0.18**	0.191**	0.41
Respondent owns a computer	0.356***	0.365***	0.354***	3.144*	3.17*	0.12
Respondent owns cell phone	0.171**	0.143*	0.17**	0.1620*	0.132*	0.23
Religious leaders should play a larger role in politics (1-completely disagree; 4-completely agree)	0.283****	0.281****	0.283****	0.275****	0.273****	2.78
There are parts of neighboring countries that belong to X. (1-completely disagree; 4-completely agree)	-0.004	0.004	0.000	-0.015	-0.0020	2.96
Influence of other religions is a threat to Islam ((thrtrsn2) (1- yes, 0- no))	0.275**	0.285**	-1.472***	0.289**	-1.463***	0.05
Bangladesh	0.146	0.076	0.075	0.233	0.109	0.0533
Ivory Coast	0.482*	0.85**	0.366	0.43*	0.697*	0.0149

Ghana	−0.253	0.031	−0.254	−0.238	−0.016	0.0058
Indonesia	−0.633****	−0.431**	−0.733****	−0.632****	−0.532***	0.1422
Nigeria	0.336*	0.532**	0.248	0.404**	0.556**	0.0311
Pakistan	−0.621****	−0.707****	−0.724****	−0.519****	−0.711****	0.1696
Senegal	−0.333**	−0.085	−0.382***	−0.326**	−0.121	0.0919
Tanzania	−0.955****	−1.01***	−1.035****	−0.945****	−1.064***	0.0209
Turkey	−1.594****	−1.355****	−1.673****	−1.508****	−1.327****	0.1096
Uganda	−0.386	−0.035	−0.414	−0.364	−0.072	0.0086
Uzbekistan	−2.149****	−1.999****	−2.228****	−2.05****	−2.05****	0.0677
Lebanon	1.093****	1.205****	1.022****	1.128****	1.179****	0.0784
Jordan	0.184	0.104	0.125	0.076	−0.06	0.1374
Bangladesh *Threat	—	—	1.67**	—	1.554**	0.0032
Ivory Coast *Threat	—	—	4.927	—	6.169	0.0005
Ghana *Threat	—	—	−2.791	—	−3.472	0.0002
Indonesia *Threat	—	—	3.118****	—	3.108****	0.0034
Nigeria *Threat	—	—	1.89**	—	1.767**	0.003
Pakistan *Threat	—	—	2.124****	—	2.218***	0.0127
Senegal *Threat	—	—	0.962	—	0.955	0.0031
Tanzania *Threat	—	—	1.774**	—	1.732**	0.004
Turkey *Threat	—	—	1.837***	—	1.828***	0.0038
Uganda *Threat	—	—	1.353	—	1.606*	0.001
Uzbekistan *Threat	—	—	2.131**	—	2.052*	0.0005
Lebanon *Threat	—	—	1.69**	—	1.673**	0.0068
Jordan *Threat	—	—	1.501**	—	1.488**	0.008
Bangladesh *Female	—	0.198	—	—	0.175	0.0231
Ivory Coast *Female	—	−0.659	—	—	−0.693	0.0077
Ghana *Female	—	−0.83	—	—	−0.659	0.0018
Indonesia *Female	—	−0.401*	—	—	−0.396*	0.0733
Nigeria *Female	—	−0.471	—	—	−0.533	0.013

Table 12.10. (Continued)

	Model 1	Model 2	Model 3	Model 4	Model 5	Sample Mean (Weighted)
Pakistan *Female	—	0.334	—	—	0.33	0.0513
Senegal *Female	—	-0.536**	—	—	-0.546**	0.0415
Tanzania *Female	—	0.121	—	—	0.115	0.0088
Turkey *Female	—	-0.455*	—	—	-0.484*	0.0546
Uganda *Female	—	-0.923*	—	—	-0.913	0.0032
Uzbekistan *Female	—	-0.311	—	—	-0.321	0.0311
Lebanon *Female	—	-0.233	—	—	-0.244	0.0369
Jordan *Female	—	0.214	—	—	0.207	0.0648
Bangladesh *OwnComp	—	—	—	-4.365*	-4.369**	0.0016
Ivory Coast *OwnComp	—	—	—	1.165	1.073	0.0009
Ghana *OwnComp	—	—	—	NA	NA	0
Indonesia *OwnComp	—	—	—	-2.309	-2.317	0.0055
Nigeria *OwnComp	—	—	—	-3.605*	-3.736*	0.0013
Pakistan *OwnComp	—	—	—	-3.494*	-3.522*	0.016
Senegal *OwnComp	—	—	—	-2.311	-2.347	0.0032
Tanzania *OwnComp	—	—	—	NA	NA	0
Turkey *OwnComp	—	—	—	-3.173*	-3.213*	0.0157
Uganda *OwnComp	—	—	—	NA	NA	0
Uzbekistan *OwnComp	—	—	—	-2.833	-2.917	0.0007
Lebanon *OwnComp	—	—	—	-2.796	-2.818	0.0376
Jordan *OwnComp	—	—	—	-2.199	-2.208	0.0405
Constant	-0.105	-0.197	-0.053	-0.096	-0.139	
N (Weighted)	6,205	6,205	6,205	6,205	6,205	
Nagelkerke R-squared	0.238	0.244	0.243	0.245	0.256	

Note: **** Indicates significant at the 0.001 level, *** at the 0.01 level, ** at the 0.05 level, * at the 0.1 level. Derived from author tabulations of data from Pew Global Attitudes Survey 2002. Unweighted sample size was 6,019.

countries for which interactions were statistically significant, computer ownership predicts a *decreased* likelihood of supporting terrorism, all else constant.

Conclusions

These analyses, at least modestly, contribute to understanding segments of the demand for terrorism (e.g., the supporters for this tactic). The descriptive and regression analyses suggest the following conclusions holding all other considerations constant:

- In uninteracted models, females are more likely than males to support the tactic. However, interaction models suggest that the effect of gender may vary within the countries.

- Older people are less likely to support terrorism. However, the predicted probability of supporting terrorism for persons over 60 is still high at over 45 percent.

- Respondents who believe that religious leaders should play a larger role in politics are substantially *more likely* to support terrorism.

- In none of the models did the territorial threat variable appear significant. (This was not the case for individual state-level models, which comprise the subject of our forthcoming work).

- While persons who are low SES (indicated by inadequate funds for food) are less likely to support the tactic, those with somewhat higher SES are more likely to support it generally.

- Individuals with phones and/or computers (which dually code for higher SES and increased accessed to information) are more likely to support terrorism than those who do not own these items in general. Interaction models suggest that the effect of computer ownership may vary across states and in some cases computer ownership may predict decreased propensity to support terrorism.

- Those who believe that Islam is under threat are much more likely to support terrorism than those who do not share this view. While the intensity of this finding varied across the states in question, there were no statistically significant exceptions.

Implications for Future Data Collection

The results of these analyses cast limited light on the impact of SES considerations on demand for suicide terrorism. The first-order effects reported here mirror those of the above-noted studies of SES impacts on supply of terrorism. However, we caution that these data do not tell the entire story about SES. It is entirely possible that it is not the level of SES, but change in SES in different time periods that matters. Unfortunately, as these data are not time series and represent only a cross section of respondents in these 14 countries at a particular time in 2002, we cannot assess this critical issue. It is also possible that such change in SES may have impacts upon other variables, such as the threat perceptions. This, too, is a consideration that remains beyond the scope of this work.

However, this outstanding empirical concern underscores the need for time-series panel data to fully illuminate the impact of SES on support for support for terrorism and specifically changes in SES across time periods.

Even though the standardized sample for our regression models contained more than 6,000 observations, in many cases the cell sizes were still too small to estimate coefficients accurately in many countries. This problem of "micronumerocity" was exacerbated in many of the models with interacted variables because of the large numbers of variables added to the analysis. More robust sample sizes are required to permit the kinds of analyses that will shed most light on the determinants of support for terrorism.

Given that many of these results appear to vary by country, it may be useful to include countries that are of specific concern to the U.S. and wider community. It is not obvious that the countries included in this Pew dataset are most appropriate or even the most interesting to U.S. policy makers because Pew included countries that are appropriate to its particular reporting mission. But the Pew data do demonstrate the "proof of concept" that such data collection is possible if limited.

The vagaries of collecting survey data of this type necessarily increases the burden of the analyst to properly understand the limits of the data employed and to properly caveat the resultant findings. Reviewers of this research note were skeptical of the utility of such survey data. Although the authors appreciate these concerns, we note that survey data are an important complement to other kinds of inquiries that are problematic in their own rights as well (small numbers of interviews with would-be, actual, or even purported militants, abstracting from press reports, reliance upon interview data with policy makers, and so forth).

Implications for Counterterrorism Activities

One of the first conclusions that can be drawn from this work is that the standard stereotypes are not altogether right. Females in general were more likely to support terrorism than males. It is possible that these effects vary substantially across states, but our sample sizes were still too small to estimate interaction effects accurately. In no model was marital status significant suggesting that married person cannot be assumed to be less likely to support terrorism than unmarried persons. This was true even in Model 1 where sample size was ample to estimate accurately. Older persons do appear less likely to support terrorism, but the decline in probability was much less than popular stereotypes would suggest. In fact, even at 62 years of age, the predicted probability of supporting terrorism was near 45 percent.

The result of the role of religious leaders is important. Those respondents who support larger role for religious leaders in politics are more likely to support terrorism, all else constant.

Territorial threats did not appear significant in this across-country model. However, we caution that this not be dismissed. Our additional analyses of country-specific models show that in some countries, this variable is significant.

Finally, the perception that Islam is threatened by other religions was associated with increases in likelihood of supporting terrorism. Many of these interactions were robust, illuminating the differential impact of this threat perception across the countries in question.

Because many of these characteristics do appear to vary by country and because several of the country-level indicators themselves were significant in many models, public diplomacy efforts and perception management campaigns need to be highly tailored to each of the key states in question. The findings of this analysis also suggest that observed country differences may reflect specific viewpoints that may be rooted to local or historical experiences as well as the larger contexts within which these experiences are situated. If so, popular aphorisms such as the "Muslim Street" or "Arab Street" may have little analytical value and may obfuscate more than they clarify.

Based on these analyses, we argue for the requirement for detailed understanding about specific populations within states to enable effective interventions. Such nuanced understanding of the demographic and psychographic breakdown of populations within specific countries may help the United States and allies prioritize its efforts not only by states but also by subgroups within states.

In conclusion, it is also important to note that these data were collected *prior* to the U.S. invasion and occupation in Iraq. Given the significance and magnitude of the threat variable (particularly when looking at country-specific affects of this variable), one wonders if the same individuals were to be resurveyed in 2004, whether we would see an increase in the support for suicide terrorism in all or a select subset of the countries in question. This question, too, underscores the need for robust time-series panel data.

Notes

1. We use the term "demand" here to refer to the public support for terrorism, which in turn is treated as a "good" produced by terrorists and their groups and consumed by the population on whose behalf they claim to act. This is in distinction to other uses of the term "demand," which could refer to groups demand for terrorist labor. For a more thorough discussion of demand-side issues, see Paxson, 2002, and Iannaccone, 1992. We are also cognizant of the debate about defining terrorism as a "good." For instance, some argue that terrorism is a "public good." However, although this debate is important to understanding terrorism and terrorist groups, this distinction is not germane to our query here. For more information about this and related analytical issues, see Iannaccone, 1992, and Harrison, 2004.

2. When this article was first published in studies in *Conflict and Terrorism*, it was the first empirical inquiry into demand for terrorism. Since its publication, a few other studies have emerged. See Bueno de Mesquita (2007). This work was overseen by Fair and USIP's Center for Conflict Analysis and Prevention to expand on and challenge the findings in this paper using additional data and more sophisticated modeling techniques. Other demand-side inquiries using descriptive statistical analyses of survey data include Wike and Samaranayake (2006), Gallup World Poll ThinkForum (2006), Mogahed (2006), and WorldPublicOpinion.org (2007).

3. Due to an error made by the authors in recoding this variable, earlier drafts of this paper found that those who believed that religious leaders should have a larger role to play were *less* likely to support terrorism. This has been corrected in this chapter. The authors apologize for any confusion this may have generated.

4. These findings also comport with those of R. Kim Craigin and Scott Gerwehr who argue that strategic influence campaigns require detailed psychographic and demographic intelligence about the target community. According to these authors, "Demographics include information, for example, on the age, sex, or occupation of potential audiences, whereas psychographic intelligence incorporates additional data on perceptions, interests, and opinions." See Craigin and Gerwehr, 2005.

5. For more information about the methodology of the survey design, sample construction, methods of fielding of the survey as well as local partners

for doing so, see the Pew Global Attitudes Project, 2002. In particular see the chapter on "Methodology."

6. This is a highly debated area in the literature. For example, see Heston and Summers, 1997, and Heston et al., 2002.

7. Due to an error in recoding this variable, previous drafts of this paper reversed this interpretation. The authors apologize for this.

References

Atran, S. (2004, Summer). Mishandling suicide terrorism. *The Washington Quarterly*.
Berman, E., & Laitin, D. D. (2004). Rational martyrs vs. hard targets: Evidence on the tactical use of suicide attacks. Conference paper, University of Chicago, October 26. http://economics.uchicago.edu/download/RatMartyrs6.pdf
Berrebi, C. (2003). Evidence about the link between education, poverty and terrorism among Palestinians. *Princeton University Industrial Relations Sections*. Working Paper #477.
Blinken, A. J. (2001, December 8). Now the US needs to win the global war of ideas. *International Herald Tribune Online*.
Bueno de Mesquita, E. (forthcoming). The quality of terror. *American Journal of Political Science*. http://bdm.wustl.edu/PDF/terror_quality.pdf
Bueno de Mesquita, E. (2007). Correlates of public support for terrorism in the Muslim world, USIP Working Paper No. 1. http://www.usip.org/pubs/working_papers/index.html
Camarota, S. A. (2002). The open door: How militant Islamic terrorists entered and remained in the United States, 1993–2001. *Center for Immigration Studies*. Working Paper 21. Washington DC: Center for Immigration Studies. http://www.cis.org/articles/2002/Paper21/terrorism2.html
Clarke, R. et al. (2004). *Defeating the jihadists: A Blueprint for Action*. Washington, DC: Century Foundation Press.
Clayton, M. (2003, September 2). Probing the roots of terror. *The Christian Science Monitor*. http://www.csmonitor.com/2003/0902/p18s01-lehl.htm
Collier, P., & Hoeffler, A. (2000, May). Greed and grievance in civil war. *World Bank Policy Research Paper* 2355.
Collier, P. (2000). Rebellion as a quasi-criminal activity. *Journal of Conflict Resolution* 44 (6).
Cragin, K., & Chalk, P. (2003). *Terrorism and development: Using social and economic development to inhibit a resurgence of terrorism*. Santa Monica, CA: RAND.
Craigin, K., & Gerwehr, S. (2005). *Dissuading terror: Strategic influence and the struggle against terrorism*. Santa Monica, CA: RAND.
Cronin, A. K. (2003). Terrorists and suicide attacks. Washington: Congressional Research Service RL3205. http://www.fas.org/irp/crs/RL32058.pdf
Cunningham, K. J. (2003). Cross-regional trends in female terrorism. *Studies in Conflict and Terrorism* 26.

Defense Technical Information Center. Perception Management. http://www.dtic.mil/doctrine/jel/doddict/data/p/04007.html

Gallup World Poll ThinkForum. (2006). *The battle for hearts and minds: An analysis of moderate and extremist views in the Muslim world*, Princeton: Gallup.

Ganor, B. (2000). Suicide terrorism: An overview. Paper, International Policy Institute for Counter-Terrorism. Countering Suicide Terrorism: An International Conference, Herzliya: Israel.

Gold, D. (2004). Some economic considerations in the U.S. war on terrorism. *The Quarterly Journal* 3 (1), 1–14.

Harrison, M. (2004). An economist looks at suicide terrorism. Working paper, January 20. http://www2.warwick.ac.uk/fac/soc/economics/staff/faculty/harrison/papers/terrorism.pdf

Heston, A., Summers, R., & Aten, B. (2002, October). Penn World Table Version 6.1. *Center for International Comparisons at the University of Pennsylvania (CICUP)*.

Heston, A., & Summers, R. (1997). *PPPs and price parities in benchmark studies and the Penn World Table: Uses*. Prepared remarks, Eurostat Conference on the Value of Real Exchange Rates, Brussels, Belgium, October 20–21. http://pwt.econ.upenn.edu/papers/paperev.html

Hoffman, B. (2001, December). All you need is love: How the terrorists stopped terrorism. *Atlantic Monthly*.

Iannaccone, L. R. (1992). Sacrifice and stigma: Reducing free-riding in cults, communes, and other collectives. *Journal of Political Economy* 100, 271–291.

Iannaccone, L. R. (1998). Introduction to the economics of religion. *Journal of Economic Literature* 36.

Iannaccone, L. R. (2002). The market for martyrs. Working paper, 2004 meetings of the American Economic Association, San Diego, CA, December. http://gunston.doit.gmu.edu/liannacc/EReI/S2Archives/Iannaccone%20%20Market%20for%20Martyrs.pdf

Kivimäki, T. (Ed.). (2003). *Development cooperation as an instrument in the prevention of terrorism–A research report for the ministry of foreign affairs*. Copenhagen: Nordic Institute of Asian Studies.

Kleinberg, M. (2003). *The national commission on terrorist attacks upon the United States, Public Hearing*. March 31. http://www.911independentcommission.org/pdf/MindyKleinberg_03_31_03.pdf

Konrad, K. A. (2004). The investment problem in terrorism. *Economica* 71.

Krueger, A. B., & Maleckova, J. (2002a). Education, poverty, political violence and terrorism: Is there a causal connection? *NBER* (Working Paper 9074).

Krueger, A. B., & Maleckova, J. (2002b, June). The economics and the education of suicide bombers. *The New Republic*.

Kulandaswamy, M. S. (2000). *Sri Lankan crisis: Anatomy of ethnicity, peace, and security*. New Delhi: Authorspress.

Maslow, A. (1970). *Motivation and personality* (2nd ed.). New York: Harper & Row.

Merari, A. (1998). The readiness to kill and die: Suicidal terrorism in the Middle East. In W. Reich (Ed.), *Origins of terrorism: Psychologies, ideologies, theologies, states of mind* (2nd ed.). Washington, DC: Woodrow Wilson Center and Johns Hopkins University Press.

Mogahed, D. (2006). The battle for hearts and minds: Moderate vs. extremist views in the Muslim world. *Gallup World Poll Special Report*, http://media.gallup.com/WorldPoll/PDF/GALLUP+MUSLIM+STUDIES_Moderate+v+Extremist+Views_11.13.06_FINAL.pdf

Organisation for Economic Co-Operation and Development, Development Assistance Committee. (2003). *A development co-operation lens: Terrorism prevention key entry points for action.* Paris: OECD.

Orvis, B. R., & Asch, B. J. (2001). *Military recruiting: Trends, outlook, and implications.* Santa Monica, CA: RAND.

Pape, R. A. (2003). The strategic logic of suicide terrorism. *American Political Science Review* 20 (32).

Paxson, C. (2002, May 8). Comment on Alan Krueger and Jitka Maleckova, education, poverty, and terrorism: Is there a causal connection? Princeton: Research Program in Development Studies. http://www.wws.princeton.edu/~rpds/downloads/paxson_krueger_comment.pdf

Paz, R. (2001, December 13). Programmed terrorists: An analysis of the letter left behind by the September 11 hijackers. *International Policy Institute for Counter-Terrorism.* http://www.ict.org.il/articles/articledet.cfm?articleid=419

Post, J. M. (1998). Terrorist psycho-logic: Terrorist behavior as a product of psychological forces. In W. Reich (Ed.), *Origins of Terrorism: Psychologies, Ideologies, Theologies, States of Mind* (2nd ed.). Washington, DC: Woodrow Wilson Center and Johns Hopkins University Press.

Rubin, E. (2002, June 30). The most wanted Palestinian. *New York Times Magazine.*

Sageman, M. (2004). *Understanding terror networks.* Philadelphia: University of Pennsylvania Press.

Sambanis, N. (2004, July 12). Poverty and the organization of political violence: A review and some conjectures. Brookings Institution. http://www.brook.edu/es/commentary/journals/tradeforum/papers/200405_sambanis.pdf

Stern, J. (2003). *Terror in the name of God: Why religious militants kill.* New York: HarperCollins.

Taylor, P. M. (2002). Perception management and the "war" against terrorism. *Journal of Information Warfare* 1 (3).

The Pew Research Center. (2002, December 4). *What the world thinks in 2002: How global publics view their lives, their countries, the world, America.* Washington, DC: Pew Research Center. http://people-press.org/reports/display.php3?ReportID=165

Princeton Survey Research Associates International. (2002). *Questionnaire Pew Global Attitudes Survey—2002.* Princeton: Princeton Survey Research Associates International.

United States Department of State. (1987). *Dictionary of international relations terms*. Washington, DC: United States Department of State.
United States Department of State. (2002). *Patterns of global terrorism 2002*. Washington, DC: United States Department of State. http://www.state.gov/s/ct/rls/pgtrpt/2001/
United States Department of State. (2003). *Patterns of global terrorism 2003*. Washington, DC: United States Department of State. http://www.state.gov/s/ct/rls/pgtrpt/2003/
United States General Accounting Office. (2003, September). Report to the committee on international relations, House of Representatives. *U.S. public diplomacy: State department expands efforts but faces significant challenges*. Washington DC: GAO. www.gao.gov/cgi-bin/getrpt?GAO-03-951
United States Information Agency Alumni Association (USIAA). (2002, September). *What is public diplomacy?* Washington, DC: USIAA. http://www.publicdiplomacy.org/1.htm
Wike, R., & Samaranayake, N. (2006). *Where terrorism finds support in the Muslim world: That may depend on how you define it, and who are the targets*. Pew Research Center. http://pewresearch.org/pubs/26/where-terrorism-finds-support-in-the-muslim-world
Wolf, C., & Rosen, B. (2004). *Public diplomacy: How to think about and improve it*. Santa Monica, CA: RAND.
WorldPublicOpinion.org. (2007). *Muslim public opinion on US policy, attacks on civilians and al Qaeda*. http://www.worldpublicopinion.org/pipa/pdf/apr07/START_Apr07_rpt.pdf
Young, J. (1999). *The exclusive society: Social exclusion, crime and difference in late modernity*. London: Sage.

Chapter 13

How Northern Norms Affect the South
Adopting, Adapting, and Resisting the Global War on Terror in South and Southeast Asia

Peter Romaniuk

Introduction

How do norms travel from the North to the South? Why are some Northern norms more influential than others in the South? How do ideational and material factors combine or interact in affecting Southern responses to Northern norms?

In this chapter, I elaborate a framework for answering these questions. I build on current debates about the role of ideas in international politics to argue that norms travel from North to South subject to two conditions: first, Southern elites are more likely to accept Northern norms when the acceptance of a norm brings relative gains, and second, Southern elites are more likely to accept Northern norms when those norms affirm their ability to construct their own identity, in other words, norms travel when elites feel that they are norm-makers and not norm-takers. I develop the concept of "normative affirmation" to capture this second condition, such that norms travel when the agency of Southern elites is affirmed. I suggest that these two conditions interact over time, determining the extent to which norms travel. When they align, states either adopt or resist norms; when they do not align, states adapt norms.

I illustrate this argument by looking at the spread of the "global war on terror" (GWOT) in the South. More specifically, I analyze the integration of the norms related to terrorist financing in India and Indonesia.

This cluster of norms—developed in the North in the immediate post-9/11 period by extending the nascent anti-money-laundering regime—has elicited different responses from states in the South. Defined in depth below, I measure the influence of Northern norms in line with a simple ordinal scale according to whether norms are adopted *in toto* by Southern states, adapted in part, or resisted outright. Initially, both India and Indonesia resisted counterterrorist financing norms. India moved to adapt them before Indonesia, but Indonesia adopted them before India. What explains this variation? As I show below, prevailing theories of international relations provide incomplete explanations. In response, my approach represents a preliminary attempt to integrate instrumental and value rationality in explaining the spread of norms.[1]

My argument proceeds in three parts. First, I elaborate the empirical puzzle regarding spread of terrorist financing norms after 9/11, describing Indian and Indonesian responses. Second, I review existing explanations of the spread of norms with a focus on constructivist approaches. I note two key dilemmas of constructivism, suggesting that the effort to integrate normative and instrumental factors remains underdeveloped, and that constructivism provides insufficient guidance on how states respond when norms conflict with each other. On this basis, I outline an original framework for explaining the spread of norms. Finally, I test my explanation by looking at the Indian and Indonesian responses to counterterrorist financing norms over time. I show that, as relative gains increase, and as elites perceive that external norms affirm their ability to construct their own identity, the more likely it is that norms are adapted and adopted.

The Emergence and Diffusion of Terrorist Financing Norms

In the immediate aftermath of the terrorist attacks of September 11, 2001 (9/11), United States President George W. Bush announced the commencement of the GWOT (see, for example, Bush, 2001). The subsequent pursuit of the GWOT has had wide-ranging effects on world politics. A broader discussion of these effects is beyond the scope of this chapter. Rather, my aim here is to summarize the kinds of principled and causal beliefs, and policy prescriptions, that the GWOT has given rise to.[2]

"Principled beliefs" are "beliefs about right and wrong" (Tannenwald, 2005, 16). The main principled belief manifested in the GWOT is simply that terrorism is wrong. Consensus around this belief has been disputed for some time, as evidenced in past debates—in the UN General Assembly and elsewhere—about the definition of terrorism. (Hoffman, 1998, chap.

1; Guillaume, 2004). However, following 9/11 there is some evidence that a broadly stated norm against terrorist violence exists or is emerging. For example, all member states of the UN have submitted at least one report to the Security Council's Counter-Terrorism Committee (CTC), repudiating terrorist violence. The resolution that established that committee—Security Council resolution 1373 (2001)—condemns terrorism in strong terms. Paragraph 3(d) of the resolution urges states to sign "relevant international conventions and protocols relating to terrorism." There are now 13 such conventions, each of which establishes a range of specific offenses, thereby identifying crimes that may be considered as "terrorism."[3] A number of subsequent resolutions of the Security Council—endorsed by a host of other international and regional organizations—affirm this position, and recent events indicate that a formal definition of terrorism may yet be concluded through debates on the Comprehensive Convention on International Terrorism.[4]

More specific than principled beliefs are "causal beliefs," which are "beliefs about cause-effect, or means-end, relationships" (Tannenwald, 2005, 16). The fact that states remain unable to conclude a formal definition of terrorism reflects the different views they share about what causes terrorism and about what causes terrorism to be suppressed. But the latter type of causal belief—beliefs about counterterrorism—have attracted greater consensus as part of the GWOT. Some aspects of the GWOT have been controversial, especially where coercive force has been used. However, far from the front of the "hot" war on terror, many—and sometimes most—states have collaborated to develop and implement new regulatory norms and rules to prevent and suppress terrorist activity. This has occurred across a wide range of issue areas, including aviation, transportation, maritime, financial, customs and border controls, police, judicial and intelligence cooperation, and measures to improve the regulation of certain weapons and weapons of mass destruction (WMD) materials. Often led by states in the North, this aspect of the GWOT is remarkable because an increasing amount of transnational activity is now subject to new or revised regulatory controls. In elaborating this agenda, Northern states have provided incentives and utilized sanctions to induce others to adopt emerging global counterterrorism standards. But just as often, and despite political differences over the Iraq war and other multilateral issues, global counterterrorism standards have been vetted through international institutions and have attracted a good deal of consensus. As Jonathan Winer describes it, "Beneath the loud shout of unilateralism present from the creation of the Bush Administration's invasion of Iraq, a veritable orchestra of institutions have continued to play sotto voce to build capacity against global terrorism" (Winer, 2003). As a consequence, the GWOT has resulted in the development and dissemination of a range of causal beliefs about the utility and substance of counterterrorism policy.

More specific still are "policy prescriptions," which are the "specific programmatic ideas that derive from causal and principled beliefs . . . [or the] precise causal ideas that facilitate policymaking by specifying how to solve particular policy problems" (Tannenwald, 2005, 16). Such "specific programmatic ideas" have proliferated in the GWOT, often in the form of "global standards" or "best practices." Although international, regional, and specialist organizations have played an important role in the development and dissemination of these policy prescriptions, they often reflect the understanding of counterterrorism advanced by states in the North, especially the United States. In this chapter, I analyze how one such set of policy prescriptions—norms and rules surrounding terrorist financing—has traveled from North to South. These prescriptions manifest both the principled belief that terrorism is wrong, and the causal belief that stemming the flow of funds to terrorists is an appropriate and effective way to suppress terrorism. I select counterterrorist financing norms here because they have their origins in the North and have elicited a variety of responses from states in the South.[5] They are embodied in the "9 Special Recommendations on Terrorist Financing" (9 SRs) elaborated by the Financial Action Task Force (FATF) in October 2001. The FATF was established in 1989 by G7 states to develop standards and share practices in countering money laundering. The rise of the FATF and the anti-money-laundering regime is described in greater depth elsewhere, (for example Gilmore, 2004) but three of its pre-9/11 features are worth restating in describing the subsequent emergence of the 9 SRs.

First, the FATF's main achievement in the 1990s was the establishment of standards for suppressing money laundering. The "40 Recommendations" against money laundering were first issued in 1990 and attracted a good deal of convergence among states over time. Second, the FATF disseminated its standards through a growing network of anti-money-laundering officials and experts, initiated within the North, but spreading across the globe. Beyond the membership of the FATF alone—which numbered 29 governments and two regional organizations in mid-2001—the FATF recommendations were endorsed by FATF-style regional bodies (FSRBs) in the Caribbean, South America, Europe, Eastern and Southern Africa, and the Asia-Pacific (Egmont Group, 2004). Over the course of the 1990s, money-laundering standards were increasingly discussed among officials from national financial intelligence units (FIUs), who initiated the Egmont Group of FIUs in 1995. In 2000, a group of private sector banks—the "Wolfsberg Group"—developed a series of principles for banks to adopt in order to comply with money-laundering standards (Pieth & Aiolfi, n.d.,

5). More generally, FATF influence was extended through its interactions with a host of international and regional organizations including the IMF, World Bank, regional development banks, the Commonwealth, the Offshore Group of Banking Supervisors, the World Customs Organization, Interpol, the International Organization of Securities Commissions, and the UN's peak drug and crime control office (FATF, 2001b, 5).

Third, the FATF utilized a range of mechanisms to enforce the 40 recommendations, including a graduated series of self-assessments and peer-review evaluations, with the possibility of sanctions for noncompliance against both members and nonmembers. Most prominently, the "noncompliant countries and territories" (NCCT) initiative, launched in 2000, provided a mechanism to "name and shame" noncompliant states, requiring that members subject transactions to additional scrutiny.[6]

Each of these preexisting aspects of the FATF's work has been extended and institutionalized since 9/11 as counterterrorist financing measures have been framed by leading states as complementary to the nascent anti-money-laundering regime.[7] In October 2001, FATF members convened an extraordinary session to consider "necessary steps for preventing and combating terrorist financing activity" (FATF, 2002, 1). At this meeting the mandate of the FATF was formally extended and "8 Special Recommendations on Terrorist Financing" were elaborated. A ninth SR was added in October 2004.

The 9 SRs (excerpted in full in the attachment at the end of this chapter) are widely acknowledged to set the global standard for counterterrorist financing and have been endorsed as such by the global anti-money-laundering network. Importantly, in mid-2002 the boards of both the World Bank and IMF recognized the (then) "40+8 Recommendations" as the relevant international standard in the area, as they developed action plans to enhance their efforts to counter money laundering and terrorist financing.[8] On the ground, this meant that the Bank and Fund collaborated with the FATF and FSRBs in developing a common methodology to assess state compliance with the recommendations. Following a successful pilot program, the Bank and Fund made anti-money laundering and counterterrorist financing reviews part of their permanent activities in March 2004.[9]

The 9 SRs now also have the explicit endorsement of the UN Security Council.[10] In citing the FATF's recommendations, the Council in effect provides mutual recognition of the FATF's work (SR I endorses of UN measures). Current UN statements of terrorist financing consist of three related elements. First, the 1999 Terrorist Financing Convention commits signatory states to take measures for the detection and freezing, seizure, or forfeiture of any funds used or allocated for the purposes of committing terrorism-related offenses. Second, targeted financial sanctions were first imposed on the Taliban in 1999 with Security Council resolution 1267. Over time, and especially in the period following 9/11, these prohibitions have been expanded and extended so that they now cover the Taliban, Osama bin Laden, al Qaeda, and associated individuals and entities. State implementation of the sanctions is overseen by a subcommittee of the Council, initially created by resolution 1267 (the "1267 Committee"). Third, as widely discussed elsewhere,[11] in passing resolution 1373 (2001) in the weeks after 9/11, the Security Council launched an ambitious counterterrorism agenda, requiring states to take measures to suppress terrorist financing, improve border security, control traffic in weapons, enhance judicial and law enforcement cooperation, and more. The resolution also created the CTC to oversee state implementation. The CTC process has had important legal, political, and institutional effects in many states, especially in the area of terrorist financing. However, enthusiasm for the CTC process has waned over time, in spite of efforts to "revitalize" the Committee (Proposal for the Revitalization of the Counter-Terrorism Committee, 2004). As this has happened, the tactical element of the Council's work on terrorist financing—namely, the sanctions implemented by the 1267 Committee—has gained greater prominence than the strategic response pursued through the CTC.[12]

The 9 SRs have now been endorsed as the global standard for counterterrorist financing by a wide range of regional and specialist organizations. Notable here is the G8's Counter-Terrorism Action Group (CTAG), established in 2003, which provides counterterrorism assistance donors with a "forum to identify priority areas of need to implement [UN Security Council resolution] 1373 and to coordinate [counterterrorism] capacity building efforts to maximize impact" (Realuyo, 2004). CTAG works closely with the FATF, the CTC and regional organizations to coordinate counterterrorist financing assistance, identifying regional priorities as Africa, the Middle East, and Southeast Asia (G8, 2005).

As my discussion to date implies, the 9 SRs are enforced in a number of ways, principally using self-assessment questionnaires, and peer and external reviews in line with the FATF/World Bank/IMF common methodology. Unlike in the pre-9/11 period, the means for encouraging convergence with the 9 SRs is more likely to involve carrots—in the form of technical assistance from the sources recounted above—than sticks. In fact, in announcing the collaboration between the FATF and the Bank and Fund, the FATF also indicated that it would not add any new jurisdictions to the NCCT list, effectively removing the "name and shame" mechanism as a means for coercing compliance for states not already on that list (Blacklist of 'Dirty Money' Havens Put on Temporary

Hold, 2002). As a consequence, multilateral institutions can only impose symbolic sanctions for failure to implement the 9 SRs. This may occur through interactions with and among the FATF, FSRBs, the CTC, and the 1267 Committee, which sometimes identify laggards in their public statements. Material sanctions for noncompliance are more likely to be imposed bilaterally. For example, under section 311 of the USA PATRIOT Act, the United States has pursued "special measures" against Burma, Nauru, and Ukraine, including enhanced record keeping and reporting obligations, and a requirement to terminate correspondent banking relationships.[13] Overall, the possibility of sanctions for noncompliance with the SRs is a real but not necessarily urgent concern for many states. However, given the benefits of market access and technical assistance, there are numerous incentives to adopt the 9 SRs.

Although adjustment costs have been high for many states, most have realized that implementing FATF recommendations is in their longer-term interests. Evidence of the adoption of the 9 SRs has been noted by a range of issue-area experts. Reflecting on the information gathered through mutual evaluations and self-assessments, FATF and FATF-style regional body (FSRB) officials have frequently commented on increases in the implementation of the 9 SRs around the world (for example, Sen, 2005). IMF and World Bank evaluators, utilizing the 9 SRs as the relevant standard, assess that 33 percent of the states in their sample are fully or largely compliant with the recommendations and a further 28 percent are partially compliant,[14] reflecting a trend toward the adoption of the SRs. UN Security Council monitors overseeing implementation of the asset freeze imposed upon the Taliban, al Qaeda and other terrorist-related entities have noted a similar trend over time.[15] Also, a wide range of researchers within (for example, Jackson, 2005, and 911 Commission Report, 2004, 382–383) and outside (for example, Council of Foreign Relations, 2004, 10–11, 29–31; Targeting Terrorist Finances Project, 2004; Biersteker with Romaniuk, 2004; Clunan, 2005) of government have discerned a trend toward the adoption of counterterrorist financing measures.

Still, as many of these observers note, within this aggregate trend there remains significant variation in national-level outcomes. In other words, there is variation in the way that global counterterrorist financing norms have traveled from the North to the South. In order to explain this variation, I propose a simple ordinal scale to measure the influence of norms: norms are adopted, adapted, or resisted by states. A state "adopts" a norm when it accepts the principled and causal beliefs, and policy prescriptions, manifested in that norm. A state "resists" a norm when it rejects the principled and causal beliefs, and policy prescriptions, manifested in that norm. A state "adapts" a norm when its acceptance of the principled and causal beliefs, and policy prescriptions, manifested in that norm is conditional or partial, such that external norms neither entirely displace nor defer to prevailing local norms.

Measured in this way, a number of puzzles emerge from patterns of adoption, adaptation, and resistance of Southern states. Consider the contrast between the responses of India and Indonesia to the 9 SRs. With its distinctive history in dealing with terrorism and political violence, India is perhaps a likely candidate for the adoption of counterterrorism norms. Since independence in 1947 a wide variety of militant groups have utilized all forms of political violence in pursuing disputes with the Indian state, including highjacking, assassination, bombing, suicide bombing, kidnapping, hostage taking, sieges, and protracted low-intensity conflict. In responding, the government of India (GoI) has utilized a full range of counterterrorism capabilities to prevent and contain terrorist violence, from negotiation and incentives for militants to participate in political processes, to the use of coercive force (Latimer, 2004; Tanham, 1992, 27). Indeed, India had comprehensive counterterrorism legislation in draft form when 9/11 occurred—the Prevention of Terrorism Bill—under which terrorist financing was criminalized. India had signed the UN Terrorist Financing Convention in 2000, although it was not yet ratified. Moreover, the GWOT was positively received in New Delhi, where some suggested that such an effort was "long overdue" (Chellaney, 2001/02, 95).

Nonetheless, India initially resisted global counterterrorist financing norms, asserting the adequacy of prevailing counterterrorism mechanisms. However, in contravention of the SRs, the Prevention of Terrorism Bill (later passed as an ordinance, then as an act), defined "terrorism" in a narrow way, referring only to acts intended to "threaten the unity, integrity, security or sovereignty of India."[16] Between 2002 and 2004, India took incremental steps to adapt global standards to Indian conditions, for example, by taking action under its UN Security Council Act to implement UN-derived terrorist financing measures. It was not until the change of government in May 2004, through which the incumbent coalition led by the Bharatiya Janata Party (BJP) was replaced by a Congress-led coalition, that India took more meaningful steps to adopt the SRs. Among other indicators, in 2005 India's Prevention of Money Laundering Bill (which had been first introduced to parliament in 1998) was finally passed, permitting the establishment of an FIU. Further, India has sought to join the FATF and the membership process is now well advanced.

If India's path to the adoption of the SRs involved a period of resistance followed by a process of adaptation, Indonesia represents a very different outcome. Compared to India, Indonesia did not have a developed domestic discourse on terrorism prior to 9/11, let alone an advanced legal

How Northern Norms Affect the South 323

and policy framework. Rather, while the history of political violence in Indonesia had given rise to the principled belief that terrorism is "wrong," that idea had not resulted in clear and consistent causal beliefs and policy prescriptions. This was especially so regarding political violence linked to the role of Islam in Indonesian politics and society, about which elites were particularly sensitive. Thus, although the U.S. State Department noted a "sharp rise" in terrorism in Indonesia in 2000, elites remained reticent to act (Patterns of Global Terrorism, 2000, 2001). Further, Indonesia was placed on the FATF's list of NCCTs in June 2001, for failing to establish a robust anti-money laundering framework.

In spite of being under FATF sanctions, Indonesia resisted global counterterrorist financing norms. What's more, it resisted for longer than India. Only after the October 2002 terrorist attacks in Bali did Indonesian elites take steps to adopt the SRs. But once that decision was taken, adoption proceeded remarkably promptly, such that Indonesia leapfrogged India. Indonesia established and empowered an FIU, made successive improvements to its legislation and became integrated into the global money-laundering/terrorist financing expert network, all in relatively quick time. These outcomes—summarized in Figure 13.1, below—yield a number of questions. For example, why did Indonesia resist norms in spite of sanctions? Having resisted norms, why did it subsequently adopt norms so quickly? India also suffered terrorist violence in this period (such as the December 2001 attack on the Indian Parliament), but those incidents failed to induce Indian elites to adopt counterterrorist financing norms so promptly: Why weren't more urgent efforts to adopt the SRs part of

Figure 13.1. Adoption of Counterterrorist Financing Norms in India and Indonesia, 2001–2006

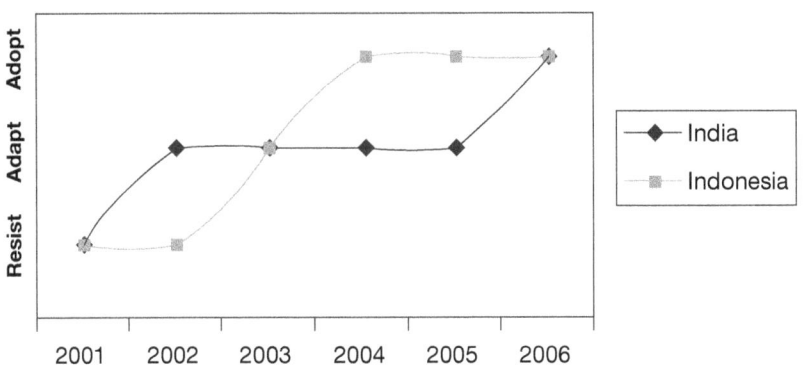

India's response to such violence? And given that India adapted norms earlier, why did it adopt norms later than Indonesia?

Adopt, Adapt, or Resist? Explaining Variation in the Reception of Norms in the South

In many ways, these questions raise counterintuitive puzzles. The prevailing North-South gap in the adoption of global counterterrorist financing norms suggests that attributes of Northern states, such as power and institutions, affect the spread of norms. But variation across the South indicates that those effects are not constant. Similarly, a number of pre-9/11 accounts of the development of counterterrorism policy had emphasized the importance of domestic factors in determining those policies (for example, see Crenshaw, 2001, and Katzenstein, 2003, 2002, 1993). Here, the aggregate movement toward global standards implies that domestic particularities now matter more in some cases than in others.

These questions also pose a challenge for constructivist theories of international relations. Among contemporary international relations (IR) scholars, it is constructivists who have the most to say about how norms spread. Archetypically, Finnemore and Sikkink posit a "life cycle" of norms (Finnemore & Sikkink, 1998). They suggest that: norms emerge when norm entrepreneurs seek to persuade others to adopt a standard of appropriateness; diffusion occurs when states, international organizations, and networks endeavor to socialize others; and, internalization occurs when states adopt a norm as habit, such that the norm acquires a "taken for granted" quality. From this starting point, the constructivist literature has developed in a gradual fashion, as constructivists have identified a range of mechanisms—beyond socialization alone—by which norms travel. For example, scholars are increasingly finding that congruence between local and global norms can facilitate the spread of norms and that local supporters of international norms are sometimes capable of overcoming preexisting differences, however wide the "existential" or "cultural match" in any issue area (Cortell & Davis, 1996, 2000; Acharya, 2004). Here, we might look to the influence of actors at the international and domestic levels to explain the spread of norms, whether they are members of epistemic communities, (Haas, 1992) norm localizers (Acharya, 2004), or members of transgovernmental networks (Slaughter, 2004, 1997; Raustiala, 2002). Moreover, mechanisms such as role playing, normative suasion (Checkel, 2005, 2001; Payne, 2001), and argumentation (Risse, 2002, 2000) have been shown to spread norms. In applying these mechanisms, constructivist explanations have become increasingly sophisticated. For example, Tannenwald has linked specific causal mechanisms to different stages of an expanded "life cycle" of norms (Tannenwald, 2005, 29–33). Checkel and his fellow contributors to the October 2005 issue of *International Organization* aim to specify "scope conditions" so that we can discern whether specific mechanisms are likely to operate. But in spite of these ongoing efforts, there remain a range of important criticisms of the constructivist research agenda. Short of an exhaustive review of the literature, I suggest that two key dilemmas of constructivism have endured over time.[17] These dilemmas are particularly pertinent to the spread of norms from the North to the South.

First, attempts to integrate normative and instrumental factors have not developed as steadily as the identification of the various normative mechanisms. Of course, it is a consequence of the way in which we frame our research questions in scholarly IR (i.e., empirical phenomena are only "puzzling" when they don't conform to the expectations of prevailing theories) that constructivists argue against rationalist accounts, often in order to make the baseline claim that "norms matter." But in doing so, constructivists have often presented an over-socialized view of actors. Constructivism has been criticized for both failing to articulate a theory of agency and for, "treating [agents] as near bearers of structures and, at the extreme, as cultural dupes."[18] Over time, structure has been a stricture, and early accounts of the spread of norms through socialization provide an unrealistically linear depiction of how norms travel (Payne, 2001, 42).

Intuitively, both material and ideational causes matter and, "Norm entrepreneurs overtly exploit material levers all the time" (Payne, 2001, 41). Constructivists have attempted to deal with this dilemma in a number of ways. Tannenwald contends that theorists simply need to make an ontological decision about whether to privilege material factors or ideas and that we should not expect consensus on this (Tannenwald, 2005, 23). But on what grounds should we make that decision? Some scholars suggest or imply a theoretical division of labor, such that, in Ruggie's words, a "core constructivist research concern is what happens *before* the neo-utilitarian model kicks in."[19] Other pragmatic responses include simply taking it as an article of faith that either material factors or ideas matters more; looking to the empirical record for guidance and; hedging our bets and endeavoring to identify "switching points" between the predominance of material and ideational factors (Tannenwald, 2005, 22–24). Whether these alternatives are useful can best be assessed by ongoing empirical research.

A second dilemma of constructivism is that, as an approach to theory, it provides little guidance on how agents distinguish among different norms that conflict with each other. After all, actors are frequently faced with decisions about which norms to follow and which to overlook. In this regard, it is telling that constructivism remains detached from substantive theories of IR.[20] "Constructivism" remains an ontology, epistemology and methodology for studying international politics. It ought to be contrasted with "rationalism" per se, and not the so-called paradigmatic theories, such as realism, liberalism, and Marxism. While neoliberals and neorealists may have little to say about norms,[21] their "classical" antecedents surely do, although we don't generally identify them as "constructivist" theories. Liberals would suggest that agents distinguish among conflicting norms on the basis of their identity as liberal or nonliberal states, wherein shared liberal ideals and institutions act as the causal mechanism.[22] Realists see ideas as part of the international struggle for power and would expect that agents distinguish among conflicting norms by maximizing relative power (Morgenthau, 1948). Constructivists have no direct response to the dilemma of conflicting norms. While constructivist researchers have arrayed evidence to show that norms matter, and while they have specified the mechanisms through which norms matter, their responses to the question "*how* do norms matter?" are ultimately indeterminate, that is, they can at best provide guidance on how to answer that question.

How, then, to address these dilemmas? In advancing an original framework for explaining the spread of norms, I make two assumptions corresponding to my criticism of constructivism. As my discussion to date implies, both of these assumptions pertain to national-level elites—the politicians and administrators who comprise the executive branch of government—which comprise my unit of analysis here.[23] Given my concern for the ways in which norms travel, these elites act as gatekeepers, resolving which norms to adopt, adapt, or resist. My first assumption is that these elites *always* exercise some combination of instrumental rationality and value rationality. Empirically, this assumption would be falsified where it can be shown that agents exercise *either* instrumental rationality *or* value rationality alone. As I discuss momentarily, I answer the "ontological question of the appropriate starting point"—material or ideational factors?—posed by Tannenwald by weighing them equally for analytical purposes.

Second, I propose a novel means for addressing the dilemma concerning the way in which agents distinguish among different norms that conflict with each other. Realists who make explicit assumptions about actors at the unit level generally refer to the goals of survival, power, and wealth.[24] By analogy, I assume that elites are similarly guarded when it comes to the ideas that constitute international politics. Specifically, I assume that agents prefer to be norm-makers and not norm-takers. Therefore, where norms conflict, agents prefer norms that affirm their ability to construct their own identity. Where agents are socially constructed, and where they know they are socially constructed, the thing that matters most to the elites is that they maintain control over the construction of their own identity. I use the term "normative affirmation" to capture this idea. "Normative affirmation" refers to the ability of elites to construct their own identity and elites prefer norms that affirm that ability, that is, presented with conflicting logics of appropriateness, elites will be guided by those norms that are more affirming. In this sense, Northern norms may be affirming where they are congruent with prevailing local norms, where they can be "localized," or where they are vetted through a consensus-generating process, such as an international organization.

Combining these two assumptions, I suggest that states are "social egoists." They are motivated by instrumental and ideational concerns, but are sensitive to the use of norms by others and the effects that has on their identity. It follows from these assumptions that Southern elites ask two questions of norms received from the North: Will we be better off if we adopt, adapt or resist Northern norms? and: Do Northern norms affirm our ability to construct our own identity (i.e., will we be norm-makers or norm-takers)? Southern elites will judge that relative gains for adopting Northern norms are either high or low. Similarly, they will perceive that Northern norms either affirm or do not affirm their ability to construct their own identity. On the basis of these assessments, we can derive some preliminary expectations about how norms travel from the North to the South.

Table 13.1 summarizes the anticipated interaction of these considerations. As this table indicates, where the twin considerations regarding relative gains and normative affirmation align, we should expect an unambiguous outcome—either adoption or resistance. Where these considerations do not align, I suggest that elites are most likely to adapt norms to their local conditions. Over time, changes in the relative gains calculation facing elites, and the extent to which elites feel that norms affirm their ability to construct their own identity, ought to produce change in the way elites

Table 13.1. Interaction of Factors Affecting the Spread of Norms

		Normative affirmation	
		Affirm	~Affirm
Relative gains	High	I Adopt	II Adapt
	Low	III Adapt	IV Resist

respond to norms from the North. Short of stating formal hypotheses, I assess these expectations in the final section of this chapter.

Before proceeding, however, suffice it to note that the account of the role of norms that I have presented here breaks with "thick" constructivist accounts by treating norms as more or less another kind of independent variable (see Tannenwald, 2005, 17–20). In other words, as Dessler and Owen describe it, I am making if-then generalizations about norms—a practice more typical of rationalists than constructivists (Dessler & Owen, 2005). Nonetheless, as I illustrate below, my approach entails a constitutive description of the origins of national identities, and an evaluation of the extent to which newly emerging norms affirm the ability of elites to construct their own identity.

Relative Gains and Normative Affirmation in India and Indonesia

What explains the pattern of adoption, adaptation, and resistance presented in Figure 13.1? In this section, I use Table 13.1 to offer a preliminary explanation of variation in the response of India and Indonesia. A detailed process-tracing account of India's and Indonesia's adoption of the FATF's 9 SRs is beyond the scope of this chapter. Rather, my approach here is simply to identify changes in the "relative gains" and "normative affirmation" variables as a way of gaining leverage over decisions to adopt, adapt, or resist.

As noted above, India had comprehensive counterterrorism legislation in draft form when 9/11 occurred. The Prevention of Terrorism Bill had been designed by the BJP government to replace counterterrorism legislation that lapsed in 1995, and represented causal beliefs about terrorism particular to Indian elites—namely, that India is a victim of terrorism perpetrated with external support. The bill entered into force as an ordinance in October 2001, the same month that the FATF elaborated the SRs. The new ordinance and the SRs were inconsistent in one critical way. Although the ordinance criminalized terrorist financing per se (as required), it provided a definition of terrorism limited to violence against India. As a consequence, raising funds for terrorism outside of India was not criminalized under the ordinance. Moreover, the SRs represented a far more elaborate policy for countering terrorist financing than contemplated by the new ordinance. For example, many of mechanisms for policing terrorist financing set out in the SRs, such as suspicious transaction reporting, are derivative of anti-money-laundering measures. Although a Prevention of Money Laundering Bill had been presented to parliament in 1998—which contained provisions regarding suspicious transaction reporting and the establishment of an FIU to oversee it—that bill remained tied up in review committees in late 2001. Indian elites acknowledged the gaps within their legal and policy framework at the time, but argued that it was of little consequence, because international norms would not suppress the kind of terrorist violence that India suffered. To the contrary, elites argued that, "[S]ince most of the terrorists commit offences like smuggling or drug trafficking, their property could be forfeited if they are either convicted under relevant laws for smuggling or drug trafficking or against them orders for preventive detention are issued" (Report of India to the Counter-terrorism Committee, 2001, 15).

Here, then, the SRs would have rendered Indian elites norm-takers and not norm-makers—they did not affirm the ability of Indian elites to construct their own identity. Also, although adoption of the SRs, alongside implementation of the FATF's 40 recommendations to counter money laundering, would benefit India in the long term, those gains were far off. Where relative gains are low, and where norms do not affirm the ability of elites to construct their own identity, we should expect to see resistance to Northern norms. So, Table 13.1 proves useful in explaining New Delhi's initial response.

Indonesia also resisted the SRs in late 2001, but in rather different circumstances. For one thing, as a consequence of being placed on the FATF's NCCT list in June 2001, there were stronger relative gains to be realized by adopting global norms. However, the normative context in which Indonesian elites made decisions about counterterrorism was hostile to the adoption of international counterterrorism norms and the GWOT generally. For example, President Megawati Sukarnoputri's visit to Washington, DC in September 2001 (by virtue of scheduling she was the first world leader to do so after the 9/11 attacks) was not well received by influential sections of civil society. A number of prominent Islamist groups within Indonesia took the view that 9/11 was effectively payback for injustices committed by the United States. On September 25, 2001, a quasiofficial body of Indonesian clerics, the Indonesian Ulema Council, released a statement suggesting that Muslims should consider jihad if the U.S. invades Afghanistan.[25] Further, the view that U.S. foreign policy was to blame for the 9/11 attacks was not uncommon among Indonesia's political elites, including Megawati's own vice president.[26] Therefore, even though the relative gains for adoption were "high" (in light of FATF sanctions already in place), the political costs to Megawati of participating in the GWOT were also very high. Under these conditions—mixed relative gains and "affirm"—my framework suggests that it is probable that Indonesia would resist global standards.

What happened, then, to put India and Indonesia on the path toward the adoption of the SRs? For Indian elites, the relative gains from adoption remained relatively static over time. Although India's market access might eventually be threatened if it failed to observe global standards, that specific threat remained distant. Further, the threat of being listed as an NCCT was removed in September 2002 by virtue of the agreement among the FATF, the World Bank, and the IMF. If relative gains remained static, though, the normative interpretation of the importance of FATF standards began to evolve in 2002. In effect, this permitted elites to slowly gain a sense of ownership over global standards. As elites perceived that they could maintain control over the construction of their own identity, India began to adapt the SRs. This occurred as a result of the issue being steadily integrated into the work of the Reserve Bank of India (RBI). These officials were able to connect post-9/11 FATF standards with integrity measures that India had introduced in the late 1990s (such as the Prevention of Money Laundering Bill) and the government's broader rhetoric on liberalizing India's economy. For example, the RBI's Standing Committee of International Financial Standards and Codes had been asked in 1999 to review India's position with regard to FATF standards. It was only in May 2002 that the committee actually reported (Standing Committee on International Financial Standards and Codes [Reserve Bank of India], 2002). Although the report offers a rather gentle criticism of India's implementation of global standards, it reiterates India's commitment to them and reframes the SRs as a "market integrity" issue, and not simply a terrorism issue.

In a similar vein, Indian elites took measures at about this time to become more integrated with the global anti-money-laundering network. India was already a member of the relevant FATF-style regional body, the Asia-Pacific Group on Money Laundering (APG), but it began the process of gaining formal FATF membership at this time and even attended plenary sessions of the Egmont Group with observer status (Reddy, 2003, 7). Becoming active in these fora meant that India would be increasingly subject to external scrutiny, although the ability of those institutions to raise the formal costs for noncompliance remained weak. Still, India's participation in FATF and Egmont meetings suggests that there were opportunities for Indian elites to be persuaded to adopt the SRs by members of a transgovernmental network. Similarly, India established or maintained a number of bilateral Joint Working Groups on Terrorism, most prominently with the United States, where terrorist financing was discussed frequently (for example, see Joint Statement: Fourth Meeting of the India-US Joint Working Group on Counterterrorism 2002; Joint Statement: Sixth Meeting of the India-US Joint Working Group on Counterterrorism, 2004).

In addition, an expert community of private sector practitioners had become mobilized around money laundering and terrorist financing issues. In fact, a working group (comprising representatives from the RBI, the Indian Banks Association and the banking industry) had been set up in 2001 to monitor global anti-money-laundering standards. They developed recommendations that were "expected to serve as a 'self regulatory code' for the banking system" (Standing Committee on International Financial Standards and Codes [Reserve Bank of India], 2002, 34). In many cases, banks took steps on their own to combat money laundering, including the creation of compliance officers to ensure implementation of anti-money-laundering regulations (INCSR, 2003, 2004).

As these various normative mechanisms—reframing, expert communities, and persuasion—influenced Indian elites, they began to perceive that the FATF's SRs might not render them norm-takers after all. Indeed, initial measures toward implementing the SRs were taken in this period, including the updating of "know-your-customer" (i.e., client identification) guidelines, the distribution of the UN's list to banks and the decision to ratify the UN Terrorist Financing Convention. Here, it is variation in the perceived "normative affirmation" of the SRs that led India to adapt, rather than resist, norms from abroad.

For Indonesia, the critical intervening event between resisting and adopting external norms was the October 2002 terrorist attack in Bali. This had the simultaneous effect of increasing demand for counterterrorism policies, reducing domestic resistance and precipitating a wide range of offers of technical assistance in areas such as terrorist financing. With that bombing, the relative gains to be realized from adopting the SRs became unambiguously "high." In these circumstances, it is difficult to discern the effect of norms on Indonesia's decision to implement the SRs. However, I suggest that the operation of a particular normative mechanism—the expert community of anti-money-laundering/counterterrorist financing officials—helps explain why Indonesia overtook India, moving from a position of resistance to one of adoption in quick time.

In the late 1990s, a group of officials within Indonesia's central bank, Bank Indonesia (BI), began to realize the importance of implementing global anti-money-laundering standards. Beginning in 1998, they opened contacts with other anti-money-laundering officials in the region, with the aim of developing "know-your-customer" guidelines. By December 2000, draft money-laundering legislation had been developed, which included a commitment to create a financial intelligence unit. This latter decision required that other agencies in the capital be convinced that the functions of an FIU could not be performed by nonspecialists within BI. By mid-2001, Indonesia had joined the APG. Also, the new customer identification regulations had been passed, although the broader anti-money-laundering bill had yet to engender enough political will to get it through parliament. The bankers' sense of urgency did not persuade others in Jakarta that anti-money-laundering policy should be a priority as Indonesia emerged from authoritarianism.

In spite of Indonesia's resistance to counterterrorist financing norms, its anti–money-laundering legislation finally passed in April 2002, creating an FIU (called Pusat Pelaporan dan Analisis Transaksi Keuangan or "PPATK") for the first time. After the Bali blasts, PPATK exercised influence by controlling knowledge and information about global standards to counterterrorist financing. Also, by promulgating legislation, and through the engagement of external and internal actors, PPATK was able to guide the formation of Indonesia's interests on terrorist financing issues after October 2002. For example, regarding legislative change, two significant amendments in 2003 indicated Indonesia's willingness to adopt FATF standards and PPATK's influence can be seen from the way in which the FATF's SRs were a direct point of reference.

First, Megawati responded to Bali by introducing a counterterrorism bill then before parliament as a "regulation-in-lieu," alongside two Presidential Decrees, creating institutional mechanisms to enable the formation of a coherent counterterrorism framework (Report of Indonesia to the Counter-terrorism Committee, 2003). Passed on October 18, 2002, the regulation-in-lieu had the force of law and became an act of the Indonesian Parliament in April 2003. From the point of view of Indonesia's adoption of the SRs, this development was important as it addressed SR I and SR II directly. The counterterrorism regulation and act went some way toward meeting Indonesia's commitments under the UN Convention on Terrorist Financing, which it had recently signed but not yet ratified. Indeed, international counterterrorism treaties (on both terrorist financing and terrorist bombing) had been a point of reference for Indonesian lawmakers in drafting the bill.[27] Regarding SR II, the regulation-in-lieu criminalized terrorist financing in Indonesia for the first time.

More importantly, PPATK oversaw amendments (passed in October 2003) to the new anti-money-laundering law, responding directly to FATF standards.[28] In order to assuage any concern about the criminalization of terrorist financing in Indonesia (SR II), the definition of "proceeds of crime" was broadened to include funds intended to be used for terrorism. This refinement also effectively extended suspicious transaction reporting requirements in Indonesia to those suspected to be connected to terrorism (SR IV). In fact, the amendment (responding again to FATF and external criticism) decreased the amount that triggers a compulsory cash transaction report, and reduced the timeframe in which reporting agencies were required to submit their reports.

Further, through PPATK's interactions with the global money laundering and terrorist financing expert network it has sought not only to "globalize" Indonesian policy, but also to "localize" the benefits of adoption for Indonesia. In securing critical technical assistance from foreign donors, and by contributing to Indonesia's campaign to be removed from the NCCT list, PPATK has helped shape Indonesia's interests. To this end, PPATK has sought out opportunities to build its capacity through technical assistance. Beginning in December 2002, PPATK has met with a core group of donors every three months. Focusing specifically on money laundering and terrorist financing issues, this group includes Australia and the U.S., as well as the IMF, World Bank, and other international organizations. Over time, such regular meetings have facilitated the delivery of a wide range of targeted and coordinated technical assistance. This forum complements side meetings—on the margins of APG and Egmont events—that occur three or four times a year, as well as the formal meetings themselves. Upon commencing operations in 2003, PPATK hosted two consultants from Australia's FIU, AUSTRAC, who assisted in the establishment of the center. PPATK officials have subsequently made the return journey to Sydney, sharing insights and advancing skills. Among other aspects of financial intelligence, capacity-building initiatives have enabled PPATK to integrate technology in the fight against money laundering and terrorist financing. Put simply, it is doubtful whether Indonesian adoption of the SRs would have advanced so quickly without the infusion of assistance from abroad (research interviews, Jakarta, April, 2005).

In this way, the perception that cooperating in the GWOT is in Indonesia's interests—to suppress terrorism and enhance state capacity—has become more widespread in the capital (research interviews, Jakarta, April, 2005). PPATK now attracts political support from the highest levels of the Indonesian government. In fact, in a sign that PPATK's agenda has now spread across Jakarta, current President Susilo Bambang Yudhoyono named four ministerial-level envoys to visit FATF member states to campaign for Indonesia's removal from the FATF's NCCT list.[29]

Overall, then, Indonesia's adoption of international counterterrorist financing norms reflects that Indonesian elites perceived strong relative gains from adopting norms. In addition, the degree to which the SRs have been internalized by Indonesian elites reflects the effect of PPATK as the domestic advocate of international norms. That advocacy has meant that, over time, Indonesian elites have seen the SRs as consistent with maintaining their ability to construct their own identity. This combination of factors explains why Indonesia was able to overtake India in adopting counterterrorist financing norms. India did not adopt the SRs until after mid-2004, when the Congress-led coalition displaced the BJP government. This shift consolidated the reframing of FATF standards as "finance"—rather than "counterterrorism"—measures, thereby affirming the agency of elites that had set India's economy on the path toward liberalization in the recent past.

In campaigning against the BJP in 2004, the Congress Party promised to repeal the Prevention of Terrorism Act as part of the "Common Minimum Programme" agreed among its coalition partners. Similar to past legislation granting "special powers" to the government, that act had been widely misused against political opponents (see Laying POTA to Rest, 2004; Mohapatra, 2004; Verma, 2004). New Prime Minister Dr. Manmohan Singh—who, as Finance Minister in the early 1990s, had introduced the first wave of reforms to liberalize India's economy—delivered on this promise in September 2004. But some of the provisions of the act, including those necessary to implement counterterrorist financing measures, were retained and rolled in other legislation. In doing so, Singh and his new finance minister, Harvard-educated lawyer P. Chidambaram, drew on prevailing local beliefs that had led India to embrace globalization over the previous decade and a half. As Chidambaram stated on assuming office, "The policies adopted since 1991 have brought considerable benefits and strengths to the Indian economy. What the new Government will now do, and what I will now do, is to factor in the experience gained during the last thirteen years" (FM Emphasizes Massive Investment in Agriculture and Manufacturing Sectors, 2004).

Reflecting this commitment, the September 2004 amendments responded directly to the criticisms of India's prior approach leveled by money laundering and terrorist financing experts. For the first time in a single act, the government criminalized terrorist financing (under an amended definition of "terrorist act" that explicitly extends coverage to acts "in any foreign country") and consolidated its power to implement UN lists, assuring its convergence around SRs II and III respectively. In another first, a series measures revising and extending the RBI's 2002 "know your customer" guidelines began to refer to FATF standards directly, noting that, "These have become the international benchmark for framing anti-money laundering and combating financing of terrorism policies by the regulatory authorities. Compliance with these standards by both the banks and financial institutions and the country has become necessary for international financial relationships" (Reserve Bank of India, 2004b). In November 2004, revised guidelines for commercial banks advanced India's adoption of the SRs (e.g., by extending customer identification requirements to NGOs and charities, and requesting banks to appoint an officer to oversee money laundering and terrorist financing policy).

At the same time, the relative gains calculation facing Indian elites began to warrant closer attention. By late 2004, an external assessment by APG inspectors was being planned, providing a rare opportunity for formal outside scrutiny of India's approach. Following that visit, in March 2005, India was better placed to become a member of the FATF in its own right. Further, private sector actors became more active in advocating that India conform to global money laundering and terrorist financing standards. In April 2005, the chief executive of the Indian Banks Association observed that India's anti-money-laundering regime was still in the first phases of its implementation and advocated that India join the FATF, to ensure that India has a say in the formation of global standards (Setup Anti-money Laundering System: IBA Tells Banks, 2005).

Perhaps the most tangible sign of India's will to adopt the SRs is that the final series of amendments to the Prevention of Money Laundering Bill were finally passed in May 2005. Framed as meeting India's "international commitments," including FATF rules, the Prevention of Money Laundering Act came into force on July 1. Importantly, the entry into force of the act was also the final legal requirement to establish FIU-IND, (Prevention of Money Laundering Act 2002 Comes into Force from Tomorrow, 2005), which became operational in September and started receiving cash and suspicious transaction reports from October 2005 (FIU to Track Deals over Rs 10 Lakh, 2005). Although India did not receive substantial technical assistance in developing its counterterrorist financing law and policy, it did consult with other states in establishing its FIU. In this regard, the Australian government offered its assistance (such that FIU-IND is modeled on AUSTRAC) and India also consulted with the U.S. and the UK.

Although points of divergence remain, it is interesting to note that RBI officials have begun to frame terrorism per se as a global and not a local concern—precisely opposite of the framing strategy deployed earlier: "Money laundering is not a new concern. The ugly face of terrorism that we have witnessed in the past makes the functioning of such a system extremely critical. Terrorism is not a local incident now but is a global phenomenon" (All Transactions over Rs 10 Lakh to be Tracked, 2005). In fact, at the recent Indo-US Financial and Economic Forum (the third such meeting since 2000), Finance Minister Chidambaram renewed India's commitment to implementing global money laundering and terrorist financing standards. In doing so, he noted the passage of the PML Act and said that, "We have complied with all the requirements. There has to be a report inspection and a report, which I believe, will take place shortly. I have told Secretary Snow that we are fully committed to curbing money laundering as well as to stamp out financing of terrorist activities" (transcript of the Joint Press Conference by Treasury Secretary Snow and Finance Minister P. Chidambaram, 2005). This renewed commitment was framed as part of a "road map" for financial sector reform, which received strong endorsement from Secretary Snow (India Presents Road Map for Financial Sector Reform, 2005).

Although this vision had its roots in the commitment to liberalization taken by India in the early 1990s, the adoption of global counterterrorist financing standards was delayed for some time by prevailing local norms about how best to counter terrorism. Relative gains calculations have increased only gradually over time, and recent moves to adopt norms reflect that the spread of norms is a function of relative gains assessments and the extent of normative affirmation that elites perceive.

Conclusion

In the period since 9/11, the development and pursuit of a "global war on terror" by powerful states, led by the United States, has shaped world politics. In the course of the GWOT, new norms have been elaborated, including a series of policy prescriptions to counterterrorist financing. These norms have been received in different ways by different states in the South, indicating that the "global" war on terror actually entails a contest between global and local interpretations of how best to suppress terrorism. In this contest, of course, norms matter. I have endeavored to show that norms matter in a specific way—namely, national elites behave like "social egoists," being concerned to maintain control over the construction of their own identity. Elites seek "normative affirmation," as they prefer to be norm-makers and not norm-takers. In resolving contests between global and local ideas of appropriate counterterrorist policies, relative gains also matter. By integrating normative and ideational factors, I have addressed what I see as two dilemmas that constructivists face. This original approach yields a number of insights in explaining India's and Indonesia's adoption of terrorist financing norms since 9/11.

In terms of locating my argument in current IR debates, I would identify it as "realist constructivist," in the sense that Barkin has used that term (Barkin, 2003). But it is at best an early attempt to flesh out what such an approach might look like. No doubt, there are other ways in which realist theories of IR, and their assumptions, can be drawn on to complement the advances that constructivism has made. It is important that such attempts at integration occur. Few actors in international politics ignore norms altogether. Fewer still are "cultural dupes," recalling Barnett's term (Barnett, 1999, 7). Explaining and predicting their behavior requires that we explicate, test, and, occasionally, revisit our premises.

Attachment

FATF Special Recommendations of Terrorist Financing (October 2001 unless otherwise noted)

Recognizing the vital importance of taking action to combat the financing of terrorism, the FATF has agreed these Recommendations, which, when combined with the FATF Forty Recommendations on money laundering, set out the basic framework to detect, prevent and suppress the financing of terrorism and terrorist acts.

I. Ratification and Implementation of UN instruments

Each country should take immediate steps to ratify and to implement fully the 1999 United Nations International Convention for the Suppression of the Financing of Terrorism. Countries should also immediately implement the United Nations resolutions relating to the prevention and suppression of the financing of terrorist acts, particularly United Nations Security Council Resolution 1373.

II. Criminalizing the Financing of Terrorism and Associated Money Laundering

Each country should criminalize the financing of terrorism, terrorist acts and terrorist organizations. Countries should ensure that such offences are designated as money laundering predicate offences.

III. Freezing and Confiscating Terrorist Assets

Each country should implement measures to freeze without delay funds or other assets of terrorists, those who finance terrorism and terrorist organizations in accordance with the United Nations resolutions relating to the prevention and suppression of the financing of terrorist acts.

Each country should also adopt and implement measures, including legislative ones, which would enable the competent authorities to seize and confiscate property that is the proceeds of, or used in, or intended or allocated for use in, the financing of terrorism, terrorist acts or terrorist organizations.

IV. Reporting Suspicious Transactions Related to Terrorism

If financial institutions, or other businesses or entities subject to anti-money laundering obligations, suspect or have reasonable grounds to suspect that funds are linked or related to, or are to be used for terrorism, terrorist acts or by terrorist organizations, they should be required to report promptly their suspicions to the competent authorities.

V. International Cooperation

Each country should afford another country, on the basis of a treaty, arrangement or other mechanism for mutual legal assistance or information exchange, the greatest possible measure of assistance in connection with criminal, civil enforcement, and administrative investigations, inquiries and proceedings relating to the financing of terrorism, terrorist acts and terrorist organizations.

Countries should also take all possible measures to ensure that they do not provide safe havens for individuals charged with the financing of terrorism, terrorist acts or terrorist organizations, and should have procedures in place to extradite, where possible, such individuals.

VI. Alternative Remittance

Each country should take measures to ensure that persons or legal entities, including agents, that provide a service for the transmission of money or value, including transmission through an informal money or value transfer system or network, should be licensed or registered and subject to all the FATF Recommendations that apply to banks and non-bank financial institutions. Each country should ensure that persons or legal entities that carry out this service illegally are subject to administrative, civil or criminal sanctions.

VII. Wire Transfers

Countries should take measures to require financial institutions, including money-remitters, to include accurate and meaningful originator information (name, address and account number) on funds transfers and related messages that are sent, and the information should remain with the transfer or related message through the payment chain.

Countries should take measures to ensure that financial institutions, including money-remitters, conduct enhanced scrutiny of and monitor for suspicious activity funds transfers which do not contain complete originator information (name, address and account number).

VIII. Non-Profit Organizations

Countries should review the adequacy of laws and regulations that relate to entities that can be abused for the financing of terrorism. Non-profit organizations are particularly vulnerable, and countries should ensure that they cannot be misused:

(i) by terrorist organizations posing as legitimate entities;

(ii) to exploit legitimate entities as conduits for terrorist financing, including for the purpose of escaping asset freezing measures; and

(iii) to conceal or obscure the clandestine diversion of funds intended for legitimate purposes to terrorist organizations.

IX. Cash Couriers (added in October 2004)

Countries should have measures in place to detect the physical cross-border transportation of currency and bearer negotiable instruments, including a declaration system or other disclosure obligation.

Countries should ensure that their competent authorities have the legal authority to stop or restrain currency or bearer negotiable instruments that are suspected to be related to terrorist financing or money laundering, or that are falsely declared or disclosed,

Countries should ensure that effective, proportionate and dissuasive sanctions are available to deal with persons who make false declaration(s) or disclosure(s). In cases where the currency or bearer negotiable instruments are related to terrorist financing or money laundering, countries should also adopt measures, including legislative ones consistent with Recommendation 3 and Special Recommendation Ill, which would enable the confiscation of such currency or instruments.

Notes

1. On the distinction between instrumental and value rationality, see Tannenwald, 2005, 17–20.

2. This typology of ideas is based on Tannenwald's (2005, 14–17). An analogous typology is offered by Goldstein and Keohane (1993). For present purposes, I omit "ideologies or shared belief systems" ("systematic sets of doctrines or beliefs that reflect the social needs and aspirations of a group, class, culture, or state") from my discussion (Tannenwald, 2005, 15, 17).

3. These are: the Convention on Offences and Certain Other Acts Committed on Board Aircraft, signed at Tokyo on September 14, 1963; the Convention for the Suppression of Unlawful Seizure of Aircraft, signed at the Hague on December 16, 1970; the Convention for the Suppression of Unlawful Acts against the Safety of Civil Aviation, signed at Montreal on September 23, 1971; the Convention on the Prevention and Punishment of Crimes against Internationally Protected Persons, including Diplomatic Agents, approved by the General Assembly of the United Nations on December 14, 1973; the International Convention against the Taking of Hostages, adopted by the General Assembly of the United Nations on December 17, 1979; the Convention on the Physical Protection of Nuclear Material, signed at Vienna on March 3, 1980; the Protocol for the Suppression of Unlawful Acts of Violence at Airports Serving International Civil Aviation, supplementary to the Convention for the Suppression of Unlawful Acts against the Safety of Civil Aviation, signed at Montreal on February 24, 1988; the Convention for the Suppression of Unlawful Acts against the Safety of Maritime Navigation, done at Rome on March 10, 1988; the Protocol for the Suppression of Unlawful Acts against the Safety of Fixed Platforms located on the Continental Shelf, done at Rome on March 10, 1988; the Convention on the Marking of Plastic Explosives for the Purpose of Detection, signed at Montreal on March 1, 1991; the International Convention for the Suppression of Terrorist Bombings, approved by the General Assembly of the United Nations on December 15, 1997; the International Convention for the Suppression of the Financing of Terrorism, approved by the General Assembly of the United Nations on December 9, 1999; and, the International Convention for the Suppression of Acts of Nuclear Terrorism, approved by the General Assembly of the United Nations on April 13, 2005.

4. At least, the UN Secretary General has recommended that Member States conclude a definition. See Report of the Secretary General (2005, 26).

5. Elsewhere, I have compared counterterrorist financing norms with analogous standards in the areas of maritime security and migration control: Romaniuk (2005, 2006).

6. Although considered discriminatory and overtly political by some (e.g., Levi, 2002, and Morris-Cotterill, 2001) it is generally credited with significant success in inducing convergence around the 40 recommendations (e.g., Drezner, 2005; Simmons, 2001; Helleiner, 2000).

7. Clunan (2005) argues that the U.S. has "succeeded in globalizing the anti-money laundering framework and recasting it as a regime to combat terrorist

financing." For a more detailed review of multilateral developments in the area of terrorist financing, see Biersteker, Eckert, and Romaniuk (2008).

8. For an overview, see Schott, 2004.

9. For an update of recent activities, see International Monetary Fund and World Bank, 2005a; 2005b.

10. See resolution 1617 (2005).

11. Among others, see Biersteker, Eckert, and Romaniuk (2008), Eckert (2005), Biersteker with Romaniuk (2004), Cortright et al. (2004), Rosand (2003), and Ward (2003).

12. The characterization of the relationship between the committees as "tactical" (1267) and "strategic" (CTC) is from Biertsteker with Romaniuk (2004, 70). More formally, the relationship between the committees is set out in "Distinctions between Security Council Committees Dealing with Terrorism" (2003).

13. Most recently, see "Treasury Wields PATRIOT Act Powers to Isolate Two Latvian Banks" (2005). Section 311 also permits action against financial institutions and is additional to preexisting designation authorities, such as the State Department's "State Sponsors of Terrorism" power (which also imposes financial prohibitions upon listed states under other legislation). The Ukraine has subsequently been removed from the "311" list.

14. See International Monetary Fund and World Bank, 2005a, 2005b. Although small (N = 18), the sample used by the Bank and Fund comprises a mix of high-, middle-, and low-income countries.

15. First Report of the Analytical Support and Sanctions Monitoring Team (2004); Second Report of the Analytical Support and Sanctions Monitoring Team (2005); Third Report of the Analytical Support and Sanctions Monitoring Team (2005).

16. This meant that the bill could not be used to apprehend terrorist financiers connected to terrorist attacks abroad, such as 9/11 itself.

17. Krasner (1999) initially raised similar criticisms.

18. The quotation is Barnett's (1999, 7). See also Drezner, 2003, and Risse, 2002.

19. Ruggie's emphasis 1998, 867. Analogously, see Checkel, 2001.

20. A point noted by Barkin, 2003, Risse, 2002, and Ruggie, 1998, among others.

21. See Checkel, 2005, 805–806, who argues that the neos are largely quiet on the topic of socialization, but recall Goldstein and Keohane (1993).

22. This is necessarily a straw-man description of what a "classical liberal constructivism" might look like and I can't think of an explicit attempt to develop such an argument. Nonetheless, my point is simply that liberalism, as a substantive theory of IR, provides guidance on how agents might resolve the second dilemma of constructivism. Harkin (2003) describes much of U.S.-based constructivism as effectively liberal-idealist.

23. This understanding of elites draws upon (and "socializes") the definition of the state posited by Mastanduno, Lake, and Ikenberry (1989, fn. 3).

24. Most explicitly, see Morgenthau, 1948. Among others, see Mastanduno, Lake, and Ikenberry, 1989, and Krasner, 1999.

25. Moderate groups opposed this position in equally strong terms: Sukma (2002, 266–267, 276).

26. Vice President Hamzah Haz cited America's "sins" as a cause of the attacks: Smith (2005b, 36; 2003a, 310).

27. Document obtained from PPATK.

28. Report of Indonesia to the Security Council Committee Established Pursuant to Resolution 1267 (1999), Pursuant to Paragraphs 6 and 7 of Resolution 1455 (2003) (2003, 10), Research interview, PPATK, Jakarta, April 2005.

29. Yudhoyono Names Special Envoys to Lobby for Indonesia's Removal from FATF List (2005). This campaign was successful and Indonesia was delisted in February 2005.

References

9/11 Commission Report. (2004, July 22). National Commission on Terrorist Attacks Upon the United States.
Acharya, A. (2004). How ideas spread: Whose norms matter? Norms localization and institutional change in Asian regionalism. *International Organization* 58, 239–275.
All Transactions over Rs 10 Lakh to be Tracked. (2005, October 22). *Financial Express* (Mumbai).
APG. (2005, May 2). Mutual Evaluation of India. *APG iQ (The APG Information Quarterly)*.
APG. (2001). *First annual report 1999–2000*. Sydney: APG Secretariat.
Barkin, J. S. (2003). Realist constructivism. *International Studies Review* 5 (3), 325–342.
Barnett, M. (1999). Culture, strategy and foreign policy change: Israel's road to Oslo. *European Journal of International Relations* 5 (1), 5–36.
Biersteker, T. J., Eckert, S. E., & Romaniuk, P. (2008). International initiatives to combat the financing of terrorism. In T. J. Biersteker & S. E. Eckert (Eds.), *Countering the financing of terrorism* (pp. 234–259). New York: Routledge.
Biersteker, T. J., with Romaniuk, P. (2004). The return of the state? Financial reregulation in the pursuit of national security after September 11. In J. Tirman (Ed.), *Maze of fear: Security and migration after 9/11* (pp. 59–75). New York: New Press.
BJP to Oppose POTA Repeat. (2004, August 12). *The Hindu*.
Blacklist of 'Dirty Money' Havens Put on Temporary Hold. (2002, September 26). *Financial Times*.
Bush, G. W. (2001, September 20). Address to a joint session of Congress and the American people.
Checkel, J. T. (2005). International institutions and socialization in Europe: Introduction and framework. *International Organization* 59 (4), 801–826.

Checkel, T. (2001). Why comply? Social learning and European identity change. *International Organization* 55 (3).
Chellaney, B. (2001/02). Fighting terrorism in Southern Asia: The lessons of history. *International Security* 26 (3), 94–116.
Clunan, A. L. (2005). U.S. and international responses to terrorist financing. *Strategic Insights* 4 (1).
Cortell, A. P., & Davis, J. W. Jr. (2000). Understanding the domestic impact of international norms: A research agenda. *International Studies Review* 2 (1), 65–87.
Cortell, A. P., & Davis, J. W. Jr. (1996). How do international institutions matter? The domestic impact of international rules and norms. *International Studies Quarterly* 40, 451–478.
Cortright, D. et al. (2004). An action agenda for enhancing the United Nations program on counter-terrorism. Fourth Freedom Forum. Joan B. Kroc Institute.
Council on Foreign Relations. (2004). Update on the global campaign against terrorist financing. Second report of an independent task force on terrorist financing sponsored by the Council on Foreign Relations (Maurice R. Greenberg, Chair). New York: Council on Foreign Relations.
Crenshaw, M. (2001). Counter-terrorism policy and the political process. *Studies in Conflict and Terrorism* 24, 329–337.
Dessler, D., & Owen, J. (2005). Constructivism and the problem of explanation. *Perspectives on Politics* 3 (3), 597–610.
Dhavan, R. (2004, October 1). Terrorism by ordinance. *The Hindu*.
Distinctions between Security Council committees dealing with terrorism (1267 Committee and Counter-terrorism Committee. (2003, July 28). UN Press Release SC/7827.
Drezner, D. (2005). Globalization, harmonization and competition: The different pathways to policy convergence. *Journal of European Public Policy* 12 (5), 841–859.
Drezner, D.W. (2003). Introduction: The interaction of domestic and international Institutions. In D.W. Drezner (Ed.), *Locating the proper authorities: The interaction of domestic and international institutions* (pp. 1–22). Ann Arbor: University of Michigan Press.
Eckert, S. E. (2005). Lessons from the UN's counter-terrorism efforts. In K. Ballentine & H. Nitschke (Eds.), *Profiting from peace: Managing the resource dimensions of civil war* (pp. 146–190). Boulder, CO: Lynne Rienner.
Egmont Group. (2004). *About the Egmont Group*. Available at www.egmontgroup.org/about_egmont.html
FATF. (2005a). Annual report 2004–05. Paris: FATF Secretariat.
FATF. (2005b). Methodology for assessing compliance with the FATF 40 recommendations and the FATF 9 special recommendations. Paris: FATF Secretariat. Initially dated February 27, 2004. Updated October 14, 2005.
FATF. (2002). Annual Report 2001–02. Paris: FATF Secretariat.
Finnemore, M., & Sikkink, K. (1998). International norm dynamics and political change. *International Organization* 52 (4), 887–911.

First Report of the Analytical Support and Sanctions Monitoring Team Appointed Pursuant to Resolution 1526 (2004) concerning al-Qaida and the Taliban and associated individuals and entities. (2004). UN Doc. S/2004/679.

FIU to Track Deals over Rs 10 Lakh. (2005, September 1). *India Business Insight*.

FM Emphasizes Massive Investment in Agriculture and Manufacturing Sectors. (2004, May 24). Press Information Bureau, Government of India.

G8. (2005, July). G8 statement on counter-terrorism. Gleneagles.

Gilmore, W. (2004). *Dirty money: The evolution of money laundering counter measures*. Strasbourg: Council of Europe Press.

Goldstein, J., & Keohane, R.O. (1993). Ideas and foreign policy: An analytical framework. In G. Goldstein & R.O. Keohane (Eds.), *Ideas and foreign policy: Beliefs, institutions and political change* (pp. 3–30). Ithaca: Cornell University Press.

Guillaume, G. (2004). Terrorism and international law. *International and Comparative Law Quarterly* 53, 537–548.

Haas, P. (1992). Introduction: Epistemic communities and international policy coordination. *International Organization* 46 (l), 1–35.

Helleiner, E. (2000). The politics of global financial reregulation: Lessons from the fight against money laundering. Working Paper No. 15. CEPA Working Paper Series III. Center for Economic Policy Analysis, New School for Social Research.

Hoffman, B. (1998). *Inside terrorism*. New York: Columbia University Press.

INCSR (various years), see U.S. Department of State (various years). International Narcotics Control Strategy Reports.

India Presents Road Map for Financial Sector Reform. (2005, November 10). *The Hindu*.

International Monetary Fund and World Bank. (2005a). Anti-money laundering and combating the financing of terrorism: Observations from the work program and implications going forward.

International Monetary Fund and World Bank. (2005b). Anti-money laundering and combating the financing of terrorism: Observations from the work program and implications going forward-supplementary information.

Jackson, J. K. (2005). The financial action task force: An overview. CRS Report for Congress, RS2 1904. Updated 4 March.

Joint Statement: Sixth Meeting of the India-US Joint Working Group on Counter-terrorism. (2004). New Delhi.

Joint Statement: Fourth Meeting of the India-US Joint Working Group on Counter-terrorism. (2002). Washington, DC.

Katzenstein, P. J. (2003). Same war—Different views: Germany, Japan and counter-terrorism. *International Organization* 57 (4), 731–760.

Katzenstein, P. J. (2002, Spring). September 11 in comparative perspective: The anti-terrorism campaigns of Germany and Japan. *Dialog-IO*, 45–56.

Katzenstein, P. J. (1993). Coping with terrorism: Norms and internal security in Germany and Japan. In G. Goldstein & R.O. Keohane (Eds.), *Ideas and foreign policy: Beliefs, institutions and political change* (pp. 265–295). Ithaca, NY: Cornell University Press.

Krasner, S. D. (1999). *Sovereignty: Organized hypocrisy*. Princeton, NJ: Princeton University Press.
Latimer, W. S. (2004). *What can the United States learn from India to counter terrorism?* MA Thesis. Monterey, CA: Naval Postgraduate School.
Laying POTA to Rest. (2004, August 12). *The Hindu*.
Levi, M. (2002). Money laundering and its regulation. *Annals of the American Academy of Political and Social Sciences* 582, 181–194.
Mastanduno, M., Lake, D. A., & Ikenberry, G. J. (1989). Toward a realist theory of state action. *International Studies Quarterly* 33 (4), 456–474.
Mohapatra, M. (2004). Learning lessons from India: The recent history of anti-terrorist legislation on the subcontinent. *Journal of Criminal Law and Criminology* 95 (1), 315–343.
Morgenthau, H. J. (1948). *Politics among nations: The struggle for power and peace*. New York: Knopf.
Morris-Cotterill, N. (2001, May–June). Money laundering. *Foreign Policy* 124, 16–22.
Patterns of Global Terrorism (various years), see U. S. Department of State.
Payne, R. A. (2001). Persuasion, frames and norm construction. *European Journal of International Relations* 7 (1), 37–61.
Pieth, M., & Aiolfi, G. (n.d.). The private sector becomes active: The Wolfsberg process.
Prevention of Money Laundering Act, 2002, Comes into Force from Tomorrow. (2005, June 30). Press Release. Press Information Bureau, Government of India.
Proposal for the Revitalization of the Counter-Terrorist Committee. (2004, February 19). UN Doc. S/2004/124.
Raustiala, K. (2002). The architecture of international cooperation: Transgovernmental networks and the future of international law. *Virginia Journal of International Law* 43, 1–92.
Realuyo, C. B. (2004, March 11). *G8 counter-terrorism action group efforts to combat terrorist financing*. Presentation to follow-up meeting to the United Nations counter-terrorism committee (CTC). Special Meeting of March 6, 2003.
Reddy, Y. V. (2003, September 21). *The global economy and financial markets*. Address by the Governor of the Reserve Bank of India to the International Monetary and Financial Committee. Dubai, UAE.
Report of India to the Counter-terrorism Committee. (2001, December 27). UN Doc. S/2001/1278.
Report of Indonesia to the Counter-terrorism Committee. (2004, August 19). UN Doc. S/2004/670.
Report of Indonesia to the Counter-terrorism Committee. (2003, March 7). UN Doc. S/2003/627.
Report of Indonesia to the Security Council Committee Established Pursuant to Resolution 1267 (1999) pursuant to Paragraphs 6 and 7 of Resolution 1455 (2003). (2003) UN Doc. S/AC.37/2003/(1455)/84.
Report of the Secretary General. (2005, March 21). *In larger freedom: Towards development, security and human rights for all*. UN Doc. A/59/2005.

Reserve Bank of India. (2004a). *Report on trend and progress of banking in India 2003–04.* Mumbai: Reserve Bank of India.
Reserve Bank of India. (2004b, November 29). *Know your customer (KYC) guidelines—Anti-money laundering standards.* RBI ref. DBOD.NO.AML. BC.58/ 14.01.001/2004-05,
Risse, T. (2002). Constructivism and international institutions: Toward conversations across paradigms. In I. Katznelson & H. Milner (Eds.), *Political science: The state of the discipline* (pp. 597–623). New York: Norton.
Risse, T. (2000). "Let's argue!" Communicative action in world politics. *International Organization* 54 (1), 1–39.
Romaniuk, P. (2006). *Global and local wars on terror: Policy convergence and counter-terrorism in South and Southeast Asia.* PhD dissertation. Department of Political Science, Brown University.
Romaniuk, P. (2005, September). *Exporting homeland security: US power, local resistance and maritime security in Southeast Asia.* Paper presented at the Annual Meeting of the American Political Science Association, Washington, DC.
Rosand, E. (2003). Security Council Resolution 1373, the counter-terrorism committee and the fight against terrorism. *American Journal of International Law* 97 (2), 333–341.
Ruggie, J. G. (1998). What makes the world hang together? Neo-utilitarianism and the social constructivist challenge. *International Organization* 52 (4), 855–885.
Schott, P. A. (2004). *Reference guide to anti-money laundering and countering the financing of terrorism* (2nd ed.), Washington, DC: World Bank and International Monetary Fund.
Second Report of the Analytical Support and Sanctions Monitoring Team Appointed Pursuant to Resolution 1526 (2004) concerning al-Qaida and the Taliban and associated individuals and entities. (2005). UN Doc. S/2005/83.
Sen, S. L. (2005, June 11). Fight against money laundering goes public. *Business Times* (Singapore).
Set up Anti-money Laundering System: IBA Tells Banks. (2005, April 19). *Indian Express.*
Simmons, B. A. (2001). The international politics of harmonization: The case of capital market regulation. *International Organization* 55 (3), 589–620.
Slaughter, A. M. (2004). *A new world order.* Princeton, NJ: Princeton University Press.
Slaughter, A. M. (1997). The real new world order. *Foreign Affairs* 76 (5), 183–197.
Smith, A. L. (2005a). Terrorism and the political landscape in Indonesia. In P. J. Smith (Ed.), *Terrorism and violence in Southeast Asia: Transnational challenges to states and regional stability* (pp. 98–121). Armonk, NY: ME Sharpe.
Smith, A. L. (2005b). The politics of negotiating the terrorist problem in Indonesia. *Studies in Conflict and Terrorism* 28, 33–44.
Smith, A. L. (2003a). Epilogue: The Bali bombing and responses to international terrorism. In I. Soesastro, A. L. Smith & H. M. Ling (Eds.), *Governance*

in Indonesia: Challenges facing the Megawati presidency (pp. 305–322). Singapore: Institute for Southeast Asian Studies.

Smith, A. L. (2003b). A glass half full: Indonesia-US relations in the age of terror. *Contemporary Southeast Asia* 25 (3), 449–472.

Standing Committee on International Financial Standards and Codes (Reserve Bank of India). (2002, May 30). *Technical report on market integrity—Issues and status*. Mumbai: Reserve Bank of India.

Sukma, R. (2002). Indonesia and the September 11 attacks: Domestic reactions and implications. *The Indonesian Quarterly* XXX (3), 263–278.

Tanham, G. K. (1992). *Indian strategic thought: An interpretive essay*. Santa Monica, CA: RAND.

Tannenwald, N. (2005). Ideas and explanation: Advancing the theoretical agenda. *Journal of Cold War Studies* 7 (2), 13–42.

Targeting Terrorist Finances Project (Watson Institute for International Studies, Brown University). (2004, June). Appendix C to M. R. Greenberg (Chair), M. Factor (Vice Chair), W. F. Wechsler and L. S. Wolosky (Project Co-Directors), Update on the Global Campaign Against Terrorist Financing: Second Report of an Independent Task Force on Terrorist Financing Sponsored by the Council on Foreign Relations.

Third Report of the Analytical Support and Sanctions Monitoring Team Appointed Pursuant to Resolution 1526 (2004) concerning al-Qaida and the Taliban and associated individuals and entities. (2005). UN Doc. S/2005/572.

Transcript of the Joint Press Conference by Treasury Secretary Snow and Finance Minister P. Chidambaram. (2005).

Treasury Wields PATRIOT Act Powers to Isolate Two Latvian Banks. (2005, April 21). US Treasury ref. JS-240 I.

U.S. Department of State. (various years). *International Narcotics Control Strategy Reports* (INCSRs).

U.S. Department of State. (various years). *Patterns of Global Terrorism*.

Verma, P. (Ed.), (2004). *The terror of POTA and other security legislation*. New Delhi: Human Rights Law Network (Delhi)/People's Watch (Madurai).

Ward, C. A. (2003). Building capacity to combat international terrorism: The role of the United Nations security council. *Journal of Conflict and Security Law* 8 (2), 289–305.

Winer, J. M. (2003, November 5). *The growing role of international institutions on vounter-terrorism and law enforcement*. Council on Foreign Relations, Roundtable on Old Rules, New Threats.

Yudhoyono Names Special Envoys to Lobby for Indonesia's Removal from FATF List. (2005, January 24) *AFX News* (London).

Chapter 14

Winners and Losers in the War on Terror
The Problem of Metrics

Michael Stohl

> Today, we lack metrics to know if we are winning or losing the global war on terror. Are we capturing, killing or deterring and dissuading more terrorists every day than the madrassas and the radical clerics are recruiting, training and deploying against us?
>
> —Donald Rumsfeld, October 16, 2003

> We're fighting the enemy in Iraq and Afghanistan and across the world so we do not have to face them here at home.
>
> —George W. Bush, July 11, 2005, FBI Academy, Quantico, Virginia

Introduction

The "Global War on Terror" commenced with President Bush's address to a joint session of Congress on September 20, 2001, with his much-cited quote "Our war on terror begins with al Qaeda, but it does not end there. It will not end until every terrorist group of global reach has been found, stopped and defeated." Much previous work within communication explores how the war metaphor has framed subsequent counterterrorism actions and how they influence not simply the use of violence and the prevention of future acts of terrorism, but also the reactions of the audience to the acts or threats (see, for example, Kellner, 2003). Less attention has been accorded the question of networks, but in a recent study Stohl and Stohl (2007) explore how the Bush administration's use of the network metaphor framed the understanding of terror and counter terror and influenced counter terrorism policies.[1]

When Secretary of Defense Rumsfeld wrote his memo to Generals Meyers and Pace, Paul Wolfowitz, and Douglas Feith on the lack metrics on October 16, 2003, from which the opening quotation was drawn, he was correct that the United States government lacked metrics by which to determine if it were winning or losing the global war on terror. Raymond Decker, the GAO Director of Defense Capabilities and Management, testifying before the Committee on Government Reform of the House, reported that the GAO review of the new or updated national strategies released in 2002–2003[2] that related to combating terrorism and homeland security, argued that "they generally lack priorities, milestones or performance measures.... The strategies generally describe overarching objectives and priorities, but not measurable outcomes" (Decker, 2003).

In this chapter I argue that they—and we as a scholarly community—still lack those measures and hence discussion of the success and failure of particular policies or even whether they are likely to bring strategic or tactical success become mired in political rather than scholarly assessment. I contend that the root of the problem of the lack of metrics is not simply the result of partisan political disagreements or policy disputes grounded in a war versus a law enforcement approach to the problem of terror[3] but rather to the failure to ground the development of metrics in a theoretical understanding of the problem of terrorism and counterterrorism.

To establish the appropriate metrics and then within that context to evaluate winners and losers—or judge success—requires an understanding of what terrorism and counterterrorism are and how terrorism and counterterrorism affect governments and populations. This necessitates that we not only apply a consistent (and operational) definition of terrorism, but also that we recognize how terrorism differs from other acts of political violence.

Terrorists seek through their acts of violence (whether perpetrated or threatened) to create fear and/or compliant behavior in a victim and/or an audience for the act or threat. That is, terrorism is communicatively constituted violence. Although there is a long debate, both scholarly and political concerning the appropriate definition of terrorism, there are some core components that figure in almost definitional attempts. Violence, fear, intent, victim, and audience are at the core of terrorism definitions. And although many would contend that definitions of terrorism are a function of political consideration (see the discussion in Stohl, 1988), Kofi Annan suggested at the Madrid International summit on terrorism, democracy, and security (http://summit.clubmadrid.org/keynotes/a-global-strategy-for-fighting-terrorism.html, 2005) a definition of terrorism "... would make it clear that any action constitutes terrorism if it is intended to cause death or serious bodily harm to civilians or non-combatants, with the purpose of intimidating a population or compelling a Government or an international organization to do or abstain from doing any acts." In short, it is the action not the actor that makes a particular act terrorism.

The focus on the actions requires then that we distinguish the victims of the violent act from the targets (the audience of that violence). As difficult as it is for us to accept in the immediate aftermath of an attack with victims in plain view, the terrorists are primarily interested in the audience, not the victims. Thus, Stohl (1983) defines terrorism as the *purposeful* act or the threat of the act of *violence* to create *fear* and/or compliant behavior in a *victim* and/or *audience* of the act or threat. In terms of approaching the development of metrics, it further requires us to consider not simply the act or threat, but also the reaction of the audience to the immediate act and the social effects, which result from this reaction and subsequent behaviors in response. And it is these reactions and social effects that counterterrorism must address.

Therefore, counterterrorism actions must always address not simply the treatment of and response to actions that have taken place and the prevention of future acts of terrorism, but also the reactions of the audience to the acts or threats. The terrorist uses their violence to communicate fear to the audience and intends also that the audience begins to doubt if the authorities can protect those who are targeted. The authorities' counterterrorism task is not limited to the apprehension of the terrorists and taking appropriate actions that make it less likely that a future attack will succeed, and thereby making the public more secure. They must also make the public subjectively believe that they are more secure and create confidence and trust that the authorities are acting toward that end. Such communicative actions are necessary not only at the epicenters of terrorist but also (retro- and prospectively) in seemingly peripheral locations where the public experience a shared empathic identity and collective loss with those stricken and also a sense of vulnerability in potentially being future victims. Failing on either to make the public more secure or having them believe that they are amounts to a victory for the terrorist but as a process, failing to make the public believe that they are safe and that the political authorities are doing what they should often presents more of a threat to the political system than particular security lapses. That many terrorist threats originate outside the geographic boundaries of a particular state and that the scope of possible operations and targets may be found anywhere on the globe, means that public and governmental perceptions and actions within the international community are also important. Thus, countering terrorism involves the use of all the security forces of the state within the context of a political process. It is not simply about destroying the threat but also by what means and how that threat and the counter-terror are perceived that are involved.

Metrics

As indicated above, Donald Rumsfeld was correct that metrics need to be established by which to judge the success of counterterrorism policies and actions. A number of authors have offered suggestions. Byman (2003) argues that there are five "genuine measures of success" by which to evaluate counterterrorist operations: the freedom terrorists have to operate (their secure geographic zone), a high level of domestic support for counterterrorist operations, the disruption of the adversary's command, and control structure, terrorist recruitment, and terrorist attacks.

Morag (2005, 319–310), examining the Israeli case, argues that one can evaluate the ability of a state to cope with terrorism using seven parameters "that fall into three categories relating to: human life (reduction in civilian casualties among both Israelis and Palestinians), *economic resources* (minimization of the negative economic impact on Israel), and *political resources* (Israeli social cohesion, international and domestic support for the Israeli government, and the extent of weakening of international and domestic support for the Palestinian leadership).

The Bush Administration established a web site that provides metrics for the operations that they have taken to wage the war on terrorism (http://lifeandliberty.gov/subs/a_terr.htm). There are six categories of operations and for each they detail their accomplishments:

1. Disrupting terrorist threats, and capturing terrorists that would carry them out.
2. Gathering and cultivating detailed knowledge on terrorism in the United States.
3. Gathering information by leveraging criminal charges and long prison sentences.
4. Dismantling the terrorist financial network.
5. Using new legal tools (the Patriot Act) to detect, disrupt, and prevent potential terrorist plots.

6. Building department of justice long-term counterterrorism capacity.

At the National Endowment for Democracy on October 6, 2005 (see http://www.whitehouse.gov/news/releases/2005/10/20051006-3.html), the president stressed five aspects of the policy with a greater focus on the international:

> "First, we're determined to prevent the attacks of terrorist networks before they occur.
> Second, we're determined to deny weapons of mass destruction to outlaw regimes, and to their terrorist allies who would use them without hesitation.
> Third, we're determined to deny radical groups the support and sanctuary of outlaw regimes.
> Fourth, we're determined to deny the militants control of any nation, which they would use as a home base and a launching pad for terror.
> The fifth element of our strategy in the war on terror is to deny the militants future recruits by replacing hatred and resentment with democracy and hope across the broader Middle East."

Finally Congressional Research Service analyst Raphael Perl (2005, 11) stresses the importance of measuring trends. He stresses measuring: (1) Terrorist infrastructure. Is their leadership being weakened; is their recruitment base, network, or target list growing? (2) Terrorist tactical and strategic goals. (3) Capabilities. What are the capabilities of a terrorist group to inflict serious damage? Are they increasing or decreasing?

Each of these approaches reminds us that metrics for understanding success of counterterrorism is not a simple matter. We need to know what these numbers mean. Further, it is not simply what the terrorists and the authorities are doing to each other but how the audience is affected and how they react. The administration's approach focuses primarily on those that they identify as terrorists and the U.S. domestic audiences. They do not present information on how their activities are "received" by others. In the context of the global war on terror and Mr. Bush's assertion that "We're fighting the enemy in Iraq and Afghanistan and across the world so we do not have to face them here at home," the importance of that global audience for impacting what Byman calls the zone of operations should be clear. The "other" may support, acquiesce, or oppose both "us" and "them" and their choice is an important component of the success of terrorists and counterterrorists. Morag considers the impact on the "other" by including as one of his measures how the counterterrorist operations are impacting not simply Israeli loss of life but Palestinian as well.

A straight arithmetic accounting is the approach most often found in government releases and media reports. There are summary statements that assert that: two-third of the al Qaeda leadership has been captured, 3,400 arrested, $200 million in assets frozen, and bases in Afghanistan destroyed. And there are also reports that take the form of listing the number of attacks, the number of killed and injured, the property destroyed. What often is missing is the meaning of such statistics. What does an increase or decrease in the number of attacks, the lethality or scope, the location tell us about the chance of successful attacks occurring in the future and the reason that attacks are increasing or decreasing?

In short do these statistics help us know if there is a greater or lesser chance of a terrorist attack today in the United States than there was when the baseline point was established? Do they help us to know if there is a greater or lesser chance of a terrorist attack against American targets abroad than there was at the baseline point?

On the counterterrorism side the number killed, injured, arrested, tried, and convicted are the most common details provided. Rarely are combined tables of information on the categories provided such as in Table 14.1, which might describe the process of terror and counterterror and rarely is the data collected by which to examine the toll of counter terror on the population at large.

In addition, rarely is such data presented in a form that allows for an understanding of trends and deviations from trends in the information provided (and even more rarely placed in an historical or comparative framework).

Number of Attacks

The single most important number from an administration perspective in counting the number of attacks is that there have been no attacks by al Qaeda on American soil since September 11, 2001. If al Qaeda had further attacks planned and they were prevented, or if al Qaeda chose to abort, that would indicate major successes for the administration. On the administration web site www.lifeandliberty.gov, the administration claims to have disrupted 150 terrorist plots around the world and at the National Endowment for Democracy speech in October 2005, the president claimed 10 plots disrupted. Cole (2006) argues that this number is much in dispute. At this point because the data that the administration

Table 14.1. Terror and Counterterror Data

	Terrorist Acts	Counterterrorist Initiatives
Killed Leaders Foot soldiers Supporters Civilians		
Injured Leaders Foot soldiers Supporters Civilians		
Property Leaders Foot soldiers Supporters Civilians		
Arrests/Detentions Leaders Foot soldiers Supporters Civilians	NA	

has presented has been so tenuous we have only the Scots verdict of not proven. We should also be mindful of George Tenet's testimony to the intelligence committees in February 2004 that al Qaeda retained the ability to carry out attacks: "Even catastrophic attacks on the scale of 9/11 remain within Al Qaeda's reach."

At the same time we do have data on attacks that have occurred. The Congressional Research Service (CRS) tabulated the number of attacks by al Qaeda in the 30 months before and after 9/11, as shown in Figure 14.1.

In that period before 9/11, there was one attack with 17 fatalities. In the same length of time after 9/11, there were 10 attacks with approximately 510 fatalities. The CRS figures do not include any attacks within Iraq.

Moving beyond a simple focus on al Qaeda, when one examines the available data from the National Counterterrorism Center (NCTC, http://www.tkb.org/NCTC/Home.jsp), the data indicate that in 2004 there were more than three times as many incidents (651/208) and three times

Figure 14.1. Worldwide Attacks Attributed to al Qaeda

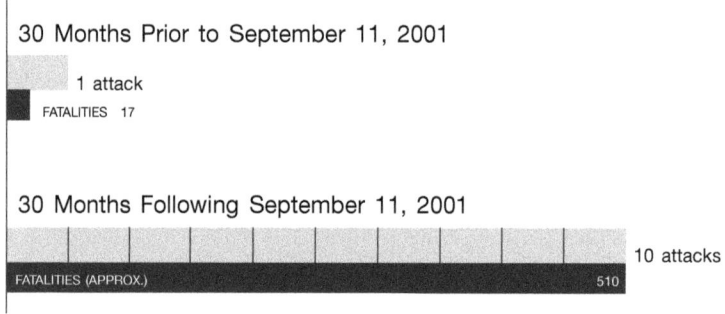

Source: Congressional Research Service (2004).

as many persons killed (1907/625) in what they define as significant international terrorism than in 2003. Thus, it appears that on a global scale significant incidents of international terrorism are increasing. When one focuses on incidents of domestic terrorism the numbers of fatalities reported is also much greater. Thus, one can support at least part of Mr. Bush's contention that we are fighting the terrorists over there. What one cannot conclude is that this demonstrates progress as there are certainly more incidents to which to respond.

Organizational Networks

Knowledge and consideration of the number of terrorist attacks, their location, and their perpetrators are related to how the "enemy" is defined in the global war on terror. At the heart of the problem is the use of the network metaphor by which the administration has defined al Qaeda and all those who are either "with us or against us." The Bush administration has never clearly and fully identified what they actually mean by a network of terror and who (beyond Osama bin Laden and the leaders of al Qaeda) actually need to be brought to justice for the "war" to be won (see Stohl & Stohl, 2007). Their failure stems from either unwillingness or an inability to clearly specify what they actually mean and some implications of the global network. In its simplest form, a network refers to the web of social relations that connect individuals, groups, and organizations.

An analysis of "networks of terror" should explain how various terrorist groups, and other organizations and states are connected, how they are organized, and how they operate as a network. We need to know what we mean by membership in the network and how the various members are linked. How the members are linked alters our understanding of what it means to be connected and how important those connections are. Not all connections are equal.

The administration argued at various points that al Qaeda had links in the past with Syria, Libya, Iraq, Iran, and Sudan. The administration also had to tiptoe around the connections between the Pakistan Intelligence Services connections to al Qaeda, the Taliban, and the Harakat al Mujahedin operating in Kashmir against India, as well as the financial connections between the Saudis and bin Laden. Estimates of the number of persons who passed through the al Qaeda training camps have ranged as high as 25,000 to 30,000 dispersed to cells in more than 60 countries. There is no easy way to determine the size of al Qaeda, the number and scale of its affiliates and proxies; or who its donors, active supporters, and potential sympathizers are. Local governments often do not know, deliberately conceal, or may at times exaggerate the al Qaeda presence in their countries. Thus if we don't know the baseline, it is difficult to determine if al Qaeda or the Global Network of Terror is larger or smaller since a particular point in time.

Estimates of the number of persons who passed through the al Qaeda training camps have ranged as high as 25,000 to 30,000 dispersed to cells in more than 60 countries. In the aftermath of the Afghanistan war the incentive to demonstrate success led to more conservative descriptions of organizational size, connections, and possibilities. For example, in June 2002, Johnson, Van Natta, and Miller (2002) of the *New York Times* reported,

> that senior officials suggest that although sworn members of Al Qaeda were estimated to number no more than 200 to 300 men, officials say that at its peak this broader Qaeda network operated about a dozen Afghan camps that trained as many as 5000 militants, who in turn created cells in as many as 60 countries.

In July 2002 Rebecca Carr, a reporter with the Cox News Service, quoting two "senior FBI officials," wrote,

> "Everyone tries to tie everything into 9/11 and al-Qaida," said one of the two officials interviewed Friday on condition of

anonymity. "There was a recent report suggesting that al-Qaida is about 5,000 strong. It is nowhere near 5,000 strong."

"While thousands of Islamic extremists and future terrorists have passed through Mr. bin Laden's training camps, it does not mean they are actual al Qaeda operatives," the officials said. The war in Afghanistan has successfully dispersed, killed or captured al-Qaeda leaders, leaving the terror network fractured and diffused. (Carr, 2002, A10)

In their public statements to Congress on February 11, 2003, FBI Director Robert Mueller III, CIA Director George Tenet, and other senior officials emphasized the number of arrests and disruptions. Mueller testified that "We have charged over 200 suspected terrorists with crimes," while Tenet noted that "more than one-third of the top Al-Qaeda leadership identified before the war has been captured or killed." President Bush himself reportedly keeps a "scorecard" that notes which al Qaeda and Taliban leaders are dead or in custody.

A body count approach is appealing because it provides a concrete measure of success and failure. Yet this approach is deeply flawed—and it is not, of course, something new in the annals of American presidents discussing success in a protracted war. A body count can be misleading because the size of the terrorist cadre is often unknown, and many of those killed or captured are low-level recruits who can easily be replaced. More importantly, it fails to reflect the impact on the adversary's morale, recruitment, fundraising, and residual ability to conduct sophisticated attacks. However, as Byman (2003) notes, "As the anonymous officer argues, Al-Qaeda's ability to recover from detentions, deaths and other disruptions make claims of its demise by officials sound like nothing so much as an arrogant ninny whistling past the graveyard." This, of course, may be because officials do not have accurate information on the al Qaeda leadership or because the organization has a ready supply of recruits and a remarkable ability to find leaders.

Building Support: The Counterterrorism Alliance

In the initial stages of preparing for the "war" on terrorism, the administration sought to put together broad diplomatic backing for its efforts. The members of NATO and the Rio Pact invoked these treaties' mutual defense clauses for the first time. Subsequently, 16 of the 19 NATO members engaged in the Afghan theater. The UN Security Council unanimously adopted Resolution 1373 requiring all UN members to freeze terrorist financing, improve border security, clamp down on the recruitment of terrorists, share information, and deny terrorists any support or safe haven. In September and October of 2001 there was clear international community support for the United States and for a collective response to the problem of terrorism. A total of 136 countries offered a range of military assistance to the United States, including over flight and landing rights and accommodations for U.S. forces. The initial cooperation led to "an aggressive international law enforcement effort [which] had resulted in detention of approximately 3,000 terrorists and their supporters in more than 100 countries and in the freezing of $124 million in assets in some 600 bank accounts around the world, including $36 million in the United States alone" (Perl, 2003, 2).

It is therefore important to examine if support has been maintained and what is the nature of the links within the counterterrorist network as well (see Table 14.2). Here it is also wise to think in comparative terms between terror and counterterror. As the 2006 Dubai Ports World deal controversy illustrates, the evidence on support by and for governments for the terrorists and counterterrorists is not always simple and straightforward. The same government that grants the U.S. its most important naval location in the Gulf region also sends millions of dollars to charitable organizations that support the families of "martyrs" in the Middle East.

Within this context it is important to distinguish states that support, acquiesce, or oppose either the counterterrorist coalition or the terrorists (and to note which particular ones) Mickolus (2001) suggests a range of measures with respect to states supporting terrorism that could easily be adapted to measure counterterrorism cooperation as well and placed in the table above. These include permitting safe havens or bases; permitting training on local soil; general training by the government; making large monetary contributions; provisioning arms; providing nonlethal operational assistance; providing direct financing and training for specific operation; providing weapons for a specific operation; adding to terrorist demands during an incident; and making payment of insurance/bonuses to terrorists after the fact.

Table 14.2. Support for Terrorism and Counterterrorism

	State	Terrorists
Domestic		
International Governments		
Public		

The Public Audience

As indicated at the start, in addition to the interactions of authorities and terrorists directly and their success in creating attacks or defending them there is also the contest for the audience. Strategies used by both sides are important in determining how the audience(s) will react. Understanding how social identity affects the processing of messages of fear and security and whether such messages produce fear or anger and a greater or lesser sense of risk and uncertainty is crucial in the contest.

Thus metrics are needed to evaluate if different publics feel more or less secure, have a more or less favorable attitude toward their governments, and have a more or less favorable or unfavorable attitude toward the terrorists or the countries allied against them, and so on. If we look at the U.S. public's confidence in the administration to protect it, we see that its evaluation has fallen "a great deal" since 2001 (see Table 14.3).

However, if you examine the data on November 4, 2004, you get an interesting and different result. Obviously there were many issues in the 2004 presidential election. But an examination of the exit polls provided by CNN indicates that support for George W. Bush over John Kerry was dramatically effected by whether the respondent defined the issue in terms of the War on Terror or the War in Iraq and if they felt that they were more or less safe from terrorism than they were after 9/11 (see Table 14.4, page 362, and http://cnn.hu/ELECTION/2004/pages/results/states/US/P/00/epolls.0.html).

Two more recent polls indicate that both the public's sense of security and confidence in the president's handling of the problem has significantly shifted.

In mid-May CBS asked "Do you approve or disapprove of the way George W. Bush is handling the campaign against terrorism?" and by *Newsweek*, which asked "Do you approve or disapprove of the way Bush is handling terrorism and homeland security?" As shown in Table 14.5 (page 362), the polls found significant drops in the president's support, although the CBS data indicate significant differences across the partisan divide.

For both sides, the development of credible messages of trust and reassurance, through both violence and the protection from violence of the other, is crucial to success. That some terrorists carefully evaluate and think not simply about the tactical uses of violence in a particular circumstance but also about the strategic effects on an audience is demonstrated in the letter published in July 2005 by Ayman al-Zawahiri, purportedly al Qaeda's second in command, to Abu Musab al-Zarqawi, then leader of the organization now named al Qaeda in Iraq.

Table 14.3. Confidence in the U.S. Government

"How much confidence do you have in the ability of the U.S. government to protect its citizens from future terrorist attacks: a great deal, a fair amount, not very much, or none at all?"

Date of Polls	Confidence				
	A Great Deal	A Fair Amount	Not Very Much	None at All	Unsure
	%	%	%	%	%
3/9–12/06	17	43	28	10	2
1/5–8/06	21	48	23	6	2
10/3–5/05	16	47	30	7	0
9/6–7/05	19	40	30	10	1
8/29–31/05	18	54	21	5	2
9/02	20	56	18	4	2
7/02	21	53	22	3	1
6/02	16	54	24	5	1
1/5–6/02	23	58	16	2	1
12/7–10/01	17	60	18	4	1
11/13–14/01	22	52	20	4	2
10/25–28/01	18	58	20	4	0
10/8/01	30	55	12	1	2
9/20–23/01	35	53	10	1	1

Further, if you examine the public's evaluation of counterterrorism efforts that, too, has registered significant drops in approval.

"As it conducts the war on terrorism, do you think the United States government is or is not doing enough to protect the rights of American citizens?"

Date of Polls	Protecting Rights			
	Is	Is Not	Doing Too Much (vol.)	Unsure
	%	%	%	%
3/2–5/06	46	51	1	2
6/2–5/05	50	46	1	2
9/4–7/03	69	28	—	3

Source: CBS News polls, http://www.pollingreport.com/terror.htm.

Table 14.4. Terrorism as an Issue in Exit Polls

U.S. President/National Election/Exit Poll 2004

Defined the most important issue in the election as:	Voted for Bush	Voted for Kerry
Iraq (15% of voters)	26	73
Terrorism (19% voters)	86	14

Do you feel we are:	Voted for Bush	Voted for Kerry
Safer from Terrorism (54%)	79	20
Less Safe (41%)	14	85

Table 14.5. Support for the U.S. President

CBS 5/16–17/06	Approve	Disapprove	Unsure
All Adults	46	47	7
Republicans	77	19	4
Democrats	21	71	8
Independents	41	48	10
Newsweek 5/11–12/06			
All adults	44	50	6

    In the absence of this popular support, the Islamic mujahed movement would be crushed in the shadows, far from the masses who are distracted or fearful, and the struggle between the jihadist elite and the arrogant authorities would be confined to prison dungeons far from the public and the light of day. This is precisely what the secular, apostate forces that are controlling our countries are striving for. These forces don't desire to wipe out the mujahed Islamic movement, rather they are stealthily striving to separate it from the misguided or frightened Muslim masses. Therefore, the mujahed movement must avoid any action that the masses do not understand or approve, if there is no contravention of Sharia in such avoidance, and as long as there are other options to resort to, meaning we must not throw the masses-scan.

Moving beyond the shores of the United States, as has been well noted, produces different results. There have been significant drops in public support for the United States since 9/11 among traditional friends and allies and with few exceptions within the Muslim world as well (see Table 14.6). Clarke (cited in Byman, 2003, 83) argues that "The war as seen on television in Islamic countries has dangerously increased the level of frustration, anger, and hatred directed at the United States. It has given radical Islamic terrorists another target, U.S. personnel in Iraq. The seeds of future terrorism have been sown."

Table 14.6. Opinions of the U.S.

	Favorable Opinion of the U.S.				
	'99/'00	2002	2003	2004	2005
Canada	71	72	63	—	59
Britain	83	75	70	58	55
Netherlands	—	—	—	—	45
France	62	63	43	37	43
Germany	78	61	45	38	41
Spain	50	—	38	—	41
Poland	—	79	—	—	62
Russia	37	61	36	47	52
Indonesia	75	61	15	—	38
Turkey	52	30	15	30	23
Pakistan	23	10	13	21	23
Lebanon	—	35	27	—	42
Jordan	—	25	1	5	21
Morocco	77	—	27	27	N/A[1]
India	—	54	—	—	71
China	—	N/A	—	—	42

1999/2000 survey trends provided by the Office of Research, U.S. Department of State (Canadian 99/00 data by Environics).

Human Rights

Finally, we explore one final metric often ignored in evaluating the counterterrorism network, the condition of human rights among the coalition member states. Have we improved or lessened the rights of persons among our global war on terror allies? Many of the nations whose assistance was thought necessary in the global war against terror were not democracies, and were engaged in the systematic violation of their citizens' human rights, and often used repression against their citizens to maintain their regimes.

Amnesty International and Human Rights Watch have documented numerous abuses in Uzbekistan, Tajikistan, Turkmenistan, Azerbaijan, Kazakhstan, Kyrgyzstan, and Georgia within the Central Asian region. These regimes routinely suppress internal dissent, arrest political opponents, and censor the media. Political dissent of any kind is harshly suppressed, and beatings and torture of detainees is commonplace.

Political Terror Scale

The political terror scale (see Stohl et al., 1984) employs the yearly reports prepared by Amnesty International and the U.S. Department of State and classifies states on the basis of their respect for human rights.

1. Countries . . . under a secure rule of law, people are not imprisoned for their views, and torture is rare or exceptional. . . . Political murders are extraordinarily rare.

2. There is a limited amount of imprisonment for nonviolent political activity. However, few are affected, torture and beatings are exceptional. . . . Political murder is rare.

3. There is extensive political imprisonment, or a recent history of such imprisonment. Execution or other political murders and brutality may be common. Unlimited detention, with or without trial, for political views is accepted. . . .

4. The practices of Level 3 are expanded to larger numbers. Murders, disappearances, and torture are a common part of life. . . . In spite of its generality, on this level violence affects primarily those who interest themselves in politics or ideas.

5. The violence of Level 4 has been extended to the whole population. . . . The leaders of these societies place no lim-

its on the means or thoroughness with which they pursue personal or ideological goals.[4]

The data indicate few cases of improvement during this period and some declines. Independently, Byman (2003) argues that

> Ironically, too, U.S. efforts to fight terrorism have sometimes fostered rather than diminished anti-U.S. perceptions. Washington's embrace of sordid governments such as the Karimov regime in Uzbekistan, its silence regarding Russian brutality in Chechnya and other distasteful concessions offered to ensure these governments' cooperation against Al-Qaeda are bolstering claims that the United States supports the oppression of Muslims and props up brutal governments.

Conclusion

This brief discussion of metrics illustrates a number of problems with the simple body count approach to measuring the war on terror that is most prevalent in governmental and media discussions. Most importantly, it affirms that the administration and the scholarly community have failed to provide adequate measures and the data by which to assess them to answer Mr. Rumsfeld's 2003 challenge. The appropriate measures will have to include the perceptions of the various audiences affected and their attitudes to both terrorism and counterterrorism in their names.

The discussion of metrics should make clear that counterterrorism cannot simply be approached with a simple or short scorecard. How you counter, with whom you counter, and against whom you counter are all also important because there is an audience to the interaction and unlike the traditional battlefield it is not simply the power to destroy but the power to persuade that is involved.

Terrorism and terrorist operations are often asymmetric and nonlinear and thus we must remember that in the short run, the terrorists don't have to win, they merely have to avoid a total defeat. As is quite clear from Horne (1978) and Crenshaw (1978) in scholarly analyses, as well as Pontecorvo's film *Battle of Algiers* of the recounting of the experience of the French in Algeria, the scorecard approach may well provide the wrong conclusion. Even when terrorists may appear to have been defeated, in the long run they may find victory because a substantial segment of the "audience" is repelled by the methods of the counterterrorists and eventually rallies to the side of the terrorist. The appropriate focus of counterterrorism must consider the messages and the audience(s) as well as the trends in violence and counter violence and the victims and the destruction.

Notes

1. I would like to thank John Horgan and Alex Schmid for their helpful comments.
2. The National Security Strategy of the United States of America, September 2002; The National Strategy for Homeland Security, July 2002; The National Strategy for Combating Terrorism, February 2003; The National Strategy to Combat Weapons of Mass Destruction, December 2002; The National Strategy for the Physical Protection of Critical Infrastructure and Key Assets, February 2003; The National Strategy to Secure Cyberspace, February 2003; The 2002 National Money Laundering Strategy, July 2002.
3. The Clinton Administration focused on terrorism primarily as a law enforcement issue while the Bush administration approached terrorism primarily as a military problem (Badey, 2006, 308). The law enforcement approach emphasizes the further prevention of the loss of life, reassuring and informing the public, gaining public support so that they assist and gather evidence for prosecution. The war approach emphasizes attacking the perpetrators and their supporters. This is not to argue that either precluded actions that would be constitutive of the other approach but that the underlying approach was defined by their definition of the problem as either military or legal. The Clinton administration sought the "collection of evidence and the clear identification of the actual perpetrators" rather than a military solution through attacks against "known targets," including, of course, full-scale military operations against Afghanistan and Iraq. This has meant also the shifting of counterterrorism coordination and resources to the department of defense and the new department of homeland security from the department of justice, a shift that dramatically reduces the importance of the Justice Department and the FBI in counterterrorism policy and actions.
4. For the data for 2001–2004, see http://www.unca.edu/politicalscience/images/Colloquium/faculty-staff/gibney.html)

References

Badey, T. (2006). US counter-terrorism: Change in approach, continuity in policy. *Contemporary Security Policy* 27 (2), 308–324.
Byman, D. (2003, Summer). Scoring the war on terrorism. *The National Interest*. Retrieved on March 1, 2006, from http://www.findarticles.com/p/articles/mi_m2751/is_72/ai_105369900

Carr, R. (2002, July 29). Only 200 hard core members. *Palm Beach Post*. Retrieved June 1, 2005, from http://why-ar.com/news/2002/07/29/onlyhard.html

Cole, D. (2006). Are we safer? *New York Review of Books* 53 (4). Retrieved on March 15, 2006, from http://www.nybooks.com/articles/18752

Congressional Research Service (2004, March 31). Terrorist attacks by al Qaeda. *Memorundum*, Foreign Affairs, Defense, and Trade Division, Washington, DC.

Crenshaw, M. (1978). *Revolutionary terrorism: The FLN in Algeria, 1954–1962*. Stanford, CA: Hoover.

Decker, R J. (2003, March 3). Combating terrorism: Observations on national strategies related to terrorism, testimony before the subcommittee on national security, emerging threats and international relations. Committee on Government Reform, House of Representatives. GAO-03-519T

Horne, A. (1978). *A savage war of peace*. New York: Viking.

Johnston, D., Van Natta, D. Jr., & Miller, J. (2002, June 16). New links increase threats from far-flung sites. *New York Times*, 1.

Kellner, D. (2003). *From 9/11 to terror war: The dangers of the Bush legacy*. Lanham, MD: Rowman & Littlefield.

Mickolus, E. (2002). How do we know we're winning the war against terrorists? Issues in measurement. *Studies in Conflict & Terrorism* 25, 151–160.

Morag, N. (2005). Measuring success in coping with terrorism: The Israeli case. *Studies in Conflict & Terrorism* 28, 307–320.

Perl, R. (2003). *Terrorism: The future and U.S. foreign policy*. Washington, DC: Congressional Research Service.

Perl, R. (2005, November 23). *Combating terrorism: The challenge of measuring effectiveness*. Washington, DC: Congressional Research Service.

Probst, P. (2005). *Measuring success in countering terrorism: Problems and pitfalls*. ISI 2005, LNCS 3495, 316–321.

Rumsfeld, D. (2003, October 16). Memo global war on terrorism to Gen. Dick Myers, Paul Wolfowitz, Gen. Pete Pace, Doug Feith. Retrieved on February 1, 2006, from http://www.usatoday.com/news/washington/executive/rumsfeld-memo.htm

Stohl, M. (1988). Demystifying terrorism. In M. Stohl (Ed.), *The politics of terrorism* (pp. 1–28). New York: Marcel Dekker.

Stohl, M., Carleton, D., & Johnson, S. E. (1984). Human rights and U.S. foreign assistance from Nixon to Carter. *Journal of Peace Research* 3, 1–11.

Stohl, C., & Stohl, M. (2007). Networks of terror: Theoretical assumptions and pragmatic consequences. *Communication Theory* 17, 93–124.

Winkler, C. (2005). *In the name of terrorism: Presidents on political violence in the post-world war II era*. Albany: State University of New York Press.

Chapter 15

Reacting to Terrorism
Probabilities, Consequences, and the Persistence of Fear

John Mueller

Introduction

For all the attention it evokes, international terrorism, in reasonable context, actually causes rather little damage, and the likelihood that any individual will become a victim in most places is microscopic. But few people, it seems, are aware of either fact. This chapter examines the process by which terrorism is measured, the fears and behavioral consequence it creates and nourishes, and the potential long-term persistence of these fears.

Calculating Probabilities

For several decades, the U.S. State Department collected data on international terrorism, defining the act as premeditated, politically motivated violence perpetrated by subnational groups or clandestine agents against noncombatant targets (civilians and military personnel who at the time of the incident are unarmed or not on duty) that involve citizens or the territory of more than one country. The data accumulated for the period from 1975 to 2003 are arrayed in Figure 15.1, next page.

Those adept at hyperbole like to proclaim that we live in "the age of terror." However, as can be seen in the figure, the number of people worldwide who die as a result of international terrorism by this definition is generally a few hundred a year. In fact, until 2001 far fewer Americans were killed in any grouping of years by all forms of international terrorism

Figure 15.1. International Terrorism and Lightning, 1975–2003

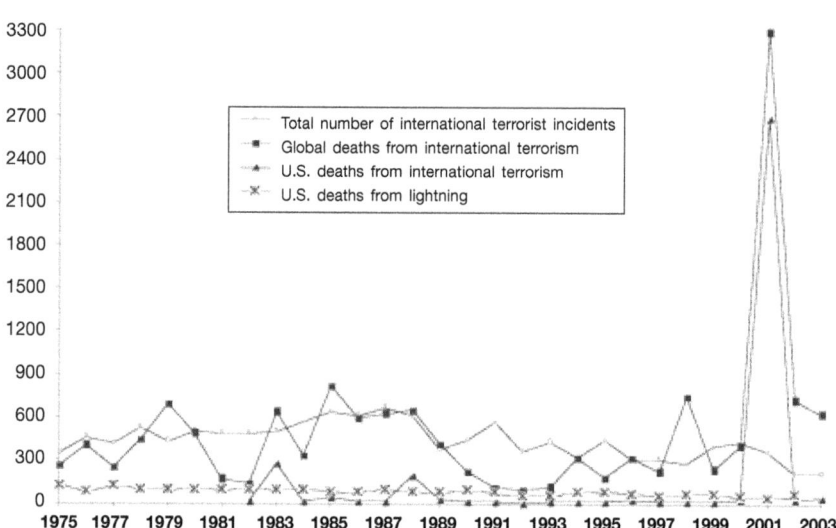

Source: Compilations by United States Department of State and by National Safety Council.

than were killed by lightning. Moreover, except for 2001, virtually none of these terrorist deaths occurred within the United States itself. Indeed, outside of 2001, fewer people have died in the United States from international terrorism than have drowned in toilets.

Even with the September 11 attacks included in the count, however, the number of Americans killed by international terrorism over the period is not a great deal more than the number killed by lightning—or by accident-causing deer or by severe allergic reactions to peanuts over the same period. In almost all years the total number of people worldwide who die at the hands of international terrorists is not much more than the number of those who drown in bathtubs in the United States—some 300 to 400.[1]

Americans worry intensely about "another 9/11," but if one of these were to occur every three months for the next five years, the chance of being killed in one of them is two one-hundredths of one percent: the posited attacks would kill 60,000, which is about .02 percent of 300,000,000. This would be, of course, an extended and major tragedy, but an individual's chances of being killed, while no longer microscopic, would still remain small even under this extreme scenario.

Another assessment comes from astronomer Alan Harris. Using U.S. State Department figures, he assumes a worldwide death rate from international terrorism of 1,000 per year—that is, he assumes in his estimate that there would be another 9/11 somewhere in the world every several years. Over an 80-year period under those conditions some 80,000 deaths would occur, which would mean that the lifetime probability that a resident of the globe will die at the hands of international terrorists is about one in 75,000 (6 billion divided by 80,000). This, he points out, is about the same likelihood that one would die over the same interval from the impact on the earth of an especially ill-directed asteroid or comet. If there are no repeats of 9/11, the lifetime probability of being killed by an international terrorist becomes about one in 120,000.[2]

For such numbers to change radically, terrorists would have to become *vastly* more capable of inflicting damage. In fact, they would pretty much need to acquire an atomic arsenal and the capacity to deploy and detonate it.

In the last few years, the State Department has changed its definitions so that much domestic terrorism—including much of what is happening in the war in Iraq—is now included in its terrorism count (National Counterterrorism Center, 2006, ii–iii). Current numbers, therefore, are not comparable to earlier ones.

However, when terrorism becomes really extensive in an area we generally no longer call it terrorism, but rather war or insurgency. Thus, the Irish Republican Army was generally taken to be a terrorist enterprise, while fighters in Algeria or Sri Lanka in the 1990s were considered to be combatants who were employing guerrilla techniques in a civil war situation—even though some of them came from, or were substantially aided by, people from outside the country. Some people, notably President George W. Bush, continually referred to what was going on in Iraq as "terror" or as "terrorism," but that complicated conflict is more properly, and commonly, labeled an insurgency. Insurgents and guerrilla combatants usually rely on the hit-and-run tactics employed by the terrorist, and the difference is not in the method, but in the frequency with which it is employed.

Without this distinction, much civil warfare (certainly including the decade-long conflict in Algeria in the 1990s in which perhaps 100,000 people perished) would have to be included in the "terrorist" category. And so would most "primitive warfare," which, like irregular warfare more generally, relies mostly on raids rather on set-piece battles.[3] That is, with the revised definition, a huge number of violent endeavors that have normally been called "wars" would have to be recategorized. Indeed, the concept of civil war might have to be retired almost entirely. Most of the mayhem in the American Civil War did take place in set-piece battles between uniformed combatants, but that conflict was extremely unusual among civil wars in this respect—the rebels in most civil wars substantially rely on tactics that are indistinguishable from those employed by the terrorist. Moreover, any genocide, massacre, or ethnic cleansing carried out by insurgents in civil wars would now have to be reclassified as an instance of terrorism.

When people in the developed world worry about terrorism, however, they are not particularly concerned that sustained civil warfare or insurgency will break out in their country. They are mainly fearful of random or sporadic acts of terrorism carried out within their homeland. For this concern, the original State Department definition, not an expanded one stemming from the sustained violence in Iraq, seems to be the most appropriate.

Another approach is to focus on the kind of terrorism that really concerns people in the developed world by restricting the consideration to violence committed by Muslim extremists outside of such war zones as Iraq, Israel, Chechnya, Sudan, Kashmir, and Afghanistan, whether that violence be perpetrated by domestic terrorists or by ones with substantial international connections. Included in the count would be terrorism of the much-publicized sort that occurred in the United States in 2001, in Bali in 2002, in Saudi Arabia, Morocco, and Turkey in 2003, in the Philippines, Madrid, and Egypt in 2004, and in London and Jordan in 2005.

Two publications from Washington think tanks have independently provided lists of such incidents—one authored by Anthony Cordesman of CSIS, the other by Brian Jenkins of RAND (Cordesman, 2005, 29–31; Jenkins, 2006, 179–184). Although these tallies make for grim reading, the total number of people killed in the five years since 9/11 in such incidents comes to about 1,000—that is, some 200 per year. That, of course, is 1,000 too many, but it hardly constitutes a major threat, much less an existential one, to countries in Europe and North America. For comparison: over the same period far more people have drowned in bathtubs in the United States alone.

Neglecting Probabilities

Thus, unless international terrorists become *far* more capable, the danger they present, particularly to people living outside war zones, remains exceedingly small. Despite this condition, polls suggest that people—or at any rate Americans—remain concerned about becoming the victims of terrorism, and the degree of worry doesn't seem to have changed much in the half-decade since the 2001 attacks even though no terrorism whatever has taken place in the country after that year.

Figure 15.2 supplies the result of a relevant question. Only somewhat less than a third profess that they do not worry at all about the chance that they will personally become a victim of terrorism—the correct response, one might imagine, to a one-in-75,000 lifetime threat. Another third worry "not too much," and fully a third worry "somewhat" or "a great deal" about this microscopic possibility.[4] Presumably few if any worry about being killed by an asteroid or meteor even though probabilities are the same and even though such an astronomical catastrophe has been vividly celebrated in dozens of books and movies over the decades.

In some respects, fear of terror may be something like playing the lottery except in reverse. The chances of winning the lottery or of dying from terrorism may be microscopic, but for monumental events which are, or seem, random, one can irrelevantly conclude that one's chances are just as good, or bad, as those of anyone else. Cass Sunstein labels the phenomenon "probability neglect." He argues that "When their emotions are intensely engaged, people's attention is focused on the bad outcome itself, and they are inattentive to the fact that it is unlikely to occur" (Sunstein, 2003, 122; Lowenstein et al., 2001).

There is also a terrorism industry—politicians, bureaucrats, journalists, and risk entrepreneurs who systematically exaggerate dangers and

Figure 15.2. Concern About Becoming a Victim of Terrorism, 2001–2006

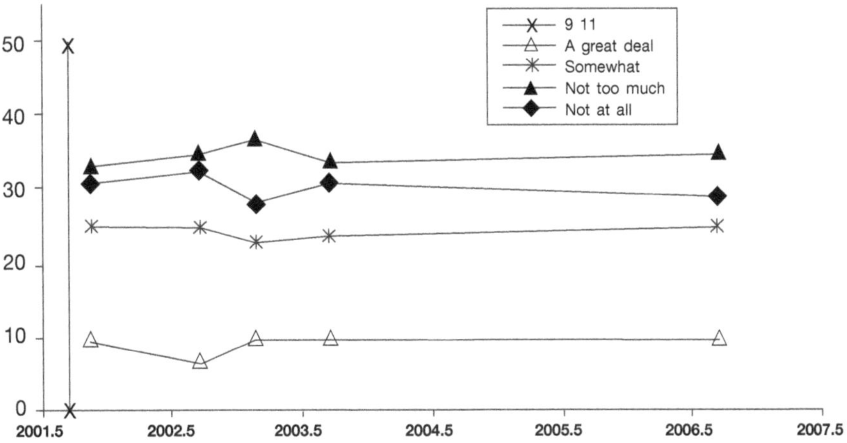

Source: www.pollingreport.com, under "terorrism" (ABC).

who often profit from their fearmongering and alarmism.[5] It is easy, even comforting, to blame these people for the distorted and context-free condition under which terrorism is so often discussed, and to want go agree wholeheartedly with H. L. Mencken's crack, "The whole aim of practical politics is to keep the populace alarmed (and hence clamorous to be led to safety) by menacing it with an endless series of hobgoblins" (Mencken, 1949, 29).

In many respects, however, the alarm is not so much aroused by the politicians and other "opinion leaders" as by their auditors. Edward R. Murrow's comment about McCarthy applies more broadly: "he didn't create this situation of fear, he merely exploited it." Jeffrey Rosen quotes Tocqueville on the phenomenon: "the author and the public corrupt one another at the same time," and he updates the lesson with a pointed observation about exaggerated fears of mad cow disease in Britain: "Unwilling to defer to any expert who refused to confirm its unsupported prejudices, the crowd rewarded the scientists who were willing to flatter its obsessions by cheering it on to self-justifying waves of alarm" (Rosen, 2004, 77, 87).

Hysteria and alarmism often sell. That is, although there may be truth in the cynical newspaper adage, "If it bleeds, it leads," this comes about not so much (or at any rate not entirely) because journalists are fascinated by blood, but because they suspect, quite possibly correctly, that their readers are. Politicians, bureaucrats, and people with things to sell to the fearful react similarly. Thus, although the terrorism industry may exacerbate the fears, it does not create them, and its activities and cries of alarm are essentially lagging indicators of the existence of the fears.

Exactly why people have managed, by contrast, to remain uninvolved emotionally by the danger of death by asteroid is far from clear. As astronomers Clark Chapman and David Morrison have pointed out, that danger carries with it many of the components widely held to inspire great fear: it conjures up feelings of dread and is catastrophic, dramatic, involuntary, uncontrollable, inequitable, due to unobservable agents, difficult to assess, and easy to visualize (Chapman & Morrison, 1989, 281–284). Indeed, Judge Richard Posner has recently and eloquently laid out the case that, although low in probability, the potential disaster from such cosmic collisions justifies not only concern, but substantial expenditures to evaluate, and potentially to avert, them (Posner, 2005).

At any rate, whatever the reason for Americans' lack of concern of death by asteroid, they certainly have become, and remain, obsessed with the 9/11 experience. Polls conducted in 2006—five years after the event—find that fully 98 percent say they can readily recall where they were when they first heard the news about the terrorist attacks, that over half think about the attacks every day or a few times a week, that two-thirds maintain the attacks changed their personal life, that over half claim the attacks changed life in the United States a great deal, and that fully 46 percent volunteer 9/11 when asked, "What would you say is the single most significant event that has happened in your lifetime, in terms of its importance to the United States and the world?" (Additionally, 38 percent remained convinced that Saddam Hussein was personally involved in the attacks.)

Behavioral Consequences of Fear

In some respects fear of terrorism may not shift ordinary physical behavior all that much, however. Thus, real estate prices in the 9/11 target areas, Manhattan and Washington, DC, continued to climb (Betts, 2005, 508). Similarly, a Columbia University study noted (with alarm) that two years after 9/11 only 23 percent of Americans and 14 percent of New Yorkers confessed to making even minimal efforts to prepare for disaster such as stocking a couple of days worth of food and water (no data on duct tape), buying a flashlight and a battery-powered radio, and arranging for a meeting place for family members (National Center for Disaster Preparedness, 2003; see also Gorman, 2003). By 2004, Americans were being scolded for being "asleep at the switch when it comes to their own safety," by the Red Cross President and CEO (Hall, 2004, 1A).

So in an important sense the public does not seem to be constantly on edge about the threat of terrorism any more than it was during the McCarthy era about the threat of Communism, when people mostly mentioned mundane and person issues when asked what concerned them most (Stouffer, 1955, chap. 3). Or during years of heightened Cold War "crisis" when scarcely anyone bothered to build, or even think very seriously about, the fallout shelters the Kennedy administration was urging upon them (Weart, 1988, 258–260).

Moreover, the potential for panic is probably not a major problem either. There is extensive evidence that by far the most common reaction to disaster is not self-destructive panic, but resourcefulness, civility, and mutual aid (Glass & Schoch-Spana, 2002, 214–215; Fischoff, 2005; Jones et al., 2006).

The main concern then is not hysteria or panic except perhaps in exceptional, and localized, circumstances. Instead terrorism-induced fears can be debilitating in three ways.

First, they can cause people routinely to adopt skittish, overly risk-averse behavior, at least for a while, and this can much magnify the impact of the terrorist attack, particularly economically. That is, the problem is not that people are trampling each other in a rush to vacate New York or Washington, but rather that they may widely adopt other forms of defensive behavior, the cumulative costs of which can be considerable. As Sunstein notes, "in the context of terrorism, fear is likely to make people reluctant to engage in certain activities, such as flying on airplanes and appearing in public places," and "the resulting costs can be extremely high" (Sunstein, 2003, 132).

Thus, the reaction of 9/11 led to a great many deaths as people abandoned airplanes for automobiles—indeed, in the three months following the attack, more than 1,000 Americans were killed because of this (Spivak & Flannagan, 2004, 301–305). It also had a negative economic impact, particularly in the airline and tourism industries, which lasted for years—a highly significant issue economically because travel and tourism has become the largest industry in the world (Chow, 2005, 1). Three years after September 2001, domestic airline flights in the United States were still 7 percent below their pre-9/11 levels (*Financial Times*, 2004, 8). By the end of 2004, tourism even in distant Las Vegas had still not fully recovered (Clarke, 2005, 63).[6] One estimate suggests that the American economy lost 1.6 million jobs in 2001 alone, mostly in the tourism industry (Calbreath, 2002, C–2).[7]

There is at present a great and understandable concern about what would happen if terrorists are able to shoot down an American airliner or two, perhaps with shoulder-fired missiles. Obviously, this would be a tragedy in the first instance, but the ensuing public reaction to it, many fear, could be extremely costly economically—even perhaps come close to destroying the industry—and it could indirectly result in the unnecessary deaths of thousands (Chow, 2005, 1; Bergen, 2007, 19).

Second, fear and anxiety can have negative health consequences. Physician Marc Siegel discusses a study that found Israeli women fearful of terrorism "had twice as high a level of an enzyme that correlates with heart disease, compared with their less fearful compatriots" (Siegel, 2005, 4). A notable, if extreme, example of how severe such health effects can be comes from extensive studies that have been conducted of the Chernobyl nuclear disaster that occurred in the Soviet Union in 1986. It has been found that the largest health consequences came not from the accident itself (less than 50 people died directly from radiation exposure), but from the negative and often life-expectancy reducing impact on the mental health of people traumatized by relocation and by lingering, and greatly exaggerated, fears that they would soon die of cancer. In the end, lifestyle afflictions like alcoholism, drug abuse, chronic anxiety, and fatalism have posed a much greater threat to health, and essentially have killed far more people, than exposure to Chernobyl's radiation (Finn, 2005, A22). The mental health impact of 9/11 is, of course, unlikely to prove to be as extensive, but one study found that 17 percent of the American population outside of New York City was still reporting symptoms of September 11–related posttraumatic stress two months after the attacks (Silver et al., 2002; see also Bourke, 2005, 374–391).

Third, fears about terrorism tend to create a political atmosphere that makes it be, or appear to be, politically unwise, or even politically impossible, to adopt temperate, measured policies. "Fearful people," notes a county official in mid-America, "demand more laws and harsher penalties, regardless of the effectiveness or ineffectiveness of such efforts" (Shields, 2006). Or, in Cass Sunstein's words, "When strong emotions are involved," as in a terrorist attack, "even if the likelihood of an attack is extremely low, people will be willing to pay a great deal to avoid it" (Sunstein, 2003, 124). Indeed, one study conducted a decade before 9/11 appears to have found that people would be willing to pay more for flight insurance against terrorism than for flight insurance against all causes including terrorism (Johnson et al., 1993, 39).[8] Most destructively, the reaction to 9/11 has included two wars that are yet ongoing—one in Afghanistan, the other in Iraq—neither of which would have been politically possible without 9/11, and the number of Americans who have died in those ventures considerably surpasses the number who perished on September 11.

We've had quite a bit of experience with this phenomenon. Exaggerated fears about the security dangers presented by domestic Japanese led to the politically desirable—if foolish, wasteful, and, ultimately, embarrassing—incarceration of tens of thousands of innocents during World War II. Exaggerated fears of the destructive capacities of domestic Communists during the McCarthy era did not cause many people literally to become concerned that there were Reds under their bed, but they did lead to, or inspire, a political atmosphere in which the innocent and, in particular, the harmless were persecuted, where liberal politicians felt they needed to advocate the wasteful setting up concentration camps for detaining putative subversives during potential emergencies, and where colossal amounts of money and energy were expended on hunting an enemy that scarcely existed. Exaggerated fears about the likelihood that international Communism would launch thermonuclear war did not impel many people to waste their personal money on fallout shelters, but they did cause majorities to support, accept, or acquiesce in colossal military expenditures in their name that were designed to confront or deter a threat that proved mostly to be a fantasy spun out by politicians and defense intellectuals.[9]

In the case of terrorism, as in those earlier instances, a fearful atmosphere inspires politicians to outbid each other in order to show their purity (and to gain votes), a process that becomes self-reinforcing as, to justify their wasteful and ill-considered policies and expenditures, they find it expedient to enflame the fears that set the policies in motion in the first place. As Ian Lustick notes of the government, "it can never make enough progress toward 'protecting America' to reassure Americans against the fears it is helping to stoke" (Lustick, 2006, 97).

However, although there may be a willingness on the part of people to pay, and although this has certainly inspired foolish and wasteful policies, the phenomenon does not necessarily specifically *require* those policies. The reaction to Pearl Harbor did not specifically make the incarceration of Japanese citizens necessary, the McCarthy scare did not specifically mandate the setting up of concentration camps, and concern about Soviet military capacity did not specifically require a fallout shelter program.

The Persistence of Internalized Fears

Reducing fear in emotion-laden situations like terrorism is difficult. In fact, argues Sunstein, "attempts to reduce fear by emphasizing the low likelihood of another terrorist attack" are "unlikely to be successful" (Sunstein, 2003, 122). As Paul Slovic, another risk analyst, points out, people tend greatly to overestimate the chances of dramatic or sensational causes of death, and a new sort of calamity tends to be taken as harbinger of future mishaps. Moreover, strongly imbedded beliefs are very difficult to modify, and realistically informing them about risks sometimes only makes them more frightened (Slovic, 1986; see also Siegel, 2005, 5–9, 206). Indeed, concern about safety rises when people discuss a low-probability risk even when what they mostly hear are apparently trustworthy assurances that the danger is infinitesimal (Sunstein, 2003, 128).

Thus, suggests Sunstein, the best response may be to "alter the public's focus." That is, "perhaps the most effective way of reducing fear of a low-probability risk is simply to discuss something else and to let time do the rest" (Sunstein, 2003, 131). Or, in Siegel's words, "we build up a partial immunity to each cycle of fear with the simple passage of time" (Siegel, 2005, 8; see also Mueller, 2006, chap. 7).

This is a plausible solution. But the evidence suggests that it may take a great deal of time for this to come about.

The closest parallel for fears about terrorism is probably with fears about domestic Communism. As Figure 15.3 indicates, domestic Communism attracted a great deal of press in the United States in the early and middle 1950s—the high point of the McCarthy era. But this interest declined thereafter, and press attention to the enemy within had pretty much evaporated by the 1970s. This may reflect in part the diminution in size of the American Communist Party itself: estimates of its membership run to 80,000 in 1945, 54,000 in early 1950, 25,000 in 1953, 20,000 in 1955, and only 3,000 in 1958 (Shannon, 1959, 3, 218, 360). Moreover, as time went by, FBI informants probably constituted an increasing percentage of that membership.

Interestingly, however, even though the party itself essentially ceased to exist, even though there were no more dramatic, attention-arresting revelations like those of the Hiss and Rosenberg cases of the late 1940s and early 1950s, and even though press attention to the threat (if any) posed by domestic Communists accordingly nearly vanished, public concern about the danger posed by domestic Communism declined only gradually. In 1954, at the zenith of the McCarthy era, some 42 percent of the public held American Communists to be a great or very great danger and 2 percent held it to be no danger at all. Ten years later, these percentages had not changed all that much: 38 percent still saw danger and only 6 percent saw none at all. When the relevant poll question was last asked, in the mid-1970s, around 30 percent continued to envision great or very great danger, while only around 10 percent saw none. (The respondents also had two safely evasive middle categories to choose from: "some danger" or "hardly any danger.")

Figure 15.3. Domestic Communism: The Press and the Public, 1940–1985

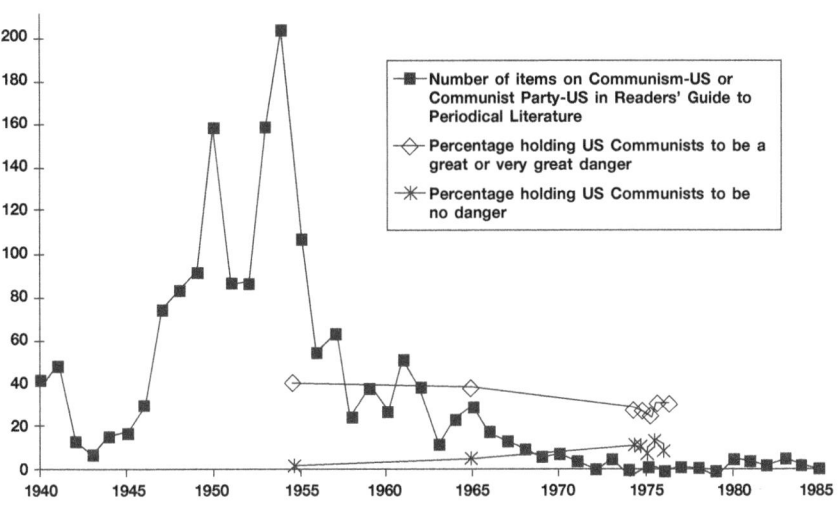

Source: Mueller, 1988.

Thus, although public opinion data do track a decline of concern, the slowness with which that decline took place is quite remarkable. Of course, the Cold War did very much continue during the period surveyed and American contempt for the Soviet domestic system continued apace: for example, between 1973 and 1984 polls found that the percentage calling Communism the worst kind of government actually rose from 43 to 60 (Niemi et al., 1989, 69; see also Mueller, 1988). But credible (or even noncredible) suggestions that *domestic* Communism was much of anything to worry about became almost nonexistent, and press attention to the enemy within—domestic Communists and the American Communist party—dropped to nothing. Yet concern about the "danger" presented by this essentially nonexistent internal enemy diminished only gradually.

Conclusion

In sum, the phenomenon studied in this chapter suggests there is a great deal in dramatic first impressions: once a perceived threat is thoroughly implanted in the public consciousness, it can become internalized and continue to resonate as an accepted fact of life. Eventually, it may become a mellowed irrelevance, but, unless there is a decisive eradication of the threat itself (as presumably happened in 1945 for the "threat" posed by domestic Japanese) the process can take decades.

Moreover, this all assumes that there are no terrorist attacks in the United States in the meantime, as there were no notable instances of efforts at internal subversion by domestic Communists in the decades after the 1950s. However, even if fears of terrorism do begin to decline, they can probably be very substantially rejiggered if a lone fanatical nut somewhere shoots up a bus, bank, or beauty salon while shouting "God is great!"

The experience suggests, then, that we are hardly likely to relax any time soon. Eventually, fears of terrorism will perhaps begin to fade. But the experience with lingering concerns about the dangers supposedly presented by domestic Communism—internalized after dramatic first impressions—suggests it may be a long wait, perhaps one of decades.

Notes

1. In almost all years fewer than 10 Americans die worldwide at the hands of international terrorists (U.S. Department of State, 1998, 85). On average, 90 people are killed each year by lightning in the United States (National Safety Council, 1997, 120). About 100 Americans die per year from accidents caused by

deer (Revkin, 1998, A1). The same number holds for peanut allergies (http://blogcritics.org/archives/2004/09/19/161029.php). Bathtubs and toilets: Stossel, 2004, 77; see also Schneier, 2003, 11, 237, 241–242.

    2. Harris explains his calculations at http://psweb.sbs.ohio-state.edu/faculty/jmueller/overblown.html. See also Schneier, 2003, 237–242.

    3. See Keeley, 1996. For more on the distinction between terrorism and civil war, see Mueller, 2004, 18–20.

    4. These and other poll data come from the information arrayed under "terrorism" at www.pollingreport.com.

    5. For an extended discussion, see Lustick, 2006, chapter 5. Also Mueller, 2006, 33–48 (this chapter draws substantially from this book).

    6. Some Las Vegas casinos report that their earnings in the last quarter of 2001 were about one third those for the same period in the previous year.

    7. One study has investigated Italian cities and towns, most of them small, which experienced a single terrorist attack. Although most of these were events minor and few caused any deaths, they appear to have had a measurable short-term impact on employment, chiefly because marginal firms went out of business earlier and because successful ones temporarily cut back on plans to expand (Greenbaum et al., 2007). Another study finds that businesses hit by a terrorist act like a bombing or the kidnapping of an executive suffer an average market capitalization drop of $401 million (Karolyi & Martell, 2006).

    8. The effect was clear though, since the number of subjects in the experiment was small, it did not achieve statistical significance.

    9. On these concerns, see Mueller, 2006, chapters 3–4.

References

Bergen, P. (2007, January 29). Where you bin? The return of al Qaeda. *New Republic*.

Betts, R. K. (2005). Maybe I'll stop driving. *Terrorism and Political Violence* 17 (4).

Bourke, J. *Fear: A cultural history*. London: Virago.

Calbreath, D. (2002, January 12). Attacks to cost 1.6 million jobs. *San Diego Union-Tribune* C-2.

Chapman, C. R., & Morrison, D. (1989). *Cosmic catastrophes*. New York: Plenum Press.

Chow, J. (2005). *Protecting commercial aviation against the shoulder-fired missile threat*. Santa Monica, CA: RAND Corporation Occasional Paper.

Clarke, R. A. (2005, January/February). Ten years later. *Atlantic*.

Cordesman, A. H. (2005). *The challenge of biological weapons*. Washington, DC: Center for Strategic and International Studies.

Financial Times. (2004, September 14), 8.

Finn, P. (2005, September 6). Chernobyl's harm was far less than predicted, U.N. report says. *Washington Post* A22.

Fischoff, B. (2005, August 7). A hero in every seat. *New York Times* 4–13.
Glass, T. A., & Schoch-Spana, M. (2002). Bioterrorism and the people: How to vaccinate a city against panic. *CID* 34 (15).
Gorman, S. (2003, September 13). Shaken, not stirred. *National Journal* 2776–2781.
Greenbaum, R., Dugan, L., & LaFree, G. (2007). The impact of terrorism on Italian employment and business activity. *Urban Studies* 44 (5/6), 1093–1108.
Hall, M. (2004, March 31). Most not prepared for attack. *USA Today*.
Jenkins, B. M. (2006). *Unconquerable nation: Knowing our enemy and strengthening ourselves*. Santa Monica, CA: RAND Corporation.
Johnson, E. J., Hershey, J., Meszaros, J., & Kunreuther, H. (1993). Framing, probability distortions, and insurance decisions. *Journal of Risk and Uncertainty* 7.
Jones, E., Woolven, R., Durodié, B., & Wessely, S. (2006). Public panic and morale: Second world war civilian responses re-examined in the light of the current anti-terrorist campaign. *Journal of Risk Research* 9 (1), 57–73.
Karolyi, G. A., & Martell, R. (2006). *Terrorism and the stock market*. ssrn.com/abstract=823465
Keeley, L. H. (1996). *War before civilization: The myth of the peaceful savage*. New York: Oxford University Press.
Lowenstein, G. F., Weber, E. U., Hsee, C. K., & Welch, N. (2001). Risk as feelings. *Psychology Bulletin* 127 (2), 267–286.
Lustick, I. (2006). *Trapped in the war on terror*. Philadelphia: University of Pennsylvania Press.
Mencken, H. L. (1949). *A Mencken chrestomathy*. New York: Knopf.
Mueller, J. (1988). Trends in political tolerance. *Public Opinion Quarterly* 52 (1), 1–25.
Mueller, J. (2004). *The remnants of war*. Ithaca, NY: Cornell University Press.
Mueller, J. (2006). *Overblown: How politicians and the terrorism industry inflate national security threats, and why we believe them*. New York: Free Press.
National Center for Disaster Preparedness. (2003). *How Americans feel about terrorism and security: Two years after 9/11*. New York: Mailman School of Public Health, Columbia University.
National Counterterrorism Center. (2006, April 11). *Report on incidents of terrorism 2005*.
National Safety Council. (1997). *Accident facts*. Chicago.
Niemi, R. G., Mueller, J., & Smith, T. W. (Eds.). (1989). *Trends in public opinion: A compendium of survey data*. Westport, CT: Greenwood.
Peanut Allergy. (2004). Retrieved July 25, 2006, from http://blogcritics.org/archives/2004/09/19/161029.php
Posner, R. A. (2005). *Catastrophe: Risk and response*. New York: Oxford University Press.
Revkin, A. C. (1998, November 30). Coming to the suburbs: A hit squad for seer. *New York Times*.
Rosen, J. (2004). *The naked crowd*. New York: Random House.

Schneier, B. (2003). *Beyond fear: Thinking sensibly about security in an uncertain world*. New York: Copernicus.

Shields, K. J. (2006, February 3). Braving the culture of fear. *National Catholic Reporter*.

Siegel, M. (2005). *False alarm: The truth about the epidemic of fear*. New York: John Wiley & Sons.

Silver, R. C., Holman, A. E., McIntosh, D. N., Poulin, M., & Gil-Rivas, V. (2002). Nationwide longitudinal study of psychological responses to September 11. *JAMA* 288 (10), 1235–1244.

Sivak, M., & Flannagan, M. J. (2004). Consequences for road traffic fatalities of the reduction in flying following September 11, 2001. *Transportation Research Part F*.

Shannon, D. A. (1959). *The decline of American communism: A history of the Communist Party of the United States since 1945*. New York: Harcourt, Brace.

Slovic, P. (1986). Informing and educating the public about risk. *Risk Analysis* 6 (4), 403–415.

Stossel, J. (2004). *Give me a break*. New York: HarperCollins.

Stouffer, S. A. (1955). *Communism, conformity, and civil liberties*. Garden City, NY: Doubleday.

Sunstein, C. R. (2003). Terrorism and probability neglect. *Journal of Risk and Uncertainty* 26 (2/3).

United States Department of State. (1998). *Patterns of global terrorism 1997*.

Weart, S. R. (1988). *Nuclear fear: A history of images*. Cambridge, MA: Harvard University Press.

About the Contributors

Tanya Alfredson is the Deputy Director of Political Training for the Department of State's Foreign Service Institute (FSI). Prior to coming to FSI, she taught negotiation courses to government ministries through the Food and Agricultural Organization (FAO) of the United Nations in Rome. She conducted research on negotiation at FAO, and on violent conflict at the Johns Hopkins University, and has served as a mediator, teacher, and/or adviser to the World Food Forum, ICARDA, and FAO. Ms. Alfredson is the recipient of a National Science Foundation Award for her research on negotiation, and served as a fellow to the Program on International Negotiations at the International Institute for Applied Systems Analysis (IIASA) in Laxenberg, Austria. The views expressed here are her own, and do not reflect the views of the State Department.

Alex Braithwaite is a lecturer in the Department of Political Science at University College London. His principal research interests focus on the causes and geography of various forms of political violence. His recent research has been published at *Journal of Peace Research, Conflict Management and Peace Science,* and *International Interactions.*

Sandra Borda is Assistant Professor of Political Science and International Relations at Los Andes University (Bogotá, Colombia). She was a visiting scholar at the Instituto Tecnológico Autónomo de México, Mexico City, and at the Munk Centre for International Studies, University of Toronto. She studies why and how domestic parties to civil wars decide to invite international actors to participate in their struggle. She has published articles and book chapters on the role of civil society and mass media in Colombian foreign policy and on the war on drugs.

Christopher K. Butler is Associate Professor of Political Science at the University of New Mexico specializing in the study of conflict and cooperation, focusing on strategic behavior and bargaining. He has examined bargaining theoretically (with publications in the *Journal of Conflict Resolution*, the *Journal of Theoretical Politics*, and *Conflict Management and Peace Science*) and experimentally (in *International Studies Quarterly*). His publication in the *Journal of Conflict Resolution*, "Prospect Theory and Coercive Bargaining," examines how prospect theory can be successfully incorporated with game theory, a topic he continues to research.

Rhonda L. Callaway is Assistant Professor at Sam Houston State University. Her primary area of research is in the field of human rights, particularly the relationship between globalization and human rights conditions. She has co-authored and published several articles on the influence of trade on the realization of human rights in the developing world. She is also an editor and contributor of *Exploring International Human Rights: Essential Readings* and the co-author of *Strategic US Foreign Assistance*, which addresses the relationship between foreign aid and human rights. Her most recent work examines the role human rights conditions play in fomenting terrorist activity.

Erica Chenoweth is Assistant Professor of Government and Director of the Program on Terrorism and Insurgency Research at Wesleyan University. She is also an associate at the International Security Program at the Belfer Center for Science and International Affairs at Harvard University's Kennedy School, and a visiting fellow at the Institute of International Studies at the University of California at Berkeley. Chenoweth's interests include terrorism in democracies, the causes of insurgent success and failure, and the consequences of political violence. Current projects include a book manuscript based on her dissertation, which explores why terrorism occurs so often in democracies; a book manuscript with Maria Stephan explaining the outcomes of nonviolent and violent protest; and a collaborative project with Laura Dugan on the outcomes of different counterterrorism policies. Chenoweth has published in *International Security, Defense and Security Analysis, Review of Policy Research, Terror and Conflict Monitor, International Criminal Justice Review*, the BCSIA Discussion Paper Series, *e-Extreme*, and multiple edited volumes.

C. Christine Fair is Assistant Professor at Georgetown University. She has been a senior political scientist with the RAND Corporation. Prior to rejoining RAND, she served as a political officer to the United Nations Assistance Mission to Afghanistan in Kabul and as Senior Research Associate in USIP's Center for Conflict Analysis and Prevention. Prior to joining USIP in April 2004, she was Associate Political Scientist at the RAND Corporation. Her research focuses on the security competition between

India and Pakistan, Pakistan's internal security, the causes of terrorism in South Asia, and U.S. strategic relations with India and Pakistan. She has authored, co-authored, and co-edited several books including *Treading on Hollowed Ground* with Sumit Ganguly (OUP, 2008), *The Madrassah Challenge: Militancy and Religious Education in Pakistan* (USIP, 2008), *Fortifying Pakistan: The Role of U.S. Internal Security Assistance* with Peter Chalk (USIP, 2006); *Securing Tyrants or Fostering Reform? U.S. Internal Security Assistance to Repressive and Transitioning Regimes* with Seth Jones et al. (RAND, 2006); *The Counterterror Coalitions: Cooperation with Pakistan and India* (RAND, 2004); *Urban Battle Fields of South Asia: Lessons Learned from Sri Lanka, India and Pakistan* (RAND, 2004), and has written numerous peer-reviewed articles covering a range of security issues in Pakistan, India, Sri Lanka, and Bangladesh. She is a member of the International Institute of Strategic Studies, London, and is the managing editor of *India Review*.

Gil Friedman, who died while this book was being prepared, was a lecturer in the Tel Aviv University Political Science Department. He specialized in conflict theory, Realist thought, and the Palestinian-Israeli conflict. His publications include a *Journal of Conflict Resolution* article on commercial pacifism in protracted nationalist conflict, a *Journal of Strategic Studies* article assessing the quality of Fatah strategic thought during the al-Aqsa intifada, a *Review of International Studies* article on rallying 'round the flag and diversionary aggression, and a book, co-authored with Harvey Starr, *Agency, Structure, and International Politics: From Ontology to Empirical Inquiry*.

Scott Gates is Research Professor and Director of the Centre for the Study of Civil War (CSCW), International Peace Research Institute, Oslo (PRIO) and Professor of Political Science, Norwegian University of Science & Technology (NTNU). His two most recently published books are: *Child Soldiers: Children and Armed Conflict in the Age of Fractured States* (Pittsburgh, forthcoming); and *Teaching, Tasks, and Trust: Functions of the Public Executive* (Russell Sage, 2008). Gates has also published in the *American Political Science Review, American Journal of Political Science, Journal of Conflict Resolution, Journal of Peace Research*, inter alia. He is Associate Editor of the *Journal of Peace Research* and serves on the editorial boards of *Journal of Public Administration Research* and *Theory and International Studies Quarterly*. Gates' current research interests include: applied game theoretic analysis, bureaucratic politics, organization theory, governance, civil war, terrorism, and other forms of political violence.

Ted Robert Gurr is Distinguished University Professor Emeritus at the University of Maryland, College Park. He founded, directed, and continues to consult on the Minorities at Risk project, which tracks the political status and activities of more than 300 communal groups worldwide. His 20 books and monographs include the award-winning *Why Men Rebel* (1970), *Peoples vs. States: Minorities at Risk in the New Century* (2000), and *Ethnic Conflict in World Politics* (with Barbara Harff, 1994, 2004). He is a former president of the International Studies Association (1993–1994). In March 2005 he convened a workshop on economic roots of terrorism for the Club de Madrid's International Summit on Democracy, Terrorism and Security.

Julie Harrelson-Stephens is Assistant Professor in Political Science at Stephen F. Austin State University. Her primary research interest focuses on the relationship among globalization, terrorism, and human rights. She co-edited a volume titled *Exploring International Human Rights: Essential Readings* and co-authored *Lone Star Politics*. Her recent research has been published in *PS: Political Science and Politics, Studies in Conflict and Terrorism, International Interactions*.

William Josiger is a PhD student at Georgetown University and his dissertation examines the relationship between terrorism and public opinion. His other research interests include the threat of European Islamist terrorism and metrics to measure progress in the war against terrorism. During the 2007–2008 academic year, he was a postgraduate student at the University of St. Andrews and an intern at the Centre for the Study of Terrorism and Political Violence.

Manus I. Midlarsky is the Moses and Annuta Back Professor of International Peace and Conflict Resolution at Rutgers University, New Brunswick. He is the founding past president of the Conflict Processes Section of the American Political Science Association and a past vice president of the International Studies Association. He is currently working on *The Origins of Political Extremism* (Cambridge University Press, forthcoming); his most recent book is *The Killing Trap: Genocide in the Twentieth Century* (Cambridge University Press, 2005). He published *The Evolution of Inequality: War, State Survival, and Democracy in Comparative Perspective* (Stanford University Press, 1999), and has recently edited the *Handbook of War Studies III*, the third in the sequence of Handbooks of War Studies (University of Michigan Press). An earlier edited volume is *Inequality, Democracy, and Economic Development* (Cambridge University Press, 1997).

Lyubov G. Mincheva is Associate Professor of Political Science at the University of Sofia, Bulgaria, and Senior Research Associate with the Institute for Regional and International Studies (IRIS). She earned her doctorate from the University of Maryland in 2000, where she is still serving as affiliated researcher. Since 2007 she has been a Fellow with the Open Society Institute, Budapest. Lyubov Mincheva has published extensively on issues of conflict, terrorism, security and peacekeeping, comparative research methodology, and democratization. Recently she has been working on a number of conflict- and terrorism-related projects, including the Unholy Alliances project, an academic initiative funded through the University of Maryland, as well as a number of NATO-, and EU-funded scholarly and policy-oriented initiatives dealing with issues of conflict databases, terrorism, and organized crime.

John Mueller holds the Woody Hayes Chair of National Security Studies, Mershon Center, and is Professor of Political Science, at Ohio State University where he teaches courses in international relations. He is currently working on terrorism and particularly on the reactions (or overreactions) it often inspires. His book on the subject, *Overblown: How Politicians and the Terrorism Industry Inflate National Security Threats, and Why We Believe Them*, was published in November 2006 by Free Press. The *New York Times* called the book "important" and "accurate, timely, and necessary." His latest book, *Atomic Obsession: Nuclear Alarmism from Hiroshima to Al-Qaeda* (Oxford University Press, 2010), to be published next year, suggests that atomic terrorism is highly unlikely and that efforts to prevent nuclear proliferation frequently have damaging results.

Rafael Reuveny is Professor in the School of Public and Environmental Affairs, Indiana University, Bloomington and Coeditor, *International Studies Quarterly* (2009–13). He is the author and co-authors of numerous articles and chapters. His work has appeared in outlets such as *American Journal of Political Science, Journal of Politics, International Studies Quarterly, International Organization, Political Geography, Journal of Conflict Resolution, Ecological Economics*, and the *Independent Review*. He is the co-author or co-editor of three books, the most recent of which is *North and South in the World Political Economy* (2008). He was program chair of the 2006 meetings of the International Studies Association, and the North American program chair of 2008 World International Studies Conference.

Peter Romaniuk is Assistant Professor in the Department of Political Science, John Jay College of Criminal Justice, the City University of New

York. He is the author and co-author of numerous chapters, articles, and reports on UN sanctions, terrorist financing, and counterterrorism cooperation. His book *Multilateral Counter-terrorism: The Global Politics of Cooperation and Contestation* recently appeared in Routledge's Global Institutions Series.

Bryan C. Shepherd is currently Senior Quantitative Analyst at a research firm in eastern North Carolina. Understanding the role of religion in motivating social action is a central theme of Dr. Shepherd's research. His recent work addresses the topics of within-congregation social support and the relationship between denominational affiliation and social agency.

David Sobek is Assistant Professor of Political Science at the Louisiana State University. He has published works in the *Journal of Politics, International Studies Quarterly, Conflict Management and Peace Science, Journal of Peace Research*, and *Journal of Conflict Resolution*. In addition, his book, *The Causes of War*, was published by Polity Press in 2008. In general, Professor Sobek is interested in the causes and consequences of political violence be it interstate war, intrastate conflicts, or terrorism. More specifically, Professor Sobek is interested in how the causes and consequences of political violence change over time and how they are influenced by domestic factors such as regime type and/or economic systems.

Michael Stohl is Professor and Chair of the Department of Communication at the University of California, Santa Barbara (UCSB). Prior to his appointment in January 2002 at UCSB, Professor Stohl was Dean of International Programs from 1992 and Professor of Political Science at Purdue University in West Lafayette, Indiana, where he had taught since 1972. His research focuses on political communication and international relations with special reference to political violence, terrorism, and human rights. His most recent publications on terrorism (2008) can be found in *Crime Law and Social Change, Critical Studies in Terrorism*, and *Communication Theory*.

William R. Thompson is Rogers Professor of Political Science at Indiana University and Managing Editor, International Studies Quarterly (2009–13). Recent books include *Globalization and Global History* (2006), *Strategic Rivalry: Space, Position and Conflict Escalation in World Politics* (2007), *Globalization as Evolutionary Process: Modeling Change* (2008), *North and South in the World Political Economy* (2008), *Systemic Transitions: Past, Present, and Future* (2008), *Limits to Globalization* (2009).

About the Contributors

I. William Zartman is the Jacob Blaustein Distinguished Professor of International Organization and Conflict Resolution at the Nitze School of Advanced International Studies (SAIS) of the Johns Hopkins University, and member of the Processes of International Negotiation (PIN) Program at the International Institute of Applied Systems Analysis (IIASA) in Vienna. He was previously All-University Head of the Politics Department at New York University, was a Distinguished Fellow of the United States Institute of Peace, Olin Professor at the U.S. Naval Academy, and Elie Halavy, Professor at Sciences Po in Paris. His numerous books include *The Practical Negotiator*, *Ripe for Resolution*, and *Cowardly Lions: Missed Opportunities to Prevent Deadly Conflict and State Collapse*. His doctorate is from Yale (1956) and his honorary doctorate from Louvain (1997).

Index

Abach, Sani, 260
Abebajo, A., 258–259
Abadie, A., 101–102, 109–110
Abbas, Mohammed (Abu Mazen), 271, 278, 281n14
Abidjan Accord, 259, 261
Abu Nidal, 244n19, 271, 281n14
Acharya, A., 324
Action Directe (AD), 222, 237, 241
Action Francaise, 39–40
Adams, Gerry, 68, 172–174, 181
Afghanistan war (1978–1989), 54
African National Congress, 220
Agami, Fehmi, 268
Agrarian Union, 43
Ahmedinajad, Mahmood, 280n2
Ahmeti, Ali, 265
Aiolfi, G., 318
akuza, 254, 256, 258, 279
al-Aqsa intifada, 193, 203, 207
Albania, political criminal syndicate, 181–186
Albanian National Army (ANA/AKSH), 185, 264
Albrecht-Carrie, R., 36
Alexander, Y., 220–221, 236
Alfredson, Tanya, 14, 19, 21
Algerian War (1954–1962), 54
Algerian Islamic insurgency, 174
All Albanian Army, 183
All Peoples' Congress (APC), 261
al Qaeda, 25, 44–45, 53, 61, 66, 91–92, 106, 150, 320–321, 349, 354–358, 365; attack since 9/11, 354–355
al Qaeda in Iraq, 360
Alternative, 222
al-Zawahiri, Ayman (Abu Musab), 360
Amal, 65
American Civil War, 58, 372
American Communist Party, 379
American Revolution, 59
Amnesty International, 364
Amnesty Law (France), 239
Andean Counterdrug initiative (ACI), 141
Andersen, R., 255
Anderson, B., 32
Anderson, William T., 68n5
anger and loss, 31–32
Animal Rights Militia, 223
Annan, Kofi, 350
Ansar al-Islam, 66
Anschluss, 40–41
Apple, R.W., 100
Arafat, Yasir, 273–274
Arce, D.G.M., 69nn8, 17
Aristotle, 31
ARM, 264
Armed Forces Ruling Council (AFRC), 260
Armed Revolutionary Nuclei, 222
Arm of the Land, 106
Arreguin-Toft, I., 54, 193
Arrow Cross, 29, 35

Arusha Accords, 254, 258
Ash, Garton, 280n10
Ashcroft, John, 99, 139
Asia-Pacific Group on Money Laundering (APG), 330–331
Assassins, 1
Asymmetric protracted conflict, 195, 211n5
AUC, 144
Aum Shinrikyu, 106
AUSTRAC, 333, 335
Austria, absence of homegrown fascism, 40–41
authority space, 33
Autocracy and Chuvah, 39
Ayoob, M., 143
Azar, E.E., 195
Azuku, 277

Baader-Meinhof Gang, 69n15
Badey, T., 366n3
Bagasora, Theoreste, 254
Bagley, B., 128
Baker, James, 273
Bali attack (2002), 323, 331–332
Balkan Wars (1912–1913), 41–42; Second (1913), 43, 47n12
Bangura, Y., 259–260, 280n6
Bank Indonesia (BI), 331
Barghouti, M., 203
Barkin, J.S., 341n20, 336
Barnett, M., 131, 143–144, 337, 341n18
Basayev, Shamil, 82, 85
Basque Nationalist Party, 225
BATNA, 251
Battle of Algiers, 365
Batum, 47n9
Bauer, Yehuda, 30
Bedie, Konan, 280n6
Beilin, Yossi, 273
Ben Ghiat, R., 28
Bergsmo, Morten, 69n9
Berkowitz, L., 31
Bergen, P., 376
Berman, E., 287

Berna, Don, 140
Berrebi, C., 287
Bessarabia, southern, 35–37
Betts, Richard, 63, 65, 375
Bharatiya Jamata Party (BJP), 322, 328, 334
Biaev, Khassan, 93
Biden, Joseph, 140
Biersteker, T.J., 321, 341nn7, 11, 12
Bin Laden, Osama, 139, 220n3, 280n2, 320, 351, 356, 358
Bio, Julius Maada, 258–259
Bismarck, Otto von, 36
Bivens, M., 86, 91
Black Hundreds, 37–39, 45
Black Shadow, 186
Black spots, 181
Bloom, Mia, 120nn3, 6
Bockarie, Sam, 262
Bodenhausen, G.V., 31
Bolshevik Revolution (1917), 39, 82
Bonner, D., 232, 234–236
Bonn Summit Declaration, 235
Borda, S., 14, 16–17, 21, 128
Bosnian War, 175
Bosworth, R.J.B., 31
Bourke, J.S., 377
Bovenkerk, F., 175
Bowers, S.R., 92–93
Bozinovich, M., 186
Braham, R.L., 29
Braithwaite, A., 14, 17, 155, 166n8
Braudel, F., 36
Broad-based Transition Government (BBTG), 254–255, 257
Brophy-Baermann, B., 151
Brotons, Remiro, 226, 228–231, 244n17
Brown, M., 193, 211n2
Browning, C.R., 28
Brustein, W., 26, 46n3
Brynen, R., 195
Brzezinski, Z., 130
Budennovsk Hospital Attack, 86
Bueno de Mesquita, E., 77, 151–154, 165n2, 278, 287, 310

Index 395

Bukoshi, Bujar, 267
Bukovinia, northern, 35–36
Bulgaria, absence of fascism, 43
Burke, Edmund, 69n13
Burke, Jason, 65
Bush, George W., 129, 140–141, 219, 316, 349, 352–353, 356, 358, 360, 371
Butler, C.K., 13, 15, 21, 55
Byman, D., 352, 358, 363, 365

Caliphate, 48
Callaway, Rhonda L., 13, 15–16, 76
Camarota, S.A., 291
Camp David Accords, 150, 159–164, 166n16
Canadian Army Recruitment Centre, 64
Carr, C., 155
Carr, Rebecca, 357–358
Carvajal, L., 127
Carrero Blanco, 226
Causal beliefs, 317
Caucasus War, 81
Cauley, J., 153
CDR. See *Coalition pour la Defense de la Republique* (CDR)
Center for Conflict Analysis and Prevention (USIP), 310n2
Chalk, P., 221, 225–226, 243nn5, 10
Chapman, Clark, 374
Charters, D.A., 219–220, 223–224, 244n23
Chechen Revolution (1991), 83
Chechen Wars, First (1994–1996), 54
Chechnya: Chechens in World War II Soviet Army, 82; deportation, 82, 89; human rights, 80; political rights, 87–88; postwar deportations, 87; security rights, 90–91; subsistence rights, 88–89; Wahabbi influence, 93
Checkel, J.T., 324–325, 341nn19, 21
Cheka, 47n13
Chellaney, B., 322
Chenoweth, Erica, 13, 16, 21

Chernobyl nuclear disaster, 376–377
Chidambaram, P., 334–336
Chinese Civil War, 59, 68n4
Chirac, J., 239
Chow, J., 376
Christian Patriots, 220n3
Christopher, Warren, 276
Cilluffo, F., 183
civil war and weak states, 66
Clark, R.P., 226–229, 244nn15, 17
Clarke, R., 376
Clausewitz, 1, 62
Clogg, R. 41
Clunan, A.L., 321, 340n7
Coalition pour la Defense de la Republique (CDR), 254–257, 270, 276
Codevilla, Angelo M., 200
Cohen, R., 31
Cold War: impact on attitudes, 380; end, 219, 272–273
Cole, D., 354
Collier, P., 170, 287
Columbian Counter-Insurgency Brigades, 133
Columbian Program Center for International Policy, 141
Common Front (MRND), 257
Composite index of national capabilities (CINC), 158
Concessions, 154
Conflict diamonds, 261
Conflict internationalization, 130–131; alliance formation, 143–144; entrapment, 144; in Columbia, 133–145; in El Salvador, 129; Guatemala, 129
Conflict resolution ripeness, 195
Congleton, R.D., 103
Congress (India), 322
Congress of Berlin, 47n8
constructivism dilemmas, 316, 325–326
Contact Group, 265–267
Continuation War (1941–1944), 47n8
conventional/unconventional war, 56–59

Convention for the Suppression of Unlawful Acts Against the Safety of Civil Aviation (1971), 340
Convention for the Suppression of Unlawful Acts Against the Safety of Maritime Navigation (1988), 340n3
Convention for the Suppression of Unlawful Seizure of Aircraft (1970), 340n3
Convention on Offenses and Certain Other Acts Committed onboard Aircraft (1963), 340n3
Convention on the Marking of Plastic Explosives for the Purpose of Detection (1991), 340n3
Convention on the Physical Protection of Nuclear Material (1980), 340n3
Convention on the Prevention and Punishment of Crimes Against Internationally Protected Persons including Diplomatic Agents (1973), 340n3
Conybeare, J.A.C., 151
Corbin, Jane, 272–275, 281nn14, 15
Cordesman, A., 183, 372
Correlates of War, 158
Cortell, A.P., 324
Cortright, D., 341n11
Coser, L., 201, 204, 214n21
Couloumbis, T.A., 42
Counter-terrorism: criminal treatment, 19; decentralized responses, 19; inter-group dynamics, 119; moderate terrorists, 150–151; oscillations in response firmness, 19; success measures, 352–354; support for, 358–359; under-reaction, 19
Counter-Terrorism Action Group (CTAG), 320
Counter-Terrorism Committee (CTC), Security Council, 317
counter-terrorism strategy: criminal justice model, 225; war model, 225
conventional/unconventional war, 56–59
covenant, 106

Coy, F., 128
Craigin, R. Kim, 310n4
Crank, J.P., 99
Crenshaw, Martha, 76, 98, 100, 104–105, 109, 324, 365
Crimean War (1853–1856), 37
Criminal enclaves, 181
criminally exploitable ties, 179
criminal networks, 176
criminal opportunity analytical framework, 176, 178
Crisana, 36
Cronin, A.K., 220–221, 243nn1, 7, 287
Cross, James, 64
Cuban Revolution, 59
Cultural dupes, 337
Cunningham, K.J., 291
Curtis, G., 171–172, 178
Cuza, Alexander, 46n4

Daalder, I.H., 269, 271
Dalmatia, northern, 35
D'Annunzio, Gabriele, 35
Darby, J., 151–152
Das, D.K., 225
David, S.R., 143
Dayton Peace Accords, 92, 266
Deak, I., 34
Decker, Raymond, 350
Deininger, K., 121n11
deKlerk, F.W., 281n16
Demaci, Adem, 267–269, 271
Democratic Party of Albanians (DPA), 262–263, 265
Demuerta security policy, 134
DeNardo, J., 152
Denial, 215n30
Derluguian, G.M., 81–82
Dessler, D., 328
DeSteno, N., 31
Deutsch, M., 214n18
de Waal, T., 82, 84, 86–88, 92–93, 94n1
DGSE, 239
DHKP, 66

Diehl, P.F., 32, 47n6
Diesing, P., 197
Diplock Courts, 234, 236
disadvantageous peace, 55–56, 68
discriminate versus indiscriminate violence, 69n10
divide-and-deal strategy, 267
divide-and-defeat strategy, 267
Dobrovin, A.I., 38
Dobrudja, southern, 35, 43
Dodd, Christopher, 140
Dollfuss, Englebert, 40
Dreyfus, Alfred, 47n10
Drezner, D., 340n6, 341n18
druzhiny, 39
DST, 239
Dubai Ports World Deal Controversy, 359
Dubnov, S., 38
Dudayev, Dzhokhar, 84, 87
Dugas, J.C., 142
Dunlop, J.B., 80–83, 88, 94n1
Dunne, J.P., 65, 69n17
Dzerzhinsky, Feliks, 47n13

Earth First!, 223
Earth Liberation Front, 223
Eckert, S.E., 341nn7, 11
ECOMOG, 260–261
Economic Community of West African States (ECOWAS), 261
Edict of Nantes, 47n14
Egmont Group, 318, 330
Elster, J., 32–33
Encyclopedia of World Terrorism, 105–106
Enders, W., 69n17, 101, 109, 151, 153–154, 158, 164
Ephemeral gain, 27, 33, 43–44
Eoka, 59
Erasmus, 53
Ertzainza, 229
Essy, Amara, 280n6
ETA, 67, 120n3, 152, 222, 225–232, 240–243, 244n14
Eubank, W.L., 78, 99

European Agency for Reconstruction and Development, 184
European fascism and political extremism, 14
European Union, 224, 260
Europol, 224
Euskera, 243n12
Evans, R.J., 34
Executive Outcomes (EO), 259
Exclusion strategies, 278
Extremism and international constraints, 46
Extremist spoilers, 278
Eyerman, J., 98–99

Fair, Christine, 14, 20–21, 310n2
FAR, 258
FARC (Revolutionary Armed Forces of Columbia), 63, 133–136, 138, 173–174
fares, 183–184, 186
fasci di combattimento, 39
fascism, 27; ephemeral gain, 35–36; paramilitarism, 37; restoration of lost worlds, 26; territorial loss, 26, 34–35; war origins, 26; willingness to initiate mass murder, 27–30
Fatah 202, 207, 271
Fearon, J., 66
Federation d'action Nationale Européenne, 222, 237
Feingold, Russel, 140
Feith, Douglas, 350
Felgenhauer, P., 94n3
Fellner, F., 41
Feng, Y., 121n11
Financial Action Task Force (FATF), 318–319, 328–330, 332–323; Special Recommendation of Terrorist Financing, 337–339
Finnemore, M., 131, 324
FIU-IND, 335
Fiume, 35
Flannagan, M.J., 376
Flemming, R.B., 102
For Tsar and Order, 39

France: Algerian War, 213n14; counter-terrorism, 236–241; proto-fascism, 39–40
Franco, Francisco, 40–41, 56, 225–227, 230, 243n12, 244n15
Franco-Prussian War, 39
Freikorps, 40
Friedman, Gil, 14, 18–19, 21
Frijda, Nico, 31, 33
Front de Liberation du Quebec (FLQ), 63–64, 152
Frowick, Robert, 263
FRY, 265

Gaitan, P., 127
Gambetta, D., 66
Gammer, M., 80, 82–83, 85n1, 94
Ganor, B., 291
Garcia, A., 128
Gartner, S.S., 56–57
Gartzke, E., 158
Gates, Scott, 13, 15, 21, 55–56, 58, 68n2
Gaza Strip settler eviction, 67
Gberie, L., 258–259
Gender and support for terrorism, 20
General Assembly Resolution, 181 II of 1947, 272
German, T.C., 82–83, 86, 89
Gerwehr, Scott, 310n4
Giap, Vo Nguyen, 63, 213n14
Gilmore, W., 318
Giscard d'Estaing, Valery, 231
Glass, T.A., 375
Gleditsch, N.P., 68n4, 99, 108–109
Global Attitudes Survey (2002), 289
Globalization and extremism, 245
Global Network of Terror, 357
Global Terrorism Risk Index, 102
Goertz, G., 32
Goga, Octavian, 46n4
Golan Heights, 275
Gold, D., 287
Golder, M., 121n13
Goldstein, J., 340n2, 341n21
Gombos, Gyula, 28–29

Gorbachev, Mikhail, 83–84, 88, 90
Gorman, S., 375
Grant, Ulysses S., 60
Gray, V., 103
Greater Albania, 185
Greater Israel, 272–273
Greco-Turkish War, 41
Greece, absence of fascism, 41–43
Greed motivation, 170–171
Gregor, P., 30, 46n1, 99
Green Line, 200
GRAPO (Spanish October First Antifascist Group), 222, 243n11
Great Idea, 42
Greve, H.S., 69n11
Grossman, H.I., 65
Grozny destruction, 76, 84–85, 90, 92
Grupos Antiterroristas de Liberacion (GAL), 231, 242
Guaqueta, A., 136–137
Guardia Civil, 229
Guerrilla warfare, 62
Guevara, Che, 92
Guillaume, G., 237, 239–240, 317
Gulf War, First, 53
Gurr, Ted R., 14, 17–18, 21, 64, 78, 99, 152, 174
Gutierrez, F., 142
GWOT (Global War on Terrorism), 315–318, 322, 329, 333, 336, 349

Haas, P., 324
Habash, George, 271
Habyarimana, Agathe, 254, 256–257, 280n4
Haidt, Jonathan, 31
Hajrizi, Mehmet, 268
Hall, M., 375
Hamas, 66, 106, 253, 271, 274–275, 277–279
Haradinay, Ramish, 185
Harakat al Mujahedin, 357
Harper, D., 62
Harrelson-Stephens, Julie, 13, 15–16, 76
Harris, Alan, 371, 381n2

Harrison, M.M., 237–241, 287, 310n1
Hart, Liddell, 61
Hattayer, Christopher, 280n8
Haz, Hamzah, 342n26
Hedges, C., 183, 267
Heimweher (home guard), 40
Helleiner, E., 340n6
Hermann, M., 170, 181
Herz, J.H., 32
Heston, A., 311n6
Hewitt, C., 226
Hezbollah, 61, 65, 156, 253, 275, 279
Hierarchy of needs, 291–292
Hill, Christopher, 268–269
Hilberg, Raul, 28–30
Hilsum, Lindsey, 257
Himmler, Heinrich, 30
Hirsch, J.L., 259, 280n7
Hirschon, R., 42
Hitler, Adolf, 29, 46n5
Hobsbawm, E.J., 174
Hoeffler, A., 170, 287
Hoffman, B., 62, 243n1, 291, 316
Holbrooke, Richard, 267
Holbrooke-Milosevic Agreement, 268–270
Holmes, J.S., 171, 174
Horgan, John, 173, 366n1
Horne, A., 365
Horthy, M., 29, 35
Huber, J.D., 101
Hudson, Rex, 121n14
Hugenots, 47n14
Human rights, 77
Human Rights Watch, 141, 364
Hussein, Saddam, 44, 375
Huth, P. K., 47n6

Iamaccone, 287, 310n1
Ikenberry, 341n23, 342n24
Imeri, Imer, 265
India: counter-terrorist norms, 322–323; norm adoption processes, 328–331, 334–336; Parliament Attack (2001), 373

Indian Banks Association, 331
Indochina War (1947–1949), 54
Indonesia: counter-terrorist norms, 323–324; Independence War (1946–1954), 54; norm adoption 329–331, 334
Inequality and civil conflict, 68n3
Interahamwe, 44, 258
Internal Macedonian Revolutionary Organization-Democratic Party of Macedonian Unity (VMRO-DPMNE), 262
International Alert, 259
International Convention against the Taking of Hostages (1979), 340n3
International Convention for the Suppression of Acts of Nuclear Terrorism (2005), 340n3
International Convention for the Suppression of Terrorist Bombings (1997), 340n3
International Convention for the Suppression of the Financing of Terrorism (1999), 340n3
INTERPOL, 224, 235
Intifada, first, 196, 272–273
Ioanid, R., 29
Ioann, Father, 38
Irish Republican Army (IRA), 69n15, 104, 120n3, 150, 152, 371
Iron Guard, 29, 35, 37n4, 46
Isacson, A., 129, 135, 137
Israeli invasion of Lebanon, 159, 161, 163
ITERATE (International Attributes of Terrorist Events) data, 109, 120n7, 153, 157–158

Jackson, J.K., 321
Jacobins, 62
Jaggers, K., 108–109
Jama'aj Islamiyya, 66
Janke, P., 244n13
Jarbawi, A., 203
J-curve, 15
Jelavich, B., 35–36, 41–43, 46n4

Jelavich, C., 42
Jenkins, Brian, 372
Jervis, R., 130, 193, 198, 211nn2, 3
Jiminez, F., 227–228, 243n11
Johnson, D., 377
Johnston, D., 357
Joint Working Groups on Terrorism, 330
Jojoy, Mono, 139
Jones, B., 256–258, 280n8
Jones, E., 375
Josiger, William, 14, 18–19, 21
Juan Carlos, 227
Judah, T., 267

Kabbah, Lansana, 259–260
Kahneman, D., 33
Kaldor, M., 130
Kalyvas, S., 57, 69n10
Kaplan, R.D., 193
Karacan, J., 178
Karmi, Raed, 200
Karolyi, L.H., 381n7
Katzenstein, P.J., 324
Kaufmann, C., 193, 211n3
Kecskmeti, P., 197
Keeley, L.H., 381n3
Kellner, D., 349
Kelly, David, 140
Kennedy, Edward, 140
Kennedy, John, 375
Keohane, Robert, 340n2, 341n21
Kerry, John, 360
KFOR, 184
KGB, 47n13
Khalidi, Rashid, 206, 214n21
Khartoum 3 Nos, 271
Khattab, Amir, 92–93
King, C., 57
Kiras, J.D., 59
KLA (Macedonian), 276
Kleinberg, M., 291
Klerks, P., 176, 178–179
Koettl, Christoph, 280n5
Konrad, K.A., 287
Kontogiorgi, E., 43

Korean War, 68n4
Kosovar (Kosovo Albanians), 265
Kosovar Democratic League (LDK), 265–269, 281
Kosovo Liberation Army (KLA), 183–186, 263, 265, 267–270 276–278, 280n11, 281nn12, 13
Kosovo negotiations, 265–271
Kosovo Protection Corps (KPC), 184–185
Kovalyou, Sergei, 84
Krasner, Stephen, 341n17, 342n24
Kratcoski, P.C., 225
Krueger, A.B., 287
Ku Klux Klan, 222
KVM, 270
Kydd, A.H., 67, 151–152, 278

Labour Party, 274
Lacina, B.A., 68n4
LaFraniere, S., 92
Lagnado, A., 85
Laitin, 66, 287
Lake, David, 193, 211nn2, 3, 341n23, 342n24
LaPorte, Pierre, 64
Laqueur, W., 30, 75–76
Larsen, Terje, 273, 281n14
Lashkar-e-Toiba, 66
Latimer, W.S., 322
Lausanne, Treaty of (1923), 42
Law Lords (Britain), 236
League of Struggle Against Sedition, 39
Leahy, Patrick, 140
Lee, Robert E., 58, 60, 68n5
Legion of the Archangel Michael. *See* Iron Guard
Leiby, M., 55
Lenin V., 45, 47n12, 87
levee en masse, 36
Levi, M., 340n6
Levy, J.S., 33, 69n16, 143–144
Lewin, Kurt, 203, 205, 214nn18, 22
Li, Quan, 98–102, 105, 107–110, 114, 116, 121nn11, 12, 13

Index 401

Liaotung Peninsula, 37
Liberal Party (Macedonia), 262
Liberation Tigers (LTTE), 25, 44
Lichbach, M.I., 58, 208
Lieven, A., 85
Likud, 272–274
Limited war, 211n5
Linz, Juan, 39
Loewenstein, 32
Loi Pasqua, 239
London Metropolitan Police, 236
London, Treaty of (1915), 35
Londono, P., 128
Loss and political extremism, 45
Louis XIV, 47n14
Lowenstein, G.F., 373
Lowi, Miriam, 174–175
Lowrey, D.C., 103
Loyola University, 63
Lustick, I., 378, 381n5
Lynfield, B., 67
Lyttleton, A., 30

Macedonian negotiations, 262–265
Machiavelli, N., 198–200, 213n11
Mack, Andrew, 54, 193, 197, 202, 210, 212n8, 213n14
Madrid International Summit on Terrorism, Democracy and Security, 272, 351
Mafia (Sicilian), 174
Magallanes, J., 171
Mahmuti, Bardhy, 280n11
Mainstreaming terrorism, 13
Malcolm, N., 41
Malic, N., 185
Maleckova, 287
Malia, M., 39
Mandela, Nelson, 220
Mankins, Darue, 139
Mann, Michael, 27, 29–30, 40
Mansfield, E., 99, 200
Mao, Zedong, 63, 213n14
Marcus, G.E., 26
Markov, N.E., 38–39
Marrus, M.R., 40, 48n14

Marshall, M.G., 108–109
Martin, J., 178
Martyr culture (Islam), 120n3
Maskhadov, Aslan, 90
Maslow, A., 195, 291
Massu, Jacques, 213n14
Mastanduno, M., 341n23, 342n24
Matthiessen, T., 128
Maurras, Charles, 39–40
McAdam, D., 99
McCarthy, Joseph, 374–375
McDermott, R., 26
McGill University, 63
MDR, 255, 257
Mearsheimer, J.J., 130
Mejia, Tirado, 128
Mele, A.R., 33
Mencken, H.L., 374
Metaxas, Ionnnis, 41
Merton, Robert, 213n10, 214n18
Meyers, Richard, 350
Mickolus, E., 109, 157, 359
Midlarsky, Manus I., 13–15, 21, 25, 28, 32, 44–45, 46n5, 104
Mikhailov, V., 82
Miller, J., 357
Milosevic, Slobodan, 265–266, 270, 276, 278, 281n12
Mincheva, Lyubov G., 14, 17–18, 21
MIPT, 105–106
Mitterand, Francois, 238, 240
Mogahed, D., 310n2
Mohapatra, M., 334
Momoh, Joseph, 258
Morag, N., 352, 354
More murder in the middle thesis, 94n2
Moreno, L.A., 139
Morgenthau, H.J., 197, 212n6, 326n24, 342
Morris-Cotterill, N., 340n6
Morrison, David, 374
Most, B., 197
Mouvement Revolutionnaire National pour le Developpment (MRND), 254–256

Moxon-Browne, E. 220, 224, 238–239
Mueller, John, 14, 20–21, 170, 378, 380, 381nn3, 5, 9
Mueller, Robert III, 358
Murrow, Edward R., 374
Multinational systemic crime, 170
Munich Olympics (1972), 159–160
Murdoch, J.C., 130
Murillo, M.A., 133
Murphy, Thomas, 173
Murshed, S.M., 55
Mussolini, B., 31, 40, 45, 46n2
Mutilated victory, 35
Mutually hurting stalemate (MHS), 19, 264, 277
Myers, Richard, 139

Nagy-Talavera, Nicholas, 29, 35–36
Narco-terrorism, 135, 171
National Christian Defense Party, 46n4
National Democratic Party (NDP), 262
National Endowment for Democracy (2005), 353–354
National Liberation Army (NLA), 133, 138, 185, 263–265, 280n10
National Money Laundering Strategy (2002), 366n2
National Party (South Africa), 281n16
National Provisional Ruling Council (NPRC), 258–259
National Strategy for Combatting Terrorism (2003), 366n2
National Strategy for Homeland Security, 366n2
National Strategy for the Physical Protection of Critical Infrastructure and Key Assets (2003), 366n2
National Strategy to Combat Weapons of Mass Destruction (2002), 366n2
National Strategy to Secure Cyberspace (2003), 366n2
National Unification Front (NUF), 185

Naxalites, 63
Naylor, R.T., 178
NCCT (Noncompliant Countries and Territories Initiative), 319, 323, 329–330, 333
Negotiation: attack frequency, 152; goal revision, 19; third party mediators, 19
Netanyahyu, Benyamin, 278
Neuilly, Treaty of (1919), 41
New Tribes missionaries, 139
Nicholas II, 38
Niemi, R.G., 380
Nisbett, R.E., 31
Nivat, A., 86
Nolte, Ernst, 39–40
Norm adaption, 321–322
Norm adoption, 321
Norm life cycle, 324
Norm makers, 315
Norm takers, 315
Norm resistance, 321
Normative affirmation, 315, 327, 336
North Atlantic Treaty Organization (NATO), 232
Northern Aid (Noraid), 173
Northern Ireland (Emergency Provisions) Act (NIEPA), 233
Nsengiyareme, Dismas, 255
Nuremberg Trials, 69nn11, 14

Obama, Barack, 140
Oberschall, A., 99
O'Connor, M.P., 233, 269
O'Hanlon, M.E., 269–271
Ohrid, Agreement, 185, 263–264
Operation Accountability, 275
Operation, Horshoe, 269
Opportunistic, linkages between terrorists and crime, 175
Organic Law (8/1984), 228, 231
Organic, Law on Citizen Security, 227
Organized crime, 176
Oslo Accords, 196, 276
Oslo Process, 271, 274–276
Ostby, G., 55

Pace, P., 350
Palestine negotiations, 271–276
Palestinian Authority, 202, 214n21
Palestinian Liberation Organization (PLO), 244n14, 271–278, 281n14
Palestinian National Council (PNC), 272
Palestinian Proclamation of Independence, 272
Pape, Robert, 43, 65, 197, 212n8, 214n15, 215n30, 287
Pardo, R., 127
Parquet, General, 239
Parti Liberal (PL), 255
Parti Socialiste Democratique (PSD), 258
Party for Democratic Prosperity (PDP), 262
Pastrana, Andres, 134–135, 138, 142
Patriot Act, 321, 341n13, 352
Paul, T.V., 54
Paxson, C., 310n1
Paxton, Robert, 27, 30–31, 40, 48n14
Payne, S.G., 29–30, 40, 46n1, 47n11, 142
Payne, R.A., 324–325
Paz, R., 291
PDC, 255
PDP, 263, 265, 280n10
Pearl Harbor reaction, 378
Pearlman, Wendy, 214nn16, 19
People's Front for the Liberation of Palestine (PFPL), 271
People's Movement of Kosovo (LPK), 183
People's Union, 38
Peres, Shimon, 273
Perl, Raphael, 353, 359
Petain, Phillipe, 39–40, 47n14
Peter the Great, 81
Pettifer, J., 183
Pew Global Attitudes Project (2002), 311n5
Pew Research Center, 288–290, 295
PFLP-GC, 222
Pieth, M., 318

Pipes, R., 47n12
PIRA, 222, 236, 243n6
PKK, 66
PL, 257
Plan Columbia, 133–134, 137, 139
Plan Columbia II, 140
Plan, Lazo, 133
Plan Patriota, 140
Plan Zen (Special Northern Zone), 230
PNC, 257
Poe, S., 79
Police Intelligence Council, 229
Policy congruence, 158
Policy prescriptions, 318
Polish-Soviet War (1919–1920), 47n7
Political extremism, 25–26; territorial loss, 45; war experience, 30–32
Political rights, 77
Political terror scale, 364–365
Politkosvskaya, Anna, 85
Pontecorvo (Battle of Algiers), 365
Popkin, S., 58
Popular Front for the Liberation of Palestine (PFLP), 106
Port Arthur, 37
Portell, Jose Maria, 227
Posen, B.R., 193, 211nn2, 3
Posner, Richard, 374
Powell, R., 101
Power, Parties, 257
Pragmatic linkage between terrorism and crime, 173–174
Predatory linkage between terrorism and crime, 174–175
Prevention of Money Laundering Bill, 322, 328, 330, 335
Prevention of Terrorism Bill, 322, 328
Prevention of Terrorism (Temporary Provisions) Acts (PTA), 233, 236, 334
Preventive Security Force (PSF), 202
Prima Linae, 104, 116
Principled beliefs, 316
Prizen Document, 263–264
Probability neglect, 373

404   *Index*

Prospect theory and losses, 33–34
Protocol for the Suppression of Unlawful Acts against the Safety of Fixed Platforms Located on the Continental Shelf (1988), 340n3
Protocol for the Suppression of Unlawful Acts of Violence at Airports Serving International Civil Aviation (1988), 340n3
Protracted conflict, 194
Provisional Irish Republican Army (PIRA), 60, 65, 173, 232
Pruitt, D.G., 277
Prunier, 255, 257
PSD, 257
PSF, 204
Public perceptions of security, 360–363
Purishkevich, V.M., 38–39
Pusat Pelaporan dan Analisis Traskasi Kevangan (PPATK), 332–333, 342nn27, 28

Qorei, Ahmed (Abu Ala), 273–274, 281n15
Quadregesimo Anno (1931), 40
Quantrill's Bushwhackers/Guerrillas, 68n5
Quebec nationalism and violence, 63–64

Rabin, Yitzhak, 271–276, 278
Radu, M., 92
RAF, 222
Rambouillet process, 265, 270–271, 278
Randall, S.J., 128
Randolph, E., 47n13
Ranstop, M., 222
Rapoport, D.C., 62
Rashid, I., 260
Rational choice and war rationality, 66
Raufer, Xavier, 186
Raustiala, K., 324
Rawson, D.C., 38–39

Realuyo, C.B., 320
Realist constructivist, 336–337
Rebellion and moral economy perspective, 69n6
Red Army (Japanese), 222
Red Brigades, 69n15, 104, 116, 222
Reddy, Y.V., 330
Reed, W., 66
Regan, P.M., 56–57
Reign of Terror, 62
Reiter, D., 61
Religiosity and support for terrorism, 20
Rempell, Ben, 280n8
Retaliation, 154
Reuveny, R., 121n11
Revkin, A.C., 381
Revolutionary United Front (RUF), 258
Reynal-Querol, Marta, 101, 114
Rich, Mark, 139
Ripeness, 264
Risse, T., 324, 341nn18, 20
Ristanovic Vesna, 175
Ritualism, 213n10
RG, 240
Robespierre, Maximilien, 62
Robin Hood effect, 60
Rogger, H., 38
Rojas, D.M., 127, 134
Romano, R., 178
Romaniuk, Peter, 14, 21, 321, 340n5, 341nn7, 11, 12
Ronderos, J., 174
Rosand, 341n11
Rosen, S.J., 197, 207
Rosen, Jeffrey, 374
Rosendorff, B.P., 67
Ross, J.I., 64, 78, 98–99, 152
Rothchild, 193, 211nn2, 3
Rotte, R., 54
Roy, Olivier, 44
Royal Ulster Constabulary (RUC), 234
Rubin, E., 291
RUF, 260–262, 264, 279

Ruggie, 325, 341nn19, 20
Rugova, Ibrahim, 265–268, 271, 281n12
Rummel, R., 69n12
Rumsfeld, Donald, 139, 142, 349–350, 352, 365
Rural Antiterrorist Groups (GAR), 229
Russell, J., 76, 92
Russia: protofascism, 37–39; War on Terror, 92
Russification, 91
Russo-Chechen War: first, 86, 88, 90, 92, 94; second, 86
Russo-Japanese War, 37, 45
Russo-Turkish War (1877–1878), 37
Rwanda negotiations (1993), 254–258
Rwandese Patriotic Front (RPF), 44, 254–257 277, 280n4

SA, 26
Sakhalin Island, 37
Salazar, 40
Salmoiraghi, G., 184
Samaranayake, N., 310n2
Sanctuary Doctrine, 238
Sandler, T., 67, 69n8, 69n17, 101, 109, 130, 151, 153–154, 159, 164
Sankoh, Foday, 260–262
Sartawi, Isaam, 281n14
Savir, Uri, 273, 275, 281n15
Schelling, T., 207, 211n5
Schivelbusch, W., 36
Schmid, Alex, 98–99, 220, 366n1
Schmidt, C., 54
Schneier, B., 381nn1, 2
Schoch-Spana, 375
Schott, P.A., 341n8
Scott, J.C., 58
Scott, James, 69n6
Schuab, D., 108
SDSM, 263
Secretary of State for Public Security (France), 238
Security rights, 77

Sedan (1870), 36
Seely, R., 81–84, 88, 94n1
Senate Appropriations Committee (U.S.), 141
September 11 (9/11), 127–129, 135, 138, 219, 287, 316–318, 324, 328–330, 336, 357, 363, 370–371, 374–377
Seung-Soo, Han, 75
Shalihu, Jashar, 280n11
Shamir, Yitzak, 272, 274
Shannon, D.A., 379
Shanty, F., 105
Sharon, Ariel, 281n14
Shaw, E.K., 43
Shaw, S.J., 43
Shepherd, Bryan C., 14, 20
Sherefi, Bilall, 280n11
Shields, K.J., 377
Shining Path, 63
Siccari zealots, 1
Siegel, Marc, 376, 378
Sierra Leone negotiations, 258–262
Sierra Leonian People's Party (SLPP), 259
Sikkink, K., 324
Silver, R., 377
Simmons, B.A., 340n6
Singer, Joel, 274
Singh, Manmohan, 334
Sinn Fein, 68, 103, 173
Slaughter, A.M., 324
Slovic, Paul, 378
Smith, Davidson, 223
Smith, M.L., 42
Snyder, G.H. 211nn2, 3
Snyder, Jack, 99, 130, 193, 197
Sobek, David, 14, 17, 21, 155, 166n8
Social Democratic Alliance (SDSM), 262
Social egoists, 327, 336
Socialist Workers Party (Spain), 228
Solzhenitsyn, A., 90
Soslambekov, Usup, 88
Sossai, M., 135, 139
Souleimanov, E., 76

Spain and counterterrorism experience, 225–232
Spanish Civil War, 56
Spanish Revolution, 225
Special Measures toward Crimes of Terrorism Committed by Armed Groups, 227
Special Operations Group (GEO), 229
Special Recommendations on Terrorist Financing, 319
Spector, B.I., 252
Spinzak, E., 104
Squire, L., 121n11
Stalin, Joseph, 37, 85, 87, 89–90, 94
Stam, A.C. III, 54
Stanislawski, B., 170, 181
Starr, H., 197
State internationalization, 131–132
State terrorism, 69n12
Stedman, S.J., 247
Stein, N., 31
Steinberg, J., 28
Steine, Michael, 185
Stern Gang, 59, 69n14
Sternhell, Z., 30
Stettenheim, J., 255, 257, 280n4
Stiles, T.J., 68n5
Stohl, C., 350, 356
Stohl, Michael, 14, 20–21, 350–351, 356, 364
Stokes, Doug, 133
Stossel, J., 381n1
Stouffer, S.A., 375
Strasser, Valentine, 258–259
Subsistence rights, 77
Suicide terrorism, 120nn3, 6; absolute terrorist type, 247; diffusion, 65–66
Sukaroputri, Megawati, 329
Sukma, R., 342n25
Summers, 311n6
Sunstein, Cass, 373, 376–378
Supergrass strategy, 235
Surprise: loss, 32; vividness, 33
Surroi, Veton, 270
Suzan, B., 237–240
Sword, 106

Szalasi, Ferenc, 29
Szeged idea, 28–29

Tacitus, 53
Tactical Question (TQ), 249–250, 253–254, 256, 259–261, 264, 266–267, 273–277
Taliban, 65, 320–321, 357
Tamil Elam (LTTE), 25, 120n3
Tanham, G.K., 322
Tannenwald, N., 316–318, 325–326, 328, 340nn1, 2
Targeted killings, 67
Tarrow, S., 181
Tartarstan, 84
Taylor, T., 173, 232–235, 244nn18, 19
Taylor, Charles, 258
Tenenoff, Rick, 139
Tenet, George, 355, 358
Terrorism, 1, 60–62, 76–77, 220, 247, 322, 351; absolute terrorists, 247; accommodationist response, 225; affluence and support, 20; age and support, 20; as industry, 373–374; categories, 221; colonial history, 16, 79; concessions, 17, 151–153; conditional terrorists, 251; contagion effects, 104; contingent terrorists, 247; counter-terrorism, 18–19; demand side studies, 287, 310n1; democracy, 16, 97–105, 118–119; emotional obsession, 21; evaluation metrics, 20; extreme terrorists, 149; foreign fighters, 16; guerrilla warfare, 59, 63, 65; human rights, 75–76, 364–365; ideological heterogeneity, 106–107; ideological linkage with crime, 173; inequality, 110; international dominance, 17; internationalization, 17; inter-group dynamics, 102–105, 118; left-wing terrorism, 221–222; marginalization, 92; moderate terrorists, 149; nationalist/separatist terrorism, 222; networks, 356–358;

organized crime, 17; political outbidding, 21; political rights, 15, 78; press freedom, 100; public support, 19–20, 64; quality of life, 15; religious terrorism, 222; repression, 77, 94; retaliation, 17, 153–154; revisionism, 156; right-wing terrorism, 222; security rights, 79; single issue terrorism, 223; social science analysis, 9–10; strategy vs. tactics, 69n7; supply side studies, 287; support due to threatened Islam, 20; technology, 15; trans-state, 169, 180–181; unequal access to military technology, 64–65; victory, 59–60; weak states, 79–80, 102
Terrorisme, 62
Terrorist Financing Convention (1999), 319
Terrorism Protection Unit (TPU), 234–235
Tetley, W., 64
Thaci, Hashim, 185
Thatcher, Margaret, 100
Thrace, western, 41–42
Thoumi, F., 136
Tickner, A.B., 128, 142, 145n1
Time horizons and strategic choice of warfare, 60
Tishkov, V., 82–83
de Tocqueville, Alexis, 78, 374
Toft, M.D., 32
Tokatlian, J.G., 128
Tolima, southern, 133
Touval, S., 265
Transitional National Assembly (TNA), 256
Transylvania, northern, 35–36
Tres Esquinas, 137
TREVI, 235, 240, 244n23
Trianon Treaty (1920), 28, 34
Tversky, A., 33

UCK, 280n9
Ulema Council (Indonesia), 329
Ulster Defense Force, 104
Ulster Freedom Fighters, 104
Ulster Voluntary Force, 104
UNAMSIL, 261
Unconventional warfare, 54–56
Union of the Archangel Michael, 38
Union of the Russian People (URP), 38
United Kingdom, counter-terrorism, 232–236
United Nations Preventive Deployment Force (UNPREDEP), 262
United Nations Security Council Resolution, 242, 271–272
United Nations Terrorist Financing Convention, 322, 331
United Opposition (Rwanda), 254
United Self Defense of Colombia (AUC), 138, 140
United States: invasion of Iraq, 317; National Security Strategy (2002), 366n2
UNMIK, 185
Uribe, Alvaro, 134 138–142, 144, 145n3
URP, 39–40
Usher, Graham, 202–203
USS Cole attack (2000), 61

Van Belle, D., 108
Van Duyne, P., 170
Van Evera, S., 193, 195, 211nn2, 3, 212n6
Vanhanen, T., 109
Van Natta, D., 357
Vasquez, J., 32, 47n6
VAT (violence, assassination, terrorism) database, 240
Vel'yaminov, 81
Verma, P., 334
Verremis, T., 42
Versailles, Treaty of, 34
Vidino, L., 86, 92
Vietnam War (1965–1975), 54, 59, 68n4
Viet Minh, 63

Villa, Martin, 229
Von Lampe, Klaus, 179
Von Lange, 171

Walter, B.F., 32, 47n6, 86, 151, 152, 211n2, 278
Walzer, Michael, 200, 208
War and territorial loss, 47n7
War Measures Act (1970), 64
Ward, C.A., 341n11
Wardlaw, G., 219, 224, 241
Warfare choices and cost of war, 67
Warner, B.W., 232, 236, 244n19
Way Out (WO), 264
Weart, S.R., 375
Weber, Eugen, 39
Weber, Max, 28, 30, 46n4, 210
Weinberg, L., 78, 99
Weinstein, J.M., 57–58
Wellhofer, E.S., 26
Westen, D., 32
White Flag, 38
Wike, R., 310n2
Wilkinson, P., 100, 221–223, 225, 238–239, 241, 243n9
Winer, J.M., 317
Winik, J., 58, 62

Winter War (1939–1940), 47n8
Wolfe, B., 37
Wolfowitz, Paul, 350
Wolfsberg Group, 318
Wood, William, 140
World War I, 45, 47n12, 68n4
World War II, 46; battle casualties, 68n4
Wright, E., 183

Xhaferi, Arben, 265

Yarborough, William, 133
Yellow Shirts (Russia), 20, 39
Yeltsin, Boris, 84–85, 88, 90
Yermolov, Alexander, 81, 89
Young, J., 291
Yudhoyono, Susilo Bambang, 333, 342n29

zachistas, 76, 90
Zak, P., 121n11
Zartman, William, 14, 19, 21, 195, 247, 249, 265, 269, 277–278, 280n3, 281n16
Zavgaev, Doku, 88
Zhironovsky, Vladimir, 46

www.ingramcontent.com/pod-product-compliance
Ingram Content Group UK Ltd.
Pitfield, Milton Keynes, MK11 3LW, UK
UKHW041921140426
5217IPUK00014B/255